Debility and the Moral Imagination in Botswana

African Systems of Thought

EDITOR
Ivan Karp

CONTRIBUTING EDITORS
James W. Fernandez
Luc de Heusch
John Middleton
Roy Willis

Debility and the Moral Imagination in Botswana

Julie Livingston

INDIANA UNIVERSITY PRESS

Bloomington and Indianapolis

This book is a publication of

Indiana University Press
601 North Morton Street
Bloomington, IN 47404-3797 USA

http://iupress.indiana.edu

Telephone orders	800-842-6796
Fax orders	812-855-7931
Orders by e-mail	iuporder@indiana.edu

The paper used in this publication meets the minimum
requirements of American National Standard for
Information Sciences—Permanence of Paper for Printed
Library Materials, ANSI Z39.48-1984.

Manufactured in the United States of America

Library of Congress Cataloging-in-Publication Data

Livingston, Julie.
   Debility and the moral imagination in Botswana / Julie
Livingston.
      p.   cm. — (African systems of thought)
Includes bibliographical references and index.
   ISBN 0-253-34637-1 (cloth : alk. paper) —
ISBN 0-253-21785-7 (pbk. : alk. paper)
   1. Social change—Health aspects—Botswana. 2. Body,
Human—Social aspects—Botswana. 3. Public health—
Botswana. 4. Botswana—Social conditions—20th century—
Health aspects. 5. Botswana—Economic conditions—20th
century—Health aspects. 6. Botswana—Moral conditions—
Health aspects. 7. Asthenia—Botswana. I. Title. II. Series.
   HN806.A8L58 2005
   362.1'096883—dc22

                                        2005005936

1 2 3 4 5   10 09 08 07 06 05

For Thatcher

Contents

Acknowledgments

I am indebted to many people and institutions that made this book possible. There is not space to thank everyone who helped me, but some individuals deserve particular mention. During my senior year in college, Randy Packard's teaching transformed me from a very disengaged undergraduate into someone with a deep interest in Africa, history, and scholarship. Over the many years since then he has continued to inspire me as a scholar, teacher, advisor, and friend. Every writer deserves to have such a committed and generous mentor. I count myself very lucky that I found one.

During my time in Botswana I incurred a special debt to the staff and clients of the Cheshire Foundation of Botswana. The warm welcome of staff members and the willingness of clients and their families to allow me to witness and participate in their visits with staff made this work possible. Without Cheshire, life would have been lonely and research exceedingly difficult. I am grateful to Sekgabo Ramsay, the director at the time, who invited me to join the staff on home visits, made case notes available to me, and welcomed me as a regular visitor to the Rehabilitation Center in Mogoditshane. Mary Leswiti took me on my first CBR trip, answered questions, shared her lunch, invited me to her home, and warmly encouraged me during my first timid moments of fieldwork. On two subsequent stays in Botswana for over fifteen months, Dikeledi Moloi welcomed me into her regular CBR routine and into her life. She patiently answered endless questions and then inevitably raised much better ones, translated conversations, offered interpretations, explained much of what to her must have seemed obvious, debated ideas and interpretations with me, welcomed me into her family, and made me laugh—usually when I needed it most. Dikeledi, friend, guide, *ausi*, teacher, remains one of the most caring and brilliant people I have ever known, and she is now central to my own moral imagination. Without her there simply would be no book.

Many others in Botswana were also helpful, hospitable, and insightful. A partial list of those who provided me with friendship, assistance, and wisdom during my repeated stays in Botswana includes Annah Banda, Petra Boekestein, Bome, Charlanne Burke, Stephanie Cohen, Danny Cooper, Diphako, Barry Eustace, Suzette Heald, Givens Kaonga, Fred Klaits, Lady, Paul Landau, Lillian, Makgoa, Maphuti, the Moloi family, Tshepiso Moremi, Condril Mosala, Timmy Motingwa, Ninki, Ntome, Neil Parsons, the late Sheilah Pule, Laura Rusche,

Onalenna Selolwane, Tiny, Tshenolo, and Ruud Van Trijp. In London, Suzette Heald, Eddie Sulimirski, and Edwina Fields provided hospitality and fun.

This book began in the wake of a friend's stunning and protracted personal tragedy. I have learned many things in the course of this research. But they all began with and inevitably return to the fundamental lessons about love, family, body, and self that Audrey Hirsch and the late Dr. Alan Hirsch taught me when they drew me into their intimate circle of care. I am grateful to them for all they taught me, to Christopher Gates who helped me make sense of such lessons, and to Randy Packard who encouraged me to see that my thoughts about my friends could be the starting point for a book.

My greatest debt is to the debilitated people of southeastern Botswana with whom I worked. They, their families, their *dingaka,* and their neighbors and friends gave of their time and knowledge to me, a total outsider. They shared some good jokes and some happy moments but also many intimate and often times painful experiences. I am forever both grateful and awed for these remarkable acts of generosity.

Many people read (or listened to) earlier drafts of various pieces of this book. I am particularly grateful for questions, comments, and suggestions from Iris Berger, Sara Berry, Caroline Bledsoe, Carolyn Brown, Claudia Castaneda, Erin Clune, Stephanie Cohen, Kathryn Geurts, Bernie Guyer, Steve Feierman, Jean Hay, Suzette Heald, Kirk Hoppe, Nancy Hunt, Diana Jeater, Nick King, Paul Landau, Murray Last, Simi Linton, Neil Maher, Sinfree Makoni, Harry Marks, David Mechanic, Neil Parsons, Stephen Pemberton, Phil Pauly, Jonathan Sadowsky, David Schoenbrun, Phil Scranton, Onalenna Selolwane, Margaret Storey, Sandy Sufian, Lynn Thomas, and Judith Van Allen.

A few people read drafts of the entire book and provided valuable input and advice: Allan Brandt, Debbie Durham, Joe Gabriel, William Gordon, Ivan Karp, Fred Klaits, Cory Kratz, Kristin Mann, Rachel McLaughlin, Randy Packard, Michelle Rotunda, Laurel Thatcher Ulrich, Keith Wailoo, and an anonymous reviewer for Indiana University Press.

This book began as a doctoral dissertation at Emory University, and I am especially indebted to Randy and the other Africanist faculty who nurtured this book from the beginning. Cory Kratz was the kind of reader a doctoral student hopes for, generous with her time and ideas, thorough in her engagement, and rigorous in her standards. I am particularly grateful for the energy she invested in the dissertation that formed the basis for this book. Kristin Mann's feedback on the original dissertation made the transformation to a book far easier. Eddy Bay provided the best kind of encouragement. I was fortunate to have Luise White around as I began to formulate my research plan. Conversations with her about oral history and field research were enormously helpful. Ivan Karp guided this project in too many ways to mention, and he has earned my deepest thanks. His course on African Systems of Thought remains one of the intellectual highlights of my graduate education.

Others beyond Emory lent special help. Suzette Heald has long been an out-of-town mentor and friend, providing intellectual guidance and support when I have been far from home. Jean Hay has been a trusted friend and advisor for many years. It was she who recommended I write Chapter 1 in its present form. Laurel Thatcher Ulrich read drafts, asked wonderful questions, and helped me see Botswana as familiar. Allan Brandt also read drafts and introduced me to the wider history of medicine. Steve Feierman, first in his writings and then in person, guided the way. Lynn Thomas shared her meticulous research notes and her infectious enthusiasm for scholarship and teaching with me. Elizabeth Guillette, Bendicte Ingstad, and Dorothy Hodgson each shared what were (at the time) otherwise inaccessible copies of their work. Elise Carpenter tracked down illustrations and gave much-needed encouragement. Stephanie Cohen shared her photographs and her knowledge. Thatcher Ulrich made the maps.

Conversations about writing with Herman Bennett, Laurie Benton, Barbara Cooper, Joe Gabriel, Alison Isenberg, Greg Mann, Mike McGovern, Jennifer Morgan, David Schoenbrun, Margaret Storey, Keith Wailoo, and Kristin Williams were most helpful. The superb editorial advice and guidance I received on other writing projects from Stacy Pigg, Caroline Bledsoe, Debbie Durham, and Jennifer Cole sharpened my thinking about this book.

Keith Wailoo deserves particular mention. He read the manuscript carefully, offered significant critique and suggestions, and provided myriad forms of guidance and counsel. Fred Klaits has been a tireless reader, conversation partner, and longtime colleague and friend whose scholarship enriched this project greatly. Debbie Durham's extensive comments on the manuscript and the countless epiphanies she has offered through her own work are examples of the kind of generosity and intelligence that has sustained me through this project. I owe Debbie a special debt for her ongoing engagement, kindness, and insight.

I was fortunate to receive funding from a number of sources that financed research trips to Botswana and London. I am grateful to Fulbright-Hays for a doctoral dissertation research fellowship, the American Historical Association's Bernadotte Schmidt award, the New Jersey Institute of Technology for a Separately Budgeted Research Grant, and the following groups at Emory University: the Center for the Study of Health, Culture, and Society; the History Department; the Institute of African Studies; and the Emory Fund for Internationalization for providing this support. The History Department at Rutgers University has provided me with a happy and productive home for the final stages of writing and revision.

I am grateful to the government of Botswana for permitting me to do research in country and to the National Institute of Research and Documentation and the Botswana Council for the Disabled for providing institutional support. This work would not have been possible without the assistance of staff at numerous libraries and archives, and I thank all those who helped me at the Botswana National Archives, the Botswana Collection at the University of Botswana, the Council of World Mission Archive at the University of London, Rhodes House Library at Oxford University, the London School of Economics, and the Royal Anthropological Institute Photographic Collection.

Many thanks also to the Royal Anthropological Institute, the Council of World Mission, and Stephanie Cohen for granting me permission to reproduce the photographs in this book. Portions of Chapter 3 were originally published as "Physical Fitness and Economic Opportunity in the Bechuanaland Protectorate in the 1930's and 1940's," *Journal of Southern African Studies* 27, no. 4 (2001): 793–811. I am grateful to Taylor and Francis for allowing me to reprint this material here: http://www.tandf.co.uk.

Working with Indiana University Press has been a great experience. I so appreciate the respect and the intellectual and practical assistance that my editor, Dee Mortensen has offered to me. Very special thanks also go to Kate Babbitt, who made this a better book. She brought a wealth of clarity, rigor, and humor to the copyediting process, which carried me through the final stages.

Finally, I am indebted to my friends and family, who have been supportive throughout. Special thanks go to Kate Gakenheimer and to my grandfather, Samuel Gutman Jr. Hazel Luo Yafang Livingston came along just in time to make the final stages of this book both hectic and joyous. Pokey has offered love, her canine sensibilities, and the need for the kind of long walks that solve writer's block. My greatest thanks go to Thatcher Ulrich. It is a good thing to marry the son of a feminist. Thatcher has moved households and continents more times than he may care to remember, lent technical support, read early chapters (until he somewhat blissfully realized he didn't have to), washed dishes, made me laugh, and given me space to write. It is to him that this book is dedicated. Any errors or shortcomings are, of course, my own.

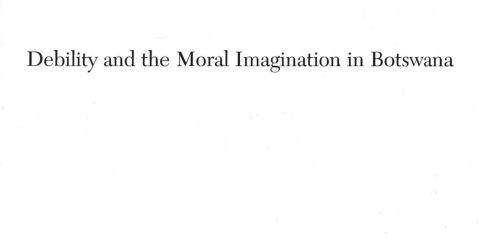

Debility and the Moral Imagination in Botswana

Map of Botswana, after 1966

Introduction
Themes and Orientation

Long ago we were all still walking when we died.
  —Alita Seati, 1997[1]

Tlhotsa pele ga e swe pele.
  —Setswana proverb: The first to be crippled is not necessarily the first to die.

In Botswana, a crisis of debility is unfolding that has been in the making for a century. Botswana is by no means alone in this regard. Debility is one of the most fundamental human experiences. This book explores practical concerns that arise in the face of debility and related epistemological and moral questions that emerge when bodily norms are profoundly disrupted. It considers how people manage bodily misfortune in a rapidly changing world. The story takes place at the intersections of culture and somatic life—it is about the ways people in Botswana experience history in their bodies and how they, in turn, make historical sense out of their changing bodily experiences.[2] My central premise is that historical transformations in southeastern Botswana have wrought important changes in the relationship between the moral imagination, personhood, and health-related discourse and practice. Such changes include the policies of British colonial rule and neglect, the emergence and increasing dominance of a migrant labor system, the political and economic shifts that accompanied Independence in 1966, problems and opportunities caused by the influx of global capital into the region, widespread and diverse forms of Christian conversion, and the pluralization of systems to deliver health care. These changes have deep bodily implications that are particularly evident in instances of debility. Because contemporary life is saturated with concern about bodies and their needs in Botswana and because the research for this book was anchored in ethnographic methods, this is, in many ways, a history of the present.

Two elements stand out in this study and will be engaged in conversation with one another throughout: social change and suffering. Over the course of the twentieth century in southeastern Botswana, experiences of chronic suffering exposed the relationship between ongoing transformations in social life, human bodies, and the plural medical system. Amid these changes, many people made sense of their experiential crises by remembering a past in which such suffering was hardly possible, a process I term moral imagination. Over the past eighty years there has been a recurring juxtaposition of themes in popular Tswana commentary on historical change: fear of moral chaos (associated with, for example, rebellious youth or new forms of sexual behavior) and its destruction of the health of society versus a nostalgic past where a clear moral order protected individual and community vitality for the common good.[3] These themes resurfaced time and again at key stages in the progression of modern Tswana history as broad historical transformations altered local health and health care, exchange relations, social categories, and domestic cycles. The history of debility provides ways of hearing and understanding the meanings of this popular commentary, its modes and contexts of expression, and the place of moral questioning in a changing society.

Bodies and Persons

Debility—the impairment, lack, or loss of certain bodily abilities—is, on one level, a profound challenge to personhood. But debility also has a history, in the sense that impairment and disfigurement arise out of particular junctures—the rise of mining and mining accidents, for example—and thus it gives us insight into a people's historical experience and changing assumptions about personhood and self.[4]

I start with a very basic fact, but one with many implications for this book: bodies are necessary but not sufficient elements of personhood. Each of us has a body and despite our incredible diversity of shapes, sizes, and features, the fact of having a particular kind of body unites us as human beings. Human bodies are the material vehicle through which we enact and experience self and the world, and they are so "good to think with" that they provide a rich set of symbols from which we organize and understand life.[5] This is a more complicated statement than it seems at first glance, because the meaning of "persons" and the material nature and cultural understanding of "bodies" vary tremendously across time and space. There are many, many ways of inhabiting a body and being a person. Moreover, among various groups at various times, certain types of bodily difference (e.g., race, sex, cognitive capacity, twinning) have posed unsettling problems to implicit notions of personhood and have forced otherwise subtle practices and ideas around the relationship between bodies and persons into view. This book is concerned, in part, with forms of bodily difference (impairment, disfigurement) that highlight such historical junctures. In Botswana, as in all places, simultaneous challenges to notions of persons and normative experiences of bodies have continually played off of one another over the course of the history in question. As the locus of personhood and the material manifestation of self, the human body is at once a profoundly moral and historical site.

Certain bodily states pose problems. Debility is one such state because it troubles, mobilizes, and intensifies social relations. When Bantle, a Motswana woman I met in the course of this research, began to develop multiple sclerosis, her mother and friends encouraged her to break off her engagement to her boyfriend, the father of her two children, which she did. She would require increasing amounts of care in the coming years, and everyone thought it better that she remain in her mother's home with her sons rather than move to her in-laws, as would have happened at marriage. Relations between the two families were good, and Bantle's former fiancé continued to visit her and support their sons for many years thereafter, even though he eventually married another woman. But with long-term care and support for Bantle at issue, the differences between in-laws, husbands, mothers, and children became explicit; the strengths and weaknesses of marriage versus parenthood were debated. In instances of debility such as Bantle's, the question of our responsibilities toward one another becomes more overt. Safety nets and moral economies are tested. Key relationships undergo both public and private scrutiny. The deep relationship of the body to the person is exposed, both for the subject and those around her. I will return to this theme in a moment.

Debility, like certain other bodily states, triggers the imagination, causing us to consider the fragile and contingent nature of bodily life. Though our bodies and our bodily capacities are forever changing over the course of our lives, and though our individual abilities differ tremendously, an element of physical vulnerability shadows us all. In what follows we will explore how people experience and make sense of this ever-present vulnerability socially, morally, and medically. We each experience physical changes over the life course, but we also collectively experience long-term changes in our bodies, their capacities, and the normative range of states. New diseases arise, old ones are eclipsed, our diets change, new technologies to assist our bodies become more accessible, and we marshal our expectations and countless moral conversations around these shifting norms. For example, in recent decades Batswana have struggled to accommodate the bodily and social needs of a growing population of elderly persons. Like their counterparts in North America, India, Japan, and elsewhere, they imagine their dilemmas around aging as moral ones.[6]

So people have bodies and yet are more than just bodies. Debility is a challenge to both the body and the person. Anthropologist Ivan Karp describes the significance of personhood as a concept that exposes the complex intersections of bodily, social, and imaginative experience:

> In the disciplines of philosophy and anthropology the term "personhood" is used as a shorthand for describing and interpreting different solutions to a universal existential dilemma: the problem of reconciling the lived experi-

ence of our changing physical bodies and sets of discordant experiences with the sense that there are unifying themes mediated through a single entity, which we call a person. . . . Ideas about the person also entail descriptions of the capacities and powers that persons have to carry out their actions and locate these powers and capacities in the image of the body.

For scholars such as Karp, African contexts offer important venues for thinking about the body:

In African cultures mental and moral capacities and powers are often located in the body rather than opposed to the body. . . . Yet we may say that . . . most . . . African concepts of personhood are relational rather than material, and that the boundaries of the body are defined as more permeable and less discrete in Africa than in many European settings.[7]

What might these observations mean for our understanding of the history and changing experience of debility?

Understanding this permeability of the human body as it works in this African context is essential for grasping the particular ways in which debility is experienced and understood in southeastern Botswana. Many readers are already familiar with what it means to have mental and moral capacities located *in* rather than *opposed to* a body that is somewhat permeable, but for those who are new to such concepts of bodies and persons, as I was when I began my research, simply reading that this is the case may not be enough to truly understand the radical implications of this cultural orientation. I hope that by the end of the book, through the examples and explanations I share, those readers will come not only to grasp this particular form of embodied personhood but also to see that it is not as unfamiliar as it seems at first glance. In the west, such intuitive notions float just under the surface of overt statements and beliefs about individually bounded bodies and Cartesian mind-body dichotomies.[8]

The crisis of debility (as remembered and experienced) stretches back in time for people in Botswana and is intertwined with the story of "modernization"—the influx of a particular web of western institutions, ideas, and capital. Explorations of debility, which take us to the margins of physicality, will help us explore changes in what it means to be an person for Batswana. What, then, has modern life meant for bodies and persons in Botswana?

Over the twentieth century, an uneasy, bifurcated sense of personhood has arisen out of the tensions between the development of a liberal sense of individualism that values personal efforts, successes, and status and the socialized notion of the person, whose sense of self is located in and continually produced through his or her relations with others. Such tensions in Tswana selfhood have a long history. Let me stress that while it was constrained, such individualism was certainly not absent in earlier times; an egalitarian ethos existed in particular relationships and domains that was in strong tension with hierarchical and kin-based identities and responsibilities.[9] A person understood her thoughts and feelings to be her own, but she also understood those internal experiences to deeply affect others (and to be affected by the actions and sentiments of others), and her ability to act autonomously was deeply constrained and shaped by age, gender, and other factors. But, as Deborah Durham suggests, the tensions between the hierarchically located and the autonomous self are reconfiguring in a changing political and social economy.[10] This is one of the most important social and cultural ramifications of "modernization" in Botswana, where the movement of global capital and the influx of western liberal ideas and institutions have combined to make self-development a highly contested and confusing terrain.[11] Through debility we will discuss the relationship between recent historical transformations and personhood via the body. Today we find more and more contexts in which bodies somehow seem to be unleashed from their social world, albeit in fleeting ways, and other contexts in which new social worlds are forged or long-standing ones are reinforced through relations of bodily care.[12] For some this is a story of success, for others one of suffering. In either case, Batswana are experiencing their history through physical culture as much as through political and economic interactions.

Modernization, of course, was not an inevitable force that simply steamrolled over society, producing individuals where once there had been only communal notions of self. Lynn Thomas has rightly cautioned against reproducing social science theories of modernization that describe social change in Africa in such terms.[13] Such implicitly evolutionary/devolutionary approaches, she points out, miss how Africans reworked colonial policies and ideas for their own ends. Thomas employs a model of entanglement that explores how bodily "struggles over wealth, health, and power" "connected and combined the material and the moral, the indigenous and the imperial, and the intimate and the global."[14] Thomas's sense of entanglement is central to this history, where the issue at hand is not *whether* self-making changed but *how* individuals, groups, and institutions struggled to control social reproduction, shifting relationships between bodies and persons in the process. For example, in Chapter 3 we will see that when returned miners, whose earnings depended on industry's perception of them as "able-bodied," redistributed their earnings by giving gifts of commodities and cash to kin in ways that mimicked ritual slaughter, they both reproduced their social relationships and repositioned themselves and their potential for autonomous action within the gendered and gerontocratic hierarchies of "communal" life.

Debility and Disability

Over the course of this project, I grappled with infertility, the by-product of a long and debilitating illness; my husband broke his hand; several friends and relatives became parents of children with developmental, physical, and/or other challenges; others suffered long and terrible years of cancer or unexpected accidents with devastating consequences; and my grandfather, much to his chagrin, began to use a cane. I made sense of these events through insights gleaned in Botswana. My point is that while this book is first and foremost about southeastern Botswana, it is also about a broad set of human experiences that promote thinking across categories of place, culture, and time. All of these events raised questions about the ways in which debility is negotiated, managed, and understood in context and in time. There is an effortless way in which our ideas and beliefs about debility intersect with our sense of self and how debility places us in some imagined communities, public spaces, and personal narratives at particular junctures. My grandfather's vigilance about independence and his presentation of self were expressed in his feelings about the cane. He was not alone in this sensibility, nor was he wrong in assuming that people would react to him differently if he walked with a cane. And yet in Botswana, canes historically symbolized the power of elderhood and the aggregation of dependents rather than the loss of independence.

The term debility denotes here both the frailties associated with chronic illness and aging and as the impairments underlying the word disability. This admittedly awkward gloss on "debility" is necessary, for it highlights the overlaps between impairment, chronic illness, and senescence. I discuss debility in terms of physical misfortune. This is not to imply that all forms or experiences of bodily difference or impairment are necessarily bad or unfortunate. They are not. Sarah Lamb's work shows how elderly Bengali women may embrace senescence; their aging bodies establish the privilege of being cared for. Their positive field of social relations with their juniors is enacted through bodily care. I am interested in how and why some forms of long-term illness, impairment, and aging are understood to be misfortune in particular times and places by particular constituencies, while others are not. Recent changes in Indian social and economic life have meant that there are more elderly women in Bengal than in past decades who lack these nurturing relationships. For those women, senescence now comes as misfortune.[15] Furthermore, people who do not recognize their own debilitated or unusually configured body or that of a loved one as evidence of misfortune must still grapple with the fact that others would characterize their lives in this way.[16] Most of the debilitated people I met in

Botswana, however, considered their own debility to be evidence of serious misfortune, as did the people around them.

Debility is similar to the widely used term disability, but it differs in key ways. Unlike "debility," "disability" has special meanings in terms of identity and capacity that we must think through if we are to use the term productively. While "impairment," like "debility," refers to functional differences or losses in the body, "disability" is a more complex term. It refers to the social challenges that stem from particular forms of bodily configuration. Thus, in America, blackness was once (and many would argue still is) cast as a disability by many whites and was used historically as a justification for both the formal and informal exclusion of black and brown peoples from particular opportunities and public spaces.[17] Disability is a biosocial identity that is at once both biologically grounded and socially parsed, an umbrella term that denotes different things in different places and at different times. Historical transformations in Botswana over the course of the twentieth century produced both impairments *and* disabilities.[18] By employing the broader category of debility, this book encompasses issues around both disability and impairments (be they associated with disability, chronic illness, or aging) but understands disability as a particular subset of experience is crucial to the history that follows.

What then is "disability," or its Setswana counterpart "*bogole*"? It is, and has been, a changing reality. How might physical or mental impairments relate to personhood? Where do we look for disability's meanings in Tswana history? These are hard questions to answer. Unfortunately, I do not have the data necessary to clearly and continuously define what disability (*bogole*) meant for Batswana over the course of a century. It is no surprise that Tswana conversations about disability rarely made their way into the archival record. Likewise, there are difficulties in defining a moving target through presentist oral recollections. Many of the older people I discussed these issues with simply "never thought about disability" until recent years or told me that "long ago there were no *digole* [disabled persons]. The *digole* came with Independence."[19] While such statements do provide clues, especially about the place of *bogole* in the moral imagination, they also remind us that disability's meanings are often buried in places with few markers. In what follows, I will attempt to glimpse meaning where possible and then anchor meaning in context. There are moments of florescence in the past where intersecting social and epidemiological changes or crises generated more intense memories and/or a more thickly laid paper trail.[20] The chapters that follow emerge in large part from these points of florescence.

To study the production of debility and its negotiation is not, of course, to dismiss somatic experience. Quite the contrary.[21] My use of terms such as "disability," "disabled," "mentally impaired," and so forth are meant not to signify a clinical status but a social identity: persons who are seen as disabled, who are called disabled, and/or call themselves disabled—that which is perceived as disability. Yet, as we will see in Chapter 1, while disability, like chronic illness or frail aging, may be, in part, socially constructed and socially negotiated, the physical and/or mental impairments (the debility) which shape the experiences of many people are quite real. I do not mean at any point to be dismissive of physical or mental experience, I merely aim to place that experience into a wider context where its depth may be perceived more holistically. Nor do I mean to deny any of the tremendous physical and cognitive capacities of many of the debilitated people I came to know in Botswana; rather, my intention is to observe why and how the lack of certain capacities or bodily configurations can trump the possession of others in social life.

While there is no fixed or single definition of *bogole,* we can sketch its contours on two levels: meanings of *bogole* vary between those located in the experience of disabled individuals and those that refer to a more general understanding of the term and its role. These meanings overlap, but it is worth exploring each of them in turn. Each has its own thematic frame of reference. For the individual subject and his or her closest associates, questions of personal history (time and context) and narrative are at the center of meaning, and for society at large, the concept of normalcy (which has its own broader history) can lead us closer, allow us to glimpse what is meant when someone is called *segole.* Each theme emerged through different aspects of my fieldwork. The diachronic nature of disability experiences was something I observed ethnographically over the period of my research; it also emerged in the various narratives I collected from and about disabled people. The second theme, normalcy, was hard to witness in a sharp or distinct way—it is the theme that gives disability its blurred edges and fuzzy meanings. One man, a paraplegic labeled *segole* by his relatives and co-workers and neighbors, deflected the question of bodily normality onto social normality when he told me "I am not disabled, I am rich in friends." Three elderly women with whom I was speaking one afternoon vigorously debated one another as to whether or not albinism was a form of *bogole,* given that it was mainly a difference in appearance, not in ability. But despite (or perhaps because of) the disagreements over what counts as "normal," when I asked various people to define what exactly disability/*bogole* meant, it was the reference point people chose—"*segole*—well that is someone who is not normal." So in these two themes—the diachronic and situational nature of the condition—we have the explicit definition of disability and the implicit (and at times contested) way in which it unfolds for the subject. These themes are woven together in the wider history of southeastern Botswana.

That disability, like other identities, would be diachronic and situational is not surprising. Nonetheless, it is worth discussing several aspects of this theme which are perhaps particular to disability. Disability, or *bogole*, is a status that arises out of a "quest for therapy."[22] It signals that this search, which may have taken many different paths, is petering out. The quest varies. Often it is an arduous one, taking patients and relatives from site to site, healer to healer, draining resources, and leaving controversy and a fractured family in its wake. Sometimes it is a measured quest that does not produce a cure but does access palliative care that eases the transition to a new state. At other times the quest is metaphoric only. Those who are involved may spend their time yearning for the reputed skill of healers long gone and yet lack the means or will to pursue any palpable action. A time will come when even this metaphoric quest for healing sputters and dies and a new identity sets in. The *molwetsi* (patient) of the quest shuffles from the foreground of local drama quietly to the back and becomes *segole* (disabled person). *Segole* is someone who can no longer be healed yet is not necessarily careening toward death. To live with *bogole* is to be stuck in the middle. This new identity is still a dynamic one. While the label of *segole* continually underscores the life of the person who is called by it, the meanings of the label change along with life situations. It means something different to be *segole* as a girl than it does to be *segole* as a mother or a grandmother. The physical or mental impairments which underlie the identity may also change, and then the identity shifts again. People who are blind can have strokes, those with rickets might lose their hearing, hemiplegia can lead to amputation, arthritis can lead to fixed joints, limping can lead to canes, to crutches, to wheelchairs, to bed.

Through these processes of quest and coping the moral imagination is engaged and a narrative is forged to explain what has happened.[23] Explanations of event and blame, suffering and coping suggest how the disabled person and others in relation to them are to be perceived. Faye Ginsburg and Rayna Rapp explain that disability entails a "rewriting of kinship."[24] Though they are focused on the United States, these kinship revisions are particularly evident in Botswana, where persons are constituted bodily through their social relationships and where historical changes have combined to strain domestic economies, as we will see in the next chapter. Through narrative explanation, the character of *bogole* interacts with the story of a person to frame which aspects of the new identity permeate the disabled person and which wash over onto family members and neighbors and caregivers. To be a *segole* is potentially to be many things: brave, idle, useless, determined, unfortunate, stupid, clever, sanguine, bitter, irresponsible (to name a few). And to be the husband, wife, mother, grandmother, uncle, boss, neighbor, daughter, nephew, or doctor of a disabled person is also open to many possibilities: generous, patient, selfish, uncaring, demanding, greedy, sad, martyred. The narrative suggests which aspects of disabled identity are relevant for whom and how the characters of both the subjects and those who are close to them interact; to be the brave paraplegic son of a patient and caring mother is different than to be the brave paraplegic son of a an uncaring greedy one.

Scholars of disability have placed great emphasis on modern western notions of normalcy in structuring the fraught history of disability in the United States and Europe. This history includes practices of stigmatization and ostracism as "freaks," eugenics and the systematic attempts to weed disabled persons out of the social body, and the struggle for rights and access to work and "normal" lives.[25] Disability is not a western invention, though in Botswana its more recent meanings have been shaped by colonial and postcolonial projects whose purpose and ideas are located in the cultures of the west. Still, normalcy in relation to disability means something much different for Batswana than it does in the west. I think all societies, be they "western" or "eastern" or "southern" have a concept of the physically and mentally normal and a normative view of themselves (and their past) which people draw on to understand bodily difference.[26] But in many societies where health and physicality are located and defined within social (particularly kin-based) relationships, notions of "normal" bodies and "normal" relationships are two sides of the same coin.[27] In Botswana, the disabled individual is the embodied nexus for a set of social relations that are open for debate. Indeed, that *segole* is "someone who is not normal" in Botswana reflects the relational and ongoing character of personhood much more than it does a sense of idealized body types or capacities.

Disability studies scholars understand relationships to shape impairment or difference into disability through social exclusion and stigma and through invocation of a medical model that classifies certain bodies as broken and deficient. By contrast, Batswana understand impaired relationships to generate bodily misfortune, which in turn is managed as disability. In both senses, disability is about bodies and social relationships, but in somewhat different ways. Likewise, much of disability activism and the medical activities of "rehabilitation" in the west are about promoting "independence," whereas in Botswana "independence" is not central to self-making and status. While people are very interested in opportunities to do for themselves, they also rightly understand themselves to be living in a web of dependencies, and they strive to manage and foster the nurturing side of these dependencies.[28] So while there are similarities between disability and *bogole,* there are also very important disjunctures.

A long history of encounters with the west informs the changing meanings of disability and debility in Botswana. Precolonial rankings of people by status—ranging from aristocrat to slave, from male to female, and from elder to child—have gradually been crosscut by new categories that were begun in the British social engineering of the "civilizing mission" that broke up attributes of the person by ranking in relation to a norm. While Batswana are not yet counting their calories or cholesterol levels, many people I know can tell you what their blood pressure is. Beginning in the 1930s, the standardization of bodies and minds became a hallmark of British colonial culture, and anthropometry gradually crept into public understandings of bodies and their capacities. This project picked up pace in the 1940s. Now every child has a clinic card with his or her height and weight measurements diligently plotted against a "normal" (i.e., metropolitan) growth curve. Apgar scores recorded at birth help identify infants at risk for "delayed milestones." While Batswana do not know their IQ scores, their schooling has been oriented around a series of Cambridge exams so that each child from primary school on is publicly ranked by a distant metropolitan order in relation to the rest. These categories, these hierarchies of capacity and averages, now unanchored from social status, are acquiring valence over historical time. The forging of the standardized normal begun through British colonialism has patterned the boundaries of one aspect of the normal. Outside these boundaries lie the meanings of disability.

Space and Affect

Debility is also a profoundly spatial phenomenon and in decisions about where debilitated bodies can go, where they are put, how they are managed—societies reveal much about their underlying cultural values, worldview, and community norms. An important part of this study will be to trace how people managed debility through public and private spaces. In Botswana, there are few obviously disabled persons in public spaces, and one rarely encounters a disabled worker or customer in local businesses, shops, and restaurants, or in the open marketplaces. Even the disabled beggars who are all too common in neighboring countries seemed strangely absent. For many, navigating through the deep sands of village paths proves too difficult and makes visiting relatives and attending social and political occasions rare events. Foreign visitors to Botswana often puzzle over the seeming incongruity between the much-publicized high rates of AIDS-related illnesses and the rarity of seeing a person one imagines to be an AIDS patient in a public setting. Yet with AIDS, as with debility of all forms, what remains invisible as a public situation (except through statistical knowledge and ubiquitous media coverage) is quite visible to many Batswana as they move within their networks of friends and relatives. There persons with disabilities join many other people who are debilitated through chronic illnesses or senescence.

The spatial dimensions of debility are about more than the practical problems of mobility, though. They are also about the meanings of particular spaces as safe, hidden, intimate, private, feminine, and/or nurturing, others as public, social, masculine, and political, and still others as dangerous, ambiguous, yet powerful. They are also about aesthetic concerns and how people anticipate that certain kinds of bodies might entail affective responses from others. Among Batswana, like many people, incontinence, inability to control saliva, and failure to conform to particular bodily norms of behavior and appearance challenge fundamental expressions of personhood and are managed spatially.

The power of the senses to affect or transform people was deep, though, as Kathryn Geurts's wonderful book on the senses in Anlo-Ewe communities demonstrates, we should be careful not to naturalize sensory experiences, which are cultural and historical products as much as anything else. The same holds true for emotional experiences, and the senses and the emotions can combine in deep ways around particular aesthetics of debility.[29] One woman told me of how she had helped her mother earn money by brewing and selling sorghum beer at parties in their courtyard. While she would serve and share gourds of beer with disabled men who came to drink, others would not.[30] It was not that these customers directly feared contagion but rather that they felt repulsed. One wealthy business manager, who was an important public contributor to an NGO that serves disabled persons, derided my practice of visiting "*digole*" in their homes, saying that the stench of urine in such a room would disgust him. Some people encouraged pregnant women to avoid looking at *maswafi* (persons with albinism) or people in the throes of epileptic seizures lest they pass along these qualities to their babies through their experiences of fright. Even among those who work with and care for disabled children today, many (not all) workers keep their own cups and utensils so that they do not have to share the ones these children have used previously, despite the fact that they have since been cleaned and dried.

Affective responses such as disgust, fear, and love are important, in part, because of the pathogenic properties of certain negative emotions in Tswana life and the sustaining power of positive ones. As Fred Klaits explains, for Batswana, sentiments that build relations between people, such as love, are nurturing, strengthening and healing, while divisive sentiments such as fear or jealousy endanger health and well-being.[31] Many people boldly challenged or simply dismissed proscriptions against looking at or being with debilitated persons, instead surrounding them with love. Yet implicit notions of pollution plague certain kinds of bodies and generate or are generated by affective responses; many people avoid debilitated or disfigured persons "like the plague."[32] Some debilitated persons, in turn, also avoid public settings—anticipating the collision of affect and sense. They fear embarrassment or potential humiliation. In one village where I worked, the previous (now deceased) chief was particularly attuned to issues of debility. He made a point of encouraging newly debilitated miners to come to the village court to participate in political meetings. One impaired miner from that village told me that while some men, like himself, did appreciate this gesture, those who were incontinent did not feel they could attend the meetings, despite the chief's encouragement.

Much of what I have just described and some of the story I will tell holds true for many people in the broader southern African region. My use of Tswana and related terms is not an attempt to bound off Tswana culture as something wholly separate or reify a complex set of ethnic processes. "Tswana" gives a homogenizing gloss to what is really a much more heterodoxical and historically fluid set of social, cultural, and political identities.[33] Instead my reliance on "Tswana" as the framework for this study is intended to streamline presentation, and to suggest the importance of a shared social, economic and political history of place. Throughout the book, I also often use the term "southeastern Tswana" as shorthand. Here I refer to those people who consider southeastern Bechuanaland/Botswana to be their home.

Yet while there is much diversity within southeastern Tswana culture and while Botswana shares many similarities with neighboring areas, southeastern Botswana is also of unique interest for historians and anthropologists of health and illness because of its rapid period of "modernization" and the nature of its particular "epidemiological transition." In the course of a single generation, Botswana went from being a colonial backwater and remarkably poor country to one of most rapidly and successfully "developing" countries on the continent. This rapid development was not without its accompanying social and biological dislocations. Exploring these processes in Botswana necessarily broadens our vision of African health issues beyond the acute infectious disease and malnutrition that dominate the attention of the international health community. In Botswana we may begin to consider the toll that chronic illnesses, aging, and impairments take on people and their families throughout the developing world; in fact, people in Botswana are insisting as much.[34] In particular, we are reminded that relying on an "African extended family" as the assumed site of long-term care amid the social dislocations of global capitalism is a tenuous move.

Work and Able-Bodiedness

The history of debility is historically intertwined with its opposite, able-bodiedness. The story of these two physical qualities together speaks to major themes in the history of Botswana and the larger Southern African region. Over the twentieth century in Botswana, the growing primacy of wage employment meant that employers became increasingly powerful in determining the meanings of able-bodiedness. From roughly the 1930s to the present, a combination of political, economic, and social transformations produced both new kinds of illness and impairment and new forms of opportunity and exclusion based on changing notions of able-bodiedness. Perhaps the most crucial catalysts for change came from a series of events rooted in the twin processes of colonization/decolonization and regional industrialization: the growth, dominance, and eventual collapse of the migrant labor system to the South African mines and the post-Independence discovery and exploitation of vast mineral wealth within Botswana that ushered in of a new era of rapid economic development. These transformations brought a reshuffling of domestic and economic relationships and new modes of health and ways of understanding one's body.

Changes in work have reshaped the ways in which persons and their abilities are valued, as we will see in Chapter 3. Opportunities in the mines (until the 1970s the primary site of wage employment) and the military were regulated by the vagaries of a system of medical examinations from the 1930s. Women as a group were deemed "unfit" for mine employment. Many men too were considered "unfit" for mine labor. The pool of men rejected from the mines as "physically unfit" grew just as mining wages became increasingly central to long-term economic strategies, and this began a process of marginalization of the myopic, deaf, club-footed, epileptic, and arthritic men from the center of economic opportunity. Such men who in earlier times may have been quite "able" and successful farmers and herders were now left with few options in the changing socioeconomic system but to seek work herding cattle for others.

The new notions of able-bodiedness that circulated amid new forms of work and new systems of wealth were highly contested, because they reoriented the relationship between bodies and persons. This point is perhaps most clearly illustrated around issues of age. Migrant wage labor was in the past and is still work for young people and the middle-aged.[35] By around ages 50 to 60, most adults expect to leave wage work behind and end their stays elsewhere with a permanent return to their natal village (or a village into which they have married), where ideally they have been "building" all along.[36] In recent decades, the ability of older Batswana to control the earnings of their juniors has become more tenuous, and they express irritation at the work culture from which they are excluded. Thus, work, which has become increasingly central to Tswana notions of success and personhood, has been replaced in middle adulthood with such tasks as herding, child care, farming, brewing, and the like. The nature of work—migrant, proletarian, and originally typed as male—has gradually reshaped the meanings of age, home, gender, and charity and the process of labor itself. Wage work has realigned age and socioeconomic power in a culture that increasingly values the money such work brings.[37]

Demand for money (*madi*) began to grow steadily during the colonial period and has become increasingly important over the past several decades in Botswana; cash-based projects and the redistribution of cash between kin are central to social reproduction. But wage labor (usually via able-bodiedness) remains the primary means to access cash. Petty trade of goods such as firewood, beans, cooked snacks, and beer; renting rooms (in those areas close to towns); and agriculture continue to bring money to many, but they are less dependable and desirable than steady wage employment. Often these activities are developed as a wage supplement.

Perhaps most significantly, cash has been used to "build." *Boaga,* or building, is an important concept in Tswana personhood and life strategy, as it is for many people in the wider African region. "Building" continually reaffirms personhood by forging connections over time and across generations—linking the doing of today and yesterday with tomorrow. Building may mean building families, herds, houses, churches, or small businesses such as tuck shops[38] or poultry runs; accumulating furnishings and crockery; or developing gardens or orchards. All are important markers of adulthood, responsibility, and success, and all build persons.[39] And all cost money. Families are increasingly built through the circulation of cash among relatives in the form of school fees, bridewealth contributions, donations at funerals, building materials, and so forth. Often a first boy in a family will be named Kago (builder), for his birth cements the building of togetherness and harmony in a young family, a sign of prospects to come. Ideally children build for their parents first before building for themselves, though the decline of this practice is becoming a marker of the now-failing gerontocracy. In Botswana, where personhood is understood to be a process, building is what one continually strives for. Through building, or self-making, as I sometimes term it in this book, people create and reinvigorate social relationships. They develop moral, economic, political, social, or spiritual capital. It is the primary means through which the promise of liberal individualism (manifest in education, entrepreneurship, wage work) can be harnessed to the making of social selves. Thus, those who earn but do not build are seen as irresponsible, unanchored, and unknowable in some ways. A friend of mine once asked me about what kinds of building I was doing back home in America. I told her that I could not build since, like most Americans, I could not afford an empty plot of land and had no fields. She looked mortified and expressed pity for Americans, since "without building there is no life."

Knowledge and Practice

Though the general trends outlined above have shaped the history of debility, the domains of medicine and health have channeled these broader transformations into knowledge and practices concerned specifically with physical misfortune and difference. Over the twentieth century, people have forged and negotiated the historical experiences and meanings of chronic debility within four overlapping systems designed to promote health and manage and explain misfortune: public health, *bongaka* (Tswana medicine), biomedicine (Western medicine), and lay nursing care. I pursue the relationship between changes in biological and social life in this book in part through transformations in these four domains of health care and the changing ways that each became entangled in the others.[40] Batswana, as patients, as disabled persons (who may or may not be patients or caregivers as well), and as caregivers, synthesize all of these elements of health care into a single, if complex, discourse within their morally imagined histories and illness narratives. Thus, the history of debility (disability, senescence, and chronic illness) provides a vehicle that brings together various elements of the total, heterodox, and hierarchical health system into a larger historical narrative.

I use the term "public health" to describe systems in Botswana by which people sought to manage the health of communities and to prevent widespread misfortune. Historically, Tswana systems of public health organized knowledge and action around spiritual relationships with ancestors; these systems provided an overlapping symbolic and material framework that united ecological and social activities around prevention of misfortune, maintenance of health, and promotion of social welfare. Tswana systems differ from the modern western discipline of public health, which organizes knowledge and action around statistical and scientific understandings. Yet despite these fundamental differences, both are systems of public health and as such both provoke and highlight tensions between the possibilities for liberal individualism and the need to sometimes subordinate individual wants to community concerns. And for all societies, provision of public health is one of the key arenas where community members expect, and often in times of crisis demand, government action in the form of laws, policies, and expert knowledge designed to promote the health of populations.[41]

Over the twentieth century, localized public health systems in Botswana that sought to strengthen and cleanse the environment of toxins and placate the ancestors broke down. By the mid-1960s, the older, chiefly led public health systems had eroded almost completely, and new national and international programs based on modern western models had taken their place. The new public health system, however, did not conceptualize the scope and meanings of health in the same way the older system had, leaving many people with a distinct sense of vulnerability to the vagaries of modern life with its escalating ethos of autonomy and evident physical perils.

Meanwhile, Tswana medicine also went through changes as new technologies and medicines came into use and diagnostic etiologies merged social changes with evolving epidemiological realities. A growing commodification of Tswana medicine occurred over the course of the century. *Dingaka* (Tswana doctors) responded to the influx of *madi* (money, blood, semen) into the region amid the atomization of local health interests that separated *bongaka* from public health and the acceleration of the need for diagnosis, cure, and strengthening needs from patients who coped with an increasingly toxic and dangerous world.

Biomedical services, which previously had been thin on the ground, grew exponentially after Independence. Initially western medicine was bundled with missionary or industrial agendas. After Independence, national and international concerns prevailed. Cross-germination between biomedicine and *bongaka* meant confused conversations and translations across a deep ontological divide, a theme we will pursue in Chapters 3 and 4.

The rise of first male and later female labor migrancy altered local patterns and methods of the nursing care that women provided for relatives and neighbors who lacked close kin. Those left behind by migrant men—women, siblings, and children—found themselves increasingly overburdened by the loss of domestic and agricultural labor. At the same time, their nursing responsibilities increased amid a rising tide of debility. As we will see in Chapters 4 and 5, many women experienced tensions between medical diagnoses that pathologized female sexuality and their public responsibilities as women to nurse debilitated husbands, children, and parents. Mother-daughter struggles over resources resulted in older women's critiques of their daughters' womanhood as manifested in the key practices of mothering and nursing.

This book, by focusing on heterodox and chronic bodily experiences (rather than on particular diseases or institutions) necessitates an integrative approach to the history of African health and medicine.[42] Since people make sense of and try to manage health in multiple domains, I do not focus on "traditional" medicine, colonial medicine, public health, or lay nursing care per se. Rather, I explore how patients and their caregivers mediate between various layers of health knowledge and practices and move through multiple domains of thought and practice as they attempt to manage an increase in debilitating misfortune and a reconfiguring of key health and welfare institutions. In the process this history illustrates the continuing incommensurability of differing (Tswana and western) ideas about health, human biology, and personhood despite increasing overlap in terminology over time. Learning how patients navigate this ontological divide between biomedicine and African medicine is critical for a deeper understanding of colonial medical experiences. It is also essential for improving the current context in Botswana, where the AIDS epidemic has generated a massive influx of biomedicine yet far less understanding of patient concerns.

But here I am interested in more than therapeutics. "Disability," essayist Nancy Mairs writes, "is at once a metaphorical and a material state."[43] In both senses, understanding debility (as well as disability per se) requires attention to social and physical experiences that ground the body and the person in daily life and in the cultural realm of ideas, images, and affect. In this way, Benedicte Ingstad and Susan Reynolds Whyte suggest, the study of disability requires a shift in focus for medical anthropologists. The same holds true for historians of medicine.

> Much research in medical anthropology has a "therapeutic theme." It has concentrated on conceptions of illness and disease, on modes of healing, and on the interaction between patient and practitioner. Studies of disability require us to move away from the clinic toward the community, where individuals and families live with deficits. Cultural assumptions about the body and personhood must be seen within the context of ordinary social interaction. We are less concerned with disease than with its long term consequences and more concerned with adjustment than with therapy. Impairments raise moral and metaphysical problems about personhood, responsibility, and the meaning of differences. Questions about autonomy and dependence, capacity and identity, and the meaning of loss are central.[44]

In an attempt to get at the depth of this simultaneously biological and social experience, I take on an expanded notion of care here, just as Batswana do. Elsewhere I have discussed how gifts of money, visits, attendance at funerals, and washing of clothes are all acts of care.[45] Fred Klaits, in his remarkably sensitive study of how members of an independent church in Botswana cope with the vagaries of the AIDS epidemic, suggests that a central dimension of caring is the engendering of love and positive healing sentiment that is so crucial in the integrated maintenance of bodies and person.[46] Through the sentiments of care as much as the material acts of caregiving, people foster the well-being and social interconnectedness of embodied persons.[47] In Chapter 4, we will look at how concepts in Tswana physiology reflect such links between sentiment, body, and society in crucial ways. For now it is enough to note that social acts that engender love and provide care have physiological and ecological effects for Batswana. Thus, much of what happens between people far from hospitals, sickbeds, and the diviner's bones has deep ramifications for health and bodily well-being.

Debility challenges the power of love and care somewhat differently than acute illness and death do. Klait's work suggests that death reminds people of the importance of love during life; funerals in particular can be key sites for sentimental processes of grief and healing but also for the playing out of unresolved social tensions that can create deep hurt and alienation. Debility, on the other hand, is about the long period that precedes the closure of death; it brings into focus the microprocesses of care. One is left with the day-to-day reality of who cares: who comes to visit, who has the time and the willingness to clean one's bedclothes, to provide a bath, to guide one to the shops, to translate one's messages, to carry one's wood or water, to provide clothes and food. Those who are present early on when impairments are new may let their participation fade over time. Such care is hard to sustain. For many of those who are severely impaired, the ability to return care with care also becomes compromised because it is especially difficult for them to initiate visits, attend funerals and weddings, earn wages with which to give gifts (or share beer, etc.), to bring tea, and the like. So while love is central to the ethos of care in Botswana and while many debilitated persons give and receive a tremendous amount of love, the chronic and diachronic aspects of debility can also lead to feelings of scorn that simmer for many years.

Moral Imagination

The moral imagination is the way we envision possibilities for a morally better or worse world than the one in which we live. Because debility serves to partially isolate experience in a single body while at the same time accentuating the human need for care and assistance and because instances of debility generate social and personal crises that must be made sense of, the moral imagination is central to any history of debility.[48] Imagination is necessary if we are to empathize with one another and if we are to make sense of why life has taken a particular path rather than the alternatives that one might have expected or hoped. Because bodies and the bodily suffering that some impairments and illnesses evidence are social and moral domains, instances of debility propel the imagination along moral lines. Disability, illness, and aging all lead to consideration of the particular paths of individual lives. The ability of the sick, the disabled, the elderly, and their caregivers to engage the empathy or interest of others while constructing their own narratives speaks not only to the power of imaginative life but also to the force of moral discourse.[49]

Many people in southeastern Botswana and elsewhere imagine morally by constructing historical landscapes. History and social memory are by no means the only sources of moral imaginative life. As Jean Comaroff and others have shown, for example, syncretic forms of Christianity and community-building are evidence of attempts to harness new and creative forms of moral power to shifting political, economic, and social circumstances.[50] But here we will focus on history and how local efforts to make historical sense of collective experiences of misfortune form a powerful nexus for exploring both historical semiotics and the relationship between meaning-making and daily coping.[51] Through the historical reckonings of people in Botswana in the late 1990s, one could glimpse the moral imagination at work.

The collective Tswana moral imagination centers on a moral order—a shared set of values held by society that guides its members in expected conduct and provides a way to judge or interpret the actions of others. This moral order links cosmological understandings of the impact of various behaviors deemed moral or immoral to social and political efficacy in the management of the vagaries of fortune and misfortune. In any given context people are forced to prioritize values; many complex situations and changing historical circumstances place words or deeds that are congruent with some values in contradiction with other values that are also held in esteem. In navigating and debating such decisions, Batswana draw on their historical imagination to make sense of present dilemmas and disappointments. This ongoing moral balancing underpins both the individual and collective sense of justice and provides the ground upon which people debate their life situations and those of others. In any individual's experience of the world, these implicit values may act as both constraint and compass. Moreover, a person's orientation on the wider moral landscape is shaped by identity: religion, urban/rural, gender, age, position in family (younger brother versus oldest brother, for example)—and is thereby situational and shifts over the life course, just as identity does. The moral imagination acts to ground cosmology in daily action and experience and bring historical analysis to bear on ongoing situations and concerns.

This study follows the examples of T. O. Beidelman and Suzette Heald, who locate morality in both daily and complex ritual and illustrate the ways in which morality maps the ambiguity of social experience.[52] By anchoring morality in ritual, they are able to explore the inherent ethical contradictions which push certain people to society's margins. Like Beidelman and Heald, I am interested in how morality is imagined and expressed by Batswana in their daily lives and in complex ritual and in how identities and actions are unified in a wider sense of social value. We usually think of moral discourse in its narrowest sense as discussions about "right" and "wrong," perhaps most commonly located in religious or legal contexts. In this case, however, I am concerned with diverse expressions of morality—their form (i.e., posture, gossip, complaining, bathing, hiding, nursing, diagnostics, proverbs, gift-giving, etc.)

and context (both historical and situational)—and with the ability of those who are marginalized in wider society to exercise moral power in certain settings.[53]

If we were to look for morality in words only we would miss much. We wouldn't, for example, understand why Batswana speak of the importance of respect for the elderly yet complain loudly when an old woman delays them in her struggles to climb aboard a bus. Or why a young man's efforts to sneak his girlfriend into his room late at night is a manifestation of his respect for his elderly aunt. Expressed values are dynamic. Though actors regularly imagine a nostalgic past as a template on which to read shortcomings in the current moral climate, this nostalgic past is always changing. The basic markers on this imagined landscape may remain the same—elders, *Modimo* (God), rain, sweeping, mothers, hearts, witches, healers, lunatics, secrets, *madi, digole,* trees, lightening, Setswana, beer, cattle, and so forth—but their shape, their context, and the norms to which they refer gradually change over historical time.

For the Tswana, as for all societies, the moral order was and is crucial for the definition and maintenance of the public's health, and on its grid one can find society's views of its own health.[54] As I suggested above, public health, by the very nature of its enterprise, generates and highlights tensions between individuals and society over moral choices. Public health enterprises ask individuals to subordinate their personal desires to the needs and projects of communities. In early-twentieth-century Botswana, health was both collective and unbounded. It did not belong to a single domain but was instead an integral part of politics, ecology, and cosmology. Shared values were expressed in social mores and practices in an attempt to maintain a veneer of peace that reaffirmed sociopolitical hierarchies and ecological harmony and managed public ill will and misfortune. Such attempts were not always successful. The health of individuals was directly linked to the social health of society through practices which varied throughout the life cycle but which sought to both discipline and nurture persons through their bodies. Both social and personal health were anchored in the wider physical context—bush, cattle post, lands, village, compound (back and front), mines—each ambiguous in its combination of healthy and dangerous elements. Public and personal health were in part managed through proper interaction with these various environments.

But the movement out of the early colonial semifeudal system and into the period of wage labor and migrancy began to unravel the threads that knit the public's health to these other elements of society. Health became a discrete marker linked indirectly through moral imaginings and moral expressions but no longer anchored directly to these facets of society. Because the sets of relationships that make up a moral order are continually renegotiated in conversation with broader historical transformation, moral imagination and moral expression provide both an index of cultural response to historical change and a force which helps dictate how and where sickness and disability are defined and the ways of coping with them. Through debility we can see this system and how it changes, how debilitated persons as well as their families and communities cope with the contingencies of bodily life. We can also see how able-bodiedness was defined and valued and how these definitions and values changed over time.

Sources and Methods

I set out for Botswana with research questions about political and economic forces that generated bodily impairments but soon realized that I could only answer them in the most superficial way. While people were unfailingly polite and answered my questions, their answers challenged my sense of history. Understanding histories of bodily misfortune requires that we integrate political economy and social history with cultural and epistemological questions.[55] Because the human body is the site of productive and reproductive labor, a source of ethnic and gender and generational identity, and a primary site for thought and experience, this integration is particularly important where questions of health and the human body are concerned.

I include the common (almost clichéd) example that oral researchers in Botswana and neighboring sites encounter to illustrate what I am getting at here. In most of my conversations about the past, somewhere in our discussion of whatever theme I was pursuing about labor strategies or marriage patterns or political changes, inevitably the person I was speaking with would mention that it had rained more in the past. At first I tried to ignore this troubling detail, not knowing what to do with it. Then after more conversations, as these details crystallized into a serious and insistent theme, I was off to the archives in search of rainfall data. Yet everything I read reiterated what I already knew about the arid and temperamental ecology of Botswana; there was no recent past of more regular and abundant rains. Instead, talking about rainfall was a way to talk about many other things at once: the power of local government and local people in community participation, opportunities for self-determination that industrialization was eclipsing, reconfigurations in social hierarchies, and so forth.[56] I had been trying to talk to people about a certain kind of history in which I was interested, only to discover that they were interested in a slightly different kind of history, one that was expressed through metaphor, nostalgia, proverbs, and bodily practices (among other things) and one that emphasized neighbors, mothers, and lovers more than mine owners and colonial officials. What you will find in this book is a merging of these two strands of historical inquiry.

Reconstructing the strands of this history and the ways they are tangled together is difficult for different reasons, but I have tried to overcome these limitations by using a combination of historical and anthropological methods. This has allowed me to piece together a rough picture of the broad changes in ideas and practices during the twentieth century. Much of this will sound familiar to other African historians and to anthropologists, who may choose to skip this last part of the introduction, but a discussion of the need for interdisciplinary methods and the limitations of this kind of research bear repeating for readers new to Africanist methodologies. Because of the paucity and the patterning of written documentation in many parts of Africa, oral sources have long been fundamental to African history. As my rainfall example shows, oral and ethnographic work together help to make sense of local categories of analysis and meaning.

Oral sources are central to this project; they provide perspectives on confinement, diagnosis, cooperation, care, and debility that are absent in the colonial and missionary records. However, because of the dynamism and disarray of this period in southeastern Tswana history and the ways in which the particular questions (especially those about sexuality and confinement) triggered morally imagined responses, oral sources often raised more questions than they answered. Patterns emerge from these popular recollections, but so do patterned contradictions. Some of the contradictions stem from the difficulties of articulating (or conceptualizing) certain western ideas in Setswana. It is no surprise that I met regular resistance to the logic of expressing fine-grained diachronic change; people preferred general periodization when discussing a discrete era of the past (*bogologolo*). The rhetorical tendency among many people in Botswana is to compare past (*bogologolo*) to present (*gompieno*) rather than past to past. The past takes on meaning and authority of its own by virtue of being the past and is thus applied to current analytic agendas. Nonetheless, I consistently made attempts to "date" the recollections of my informants by cross-indexing them against major historical events—the year of the black sorghum, the start of the war with Hitler, the opening of a clinic, and so forth—or to personal events—the birth of a child, the first year at the mines. The reader should be aware that the history I tell was in many ways dictated by my own (not my informants') sense of time.

Other contradictions stem from positionality: people who were children in a given period remember it differently than those who were adults, men remember it differently than women. Especially because so many men were absent for much of the time, male impressions are interrupted ones, forged as much in distant mining compounds as at home in their villages.[57] Yet this positionality also allows me to compare oral responses to identify essential or core elements of what happened in the past and to glean the importance of life experience in shaping how people viewed their world.

Still other difficulties stem from the sensitivity of the topic. Some people whom others identified as having had "hidden" disabled persons in their households did not mention this during our conversations and I thought it insensitive to question them directly on this issue. Others admitted freely that a disabled family member had been confined in the family compound but were either unwilling or unable to provide much in the way of description or analysis of the diagnostic and nursing practices that led to such confinement. Few people who were confined themselves are still alive today, and the tiny handful whom I met who could communicate cogently did not wish to discuss those experiences. Sorcery, illicit abortions, and infanticide were all issues I found difficult to probe with many people, though references to all these practices appeared in the colonial record and occasionally people would speak freely on these matters. The types of experiences and the constellation of people and events that forged diagnosis and coping in the cases I witnessed and got to know in the late 1990s through ethnographic observation, a method which I will describe in greater detail in Chapter 1, were not available to me solely through a process of oral recollections.[58]

A similar set of issues confused me in my historical exploration of local medical knowledge. Tswana medicine (*bongaka*) clearly evolved over the twentieth century, as all therapeutic systems do. But in discussions with elderly healers it was difficult to disentangle which of the disparate elements that entered into local medical thought and practice did so, and when and how and which techniques and ideas were reoriented or dropped.[59]

Oral histories are not the only complicated sources here. Statistical data on various health-related phenomenon, the bread and butter of historical epidemiology, is either nonexistent or incomplete and problematic in this case. Though the colonial medical service tallied and assessed statistics on clinic and hospital attendance, diagnoses, and health outcomes throughout the colonial period, such statistics tell us more about the predilections and practices of colonial doctors and institutions than about patient experiences. Colonial medical settings, where language and cultural barriers greatly confused the taking of case histories and where laboratory and other diagnostic technologies were primitive and subject to repeated breakdowns, generated serious problems in differential diagnosis. Racist assumptions about African bodies and behaviors shaped diagnostic trends. Also, colonial medical institutions were remarkably few, and their reception by local persons had much to do with the personal reputations of individual doctors and nurses. Since many medical personnel were regularly reassigned or returned home, we might expect that clinic and hospital attendance responded in part to local assessments of current staff, thus creating an uneven flow of patients into many such sites. We also know little about when and why certain people came to such sites for treatment while others eschewed biomedicine altogether. In the end, statistics and other colonial-era medical records tell us most about transitions in colonial medicine itself, an important piece of this larger story. They have more limited utility, however, in illuminating the pathways in and out of debility for the people on the ground.

With these various concepts and themes laid out, we now move to southeastern Botswana in the late 1990s, where our story both begins and ends. We will begin in the context in which the memories that are central to this book were told to me. It was a moment when the issues of bodies and persons, debility and disability, self and society, medicine and power, and the moral implications of historical change were very much at the center of bodily, imaginative, and social life.

1   Family Matters and Money Matters

Motse mongwe le mongwe o na le segole.
— Setswana proverb: Every village has its cripples.

Khumo le lehuma di lala mogo.
— Setswana proverb: Wealth and poverty lie together.

The village of Diphaleng is located less than twenty kilometers from Botswana's rapidly expanding capital of Gaborone.[1] The tarred road that links Diphaleng with the city was not built until the early 1990s. Before then, the village was oriented more toward its sister village, Medupe, which is clearly distinguished on the horizon by its rocky hills. But now Diphaleng and Medupe are on separate spokes radiating out from the capital via the sprawling urban village of Mogoditshane. Lodgers and new plot-holders have come to both villages, hoping to live near the city with all its opportunities while avoiding the dangers and expenses of "town life." The young are now oriented toward Mogoditshane and Gaborone with their shopping malls, discos, and bars. Medupe and Diphaleng seem increasingly far apart; people now count distance by the number of combis (minibus taxis), and combi fares it takes to reach a destination. One young friend relayed to me with amazement that her grandfather had regularly "barefooted" it all the way to Mogoditshane (under fifteen kilometers, or about nine miles) to visit relatives until his death in 1996.

Within Diphaleng the old and the new exist side by side. Women and girls gather water from the village taps in buckets carried on their heads or in wheelbarrows stuffed with 40-liter plastic drums. Donkey carts, often made from the discarded flatbeds of old Toyota pickup trucks, move up and down the dusty paths crisscrossing the village, laden with people, firewood, and water. Many times each day from my house high on Moretologa hill I saw them briefly slow the fast-moving traffic on this easternmost bit of the Trans-Kalahari Highway as their drivers crossed the tarred road, moving people and goods between village residences and "the lands" (the agricultural zone; site of fields and farmhouses). Donkeys stand facing every which way scattered about the village, staring off into the distance. They are what is left of the progressive government program to provide cheap draft power to families without cattle. One friend told me that her grandmother says donkeys are angels put here by *Modimo* to watch over the people. The series of paths lead into vaguely circular "wards" where a number of compounds center on a large tree or fireplace for local meetings. Many of the homes are thatched-roof mud rondavels painted in earth-colored geometric designs surrounded by the traditional low mud-walled courtyard called the *lolwapa*.

Other women and young men gather water into plastic drums loaded into the backs of their pickup trucks or station wagons or simply draw water from the taps they have paid to extend into their courtyards. More and more rectangular cement houses with tin or even tiled roofs have sprung up in the village. Some of them are quite extensive with five or more rooms and a veranda. Televisions abound, evidenced by the antennae and satellite dishes fastened to many of the buildings, and more people have electrified their homes, eschewing the laborious task of recharging the car batteries they previously used for power. Between five and six P.M. many people can be found inside their homes or those of friends and relatives, sitting on the overstuffed furniture, glued to their daily dose of *The Young and the Restless* and *The Bold and the Beautiful*.

In one home, grain is pounded by hand and cooked over a fire. Next door, the cook opens a giant plastic bag of Tastic Rice and lights a stove fed from gas cylinders. Young mothers regularly give their infants and toddlers large spoonfuls of mayonnaise and sips of Coca-Cola or cellophane packets of "peri peri" or cheese-and-onion-flavored snacks with names like Nik Naks or Shooters, believing what they have learned from the clinic, that costly European foods will be beneficial to a child's development. Meanwhile, grandmothers attribute their own "high blood," aches, and pains to the changes in diet brought by "foreign foods" such as cabbage, tomato sauce, and pasta.

This was southeastern Botswana in the late 1990s. It was the context in which the debilitated people of Diphaleng lived and the one in which their problems and solutions were forged. Here I will present several narratives, or case studies, of people I came to know in Diphaleng and two neighboring villages in an attempt to illustrate the social, economic, moral, and experiential complexity of debility in contemporary Botswana. None of these cases are "typical," but then no debilitated person whom I met had a "typical" story to tell. Though many people cope well with their impairments, stories of bodies, minds, and families unraveling or reconfiguring are never "typical." Cases of debility are always complex because they provide a site in which the latent socioeconomic, physical, cultural, and moral planes of a society intersect in explicit ways. The value of examining narratives such as those below lies not only in what they tell us about the situations in which large numbers of people find themselves but also what they show us of the outlines of community and the mechanisms and semantics of social relations in action. These cases show what happens when that which is normal and expected—the birth of a child, earning a wage, marriage, building a new home, a mother's aging—become "abnormal" and contested. They allow us to glimpse how cultural and moral conceptions of the world are grounded experientially. Case studies are also important, since debility is a diachronic process. In each case, modes of interpretation, care, conflict, and coping are all rooted in the time before the impairment or illness started and evolve as the period of illness or impairment lengthens. Narratives enable us to explore some of that temporal progression.

Perhaps most important, case studies allow us to see how local meanings of debility are negotiated through relationships. In Botswana, debilitated individuals and their family members and caregivers alike read the meanings of debility as the product of relationships. Such meanings are often displaced from the social world and are manifested in the body of the debilitated subject instead of originating in a notion of individual experience. This conception of debility is a dynamic one in which ongoing physical and social processes interact to shape and reshape one another.

Below I will present four cases: two of childhood disability, one of a 45-year-old ex-miner, and one of an elderly stroke patient. I selected this range of material to highlight the importance of age in health-related contexts. I have supplemented my discussion of each narrative with reference to similar cases which point out common themes and alternative outcomes. Together all these stories highlight themes about family, community, and health that will be traced historically through the rest of the book. Family (including the debilitated subject) is the key context in which the experiences of disability, aging, and illness are negotiated. Conflicts over debility in the late 1990s usually took place within families, and inevitably crystallized around struggles over morality, money, and care. While health care professionals, community leaders, neighbors, and friends all play a vital part in the lives of debilitated persons, they do so in part out of their capacity to affect internal family dynamics.

Families shape the outcome of professional health care, be it Tswana or biomedical in orientation. Through internal familial struggles over the meaning and validity of diagnosis and treatment, family members together define the nature of a particular case of debility: who, if anyone, is to blame and what type of future onus is to accompany that blame; what is to be done given the interpreted nature of the problem; how much self-determination is to be accorded to the debilitated subject. Though men do play vital roles in families with disabled, frail, or ill members, women play a leading role in the two key semantic arenas that determine the experience of debility—morality and nursing. The gendered nature of nursing care means that women are at the center of debates and struggles over many cases of debility regardless of the gender of the subject. Likewise, debility provokes moral inquiry into causation and care. It is often taken to be a manifestation of a breach in moral codes, and even when men might be a catalyst for this breach, blame usually aggregates in women. Women, in turn, take the lead in shaping the public debates over the morality underlying a given case. Obviously the personality of the debilitated subject, the specifics of their physical and mental impairments, and their position within a family all affect how a family perceives and copes with the situation. But debilitated subjects will almost never be alone in their perspectives; they will be in a faction or entire family of relatives who sees the problem as they do. Part of their success in self-determination will have to do with their ability to influence family politics.

During my stays in Botswana from 1997 to 1999,[2] I met some of the disabled people of Diphaleng on my own. But I met most through my work with the Cheshire Foundation, an NGO which provides community-based rehabilitation services (CBR) in southeastern Botswana. Cheshire generously welcomed me aboard and allowed me to accompany Dikeledi Moloi, a rehabilitation technician, on her mobile trips three times a week. On Mondays we worked in Diphaleng or another small village farther up the tarred road. On Wednesdays and Thursdays we were in another larger village, yet one more stop up the road.[3] This work allowed me to get to know a number of debilitated people and their families and to watch their life situations change over a two-year period. In addition, the administration at Cheshire made their CBR case notes from 1991 to 1999 available to me. Patients also regularly showed me their health cards, on which clinic and hospital staff made notes summarizing each visit, prescribed drugs, and noted test results. I tape-recorded formal semi-structured interviews with approximately sixty of Cheshire's clients and/or their family members and another thirty-five or so other people: missionary doctors, traditional doctors, healing prophets, disabled activists, elderly people, and so forth. I almost always had a Motswana research assistant to help translate during these interviews, though I checked their translation when I transcribed the tapes. I have taken numerous classes in Setswana, and my ability with the language improved greatly over my time in Botswana, but I never became completely fluent. I easily lost the thread of a conversation when the pace of speech was too rapid or when the speaker was particularly eloquent and exercised his or her knowledge of deep Setswana.[4] Sometimes Dikeledi would translate for me, and I always benefited from the questions she would add to the interview.[5] Often visitors or other household members would participate in part or all of the discussion, and conversations that had begun as two-on-one interviews often wound up as group discussions. I also had countless informal conversations with Dikeledi, the family welfare educators (FWEs) from the local clinics, patients, family members, and neighbors. More important, I witnessed many such conversations in which I played no part. When I failed to grasp the Setswana in these conversations, Dikeledi and the FWEs would review for me what had transpired and we would debate its meanings as we drove in our pickup truck to the next client's home. The following observations are based on a combination of all of these sources.

The cases that I came to know best were all in villages that were served by the CBR program. The presence of such a program locally obviously affected the experiences of patients and their families, and therefore certain aspects of these cases cannot necessarily be generalized to areas without such programs. I did get to know several disabled people who were not served by CBR programs and made a number of trips to Kubung, a tiny village which had no CBR program, located twenty kilometers or so down a dirt road from Thamaga. There I conducted interviews with disabled people whom Stephanie Cohen had identified in her survey work. But though I learned some interesting things from my trips to Kubung, a single interview with a person did not provide the richness that came from visiting someone over a two-year period and meeting their relatives, neighbors, and friends. In Diphaleng and the other two villages, I was also able to be present when several persons first developed their impairments, whether through accident, disease, aging, or birth. This type of diachronic observation proved much more revealing than the cross-sectional or snapshot-type data I got from my visits to Kubung. Therefore all of the case material provided below comes from the three villages in which I worked with Dikeledi.

Economic Contexts

Few debilitated people that I met were able to find employment, though some ran small businesses making dresses, doing screenprinting, selling fruits and vegetables, or working as graphic artists. Many disabled persons expressed the tragedy of their situation through their fear or certainty that they would never work again. Wage work in Botswana, as in most places, brings social power through "building" and redistribution of cash and gifts. Usually the disabled person believed that he/she would be able to do a job well but feared they would never be given a chance.[6] There would always be an able-bodied person who was also looking for a job and preference would be given to them. This fear was well grounded, and though the Cheshire Foundation worked hard to find employment for many of their clients, their successes were few (but significant).

Still, disabled persons, like the frail elderly and those debilitated by chronic illnesses who were home all day, were not alone. Unemployment in Botswana is high by western standards, yet at 21 percent in 1994 and dropping to 15.8 percent a decade later, it remains low compared to the rest of the region.[7] The employment figures are calculated as "persons aged 12 and above who did some work for payment in cash or kind or who were in self-employment for profit or family gain during the reference period." This definition masks a large degree of underemployment. If someone found a few days of work weeding another person's field in exchange for sorghum, they were, by national standards, considered employed.

Furthermore, the definition of unemployed excludes discouraged jobseekers; these people are defined by official terminology as "economically inactive." This category includes many of the country's debilitated persons. "Economic inactivity" rates rose from 37 percent in 1986 to 65 percent in 1994. It is no surprise that more employed persons and jobseekers were in the city and large towns, where most jobs were, than in the rural areas. Women are more likely to be "economically inactive" than men and their rates of participation in the labor force fall precipitously after age 39 in urban areas and age 25 in rural areas; men continue to participate in the job force at rates over 50 percent as they age. In 1991, this meant that there were 402,799 "economically inactive" adults in a country of some 1.4 million persons. Add to this 61,265 people actively seeking work, and the resulting total of 464,064 unemployed persons outweighs the 441,203 persons who are earning in either cash or kind.[8] Thus, those who are unemployed, which includes many debilitated persons and their caregivers, are in good company, and though they may regret their situation and long for the consumerism and redistributive powers money makes possible, they do not necessarily carry any social stigma from their unemployed status.

Unemployment does not in and of itself bring exclusion from the social world, and the villages remained vibrant places during working hours. A significant percentage of rural residents were supported at least in part through government welfare schemes. Many of the men and women we would find at home in the villages during the day did piecework jobs when they were available or earned cash through the seemingly perpetual program of drought relief. Drought relief is one of the state-funded social welfare programs through which participants are remunerated for labor on local public-works projects such as building roads or enclosures around water taps to keep livestock out. It is open only to the able-bodied, and many elderly and disabled people complained of their exclusion from the programs, which provide up to 20 percent of the employment for rural residents.[9] The elderly are covered by an old-age pension scheme, while a small portion of the disabled population, those determined to be without assets and unable to work—the "deserving poor"—are provided with a monthly allowance for food and other essentials.

Despite the relative wealth of Botswana compared to other African countries and the government's commitment to social welfare programs, a third of all households (and 43 percent of the population) still lived below the national poverty line in 1994.[10] This was down from 46 percent of households in 1986.

The president, a trained economist, has suggested that a shift from income in kind to cash-based income is at least partly responsible for this increase in real household average income.[11] The prolonged drought of the 1980s in part precipitated this shift; in its wake, many women abandoned agriculture altogether. The current AIDS epidemic has further compromised farming as many older women (i.e., farmers) are busy nursing sick relatives and caregiving is easier in the village with its water taps, pit latrines, and shops, than in the more rustic and scattered setting of agricultural homes used during the growing season. The movement toward cash income advances a trend begun in the 1930s and has brought a further reconfiguration of economic power within in the household; men earn more than women and the old are increasingly seen as "economically inactive." Thus, those who do earn, particularly those who earn in cash, have both increased social power and tremendous demands on their earnings. For those who had regular employment, stretching each paycheck to meet the demands on it was difficult. Payday at the end of each month in Botswana was celebrated with visits "home" to see relatives and attend parties of all sorts. Early into the Saturday morning of "month end," I could hear the sounds of revelers, often screaming up the unlit single-lane highway in overly full pickup trucks. At the start of each new month we arrived at work to be greeted with a story about someone's relative, neighbor, or friend who had been killed or seriously injured in a car accident during month end. Month end, Christmas, New Years, President's Day, and Easter Weekend, while relieving the pressures of work and economic demands, also continually supplied new members to Botswana's disabled population.[12]

Professional Health Care Contexts

In 1991, the Cheshire Foundation of Botswana, a small branch of an international organization, began to provide community-based rehabilitation services to Diphaleng and fifteen or so other villages in eastern Botswana. Their program was modeled after the one designed by the WHO during the late 1970s during the heyday of programs which relied on community "participation." The CBR program at Cheshire provided rehabilitation technicians to local communities. These technicians underwent a two-year course in which they were trained in a variety of techniques such as physiotherapy, occupational therapy, speech therapy, manufacture of technical aides, social work, and community organization. Other NGOs operated in different villages in Botswana, though they covered only a small fraction of the nation's debilitated population.[13] Due to problems with transportation, villages such as Diphaleng which are supposed to be covered can go for weeks or even months at a time with no CBR services, and most villages in Botswana had no services.

An elderly man receives community-based rehabilitation from a rehabilitation technician (in white coat) and a family welfare educator (seated in chair). His wife is seated next to him. Photo by Stephanie Cohen, 1999.

Dikeledi, a 30-year-old Motswana woman who trained in Zimbabwe, was one of the best rehabilitation technicians in the country. She worked in conjunction with the family welfare educators at the local clinics to identify and "rehabilitate" her clients. The FWEs, all women, provide the vital link between the community and the health care system, working in the same villages where they had always lived. Along with providing health education and manning the clinics, under the direction of a supervising nurse, they also move about their section of the village providing basic nursing care and clinic referrals. Hardworking, amazingly persuasive, yet remarkably subtle, they are the backbone of Botswana's government health care system. Their work blurs the lines between relatives, neighbors and patients and professional health workers, bridging two cultures of health etiquette and knowledge production—the professional culture of the clinic and the lay one of the village.

The FWEs were part of a national health care system which was at least partially administered at the district level. In the thirty-plus years since Independence, Botswana has developed an amazingly broad health care infrastructure with a health post or clinic in every village, several regional primary hospitals, a handful of secondary hospitals, and two referral hospitals. Diphaleng's clinic, a cement building painted in the district colors—mustard yellow and green—was near the center of the village. It fed into the country's largest hospital, Princess Marina Hospital in Gaborone. When I left the village in 1999, building work had been completed on a second clinic that would soon open to ease some of the overcrowding at the old building, which was then serving a population estimated at 7,500 people. The other villages where I worked were also well served. The large village had two clinics and a primary hospital, while the smaller one still had its own clinic. Technically the FWEs were supposed to provide CBR services as part of their regular work, based on techniques and knowledge they gleaned during brief training seminars. This was a practical impossibility given their level of training and the already great burden of work these women had. In addition to providing care before and after births, family planning services, first aid, and primary health care, these clinic staff also helped organize public health campaigns such as TB Awareness Day, Sanitation Day, and AIDS Awareness Day.

Clinic workers are also often community leaders, in part since their work brings them into contact with the majority of people in the village. In 1998, the Diphaleng clinic staff began working with local church groups to organize a voluntary Home Based Care Committee to provide assistance to people with AIDS. But church leaders controlled the group, and their religious politics were made clear to me when they rejected a donation pledge of 1,000 meals from a group led by an Indian schoolteacher who worked at the local junior secondary school. His vegetarian meals, which I imagine would have been welcomed by the many patients I saw with little or no food in their homes, were suspected to be a thinly veiled attempt at religious conversion.

The Ministry of Health also maintained a division devoted to disability, the National Rehabilitation Services Division, but given the massive demands on the national health budget, the vastness of the country, the amount of time required for meaningful rehabilitation, and the unit's commitment to generating a national awareness of disability, they were unable to provide much in the way of ground-level services. In my total of sixteen months working with CBR, I only encountered the government rehabilitation team once. They announced their visit the day before their arrival and requested that all the disabled people in the village congregate at the clinic, where they would be treated. When the rehabilitation team arrived, disappointed at the lack of patients, they were counseled about the practical difficulties of transporting well over 100 people with physical impairments on short notice. They settled for a spontaneous roundup of the deaf population, only to discover that the clinic had no electricity to support their audiology equipment.

The clinics never seemed short on patients, but people also made extensive use of the networks of *dingaka* (Tswana doctors; singular *ngaka*) and *baprofiti* (healing prophets). Members of the small independent churches and the powerful ZCC (Zion Christian Church) also used healing services available through their churches. Much has been written on health-seeking behavior in Africa, the ways in which decisions are made not by individuals but among kin groups, and the movement of patients and their families through an increasingly pluralized set of health care options.[14] Botswana is no exception (I will return to these issues in Chapter 5), but it is worth making a few points as they relate to debility. Debilitated persons and their family members are interested in two types of medical care. First, they have searched or are still searching for a cure for their problems. Second, they seek assistance in coping with their physical and economic limitations; this includes palliative care with its promise of relief from pain and discomfort and the at-least-theoretical potential for acquisition of canes, crutches, glasses, wheelchairs, and prosthetics.

But while people might look in any number of health care settings for a cure, they limit their search for palliative care and coping to local church communities and institutions run by the government, missions, and NGOs. I met no one who sought out a *ngaka* or *moprofiti* for assistance to cope with a chronic illness or impairment. People approached these practitioners for diagnosis, cure, or prevention only, and when they found relief but no cure they considered the process a failure. Comparisons of such doctors to the powerful *dingaka* of the past were common. Like Evans-Pritchard's Azande, failure to cure did not suggest a failure of Tswana therapeutics.[15] Rather, to many Batswana, it meant that the profession had become polluted with charlatanism and shoddily trained practitioners. Independence, with its newfound money and flouting of convention, had chipped away at the strength of the therapeutic system, as had the years of colonial rule in which key Tswana medical practices were criminalized, and it was getting increasingly difficult to find a powerful doctor. Likewise, there was a healthy degree of cynicism among many about the efficacy of diagnostics and the promise of cure at the clinics and hospitals. Many people explained that care in such sites might combat symptoms but not fully cure the patient of their illness.

People also looked to the government to provide financial assistance to disabled people. Many people, including those with large homes, livestock, or even cars, complained bitterly about the government when they found that disability did not automatically qualify them or their relative for a "destitute" ration. Beginning in the 1930s, churches became an important source of supplemental social support. Though churches usually lacked the capital to contribute financially to their debilitated congregants, they did provide a perpetual check against the often socially isolating life of debility. Church members would regularly come and pray and dance for bedridden patients, thus helping patient maintain a foothold in the community.

For those in dire straits, church groups might also provide labor to the incapacitated. Tebogo, a 45-year-old woman whose stroke left her hemiplegic, had been living in a Red Cross tent with her adolescent daughter for seven years after her rondavel crumbled during the rains. Her family refused to help her rebuild though they lived in neighboring compounds and some members enjoyed such luxuries as a car and cement house. She was finally granted money by the Village Development Committee for a one-room house, and her fellow ZCC church members came to weed her compound and plant a hedge around her plot in preparation for the building project; they also regularly helped her fetch water.

Demographics of Disability

The statistics for disability are dubious at best. I could find no one in Botswana who trusted the available data on the size, diversity, and distribution of Botswana's disabled population in anything but the crudest sense. This is understandable since counting disabled persons is difficult for methodological, political, and ethical reasons.[16] The ethical problems arise on two fronts: first there is a fear of generating a false expectation for services when a government or NGO registers disabled persons in a survey, a problem the Botswana government grappled with in the late 1970s when they were first beginning their pilot community-based rehabilitation program. Second, there is fear of attaching potentially stigmatizing labels to people who might not wish to be so identified. Add to this the methodological difficulties of both defining what is meant by "disabled" and what medical anthropologist Benedicte Ingstad has described as "drawing a line between mildly disabled persons and what one might call variations within normality. This is especially clear when it comes to sub-normal intelligence, psychiatric and social problems, but it is also present when it comes to physical handicaps. For instance, how stiff should a leg be before the person is considered to be disabled?"[17]

The 1995 disability statistics from the Ministry of Health provide a good example of how methodological difficulties produce inconclusive results. That year, several districts failed to return their results, but of the remainder the totals are dubious at best. The Ministry of Health counted 198 men and 177 women with visual impairments in their reporting districts. Of those 375, only two people were aged 65 or older![18] This seems doubtful given the widespread problem of cataracts in a country with such strong sun.[19] This seems to be a clear case of reporting error, in part arising from difficulties with translation from English to Setswana. Oral sources suggest that blindness in the elderly is not considered to be a disability, while in the young it is. Therefore, blindness that develops late in life, for example from cataracts, might never be brought to the attention of Ministry of Health rehabilitation staff, who inquire only about people who are disabled in a given community. Though these people might not be called *digole* locally, many of them might still benefit from services the Ministry of Health or an NGO could provide, such as the provision of glasses or even a cataract operation.

Given such difficulties with the government data, therefore, I will limit myself to observations about prevalence drawn from a thorough but small-scale study. In 1999, a fellow researcher, Stephanie Cohen, along with local clinic staff and a Motswana research assistant, conducted a series of three ward-level house-to-house surveys to gauge the prevalence of disability. Each survey covered all compounds of a single ward of a village. All of the villages were in the southeastern zone of the country. Two of the villages chosen were rural and one was the peri-urban village of Mogoditshane. Survey respondents were not necessarily household heads, but all were resident household members. They were asked to report the number of disabled persons in the compound and their responses were probed through discussion. The results showed a reported incidence of 4 percent in the peri-urban village and 8 to 9 percent in the rural villages.[20]

A more telling statistic is the household distribution of disability. Cohen found that one out of every six to seven households she visited had at least one disabled resident.[21] However, in these one out of six or seven households, there is often more than one disabled resident. It is easy to think of compounds where two, three, four, or even five disabled persons live. Of course households do not exist in isolation from one another; the webs of disability are more dense than at first glance.[22]

For example, soon after we moved to Diphaleng, I employed a woman of my age, Frances Ditaba, to help me learn to better translate some documents I had photocopied from the Botswana National Archives. My husband and I soon became friends with Frances, and we continued to see her long after the translation project was completed. She lived in a nice cement house with electricity and running water and a giant yellow bougainvillea arbor in the *lolwapa*. Frances had suffered from painful and debilitating juvenile arthritis and had undergone a number of operations at Baragwanath hospital in Johannesburg, which had left her with several fixed joints. She had worked in an office in Gaborone until 1997, when she was no longer able to climb the stairs to her office and was forced to remain at home in a wheelchair. Frances, an avid reader who had wonderful taste in literature, was incredibly resourceful and soon began a graphic-arts business out of her house, designing greeting cards, invitations, school certificates, and the like on her Macintosh computer. She lived with her mother, who was in her early 70s; her older sister Ruth, who worked as a schoolteacher; a nephew; and two nieces, including Frances's favorite, Mmalebogo, a successful beauty queen who was crowned Miss Diphaleng for a stretch in the 1990s.

Frances's only child, her five-year-old son, was at Baragwanath himself, undergoing treatment for leukemia, of which he eventually died in 1999. Her oldest niece was mildly mentally impaired and so unable to excel at school. She helped Frances by doing errands, fetching things, and wheeling Frances between rooms. In the back of the compound, in his own one-room house, was Frances's cousin. He had been living with the Ditabas since his mother died two decades before. The nephew suffered repeated bouts of mental illness and could often be seen talking to himself erratically, especially if he had been drinking, but they gave him work running the small mill in the backyard in which they ground the neighbors' grain for a small fee. Frances's cousin, Cindy, and her best friend, Boitumelo, who both worked as schoolteachers, had young daughters with cerebral palsy.

Frances was aristocratic, from a chiefly family, and so her compound was in the central ward of the village, near the *kgotla* (the village meetingplace). Up the hill behind Frances lived Matshediso, the dressmaker who was deaf in one ear and walked with crutches due to the congenital rickets that ran in her family. Matshediso was unmarried, but both of her children had the same rickets and helped their mother with her business. Three doors down from Frances was a "hyperactive" 10-year-old boy with cerebral palsy, and across the road lived one of her mother's oldest friends, who had a severely arthritic hip and was forced to use a walking frame. This woman lived with her sister-in-law, who was caring for her granddaughter, who had post-meningitis cerebral palsy, and her extremely elderly and senile mother. Behind them were the Diphutis, who had seven children. Five of them had microcephalus. They were well known around the village for this. The oldest son, Goodson, did not have the condition, but he was severely myopic and required special glasses, which were extremely costly. When they broke he was forced to tape and glue the pieces together for several months while he ran his fruit stand, upon which the family depended for their livelihood. And so Frances, who rarely left her home due to her impairments, was nonetheless living within a sociogeographical network of kin, friends, and neighbors rife with debility. In a large village such as Diphaleng, this was typical.[23]

Frances herself and some of her friends and neighbors were beginning to see themselves as an emerging subcommunity and often talked about beginning a group that could advocate for their interests. They thought their group could fall under the umbrella of the Botswana Society for People with Disabilities, but the bureaucracy involved in starting such a branch proved greater than their organizational commitment. After a few months, talk of forming a group subsided. This emerging consciousness of a community of suffering, which certainly did not encompass all the disabled people in the village or even a majority of them, stood in contrast to the views of many of the non-disabled, who failed to recognize the ways that the identity of *segole* crosscut other important aspects of community identity such as class, gender, religion, educational level, and age.

This point was brought home to me one day as I sat in Frances's living room drinking beer (I was actually having a wine cooler) with her and several friends. One of the Diphuti children had recently returned from a government-sponsored trip to North Carolina, where he had earned a gold medal in the long jump at the International Special Olympics. His picture had been featured in the newspaper. One of Frances's friends, Lebo, who was drunk, started joking about the boy, imitating him. He said, "All Batswana know that if you see a boy with a tiny head, that one is from Diphaleng. Why must he make us famous for these *digole*?" Frances rolled her eyes. Lebo seemed oblivious to the icy stares he received from Boitumelo and Cindy, both of whom had children with cerebral palsy. Then again, Lebo seemed oblivious to many things.

Even among those whose lives were intimately affected by disability there was often judgment, insult, and estrangement. For example, the identity of *bogole* was not enough to necessarily surmount the rhetoric of blame, shame, and gossip which accompanied the diagnosis of *mopakwane*. *Mopakwane* was a Setswana disease that afflicted infants and small children; its constellation of symptoms encompassed such biomedical conditions as cerebral palsy and Down's syndrome. Parents caused the condition by breaking key postpartum sexual taboos. In later chapters I will discuss the condition in greater depth, but for now suffice it to say that for many mothers, having a child with *mopakwane* meant being regularly regarded as a slut. Public self-righteousness toward those with *mopakwane* children was no less prevalent among those in the wider community of disability than it was among others with only able-bodied kin.

In July 1999, we organized a Day for the Disabled at the chief's *kgotla* on behalf of the Gaborone Lion's Club, where many of the disabled people of Diphaleng and their families gathered to receive donations of blankets and food and to enjoy a program of speeches and music. A few days later I was talking with Nonyane, an old woman who had attended the program to receive a blanket on behalf of her great-granddaughter, who was away at the School for the Deaf in Ramotswa. While we were discussing the day's events, she looked at me with a conspiratorial expression and in a stage whisper asked,

"Did you see Boitumelo there with that child who was like [she gestured, contorting her face to imitate MmaPula, Boitumelo's child with cerebral palsy]? Imagine showing her to everyone. Boitumelo, she slept around and ended up making this child to be a *mopakwana*!"

The Cases

I first met Kago in October 1998 at his mother's house, where he lay on a mattress covered in blankets, despite the grueling heat. His speech was slow and slurred and he could only speak a few words at a time, but we exchanged the proper greetings. He was tall and skinny with graying hair and a beard, and he was dressed only in a thin striped T-shirt and blue underpants. He had always been light-skinned, I assumed from looking at his mother and sister, who were also in the room, but he looked completely yellowed and ashen to me as he lay beneath the blankets trembling violently. The air was so hot and stale in the small cement room that I thought I might pass out; his mother kept the windows and door closed even in the sweltering heat to protect against the dust. Though his mother and sisters bathed and changed Kago regularly, the odor of urine nonetheless hung in the air. His wheelchair was parked in the corner of the room, but the pile of folded blankets on its seat suggested infrequent use. Behind it hung his mother's church uniform, a long green tunic with a white cross stitched to its front.

Kago was depressed. He hadn't seen his wife or children in close to a year, since the day his relatives chased them out of the compound. Though Dikeledi had previously trained him to feed himself and walk with the aid of a walking frame, he now could barely sit up in his mine-issued wheelchair. He might go hungry for a stretch; a few times we found that there was no food in the house and that he had only taken tea with milk the past day. Once we brought the family a huge sack of beans, another time a basket of lemons. Later they reciprocated with a plastic bag of morula fruit harvested from the tree in their compound. At night Kago would sleep in fits and wake up sweating and screaming, fearful that witches were coming to kill him. In his delirium he feared that the doctor he had paid to strengthen his home with traditional medicines was angry over his fee and was now sending witches in the night to finish him off. By January he was refusing to eat or drink, saying that he missed his wife and only wanted to die, and on two occasions I accompanied the clinic staff to his home to forcibly administer oral rehydration salts to him in his delirium. In late January he was admitted to the hospital in town, but he was home again in a few weeks. After that he had his good days and his bad ones. Dikeledi encouraged his sisters to take him out into the *lolwapa* on a mattress where he could get some air, and sometimes he would even joke around with us for a bit. But other days he was quite depressed and might cry to himself or barely raise his head for greetings.

Kago, then 45, was the oldest of seven children. He lived up to his name, which roughly translates as "breadwinner," when he went to work in the South African gold mines in 1976 at the age of 21. He continued working in the mines for his parents, continuing to work for his mother when his father died in 1984, until he married Onkaetse, a 21-year-old woman from a neighboring ward and mother to his two children, in 1987. They then moved in with Kago's mother and his three sisters and their young children. Onkaetse had been friendly with the family, but tensions soon developed over who should control her husband's mining wage. While Onkaetse felt that she was trying to be generous, she also saw that there wasn't enough in one salary to support their own children and those of her sisters-in-law equally. Nonetheless, the single paycheck was regularly stretched to feed a large household and to save a bit for "future," until Kago's younger brother got work as a mechanic and a second income came into the household.

By 1992, Kago and Onkaetse had saved up enough money to fence their own plot and build a two-and-a-half-room house and pit latrine. Before moving in, they hired a *ngaka* (doctor) from a neighboring village to strengthen and protect their compound. The move made the wage distribution more clear-cut, since the women no longer cooked together. Kago's mother expressed some of her resentment with hushed rumors that Onkaetse was "sharing her blankets" with other men in Kago's absence. I don't know if these stories were true or not, but as one neighbor said, "His mother was always jealous and nosy about who was there visiting at the two-and-a-half, gossiping that maybe she had some men there. . . . Who knows what the husband was up to when he was gone all those months? We only know what they will say about the wife, never about the husband."

Then, in 1995, Onkaetse and her mother-in-law each received a letter from Onkaetse's brother, who was working at the same mine as Kago. He explained that Kago was in the hospital and asked them to come immediately. Onkaetse left right away along with Kago's two brothers and oldest sister and his uncle— Kago's father's younger brother (*rrangwana*)—since his mother at age 61 was considered too old to make the journey. There they found Kago in serious condition. He had apparently been struck on the head in a mine accident several years earlier and now one of the veins in his head had ruptured so that "blood went onto the brains." His medical card read "massive cerebral hemorrhage." The doctors in South Africa wanted to operate immediately, and Onkaetse's brother was preparing to sign the release form for the operation when the relatives arrived. Led by the uncle, Kago's family refused. They insisted that they wanted him back in Botswana. As Dikeledi explained, "so much so that they ended up asking the hospital to release him without going through the right channels—so much so that they even wound up bringing him down here using their own transport," a costly endeavor.

A fight soon ensued because Onkaetse and her brother disagreed with this course of action. The struggle intensified when it became clear that Kago's family was not going to allow him to return to his own compound to be nursed by his wife. During the fight, accusations surfaced that Onkaetse had caused the illness. The uncle accused her of having aborted a child conceived with one of her supposed lovers, a grave charge. She then passed on her dangerously hot blood to Kago, causing his illness. Why else, his relatives asked, had his sickness happened so soon after a visit home? Others did not agree, but few followed Dikeledi's way of thinking: "So if you look at the brain and abortion they are two parallel things which will never meet."

The mines awarded Kago a one-time lump sum of 5,000 pula (approximately $1,000 at the time). I felt that they were hardly taking proper responsibility for the situation, given that Kago would most likely never work again, but the family was focused on a different causal etiology than one anchored in the political economy of occupational health. The family wanted Kago to turn the money over to them, not Onkaetse, since they hardly felt that a selfish culprit should be rewarded financially for her transgressions. His mother went to Onkaetse's home and took all of Kago's papers and passport, saying that Onkaetse would only spend his pension money on her boyfriends. But they soon found that they needed either Onkaetse or Kago to sign for the money. They went to the village *kgotla* to request that the chief ask Onkaetse to go sign for the money at the local mine recruitment office. But Onkaetse refused, saying that they should wait for Kago to decide what was to be done with it. The family was still dissatisfied, so they moved up the judicial hierarchy, taking Onkaetse to the paramount chief in Molepolole. He sided with her, telling the relatives that she and her husband should be the ones to decide how to use the compensation money.

The matter rested uneasily for a short time, during which Kago was admitted to Princess Marina Hospital in Gaborone. While he was there, Onkaetse's sister passed away, and she went to stay at her mother's compound to prepare for the funeral. During the funeral preparations Kago was discharged, so his mother and uncle took the opportunity to bring him to the mine employment bureau office at Kgale, where they made him sign for the money with a thumbprint, then took it. When Onkaetse returned, Kago told her everything as he pressed his mother to give his wife some money to buy clothing for his five children. His mother refused, immediately accusing her daughter-in-law of trying to manipulate her son. Before long the money was spent.

Kago's mother then took her son to "the lands" with the family for the agricultural season.[24] Onkaetse was not invited to accompany her husband, but she came anyway and was tolerated. Had she not, she could have been rightly accused by family and friends of ignoring her responsibilities as a wife. At this point Dikeledi joined the case and began helping Kago with a program of rehabilitation. As in so many cases of chronic illness and disability, the tensions in the household already present over money and morality now crystallized around nursing and rehabilitation. Dikeledi's mission was to make Kago as "independent" as possible. Tswana values, on the other hand, dictated that his female relatives were expected to make him as comfortable and indulged as possible, in keeping with Tswana nursing practices. Onkaetse worked with Dikeledi to teach Kago to walk to "the toilet" (which out at the lands meant the bush) with the aid of a walking frame. They worked on restoring his fine motor skills by having him feed himself with guided movements; both Onkaetse and Kago would hold the spoon and carefully move it from the bowl of food to his mouth. To his mother this was further evidence of Onkaetse's failure as a wife. As Dikeledi explained, "The mother would start complaining, saying, 'Hey, she is married to him she should be feeding him [not making him feed himself]. So now if he was to walk to the toilet she would say no he is to be lifted.'"

This conflict over the value of rehabilitation was one I witnessed countless times in Botswana. Parents often refused to put their children into the orthopedic shoes or calipers meant to help them learn to walk because the children cried from the discomfort of adjusting to the stiff boots. Or adult children might carry their mother if she was a recent diabetic amputee rather than watch her struggle, since adjustment to the prosthesis was a profoundly awkward and painful process. A child with Down's syndrome might never learn to dress herself, and one with cerebral palsy might not be sat up in the corner seat Dikeledi had specially built to train the child to hold her head and spine straight if the new posture made the child cry. This resistance stemmed from emotional and intellectual responses to debility and family that ranged from love and concern to apathy and ill will or resulted from a simple lack of confidence in complex rehabilitation regimens. But it was also clearly reinforced by fear of social sanction in a community in which women's nursing was a semipublic affair. As Ingstad and Bruun found,

> A family that lets its elderly person do too much on their own may easily be seen as one that does not give proper care. Thus in a previous study of disabled people in Botswana we found one daughter-in-law who simply refused to teach the old blind lady to move around alone with the help of a stick outside the compound, because "what would people say if I let her go out alone."[25]

Kago's mother, sisters, and wife all loved him and wanted the best care for him but did not agree on what that meant. This was also true in terms of cure. Onkaetse and her brother had wanted the doctors in South Africa to operate on Kago. His relatives, however, decided on another course of action. Though they repeatedly had him hospitalized when his condition worsened, they also took Kago to a series of *dingaka* and *baprofiti* in their search for a cure. I suspect his mother spent a significant portion of the compensation money in such attempts to find a cure to her son's illness.

By the end of 1997, when the family returned from the lands, the tensions were running high. Finally, in early 1998, a major fight ensued in which Onkaetse and her children were "chased out of the house." They returned to their two-and-a-half room home and Onkaetse began working. Initially she worked as a cleaner, but then her brother got her a job as a security guard at a store in Gaborone. Even after she had returned to her home, the tensions continued. She told me that Kago's family does not care about her and her children, "because even if they could be in the village and they meet me or they meet the children, well, they don't even say hello, they just pass—even the sisters."

Failure to greet relatives is a significant act in Botswana. It is the stuff of gossip and severe social rupture. In rural Botswana, one exchanges greetings with anyone encountered on a path or public space or any compound resident seated in the *lolwapa* one passes. Greetings reaffirm personhood and common humanity; through their particular semantics they establish degrees of social distance or familiarity and age-based respect, and they often convert everyone—from strangers to neighbors—into fictive kin through their language.[26] Even greeting a friend as though she were a stranger was a serious affront, but hurrying by someone and denying them greetings indicated complete social breakdown. It was a public means of telling that person that they are now dead to you. This was a mode of expression I witnessed or heard tell of on several occasions during my collection of case material. That many cases of family strife which emerged in the wake of debility culminated in failure to greet was a comment on how seriously such situations could destroy social relations and public civility. As Kago sunk into his depression, his wife struggled to cope with her worries about her husband and the animosity directed at her. When we would run into her in the village she would immediately begin asking if we had seen Kago. How was he feeling? Would we look out for him? She usually left such conversations feeling dejected.

The battle for resources did not end when the compensation money was exhausted. In March 1999, Kago's uncle (*rrangwane*) approached Onkaetse and asked if she would give him the concrete blocks stacked in the corner of her yard. She and Kago had been investing in bricks before his accident in the hope of building an extension on their home. The bricks were her savings, and she refused. She relayed the story to me:

> Those people it seems they want to harass me so that I end up leaving that two-and-a-half—you know the place—because recently the uncle—the one we had gone to Johannesburg with—he came asking for some stones, the concrete which was there. Then I said "Nnya, I can't give you this because maybe in the long run we are going to build; the owner of this compound, you know he is sick so these things have to like wait for him." Then he asked if he could buy it and again I refused. Then he ended up saying Hey he's going to get it because it's his son [*ke ngwanake*] so he will get it. So then the other day we were going to church. So then when we were getting ready to leave the house we just heard him loading in the concrete, which is within the compound. So he just took it.

By winter 1999, Kago was depressed, his mother was exhausted from caring for her son, and his sisters were increasingly disengaged from the conflict, which they indicated was rife with misunderstanding. The family hadn't gone to the lands to farm in 1999. The old lady said it would be too difficult to care for her son and farm, especially while her youngest daughter was in post-partum confinement and not only could not help with the farming but also required special meals and care. So the case was costing them their harvest. Relatives who had tried to intervene to bring about harmony had failed, as had past recourses to the chief at the *kgotla*. Yet to my amazement, Onkaetse and her mother-in-law each approached Dikeledi in her own way to see if reconciliation was possible. Onkaetse invited her mother-in-law and Kago to move into the two-and-a-half with her and her children while she continued her job. Plans for the move were in progress when I left Botswana in September 1999.

At its heart, this new process of reconciliation was pragmatic. By the winter of 1999, it seemed that attempts to cure Kago were almost exhausted. His mother and sisters always denied to me that they used Tswana *bongaka* for Kago; I guess they assumed that as a white woman who often visited with local clinic staff I would scorn such attempts. But a *ngaka* in a neighboring village with whom I talked knew of the case. It was his son who haunted Kago's delirium. And sometimes when I visited I would find Kago with new pieces of yarn tied round his wrists and neck and maybe even waist beads, all signs he had been to a healing prophet. There were even times when we weren't invited in but could see through the doorway that he had been coated with medicines and was unable to bathe them off for a period of some days. But by June and July we noticed no more signs of these efforts and talk had turned to coping, not cure: how to get to the lands for the next rainy season, how to keep him comfortable, how to get food into the house. While his mother had staunchly denied to me that her son was *segole* (disabled) in 1998, saying that no, he was only ill (*molwetsi*), once all possible cures and resources had been exhausted the family was beginning to face the fact that Kago might be bedridden for the rest of his life. And so his mother began wondering aloud how this misunderstanding between her family and Onkaetse, the only other person who could lighten her nursing burden, had come about.

Kago's mine-related disability put him in good company. Most men in wheelchairs I met were "from the mines," though a growing epidemic of road accidents is currently replacing the mines as the primary source of paralytic and amputative injury among Tswana men. But many of these former miners were able to adjust more easily to their new bodies and situations than Kago. There are two primary reasons for this. First, most men did not have the communication problems that come from brain damage and so were able to play a central role in the negotiations over their own care, compensation, treatment, and future. Second, in many other cases there was either no compensation money to grapple over or monthly compensation money that secured the man's position in the family as a perpetual wage-earner.

For example, Rra Molefi, a 56-year-old man whose spine collapsed from tuberculosis in 1991, did not receive a pension, though he was sure that he had contracted his TB during his twenty-seven years in the mines. He directed his family in their agricultural, pastoral, and building tasks from his wheelchair. Rra Molefi had been able to maintain his role as household head through three decades of distant mine work, even though now his wife told me point blank in front of her husband, "Look at him—he is useless! You will find him always seated." His wife and adult children continued to invest in projects he oversaw, such as building a latrine he could access from his wheelchair. In conversation, all deferred to him as the household head.

Or take the case of Moreki Morwa, a remarkably handsome and very hip man who regularly dressed in Nike and Adidas clothing and listened to Kwasa Kwasa music. Moreki was only in his late 20s when his spine was crushed in a underground rock burst in 1990. But Moreki controlled his compensation money. He received both a lump sum and a monthly pension, so he used the lump sum to purchase an old car, which he and his brother-in-law converted so that Moreki could drive. I often saw him driving around the village with friends, music booming out of the green Toyota, heading to a party or to the bars, or with his small children and girlfriend out visiting friends and relatives. He explained his reintegration into his social world to me in terms of his friends and neighbors, not his family, who clearly accepted him and benefited from his monthly pension and his car.

The people I used to be friends with they are just accepting me as a normal person, because some of them, they are even coming here sharing jokes with me. They are the ones I am going out with. Others they are just, some of them, well they are two different types, others they are just ignoring me ever since my accident. They are no longer coming here. I am just meeting them at the road we just greet each other just like that as if we don't know each other. But with the neighbors they are just okay, they are coming here trying to know how I'm living, trying to know whether I'm sick or not.

Though Moreki appeared to be coping well with his disability, he nonetheless continued to see *dingaka* in the hope of curing himself so that he could walk again. He was also taking his son, who had hydrocephalus, and his nephew, who was born without fingers on his right hand, hoping that they too could be cured.

The struggles which consumed people such as Kago and his family were also anchored in the case history. Initially caregivers wanted to nurse patients who were considered *bolwetsi* while seeking a cure for the illness. Cure-seeking was a moral imperative, and customary law suggests that provision of medical care was a basic parental obligation.[27] In the 1990s I never heard of a formal case before the *kgotla* charging neglect for failure to access professional medical care (though I failed to systematically inquire about such cases), but gossip among neighbors and friends indicated that ignoring the illness of a close relative was an important breach of local values. But cure-seeking did not always result in cures. In many cases it led to webs of accusation and counter-accusation that reoriented care-giving resources available to the patient while "healing" continued to elude. After the search for a cure had been exhausted, if it ever was, then people might turn to coping. But sometimes the quest for therapy left the family so torn apart that there was little in the way of emotional or financial resources left to devote to the tedious and stressful process of rehabilitation and daily nursing.

This was the case with Nanki, a young girl with post-meningitis cerebral palsy I first came to know in 1997. Before I met her I had heard about her case from Dikeledi and Lillian (one of the FWEs) as a clear-cut example of the pitfalls of spending time and money searching for help from *baprofiti* and *dingaka*. When attempts at cure had failed, Dikeledi sat with Nanki's parents and added up all the money they had spent on these healers. It came to 4,000 pula (close to US$800 at the time), a tremendous sum, enough to buy a used car or build a one-room house at least. When I met Nanki I could see why. It was painful just to look at her. Every few minutes she would begin whimpering and a spasm would set in, her back arched, her mouth agape, her eyes open wide, frantically searching for her grandmother's face as the old lady rocked her back and forth and patted her bottom, quietly begging her to hush.

Nanki was born in 1990, the first child to her mother and father, who were from neighboring wards of their village. Her parents were unmarried at the time Nanki and her young brother were born. Her mother worked as a cook at a local school, and her father worked in the South African mines. Nanki was a healthy child until she was about fourteen months old, when, according to her clinic health cards, she contracted meningitis, which left her paralyzed and drooling. She had frequent painful convulsions and was unable to walk, talk, feed, or toilet herself. Much of the time she appeared to be in agony. Her father returned from the mines to assist in the search for a cure. Her distraught parents took Nanki to a series of *dingaka* and healing prophets. Nanki's mother lost her job because her daughter required constant care, and her father, who had left his job mid-contract, was now unemployed. Borrowing from relatives and depleting funds for building a compound of their own, they finally gave up searching for a cure a year and a half (and 4,000 pula) later and accepted that Nanki was a *segole* (disabled person).

Meanwhile, Nanki's paternal relatives and many of the neighbors suspected that her mother had broken important taboos prohibiting sexual relations with multiple partners and had thus brought about Nanki's condition, *mopakwane*. Yet Nanki's paternal grandmother, Lorato, continued to accept the child and shared in childcare responsibilities. Nanki's maternal relatives, however, suspected that Lorato had bewitched Nanki's mother because she was jealous of the access she had to her son's income, causing her child's disability and throwing her fidelity into question. Whispered rumors circulated among neighbors and kin until one day Nanki's mother brought the child to Lorato's compound, asking her to take care of Nanki while she went to the shops. Days went by and she never returned to pick up her child. Messages were sent and relatives tried to intervene, but Nanki's mother was through with her. She had the support of her own mother in her decision and both held firmly that since Lorato had caused Nanki's illness, she should bear the burden of caring for the child. From that day on, Nanki's mother never saw her again. Nanki's maternal relatives would ignore Lorato, her sisters, and her friends when they would meet accidentally in the village. Occasionally Lorato would see Nanki's mother hurrying past her compound on her way about the village. Meanwhile, Lorato's son, who had found employment with the district land board, had moved out of his girlfriend's mother's compound, though he continued to see her for another few years until they eventually parted in 1997, when she had a child by another man.

Lorato had little available help in caring for the sick girl. All but one of her children were living in town. Her husband spent much of his time at the distant cattle post caring for the family's livestock and made limited attempts to farm the family's fields without his wife's help. Lorato could no longer attend church, farm her fields, visit her friends, attend weddings and funerals, or visit the shops. She was isolated in her compound, caring for her granddaughter. Some of her neighbors told me that Lorato had gotten what she deserved, since they suspected that it was actually her son who had "broken the rules," thus causing his daughter's disability. When I asked why a son's transgression should result in a mother's burden, they explained that the father couldn't look after the child himself; he required a woman to nurse Nanki. That woman should be his mother, since she had failed in her parental responsibilities to raise a child who respected the rules. But Lorato's church group and her friends and relatives continued to visit her in her home, often gossiping about Nanki's mother and her many boyfriends and her irresponsibility and supporting Lorato's innocence in the matter.

Like Nanki's maternal relatives, Lorato saw the situation in moral terms. But in contrast to them, she saw herself as the righteous one and cast Nanki's mother in the role of the sinner. Her version of the story erased the marriage plans Nanki's parents had once had, emphasized the alcohol consumption in Nanki's mother's compound, and looked to God for ultimate salvation. When asked her feelings about how Nanki's mother had brought the child to Lorato, she explained,

> When I think of the mother really—I am somehow afraid or scared of what would she really do. For instance, others are always telling me that I should be taking the child back. But then I think like, "Well, that lady wasn't married yet to my son—so they were just still going out together." Of course we had accepted the pregnancy, we knew that our son actually impregnated her—but there were no plans yet like marriage. But dumping the child just like rubbish—like they were just dumping their rubbish—so much so that I don't know what will happen—like if I take the child back. It's like maybe if the child was dumped, it's maybe because of something she did—or because she is not married. So whenever I think of taking the child back I'm just afraid—like somehow I am afraid of doing a really sinful thing. I am thinking that maybe if I do that I can end up suffering—punished by God if I take the child back—so I never think of it really.

> J. L.: But what will happen when you are too old to take care of this child?

> So I'm just wishing that maybe old age can be set aside for me so that I am actually able to take care of the child. Because if at all it can't happen, we will both suffer. But I am actually trying to do a lot of things, wishing that maybe God can help me so that maybe God can help this child to learn to

speak and even maybe walk. Even if she will be just limping that is okay, as long as she can walk from one side to the other.

Nanki died in 1999. By that time her parents had long since broken up and her maternal relatives had gradually reinterpreted Nanki's illness as *mopakwane* caused by the father. Nanki's maternal grandmother, Esther, explained how she had been misled by both Nanki's father and amateurish *dingaka* into her original misinterpretation of the condition,

> These days sometimes there are very few those [*dingaka*] who learned, like went through the whole training and copied from the olden days. So then some of them you find that they learned but they didn't go through the whole educational procedure, so they end up not knowing. So now it's like if you go to a *ngaka* or to the hospital and then you don't tell them exactly what is wrong, they won't wind up being able to give you the right treatment. Because let's say one has disobeyed these beliefs [*mopakwane*] and then you go and don't tell exactly what you did, yeah of course the doctor won't be able to give you treatment, and even if you go to the hospital and you are having this kind of venereal disease and you are shy to tell exactly how it is—you are shy to talk about these private parts—then obviously you won't get the right treatment.
>
> J. L.: So then they are no longer as good at diagnosing?
>
> Yes, yes!

Esther now saw Lorato not as someone involved in witchcraft but merely as a mother of an immoral son who was too self-absorbed to confess his transgressions to the doctor. But the quarrels over Nanki and her care were not quite over. Lorato sent word to Nanki's maternal relatives when she died. She received no reply and so arranged for a very modest funeral, exhausting what little money she had or could collect from relatives. But the day after Nanki's burial, she received an angry rebuke from Nanki's mother's kin. She had buried Nanki incorrectly. Esther explained why,

> Actually if anyone of that condition [*mopakwane*] is to die he or she is buried just like anybody else, but for Nanki she wasn't buried properly because usually the mother has to be there—especially when she is alive—she is the one who people should be coming to mourn for. But you know she came when the child was already buried—and then the other thing again—these days things have changed again. If anyone dies after the age of one year because now this is really a human being—really they have grown up—but if it's a small baby or maybe miscarriage or the child is born not alive those ones are just wrapped in a blanket and would be actually buried at home, but

these ones with the coffins they would actually be taken to the graves. So it might be that all those things Nanki was denied—she was deprived of all those rights—she was buried in the mother's absence. She was buried in the compound and she was buried without a coffin.

J. L.: At what age should children still be buried in the compound and not the cemetery?

Two, three, four years old they have to be within the compound. That person would still be young, they would need mother's love, mother's care—so once he or she is buried within the compound he or she is still near the mother. But then it depends on the parents. If they feel that they can take care of that child at the grave it's still okay, depending on how they want to do it.

Lorato felt that Nanki would still need her love and care after death and so she buried the child in the back of her compound, but in this act she usurped the mother's role. Grieving is an important public affair in Botswana, and by burying Nanki in her own compound, Lorato established herself as the primary recipient of sympathy and attention. Nanki's maternal relatives threatened to take Lorato to court for this misdeed, so she went to the chief and explained her case. This preemptive move was successful and the chief assured her she had done the right thing. He made it clear that no one would be able to extract money from Lorato over Nanki's burial. After several years, Nanki's case was finally over, though her life left a series of social ruptures in its wake.

Mopakwane was one of the most common forms of disability I saw in Botswana. All childhood disability affected parents and siblings as well as the children themselves, but few problems were as divisive as *mopakwane* had the potential to be. Some families coped well with this problem and the potential for moral questioning it invoked, but many others, like Nanki's, fractured in the wake of the diagnosis. *Mopakwane* might divide the child's family into opposition between maternal and paternal relatives, as it did in Nanki's case. In other cases, the father and his family play no role at all; they are often not identified. In such situations, if the mother and her close female relatives are "in good books" as they say in Botswana, together they can often piece together a moral logic and a system of support that enables both the mother and her child to cope both practically and socially with the situation. On the other hand, if there is already tension between the mother and her female relatives, the mother's own family may start collapsing around her. This was the case with Senowe Mmilo, mother of Obakeng, a small girl with cerebral palsy.

The case of Obakeng Mmilo was a complicated one which spanned many years and several generations, beginning long before Obakeng was even born. Obakeng's mother, Senowe, was born in 1959 to her unmarried mother. Not long after her delivery, Senowe's mother developed an abscess on her breast and her older sisters took the baby to the senior sister's house, where she was weaned. Senowe thus grew up with her aunt and cousins. Her mother was something of an anomaly in Diphaleng. She enjoyed the highly unusual distinctions of both having only one child and living by herself in a small rondavel near one of the major dirt paths connecting the two sides of the village. It was difficult to find people who wanted to talk directly about Senowe's mother, but from what I gleaned from neighbors, medical notes, and Senowe herself, her mother was mentally ill and rumored to be a witch. The sisters' actions would make sense in this context, since even long after the abscess healed Senowe remained with her aunt. Senowe's mother was poor with no money and little food, but the sisters did not take her in, only her child. Usually children would be given to a woman living alone to help with the domestic chores, not taken away from such a person. Senowe remembers feeling stigmatized as she grew up in her aunt's home. "The treatment [by my foster family] it wasn't really equal. It was because they had not really any other alternative—just they had to accept the situation as it was."

So Senowe grew up and lived with her aunt's family until she was pregnant with her third child in 1987. At that point, she moved into her mother's small rondavel. This situation worked out well, since her mother would mind the children while Senowe went to work her job. She was employed by an agricultural project of a local development scheme begun by a missionary. But then her mother's "heart problems," as Senowe described them, started acting up again. Her mother, who had taken Senowe's baby to the monthly child welfare clinic, was accused by her neighbors of stealing a welfare ration from the clinic. As the level of gossip escalated, Senowe watched her mother grow increasingly agitated.

> As people were saying that [she was a thief], really she got hurt. So much that she started saying that she is seeing the police car coming to collect her since people say she stole from the clinic. Then she started running around. She wasn't staying at her place. She was always on the roads saying she is running away from the police. Then at last she was given some pills from the clinic. Those pills were making her sleep—but then it didn't make any much difference because she would now spend the whole day sleeping. I was by myself that time, by myself, myself, myself (*ke a le nosi—nosi, nosi, nosi*). I was just by myself—even though I was going consulting my uncles and aunties, but they were not coming in to help me.

With her mother medicated into semi-consciousness, Senowe was forced to return to her aunt's home to deliver her third child, Obakeng. When she emerged from her two months of confinement, it was already becoming apparent that Obakeng was struggling. By five months, when the child couldn't be trained to sit upright, Senowe began taking her daughter to a series of *dingaka*. Without her mother to explain to her what *mopakwane* was, she remembers not fully understanding what the various doctors and neighbors were implying when they discussed Obakeng's case.

> I didn't know what was wrong really—that's why I consulted these traditional healers—because I wanted to know what was wrong with the child really. Then with the traditional healers they tried all their things like tattoos and marks but it didn't make any difference. Then I went for this spiritual healers also they made their own things—this woolen necklaces—but it didn't make any difference. But they never told me anything—instead they kept on saying we will try and help you—but then behind my back they started gossiping—she, she, she did this—she broke the rules—but they never told me in face to face. My relatives were also supporting those rumors, but they wouldn't come to me to tell me. Okay to my face they would say a different thing, but when they go out they were supporting those rumors and spreading them, saying I didn't obey the rules. Then some people, friends, were coming to me and telling me that my relatives were saying one two three four about me.

> J.L.: So that is very painful—what did you do? Did you go and confront those people or just stay quiet? I mean what can you do when people are saying bad things about you and you know it?

> Yeah I felt pain like sad that those people were saying those bad things about me—but I couldn't just go confront them—because—well I couldn't go confront them because they are adults, older than me—so I felt really like scared to go and confront them.

She returned to her mother's home in late 1990, where Sarah, the rehabilitation technician who had just begun the pilot CBR program in Diphaleng, came to visit her. Sarah brought Senowe and Obakeng into the new cerebral palsy mother's group she had started, which was designed to be both a support group and a way for Sarah to teach several mothers at once to perform stimulating exercises for their disabled children. Senowe, like most women in the group, found the experience very liberating, in part because Sarah provided an alternative explanation for the cause of *mopakwane*. "Sarah counseled us in a group as mothers—that we shouldn't be listening to all those things [about *mopakwane*]—it's the brain paralysis that actually occurred during delivery—so then later on that's when I forgot about what those people were saying about me."

I met many other women who, like Senowe, found ways to reject a *mopak-*

wane diagnosis. Christianity and biomedicine offered alternative explanations for many. In other cases, mothers might publicly defend their daughters, advocating on behalf of their daughter's virtue. But a few very poor women did in fact accept the diagnosis and their own culpability. Women who depended on a series of boyfriends to provide food for their children reluctantly accepted the risk of *mopakwane* as the price of survival.

Unfortunately, Senowe's boss at work was one of her relatives. He had already proved difficult in his role as the older brother of Thuso, a woman with below-waist paralysis whom Senowe called *ausi* or older sister, and he had different ideas about disability than those Sarah was espousing. He docked Senowe's already meager pay (pula 120 per month) for each hour she spent in the cerebral palsy group. He also docked her for taking Obakeng to the monthly child-welfare clinic, though I was told that this was against the law in Botswana.

So Senowe, who was already struggling to feed her family from her wages and the class A destitute rations she received, had to stop attending the group. Sarah continued to visit Obakeng at her grandmother's home, but a sampling of her case notes reveal how Obakeng's condition began to decline.

> 17/12/90: Obakeng still floppy and weak. She was hungry and found with the granny. . . . Condition is deteriorating because granny is getting worse, but she is the one remaining with Obakeng while Senowe is at work.

> 7/12/92: No progress at all. Senowe doesn't have time because of granny's illness. Obakeng always on her back and has lost her hair. Now it will be difficult for Mom to start all over again. Senowe said at present she can't help it; she has to be with her sick mother.

> 1/2/93: Obakeng's condition deteriorating. Mother has noticed. She said it's because she doesn't have time. She is nursing her very sick mother who has cirrhosis of the liver. I cannot blame her for this because she is the only child, she has to take care of her mother.

When Senowe's mother finally passed away, things got a bit better for the family. After discussion and intervention by Sarah, the village social worker, and one of the family welfare educators from the clinic, Senowe was able to move back in with her aunt in late 1993. Then, in late 1994, the aunt had a serious accident when she was struck by a passing car while crossing the road. This brought on a long bout of "mental illness," and she kicked Senowe out of the house. Another aunt couldn't take in Senowe or her children since her own husband had suffered a stroke and was now hemiplegic and drinking heavily, bringing on bouts of delusion. She was doing all she could to support her own family by selling fat cakes and oranges in front of the bus stop.

Senowe was fired from her job, but after some months working for the drought relief program she found a new job in a cafe. She had moved into a small rented room with her four children and was struggling to support them. All her efforts to secure a residential plot in the village had been thwarted by local politics, despite the efforts of the social welfare office. Two of her uncles were headmen in two different wards of the village where plots were given, and they seemed to be hindering Senowe's efforts to succeed. They also prevented her from inheriting her mother's plot with its decrepit rondavel, claiming the plot for themselves, though years later it is still sitting unused and the rondavel has crumbled beyond repair. Senowe also struggled with child care. She drew from her wages to hire a series of maids, young women who would live in her rented room with the family and care for Obakeng. Hiring of maids even by women with limited earnings was common in Botswana. But most of the women Senowe hired didn't last more than a week. She explained why.

> I had to employ the maid—then within the places I moved into it was difficult for them to accept Obakeng as disabled—even the maids were not accepting their work, some only staying for a week or two then I would have to run around looking for another person to look after her—so it has been quite difficult for me really.

> J.L.: Why weren't the maids lasting, were they afraid somehow?

> They were not afraid. But it's hard for them to look after her because of the way she messes herself since she can't take herself to the toilet so for them to be looking after her it's too much so that's why they ended up leaving.

By late 1995, Senowe had given up on finding help. She was forced to leave Obakeng at home locked in the room until the other children returned from school each day. Dikeledi had taken over the case from Sarah by this point, and she would stop by the home to try and check in on Obakeng through the window. In November of 1995, Obakeng suffered from severe paraffin burns which blistered her back, neck, shoulders, and chest. She had grabbed for the lamp while alone in the house. After much intervention by the clinic staff, in 1996 Senowe and her children returned to her aunt's home, but after a year, they were again ejected by the old woman. One of her own children had moved back home with her family, so she protested that there was no room for Senowe and her kids.

Then, in 1997, Senowe got work taking care of Pelonome Kebafetse, an old woman who was bedridden with a severely arthritic spine. Pelonome had nine adult children who were working to support her, and they hired a caretaker in addition to their maid so that their mother would be comfortable. One of Pelonome's children worked at the clinic as a cleaning woman, and Dikeledi and the FWEs urged her to hire Senowe. Another of Pelonome's children, her youngest daughter, had a plot of her own with an extra room in it, and she allowed Senowe and her children to move in and stay rent free as part of her employment. Senowe would work until lunchtime, when she would walk home to feed Obakeng and then return to work for the afternoon, knowing that her children would soon be home to help out. The family settled into this new routine until early in 1999, when Pelonome moved to stay with another of her daughters in the village of Kanye. Fortunately, the Kebafetse's youngest daughter, who had befriended Senowe, allowed her to stay in the room in her plot for free, but she was now back on the drought-relief program while also attempting to farm her one field during the planting season. This meant rising long before dawn to walk the long distance to the lands and be back by midafternoon to feed Obie. Though she was getting by, she was unable to "build." Her future was always precarious. She assumed, as did we, that eventually the plot owner would marry or want rental money for building and so would evict Senowe. Living with non-kin rent free or even for reduced rent was not common in Botswana. Without a residential plot of her own, Senowe could hardly afford to dream of great works and betterment.

> I am not really clear about my future or that of my children—because I don't have anything like a plot or anything. So I might be thinking I want to do one two three four, but since I don't have my own home really it is quite difficult. Moreover I know I am going to stay like that without a home until I die.

Despite all of this, things were looking up for Senowe when I last saw her in August of 1999. Her oldest son was doing well in Form 3 and would be going on to senior secondary school. In two years' time, he would be old enough to apply for his own residential plot. They all hoped that he would be able to avoid his mother's stigma and succeed in acquiring land. Then, at long last, the family could "build." As for Obakeng, she had developed painful contractures of the hips from spending her days lying down, and her limbs were becoming increasingly stiff and twisted over time. She still couldn't speak, but she clearly understood all that was going on around her. Dikeledi and I would often stop by and visit her through the window of their room, and she would always laugh at Dikeledi's jokes. But her situation was depressing as hell, and there was little hope that it would be otherwise.

Though all the people I talked to stated unequivocally that the primary burden for caring for sick, impaired, elderly, and destitute persons should fall to family members (and many people thought this care should be supplemented by the government), this was not always the case. Not all families were supportive of all relatives. Some lacked the means, others lacked the will, and some people lacked the necessary advocates in the family hierarchy to push for their welfare. But there was little room for the possible lack of familial support in public rhetoric about care for the sick, the disabled, and the elderly.[28] Despite the stated ethos, the arena of "family" from which care is drawn is shrinking. Historically, residential wards were established by lineage segments, so residence overlapped with kinship. The semantics of greeting and social interaction recast more distant kin as closer relatives, which further solidified the dual identity of neighbors and kin, an identity which brought a responsibility of caregiving. Neighbors might regularly bring food to the single elderly man in their ward, calling him *ntate mogolo* (grandfather) as they did so. This is not necessarily the case today. More and more people see those in need as the responsibility of immediate family members only or, in their absence, the state.

Likewise, people find the social and judicial sanctions which once ensured a greater degree of care for the sick and the elderly weakening in the face of the self-determination of individuals. For example, I heard rumors of a few cases in which the *kgotla* failed in its attempts to compel a person to aid a close relative who was destitute by virtue of age or illness. In these stories, the chief and his councilors tried to enforce compliance by garnering the wages of the recalcitrant person and turning a portion over to pay for the relative's care. But such instances were relayed to me as evidence of the determination of some people to be selfish in the face of guidance. In the anecdotes I heard, the people brought before the court quit their jobs and suffered the consequences rather than have the court determine the redistribution of their wage—even if this redistribution was in accord with "traditional" Tswana values. The moral of these stories was clear: in the new economy, some people would rather be broke than share with relatives.

The state endorses the public rhetoric of the sanctity and strength of family-based care, though it has taken steps to supplement this familial support with their own inputs. In 1996, it began a program of old-age pensions. Seniors and their families welcomed this development. The small pensions were originally intended to be supplemental, but they have become the primary means of support for many elderly Batswana. In the poorest of households such pensions may be the primary cash input, thus allowing the elderly to reclaim some social and economic power. But these pensions have other unintended ramifications as well. Gifts of food from neighbors are less frequent. Though the aim for children is still to "build" first for their parents and later for themselves, small gifts within families are also less likely. Many juniors prefer to give their parents larger material objects as gifts: blankets, clothing, or furniture which they will inherit when their parent's possessions are divided after death, unlike goods which will be consumed immediately. Seniors are expected to use their pension each month to purchase their own tea, soap, paraffin, sugar, cooking oil, and meal. If they do not, they might be accused of "drinking" the pension money. Lessons about economic prudence are now flowing from juniors to seniors, not just in the other direction. This is clearly not the case in all families, but realistically the pension scheme has enabled a further reworking of the age-based hierarchies of wealth redistribution.

Where debility is a major factor, control over care in some cases has come to mean control over the pension. This was the case with Lesego Dinare, whose pension was coopted for several years by one of her daughters. Lesego is a 69-year-old single woman with five children, and hers is the last case I will present here. She suffered a stroke in 1995, and when I met her in 1997 her speech was limited to "ee" (yes) and "nyaa" (no), but she was able to move about slowly with the help of a tripod cane and the physical support of a relative, Dikeledi, or one of the FWEs. In 1998, when I returned to her village after a nine-month absence, she was for the most part bedridden and depressed. In 1997, she had been quick to laugh or smile at a joke and wanted to be included in conversation, but by 1999, she refused to get out of bed and would sleep, stare, and cry for most of the day.

Dikeledi was very concerned about Lesego, and in 1998 went so far as to bring Kate, another stroke patient from a neighboring ward, to visit with Lesego to give her encouragement. Kate was coping much better with her hemiplegia. Though she too was unable to talk, she worked with a "communication book" Dikeledi had made. In it were photographs of the various objects and people in Kate's life: her rosary, her husband, a bowl of food, the toilet, her children, and so forth. Kate would point to the one she wanted. Kate's visit encouraged Lesego, who perked up for a few weeks afterward, but another visit was not possible. Kate developed gangrene in her right leg, which was amputated first below the knee and then, six months later, above the knee. Visiting was now out of the question.

Lesego's depression came as much from the conflicts in which she was embroiled as from her physical condition. In order to understand why, it is best to start at the beginning of her story. Lesego never married, though she had five children. She spent most of her adult life working as a maid in neighboring South Africa to support her family, though she returned home for good in 1979 to work in the fields of her relatives. She had a reputation for being a particularly hard worker and an excellent farmer. In 1995, she suffered a minor stroke while harvesting her brother's crop. Her relatives brought her by donkey cart from the lands all the way to the nearest primary hospital (a distance of tens of kilometers), where she was admitted. After two weeks in the hospital she could move about and bathe herself; her prognosis looked good. Then she had a major stroke, which left her paralyzed on her right side and unable to speak. She was to remain in the hospital for longer, but now a fight ensued among her family over who was accountable for Lesego's misfortune and who should take responsibility for her care.

Lesego had two daughters and two sons who were still living in her village. I met only one of her sons; he remained somewhat neutral throughout the struggles over his mother's care, since as a man he would never be expected to nurse an older woman, to bathe her, empty her chamber pot, and change and launder her linen unless there was no other alternative. Her daughters, Tshepo (the older) and Boitumelo (the younger), however, blamed their wealthy uncle and his wife for their mother's condition. They had long resented the time that Lesego spent working for her brother and sister-in-law, since she did not receive an equal share from the harvest. Moreover, they were jealous of their uncle's conspicuous wealth. He and his wife, Mary, lived in a large, electrified cement house with a satellite dish and an indoor toilet. They each drove their own car. Tshepo and Boitumelo thought that since their aunt and uncle had gotten wealthy from their mother's labor, Mary should be the one to nurse Lesego. Besides, they argued, Mary was a former nurse who now owned a shop in the village selling traditional and patent medicines, and their house was better suited to caring for a hemiplegic woman since they had a toilet. Neither Tshepo nor Boitumelo, who was living in Lesego's compound, had a latrine, much less an indoor toilet.

Mary and her husband saw things differently. They felt that it was actually the stress and worries over her children that had caused Lesego's stroke, not working in their fields. By "children," I think they meant the oldest daughter, Tshepo. Tshepo was unemployed, a heavy drinker with eight children. She would visit the bars around the village, often returning home late with different men. Lesego's other daughter Boitumelo was different. She had been living in a neighboring town and working as a shop clerk there but had quit her job and returned home to stay in her mother's compound when Lesego fell ill. She was able to get work as a cook for one of the local primary schools, though the pay was meager in comparison to her former job in town. Mary asserted that it was the stress of having problem children that brought on Lesego's major stroke.

> After the stroke—I saw her when she was from the lands but it was quite a mild stroke. I will call it a mild stroke, it seems like you could only realize it when you know her—she had been just an active person before that. Apparently she had high blood pressure which we didn't know—we didn't know she was hypertensive until she had this—it was just the tongue—the speech wasn't perfect, but she walking just all right. You have heard the speech of a drunken person—it was just like that. Anyhow, she was just all right and then somewhere along the line she must have been terribly disturbed—no,

annoyed—*ke bana*—*mathata ke bana*—[it is the children—the problem is the children], because it was after that she was too ill. She was admitted to hospital. I went to see her—she was too ill. . . . If she could have lived with the mild stroke that she had it could be fine now—she could really be fine— but along the way I think she must have had two or three until she ended up like this.

Though Mary and her husband blamed Tshepo and Boitumelo for Lesego's condition, they thought that her mother, Joyce, should actually be the one to care for Lesego, since mothers are expected to nurse their sick daughters even in adulthood. A child could be given to the old lady to assist her in taking care of Lesego, and the transition would be an easy one since Lesego's compound was next door to her mother's place. But Joyce resisted this. Stroke, or its Setswana equivalent, *go swa mogama* (to be half dead), implied a movement into *botsofe,* or old age. If Lesego was now elderly, it would be her daughters' responsibility, not her mother's, to care for her, since daughters are expected to nurse their elderly parents. So Lesego was eventually moved back into her own compound, where Boitumelo took charge of her nursing care with occasional assistance from Mary.

Mary and Boitumelo together paid to build a latrine in Lesego's plot, since Lesego could no longer go to the bush. Boitumelo and some of the relatives wanted to take Lesego to a doctor in Ramotswa who could "untie" her tongue by cutting the tendon which tethered her tongue to her lower palette, which they hoped would enable her to speak again. Her brother, however, vetoed such a move, and instead Mary took her sister-in-law each week to Gaborone for acupuncture and physiotherapy. By 1997, though, Tshepo and Boitumelo were fighting over their mother's care. Boitumelo complained that her sister was not helping to ease her nursing burden; Tshepo complained that her sister was "eating" her mother's pension. In 1996, when the government introduced its old-age pension scheme, Lesego began receiving 100 pula per month (it was raised to 110 pula in 1998). Boitumelo collected this money on behalf of her mother each month, but Tshepo wanted a share. Tshepo had also brought one of her daughters to Boitumelo to help her in caring for Lesego, but now this daughter was pregnant and unable to assist, instead requiring care of her own. Boitumelo was recently widowed; her husband had died soon after the wedding, a suspected early victim of the AIDS epidemic. Boitumelo was depressed and eventually gave in to her sister.

Lesego, crippled with hemiplegia and unable to speak, was thus brought to Tshepo's dilapidated and already overcrowded compound. Tshepo's compound had two small mud rondavels and the foundation for a three-room house which her brother, who was a builder, was working on intermittently. It lacked a latrine. There Tshepo lived with her eight children and three grand-children. Tshepo put Lesego into one rondavel with her pregnant daughter, who soon gave birth. Lesego continued to stay in the confinement hut. It was shortly after this move that I first met Lesego.

Joyce never came to visit her daughter. Not in the hospital, not when she was next door, nor when she was eventually moved into Tshepo's compound. This was part of the reason that Lesego was so depressed. She thought her mother didn't love her or care about her. I suspect that this was not the case, that rather the old lady was angry that Lesego had usurped her own movement into *botsofe,* with the spiritual transcendence it implied. She complained that she too had high blood and so couldn't physically manage to visit her daughter. Though her family questioned her actions, Joyce was in good company in her decision not to visit her daughter. Many mothers of adult children with *go swa mogama* (hemiplegia; stroke) refuse to visit them, deny responsibility for their nursing care, and complain of their own ignored ailments and problems. Having two generations of *batsofe* (elderly persons) at once challenged the very nature of family and the life cycle, and the senior generation resisted it with all their might.

Within a short time, it became obvious that Tshepo, who had begun by tak-ing good care of her mother, was overwhelmed with the task. Boitumelo, who worked from early morning to one in the afternoon, began spending much of her time at Tshepo's place, helping her often-absent sister to care for their mother. Fights ensued, as the family soon surmised that Tshepo was spending the pension money on alcohol. Mary and her husband sided with Boitumelo and began questioning the type of care Tshepo was providing. Dikeledi, Lillian (one of the FWEs), and I were aware of Tshepo's drinking, but Mary empha-sized it as she explained the situation to us in mid-1999.

> You know what I have realized? The elder sister Tshepo is an alcoholic. Tshepo is an alcoholic, she drinks a lot. I am sure that that is where she squanders the money—the 110 because the extra the daughters are giving her. So there is no food in the house—*wa bona?* (you see?) And *molwetsi* (a sick person) needs food in the house. Do you realize that there is no toilet in the place? I was asking them—how are you coping with *molwetsi* and the kids and everybody without a toilet?

Eventually, in May 1999, Tshepo, who was overwhelmed by her caregiving responsibilities, complained to us that she already had children of her own and grandchildren to care for and that the burden of nursing her mother was too much. She no longer gave Lesego the pills the clinic had dispensed to con-trol her high blood pressure. She also stopped providing proper hygiene for her, so that when we visited we found Lesego with a massive weeping rash on her thighs from lying in her own urine for days at a time. Dikeledi and Lillian brought cream for the rash and took Lesego's mattress out to dry in the strong sun.

Dikeledi asked Tshepo's brother who was there working on the house to encourage his sister to change the soiled linen and bring their mother out into the *lolwapa* each day. Dikeledi explained to me why he felt he had no control over the nursing situation: "Then he was saying 'Ah! these people, each time you try to tell them something they feel that they are being bothered, they will start shouting at you. So they never agree to anything I tell them.'" Mary and her husband had tried to intervene, but Tshepo had insulted her uncle to his face and now he refused to visit his sister. Lesego's relatives had been trying to bring her gifts of food all along since "*molwetsi* needs food in the house," but they stopped soon after Lesego moved to Tshepo's place. They reported that they no longer felt sure that the food they brought would go to Lesego. They feared it would be eaten by Tshepo's family instead, and they wanted to feed a sick/elderly relative, not the children of a woman who was busy drinking.

Eventually, after much debate within the family and between family members, Dikeledi, and the FWEs, they resettled Lesego in her former compound, which Boitumelo had since taken over. Meanwhile, Dikeledi and I concerned ourselves with reuniting Lesego and her mother. We visited Joyce in her compound one morning and asked for her help with Lesego. She lied to us, saying that she had been visiting her daughter all along, only now she was sick with high blood and so couldn't make the journey to Tshepo's place. Dikeledi told her that Lesego was sick and needed a "mother's love" to help heal her. I often heard this rhetoric in Botswana, which was based on more than sentimentality. The special qualities of a mother's heart are a powerful force and are often referred to in relation to healing and nursing. Lesego's depression meant that family members had begun to consider her *setsenwa* (mentally ill). Perhaps motherly love could deliver her from this encroaching illness of the heart. Joyce hesitantly agreed, and we brought her in to begin visiting with Lesego shortly before I left Botswana.

These cases illustrate the complexity and texture of the experience of debility and the role of family in shaping that experience. As the narratives suggest, disability, illness, and aging are not static; instead they are constantly changing processes of meaning-making, pragmatic initiative, and power-brokering. Women are at the center of debates in all of these cases, exercising their moral authority through nursing, gossip, prayer, greeting (or its absence), and public debate. Even male morality in these cases is ultimately negotiated through women. Money also plays a crucial role in all of these cases. As in so many instances of debility in Botswana, struggles over money that were present before any debility began underwent a florescence in the wake of a disabling accident, illness, or birth. Cases such as these open a window into the dynamics by which family members grappled with their responsibilities to one another in late-twentieth-century Botswana. They highlight the tensions that have resulted from the rapid historical reconfigurations in communities and families that have enabled persons to perceive their responsibilities and those of others in a variety of ways. They also illustrate how diverse sets of sociocultural practices and ideas that at first seem to be unrelated to health and physicality are funneled through bodily experiences and illness negotiations. The negotiated experiences and meanings of debility provide a nexus in which a wide array of historical circumstances converge and are interpreted. To decipher the historical meanings encoded in these types of narratives, I will begin by returning to a much earlier historical time, the early decades of the twentieth century, when the roots of the current sociocultural and medical system were beginning to take shape.

2   Public Health and Developing Persons

Goo segole ga go lelwe.
  —Setswana proverb: At the home of the cripple there is not weeping.

Moeng ngaka, o sidila babobodi.
  —Setswana proverb: A visitor's arrival, like a doctor's, heals the sick.

Upon entering any of the six early-twentieth-century Tswana chiefdoms (*merafe*; sing. *morafe*) which British colonial rule had amalgamated into the southern districts of the Bechuanaland Protectorate during the dry season, one would first be struck by the dust.[1] It gathered in clouds swirling over the veldt; it entered eyes, noses, ears, blankets; it covered cattle; and if you were not careful to shield it with your back, it covered your meal. Here on the outskirts of the Kalahari Desert, the dry season was long. It stretched from March or April to the little rains of late September (if they came at all) and didn't really end until the first good drenching of the big rains, causing both the hopeful and the pessimistic to start craning their necks skyward in late October. The dust was sharp and ever moving in the cold winter winds of June and July. By October it was scorching hot underfoot. After the rains the dust lay down. On a clear day, one could discern the rocky outcrops surrounding the central villages.

When one climbed to the top, one could see the larger geography. Rivers, which flowed only briefly each year, if at all, wound near major villages. Here women and girls dug wells in the dry riverbeds and hauled water in earthen jars for cooking, drinking, and bathing. Herd boys too sometimes dug these wells to water their cattle. The tightly settled central villages, some of the densest and most populous on the continent, consisted of constellations of circular wards of compounds centering on the chief's ward and the village meeting-place, the *kgotla*. The *kgotla* was the heart of the village, where the chief tried cases and met with the public. In its adjacent kraal, the chief kept stray cattle and those collected in fines on behalf of the commonweal. In a wide band around the village, often several miles thick, lay the agricultural lands where villagers kept rudimentary farmhouses to live in during the planting season. From here women worked their fields, harvesting staple crops of millet, sorghum, pumpkins, melons, sweet reed, beans, and, more and more often, maize. In a still wider band around the fields lay the *meraka*, or cattle posts. There, in the wet season, sons, grandsons, nephews, and servants tended their male seniors' cattle, living in crudely erected shelters, their stays at the *meraka* punctuated by visits from their elders come to check on their herds and their juniors. The grazing lands then gave way to the bush, where wild foods—greens, fruits, mopane worms, and roots—were all gathered in their seasons to supplement the diet and build physical strength. Here also men procured game meats and birds through hunting, though Tswana hunting culture was already on the wane in these first decades of the twentieth century.

The scarcity of surface water concentrated the population during the dry season. Central villages were massive places with many thousands of residents who were broken up into wards, though many also lived in smaller satellite villages. Wards, which were distinct social and administrative units, consisted of a number of closely related patrilineal households that were grouped under the leadership of a hereditary headman. Wards ranged in size from roughly 100 to 400 people, though some were smaller and others significantly larger.[2] Royal wards originated from the respective groupings of a chief's wife's sons; the eldest sons presided as the ward headmen. Each generation of chiefship spawned successive wards, the number depending on the number of wives a given chief married. Each ward was organized in a circle around a *kgotla*, often a central fireplace or large tree. There male ward members met to discuss local issues and settle disputes. From the air, a Tswana village looked like the cross-section of a honeycomb.[3]

We cannot grasp how or what Batswana imagined in the past, much less why they imagined the world as they did, without first ourselves picturing their world. In order to understand how and why ideas about bodies, persons, misfortune, and care changed in the historically contingent ways they did, we must start with a snapshot from which we might begin to discern how these categories fit into the overarching logic of the ever-changing southeastern Tswana world. This is an artificial task. In some sense, the effort to establish a baseline implies a static society, which of course was never the case. Nonetheless, in order to make sense of the processes of community fracture and reconfiguration, of pluralization of medicine and epidemiological changes that were ongoing in the twentieth century and local analyses of these transformations, we need to know something of how that world looked and felt in earlier times.

The decades leading up to this period had been turbulent ones. In the nineteenth century, repeated wars and cattle-raiding, large-scale migration, the political ascendancy of splinter groups who migrated from central *merafe*, ecological disruptions, and the reverberations of distant slave raids, wars, and missionary and colonial expansion continually shook local society. These events and processes brought new groups of people into contact with one another and opened up new economic, social, cultural, biological, and intellectual opportunities while foreclosing others.[4] Yet anthropologist Isaac Schapera found people in the late 1920s nostalgic for the mid-nineteenth century, just as one finds people in the 1990s longing for the imagined moral clarity of the 1920s and 1930s.[5] The following description does not suggest a primordial and timeless southeastern Tswana world; rather, it is a frozen moment of a world in motion and a starting point for our extended discussion of debility and the moral imagination. In what follows, I will suggest the social complexities, tensions, and ambiguities that underlie the nostalgic snapshot to which contemporary rhetoric refers. In the interests of space, however, I must consolidate much of the discussion around issues of health and the human body (two *very* expansive domains in early-twentieth-century Bechuanaland). I will only hint at the full array of factors that shaped such a complex and dynamic social world.

Space and Season

Southeastern Batswana in the early twentieth century carved out their lives through actions in prescribed spaces. Tswana organized their lives within a set of concentric circles: village, lands, cattle post, and bush. As with many other African communities, each of these zones and its constituent elements embraced internally contradictory sets of practices.[6] At the heart of human life was the domesticated space of the compound and village, which gave way to the liminal zones of seasonally tamed fields and open grazing land and finally to the bush. The boundaries of spaces—compounds, fields, cattle kraals, even the geographical boundaries of the *morafe* itself—were all regularly ritually strengthened to preserve their inherent potency and to disarm the effects of potential sorcery and other toxins. This ritual maintenance of boundaries was necessary to maintain the health of fields, homes, cattle, and humans.

The bush (*naga*), arguably the most powerful cosmological space, lay at the geographic margins of the Tswana world. The bush was and remains the antithesis of the human world. When I lived up on a rocky hill on the periphery of Diphaleng village, one of the first jokes I learned to make in Botswana played on this—I stumbled on its humor quite by accident. When I was asked *O nna kae?* (Where do you live?) I wanted to convey that I lived up on the hill (*mo ditabeng*), but, confused about my Setswana, I told two women *Ke nna mo nageng* (I live in the bush). They doubled over with laughter, for what person (especially a white lady) could ever live in the bush? This joke became a regular favorite in my repertoire.

The bush, though physically remote, was crucial to Tswana well-being. The bush was the place where the spirit world infused the natural world with power. This made the plant and animal products of the bush potent substances that could strengthen bodies and physical boundaries. Elderly Batswana impressed upon me the historical importance of wild foods gathered from the bush as regular dietary elements, labeling them as special "body protective, body building" foods.[7] Daily life, physical maturation, and sexual activity all converted the *madi* (blood, semen), the vital life force of the body, into productive wealth on behalf of the family and the wider community. Foods gathered in the bush were part of this vital rejuvenation of the body necessary for the proper pace of aging. Ingestion of bush foods was a delicate matter, however. It required mediation—through proper processing—and intimate knowledge of the local environment. In present-day Botswana, the elderly lament the loss of this knowledge, remarking that children today do not recognize the plants of the bush well enough to select benign rather than poisonous foods.[8]

Medicines were also collected from the bush. While the knowledge needed to acquire and process wild foods and some basic medicines was widespread, knowledge of the Tswana pharmacopoeia was more specialized. *Dingaka* (doctors) were trained to identify, harvest, and process items from the bush under the tutelage of an experienced *ngaka*.[9] The substances often required a great deal of skill to procure, and though there was flexibility when a given substance was unavailable, access to particularly potent ingredients was part of the doctor's strength. In using these medicines, the doctors brought the dangerous substances of the bush into the ordered space of the domestic world, a delicate matter that required expertise in collection, processing, and timing.

The untamed power of the natural world permeated the plants and animals in the bush, which could be harnessed by humans for both benevolent and malevolent ends. Most of the substances used for sorcery were also found in the bush. *Dingaka* today state two reasons why medicines—whether intended for healing or harming—come from the bush. Most important, plants that grow wild are the trees planted by *Modimo* (God/the original ancestor) or the *badimo* (ancestors). This first rationale is not unlike the one Schapera reported. He quotes the *ngaka* (Rapedi) as saying that while he was preparing his medicines he couldn't take any food or snuff without first putting a little into the pots of medicines as a "prayer" to the *badimo* "because the medicines belong to them."[10] A second reason helps to distinguish a *mmilo* tree growing in the village from one growing in the bush, for example: the one in the bush does not get polluted by having many humans passing by it each day.[11]

Between the bush and the village lay the cattle posts and lands, where families would maintain satellite homes. Such spaces were allocated and developed along ward lines, so one's neighbors at the lands were often relatives or neighbors from the village.[12] Cosmological and symbolic power congealed in the material products of each of these respective spaces—just as with the bush.

Cattle posts and grazing lands were male domains. There boys, young men, and servants worked for their fathers, uncles, grandfathers, and bosses. Adam Kuper has explained how for the Tswana, as in much of Southern Africa, cattle were vital to community health and social reproduction. Aside from their utility in pulling plows or oxcarts (both of which were nineteenth-century introductions), their milk and meat and the use of their skin and dung for building, clothing, and fertilizer facilitated the conversion of labor and social relations into fertility and wealth through the exchange of bridewealth, and the use of cattle in ritual sacrifices included many healing practices.[13]

Fathers provided their sons with cattle to offer in-laws in exchange for a new wife's movement into their lineage. In giving cattle as bridewealth (a process that could take many years to complete), a lineage generated new forms of consanguinity, bringing a bride's blood (*madi*) into accord with that of her husband's family and making her children members of their father's lineage. This was accomplished both through the actual exchange of cattle (creating legal rights and obligations) and through the ritual slaughter of the marriage ox by the bride's father. After the slaughter, certain pieces of meat from the udder or breast were eaten by the married couple and a sheet of fat from around the intestines was doctored with medicines, cut in two, and placed around both bride and groom.[14] Because intestines were central to diseases of widowhood and breasts and udders were central to milk and nurturance, I suspect that these rituals were necessary for creating the consanguinity of the married couple necessary for safe and effective reproduction, which entailed the mixing of *madi*.[15] Cattle were necessary for marriage and parenthood (and many other ritual processes), and through their control over cattle, senior men controlled their juniors.

This system underwent extreme stress in the early part of the period in question. In 1898, the Rinderpest epizootic swept through the region and over 90 percent of the cattle in the area died of the disease. The wealthy, who held larger herds, were better positioned to recover than their poorer neighbors, but no one escaped the severity of the situation.[16] The death of so many cattle had an incredible effect across an array of domains, but one of the most important was its impact on the relationship between fathers and sons. Benedict Carton has described the generational dynamics for this period in Zululand, where the decimation of the cattle population exposed the contingencies of social aging for young men. Historically sons labored on behalf of their fathers with the expectation that their fathers would provide them with the cattle necessary to marry and become fathers in their own right. As these expectations collapsed, young men began subverting or challenging patriarchal authority. Many young men (though at this stage far fewer in Bechuanaland than in Zululand) inverted the dynamics of reciprocity and began migrating in search of wage work to rebuild herds.[17]

The agricultural lands were a female space.[18] Though men provided assistance at key moments in the growing cycle (especially after the ox plow became widespread), women and girls performed the bulk of agricultural labor. Through farming, women combined the fertility of the land with the fertility of their bodies and reproduced the lineage. The grain and vegetables women produced and processed formed the bulk of the local diet. Agricultural products, like cattle, also had important uses beyond sustenance. For example, beer drinks reinforced a sense of both community and hierarchy, as did the giving and sharing of grain in a ritual that was reenacted each year at harvest time under the direction of the chief.

While healing and strengthening brought substances from the bush into the ordered world of the village, palliative care or nursing took place within the domestic and very female realm of the compound. Jean Comaroff describes spatial organization of these homes as uterine—in both their architectural and social forms—reminding us that "the term for the inside of the house (*mo teng*) also meant *in utero*."[19] Her illustration of the symbolic qualities of the homes strikes me as equally descriptive of the sense of nurturance experienced within the homestead. This is not to suggest some idyllic lack of domestic conflict or strife or the dominance of European bourgeois notions of domesticity that the missionaries sought to impart; I only suggest that for the sick or frail, the fixtures and rhythms of the home most likely provided comfort.[20]

These homes were at the center of each family's domestic life and were built by the women of the household.[21] Each compound was organized in an arc with a low mud wall with a single opening surrounding an outdoor *lolwapa* that faced outward into the ward. In the *lolwapa*, the public life of the family took place. As one walked through a village, one might pass small groups of women and young children at work in their courtyards or men gathered to talk. People would exchange greetings at each homestead encountered, reaffirming through openness and face-to-face interactions their benign intentions and the public nature of life. Such openness manifested through greetings was a crucial affirmation of personhood. Greetings and face-to-face interaction stood in stark contrast to the secrecy and isolation associated with the malfeasance and sorcery that brought misfortune.

Entering such a courtyard after the end of the agricultural season, one might find a variety of activities in process, depending on the time of day. Dogs patrolled the compounds to ward off intruders at night, and cats kept away snakes and rodents. Often one would encounter other visitors to the compound, since visiting was as important as greeting in affirming interpersonal connections.[22] Here men, if they were home rather than in the *kgotla* or visiting the cattle post, might be seated in special wooden folding chairs they had made with seats woven from leather thong. No one else would sit in the household

A compound courtyard (*lolwapa*) in Gakgatla. Photo by Isaac Schapera, c. 1920–1930. Courtesy of the Royal Anthropological Institute.

head's chair when he was away. Women sat on the ground or on skin mats. In the mid-afternoon, one might find the household asleep on skin mats beneath the shade of a large tree in their compound.

Behind the *lolwapa* stood at least one or more often a series of round mud houses with conical thatched roofs. Older children would often be given their own houses to sleep in, so that ideally there would be one for boys and another for girls; in polygynous families each wife would maintain her own house. The interior of the buildings were intensely private spaces, and most indoor visiting implied secrecy and could easily become the subject of gossip. As Chief Seepapitso explained at a public meeting in 1912, "obviously, a person goes indoors only to talk scandal."[23]

Women sought to preserve the forward-facing exterior of the homestead for public view. They could display their creativity and building skills for personal satisfaction and public approval, molding decorative shapes and useful shelves and cubbies into the mud walls of the *lolwapa*, which they regularly smeared with cattle dung to create a smooth surface. They might also use different colored clays dug from various spots in the surrounding hillsides to paint patterns and figures onto the walls of the *lolwapa* and huts, or they might etch patterns into the clay.[24] It was vital for women to keep the outside of their compounds looking pristine, and any weeds that emerged in compound courtyards were swiftly uprooted. Women swept courtyards each morning with long brooms, removing any fallen leaves or thorns and maintaining the crucial distinction between domesticated space and the untamed growth of the bush. Weeds, of course, provided a habitat for snakes, rodents, and insects, and an unswept compound marked discord—the violation of the spatial boundaries between the human world and the natural/supernatural world—and would be met with gossip and disapproval, while a tidy compound showed off the skills and domestic qualities of the woman in charge, earning her praise.

The backyard of the compound (*segotlo*) was a different matter, however. It faced the bush, not the village or neighbors, and so was the most private space in the home, as well as one which underscored the symbiotic relations between domestic and wild. Writing about the nineteenth century, Jean Comaroff describes it as a female sanctuary where the women of the house and their children and matrilineal kin "consorted and ate together without the risk of contamination by rivals, and where they were protected by the female 'living dead' (*badimo*) buried beneath the floor."[25] By the twentieth century, the *segotlo* may have been more ambiguous than the emphasis on nurturance and sanctuary that women promoted in the moral imagination or than the analysis of it as "the site of the transformation of presocial elements [grain; children etc.] into more decidedly social form" would suggest.[26] Privacy and secrecy were two sides of the same coin, and family members may also have gone to the back of the compound to work out tensions and emotions they didn't want to air in public without arousing the suspicions invoked by the secrecy of meeting inside a hut.

Along with the bush/homestead division was another ecological opposition that was central to southeastern Tswana life. The experience of two opposing ecological phenomenon lay at the heart of Tswana understandings of their world: heat and dust and the cooling drench of the rains. The southeastern Tswana directed much of their cosmological speculation toward effecting the seasonal change that cooled the heat and dust into nourishing life. The rains were brought by the ancestors, who expressed their pleasure or displeasure with their human descendant communities through rain. Here too, the uterus was invoked. Clouds could become pregnant with rain and "labor" to deliver it; thus efforts focused on preventing their "miscarriage."[27]

Rain was a highly nuanced marker. Soft, extended, regular rain was the ideal, often referred to in song as rain that goes "pitter pat," but rain also came in short, dangerous, lightening-filled bursts, hail storms, or torrential downpours which destroyed houses and crops. When the rains came they could be seen from a long way off. The great open sky allowed all to witness far-off lightening

The backyard (*segotlo*) of a compound in Gakgatla. "The poles on the ground indicate that a sick person is confined in the hut to the right." Photo by Isaac Schapera, c. 1920–1930. Courtesy of the Royal Anthropological Institute.

storms moving swiftly across the veldt and to monitor the unevenness of the rains; often as a farmer watched the rain clouds open onto a neighboring section of the veldt, she stood in her dry fields knowing that the rains might pass her by entirely. With the first big rainstorm, the earth that had baked into a hard crust in the winter sun became soft enough to plow, and farmers began to wait for the chief to open the plowing season. All at once, it seemed, the desert came alive, with green leaves, shoots, buds opening, insects everywhere, and tough thorny weeds emerging in compound courtyards overnight. The Setswana language mirrored the dynamism of these seasonal changes with language: the verb for "bloom" (*go thunya*) is the same as the verb for "explode," and the derivative noun (*sethunya*) is used for "flower" as well as "gun" and "pain."

The transition from dry to wet was a profound one. By the 1920s, this yearly change was called the "season of mental illness" or, as many European expatriates later called October, "suicide month." Each year at this time as the buds began forming and the first small rains enabled them to explode into bloom, a small number of people would exhibit signs of mental illness: talking aloud to themselves seemingly unaware of others; undressing in public; becoming suddenly, inexplicably violent or just quiet, weepy, and exhausted; receding from their social world. Often they were the same people who in years past had succumbed to similar illnesses but who had recovered under the lengthy and intensive care of a local doctor, only to yield again to the power of the season.[28] Others remained sick indefinitely.

The changes the rains brought were powerful in many other ways: they caused the people to move residence from village to farms, dispersing the social nexus across a wide area and relieving the tensions of town life. They brought sustenance—crops, grazing, water. They brought misfortune in lightening bolts that set huts on fire and struck people down in the their fields and in the potential for drought if more rains failed to come. The rains also reaffirmed or called into question the powers of the chief, whose job it was to provide rain for the people through his relationship with his ancestors, the *badimo*. Harnessing these seasonal changes, taming them into benevolence, was a delicate matter that entailed community cooperation and effort both through hierarchical control centered on the chief and the wider, more diffuse discipline of kin and neighbors to ensure that all were doing their part to maintain proper ecological and cosmological balance. Despite contemporary nostalgia for the past as a time of abundant rain, this was not easily or always achieved.

Chief and Community

Heat and rain were opposites, and maintaining a balance between them was of the utmost importance for community health and vitality, which the people saw as embodied in peaceful coexistence, successful procreation and aging of humans and cattle, and well-watered productive fields. The "misbehavior" of individuals could easily upset the *badimo*, and ecological balance was necessary for interdependent meteorological, agricultural, and cosmological success. Poor conduct could also offend others, breeding tensions that spawned acts of witchcraft. The hierarchical, gendered, and age-based political structure of society prescribed the boundaries and conduct for individual lives in an attempt to tie them together into a peaceful, productive community. Given the (at times) competing interests of agnatic groups or various gender-, age-, and class-based groups and their correspondingly uneven access to social, political, and cultural capital, this harmony was more a perpetual but elusive goal than a daily reality. Chiefs, councilors, and the commonweal debated adaptations of the implicit moral code of community life as novel situations and personalities brought tensions to the fore. Balance was difficult to achieve, especially over historical time, and required disciplined cooperation by all citizens, guided through relations and acts of mediation.

The *badimo* mediated between the human and the spirit world; while the chief, *dingaka,* and lineage heads mediated between the human world and the *badimo.* Seniors mediated the behavior of juniors. Women ensured that political machinations did not disrupt the necessary mediating activities of men, through their unique social position and ritual activities. Through their fertile and nurturing qualities, women also extended the system to the ground, turning rain into food, *madi* (blood) and *mashi* (milk) into people, and the doctors' power into the experience of care and well-being. Within this cosmological system, individual health aggregated as community health. Perpetual tensions and differing interests among individuals or lineages and between age-, gender-, and class based groups were subsumed under a metalanguage that dictated a reading of sociopolitical and supernatural relations as either nurturing and mediating or consuming and dangerous.[29] Within that larger cosmological language, people made sense of their experiences of misfortune, disability, and aging.

Through the chief, seniors tried to maintain a moral compass for the *morafe* as a whole, though the value of this mechanism depended in part on the chief's own personal conduct. This was necessary for cosmological harmony between the people and their ancestors, the *badimo,* who governed both the natural and supernatural world. The *badimo* concerned themselves with maintaining a moral society among the living and would show their displeasure with the moral failings of their descendants by bringing misfortune to them. As elders of the living, the *badimo* required propitiation through word, deed, and sacrifice, acts that knit together the moral fiber of a hierarchical community toward a common purpose. This sense of community cohesion and moral cooperation had always been tenuous, as the misfortunes of war, drought, locusts, political fissures, and the like had shown the people of the previous century. In the early twentieth century, the economic, social, and religious upheavals stemming from colonization, missionary activity, and the opening of new markets following economic growth in neighboring South Africa and Rhodesia reinforced the perceived need for a *morafe*-level sense of moral stability in changing times.

A paramount chief (*kgosi*) stood at the top of the regional power structure of each *morafe.* As in other areas of Africa, the politics of chiefship and the cosmological importance of the chief were intertwined. As Feierman has described for the Shambaa and Packard for the Bashu, chiefs sought and maintained political control by providing ecological well-being for their communities. This process was most powerfully demonstrated through attempts to control and exercise rainmaking. As these authors show, the historical transformations of the early twentieth century continually reshaped the spiritual and political functions of chiefship in response to changes in the sociopolitical and ecological world.[30] Over time, British colonial rule succeeded in separating the ritual and political functions of chiefship, exposing communities besieged by drought and labor migration to cosmological upheaval and fracturing the social order.

Chiefs, usually male, were chosen through descent. But the measures of kinship and the interpersonal relations that operated through the idiom of kinship could be manipulated and contested through marriage choices and the recasting of preexisting relationships in new terms, a process facilitated by marriage practices that linked people to one another in multiple ways.[31] The choice of chief and the degree of power exercised by regents on behalf of chiefs who were still minors were not always cut and dried. The chief worked informally through consultation with senior kinsmen and formally with a council of senior advisors drawn from both royal relatives (usually uncles) and headmen commoners. The chief's role was modified somewhat through the imposition of colonial rule, interactions with the scattered mission stations, and the end of the wars and ensuing migrations that had characterized the previous century, but in the early decades of the twentieth century he was still the central figure in political, legal, and cosmological aspects of society. He presided over court cases, distributed land, made new laws, extracted surplus, and played a crucial role in various rituals such as initiation and rainmaking.[32]

Much of this work was public. The chief called and conducted public meetings and settled disputes in the village *kgotla,* through which all new legislation and ideas had to pass, and the massive *letsholo* (public assembly) meetings in the veldt, which brought in citizens from satellite villages. But other aspects of the chief's work were private, mysterious, and secretive. As a mediating link between the spirit world and the human world, the chief and many of his activities were necessarily unknowable to the majority of his subjects. In all of this there was a profound tension between an egalitarian spirit of public consultation and consensus-building and attempts through participatory public theater to legitimate a very hierarchical and factionalized political system. Isaac Schapera reminds us that the balance between such tensions and the specific character of chiefship depended in no small part on the distinctive personalities of the various chiefs and their councilors. The chief needed to garner and maintain popular compliance and cooperation; his position was powerful but by no means autocratic.[33] This was equally true in terms of his perceived cosmological responsibilities.

The chief presided over a council of *dikgosana* (sing. *kgosana*), or smaller chiefs or headmen. These men were the official intermediaries between the chief and the populace. They judged cases at the ward level, distributed residential land, enforced the chief's orders, and presided over ward meetings. Each of the *dikgosana* headed a ward of the central village or one of the smaller outlying villages. Some of the *dikgosana* were actually the chiefs of these smaller villages who sat under the umbrella of the *merafe* and the paramount chief. Many of these villages were settled as vanguard defensive areas during the period of intense warfare of the first half of the nineteenth century. Others were settled by immigrant groups—some of whom were dissidents from other *merafe* who had come seeking refuge from one of the Batswana paramount chiefs.

Headmen, like chiefs, were usually male. Women were excluded from most public political meetings in the village *kgotla,* though they did attend the less-frequent veldt assemblies or *letsholo.* This does not mean that historically women lacked any political power at the top echelons of the polity.[34] Most notably, women occasionally acted as regents. In 1917, in Gangwaketse, the location of the Bangwaketse *morafe,* after Chief Seepapitso's younger brother shot him to death in the *kgotla,* his senior son, Bathoen II, was only eight years old. A series of troubled regencies followed for several years until Seepapitso's mother, Gagoangwe, the young chief's grandmother, the infamous "one-eyed queen," worried about the fate of her *morafe,* seized control of the regency.[35] She lasted only a year or so before dying of cancer, but before her death she installed her daughter, Ntebogang, as the succeeding regent. Ntebogang, like her mother, was a very powerful ruler and had a remarkably successful though brief reign during which she was able to reconsolidate power in the chiefship. She ruled only four years before she handed over power to the young chief, Bathoen II.

Women exerted power within royal politics in less public ways as well. The district commissioner's report from 1934 reveals long-standing tensions between Isang, the Bakgatla regent, and his sister, Kgabyana. When Chief Lentswe, their elderly father, suffered a stroke and the resulting hemiplegia in 1920 he left the chiefship, though he was to live for another four years with his debility. Apparently he had already secretly taught Kgabyana to make rain and to ritually doctor a new chief with lion fat. She hid the *morafe*'s rainmaking materials, which had been entrusted to her for the time when Lentswe's heir to the chiefship, Molefi, was old enough to take the office, expecting that she could teach him to make rain and hand over the materials. Lentswe had anticipated the tensions between Isang, the regent, and his young heir Molefi, and he realized that Isang could have used his ability to make rain as effective leverage to keep Molefi from the chiefship. Thus he trained his daughter, whose character he trusted more than that of the overly ambitious Isang. In the end, although these tensions between Isang and Kgabyana led to mutual accusations (and quite possibly acts) of witchcraft and various other forms of aggression, Kgabyana stood her ground with Isang and the young Molefi. Isang, unable to make rain, instead turned to the British colonizers to sink a borehole in the village, bringing engineering into competition with cosmologically based water technology.[36]

These and other examples which have filtered down through the colonial records suggest that royal women played key mediating roles in politics and ecology. At times they acted to check the strife that undermined ecological harmony.[37] As Paul Landau has shown us for the major *morafe* of Bangwato, by the 1910s and 1920s many women were finding a new nexus of power in the church.[38]

Wealthy men and women often had *batlhanka* (servants/slaves) who labored for them in their fields or at their cattle posts. *Batlhanka* were often Bakgalagadi or Basarwa (San), two subordinated ethnic groups who had lived in the area long before the various Batswana *merafe* immigrated to Bechuanaland from the South African high-veldt. Women were employed to ease the burden of domestic drudgery and as farmhands during the agricultural season. Herdsmen might work through a system of labor called *mafisa*, whereby a man (and often his family) herded another's cattle. He would be allowed to take all the milk produced for his family, and at the end of the season, if all had gone well, he would receive a cow. Though these systems provided for the exchange of labor and food, they were rarely paths to significant accumulation and upward mobility.

The chief stood at the top of this hierarchy and directed its most crucial activities. He regulated the agricultural season, announcing when plowing and "biting of the first fruits" could begin to ensure that all farmers observed the same seasonal work rhythms. Certain trees that were considered "female trees" could not be cut during the rainy season or they would disrupt the rains.[39] Particular foods were to be avoided, and the hot blood of widow(er)s and women who had recently miscarried needed to be cooled lest they scorch the earth into drought through their footprints. Premarital pregnancies were to be avoided, and the land had to be cleansed of abortions and other toxins (*dibeela*) lest the rainclouds "miscarry" from the sight of such an abomination.[40] The chief retained a number of *dingaka*, who were dispatched to the homes of widows immediately following a death to begin the purification of the surviving spouse.[41] By the early decades of the twentieth century, these practices had eased in their severity, but their historical force persisted in memory. In "the old days," a Mowkena man explained to the missionary Willoughby,

> They would be sent to the chief—he who slept with a widow would be sent with the widow to the chief, and he who had impregnated a marriageable girl, and she who had had a miscarriage in the veld. And a great Civil Assembly would be convened, with women and girls and boys present. And the

"pot of the rain," which has the rain medicine mixed with water, would be brought to the Assembly, and the urethra of each would be cut so that blood flowed into the pot. They would be cut badly, the razor entering deep, it being said, "Let the blood flow freely." These people were so treated in public before the eyes of men, women, girls, and boys so that whose who saw it might be warned that there must no longer be any one who could do such a deed as lying with an unpurified widow, or impregnating a marriageable girl, or aborting in the veld and hiding her deed. They would fear the shame of being cut with a razor in public.[42]

In the late 1920s and early 1930s, disabled bodies (rather than such shaming rituals) might operate as public symbols to remind observers of the perils of "breaking the rules." In Gakgatla, Schapera observed that "Moeketse, whose legs are completely paralysed, is pointed out as an example of what can happen to a person sleeping with a widow newly bereaved."[43] We do not know how Moeketse understood his paralysis or how he felt about his public role as a cautionary figure.

But the chief did more than maintain the parameters of his people's specific ecological activities. In his role as mediator between the ecological and the human worlds, he needed to make sure that key Tswana social values that he saw as crucial to community vitality were upheld, otherwise suffering and ancestral anger might ensue.[44] The chief's pronouncements were not always heeded.[45] Extreme social disruption manifested itself in ways that drained community vitality: political disunity and negative emotions such as jealousy and anger could generate sorcery or bodily misfortune and or anger the *badimo* into effecting drought, while unchecked sexuality weakened the sociophysical strength of the *morafe* and opened way for the buildup of pollution and toxins in individual bodies or across the landscape.

The moral discourse the chief used was part of the larger project of public health in ways that extended beyond the immediate social concerns they echoed. This can also been seen in law, where personal insults were grounds for court cases.[46] Social accord was always a delicate matter in the southeastern Tswana *merafe,* as in all societies, and secrecy, jealousy, and competition regularly threatened the community health. Despite what was seen locally as an efficacious system for the procurement of rain and health, the rains did not always come as everyone hoped they might. Still, a system for responding to these difficulties existed, drawing the community into a complex set of relationships that subverted or crosscut and rebalanced the at-times-troubled hierarchical community.

Three groups—women, able-bodied men, and doctors—played a significant role in community health and cosmological success, though each group was ultimately subject to the authority of the chief. They each had the capacity to subvert the chief's power, and their particular qualities were necessary elements of cosmological activity. Women's quality of nurturance and their supposed distance from political structure, able-bodied men's labor, and doctors' specialized knowledge and skill were all crucial elements of the balanced interaction of people and ancestors that the chief sought to mediate.

Just as the chief admonished the people when they were violating important social values, the people admonished the chief when he failed in his political and cosmological duties and the rain failed to materialize. The chief's personal conduct as well as his ability to maintain the conduct of others was necessary for the preservation of his relations with his ancestors, who accessed rain from *Modimo,* the most powerful and distant ancestor. *Modimo* was the entity that the missionaries who first began to live and work among the Tswana in the early decades of the nineteenth century recast as a supreme being or God in the Judeo-Christian sense.[47]

The language with which people appealed to the chief during dry years suggested the possibility that the chief was purposefully withholding the rain. Prolonged drought or late or erratic rains usually met with demonstrations of unease. Sometimes men would bring the chief an ox and ask for rain. Women, however, were far more direct in expressing their impatience with the chief, subverting the customary gender hierarchy. Women as a group, especially older women, would intervene when they thought it necessary to end the heat and dust and bring rain back into their world. They would gather and dance while singing songs that questioned the chief and his motives. Schapera tells us that "men were not allowed to be present; if they came near, the women thrashed them and drove them away."[48] Despite the growth of Christianity, which threatened the rainmaking rites as new Christian prayers for rain usurped the role of the rainmakers, women's demonstrations persisted well into the 1930s in Gakgatla. Two old women who had participated in such protests relayed their experience to Schapera:

> They said that "in 1926 or 1927, when there was a serious drought," the women of Mochudi gathered in the central *kgotla.* They sang there and then, still singing, proceeded to Isang's home. They complained to him that "they were thirsty and wanted rain." He told them to go with new clay pots, not yet used, to 'Kgamanyane's *lapa* [courtyard]. There they filled the pots with water. Then, led by Isang's wife and Molefi's mother, they returned to the *kgotla* singing. They entered the adjoining cattle-kraal, where Lentswe had been buried, and poured out the water on the site of his grave. They

Bakgatla women dancing for rain in Sikwane. There was a drought at the time. Photo by Isaac Schapera, c. 1929–1934. Courtesy of the Royal Anthropological Institute.

remained there for some time "dancing on the grave" and singing, together with some men who came to join them. They did all this on one day. "Soon afterwards the rain fell."[49]

The songs sung on this occasion directly blamed the chief for the lack of rain and called his rainmakers sorcerers.[50] Though this protest appears to have been spontaneous, sometimes the chief himself would organize a women's demonstration during a drought if the rainmaker's divining bones indicated that it was necessary. The women would be given pots of water mixed with rain medicines and pots of beer and would dance and sing rain songs on the grave of the late chief. The rainmaker Rapedi explained to Schapera that then he would expect rain to come "because the noise of the songs is heard in heaven."[51] They were directly propitiating the ancestors through the principle ancestor, the deceased chief, for rain. Women, as mothers, as people who converted heat and rain into life and milk, had their own relationship with the *badimo* and could play a role in effecting seasonal change.[52] Thus at times women successfully subverted the gendered hierarchy, cutting through the mediating role of the current chief to exercise direct cosmological power. At other times, the chief attempted a preemptive strike. He undercut women's subversive power by coopting them directly into the chiefly system of rainmaking, thus obviating the need for publicly performed critique of his motivations and efficacy.

Women were also enlisted to cleanse their homes and the village during epidemics. Willoughby, a missionary to the Bangwato for many years in the early twentieth century, explained that "if an epidemic prevailed in the town, it was usual for the chief to order all fires to be extinguished; all hearths swept, and ashes taken out of the town; and when each woman had laid a stick of *monololo* and another of *mokompatla* (both of which are bushes) across the threshold of her courtyard, as a sign that she had completed her task, the chief lit and distributed new fire as if founding a new town. This same ritual was observed at the Feast of the First Fruits."[53]

Though age- and gender-based hierarchies were central to community cohesion and thus to cosmological well-being, they were balanced by a system of age-grades or regiments which crosscut the generational order while reaffirming the sociopolitical hierarchy. The regiments were a critical vehicle for community-wide cooperation and provided a mechanism for redistributing able-bodied male labor for the benefit of the *morafe*. Young men and young women were initiated into regiments (*mophato*; pl. *mephato*) in rituals called *bogwera* (for men) and *bojale* (for women), which reinforced the greater social hierarchy while creating age-based ties across the community. New regiments were formed roughly every five years in ceremonies, which for men included circumcision. After its formation, the regiment became the vehicle through which members provided physical and ritual labor for the commonweal. Each regiment had its own leader chosen from among the initiates for his close agnatic relation to the chief. While the age-grade system was used to organize men for battle in the previous century, colonization had effectively ended this need by the twentieth century.

Though both men and women underwent initiation, male regiments were more often called upon to provide labor for the chiefdom in the early twentieth century. Through regimental labor the physical strength and labor of men was directed toward the well-being of the *morafe*. It seems that many disabled men, whether or not they were initiated, were excused from regimental work and elderly regiments were retired from their obligations en masse.[54] Through the regiments, health and vitality was returned to the community. The chief controlled regimental labor, which he used for a variety of tasks that included policing, public works, and public health.[55] But the chief's power depended in part on consensus.[56]

Chiefs also employed regiments to farm their fields. During the official agricultural season, the chief's tribute fields were plowed first. In addition, citizens were to bring tribute corn from their own fields to the chief each harvest season. He would then return a portion of it to the women to brew into beer. When the beer was ready, the whole village was summoned to the *kgotla* to drink their beer together as part of the annual harvest celebration.[57] Although the chief might help feed one or another of the destitute members of the *morafe,* in general, this was considered the responsibility of kin if the individual was unable to find employment helping in someone's fields or with their cattle in exchange for food.[58] In lean times, though, tribute grain might be redistributed to those in need. After colonization, the British added a hut tax targeting men to the traditional tribal levy of corn. As taxation came to be more strictly enforced in the 1910s and 1920s, chiefs often sent defaulters to the mining areas of South Africa to earn their tax. There they joined young men who had run off to the South African mines in search of their own wealth, escaping the gerontocracy at least temporarily. In the early decades of the twentieth century, the number of men leaving to work in South Africa were still small enough that regimental labor was not significantly disrupted.[59] But by the 1930s, households that lacked a wage earner had difficulty raising the necessary cash for hut tax payments.

Dingaka and Bongaka

The last group necessary for the public health and well-being were doctors. *Dingaka* were ambiguous figures. They embodied enormous potential for cure, protection, and strength, but they also could be the vehicle for sorcery, converting the jealousy of humans into illness, accident, and anguish. Much of their work was mysterious and secret in a society where secrecy was inherently suspect. Powerful doctors could inspire fear or confidence or both. In the first decades of the twentieth century, *dingaka* could be of either sex, but most often they were men, with the exception of the midwifery specialists and pediatricians, who were exclusively female.[60] Informants in the 1930s reported that in the past the doctors (including the rainmakers) of at least one royal family had historically been female.[61] The community relied on doctors to maintain its well-being, but there was a persistent tension between *dingaka* and political leadership. Chiefs sought to control the *dingaka* of their *morafe,* upon whom they were ultimately dependent in some senses, but this control could not be

Rapedi Letsebe, a *ngaka* and rainmaking specialist of the Bakgatla, preparing rain medicines. Photo by Isaac Schapera, c. 1929–1934. Courtesy of the Royal Anthropological Institute.

absolute. *Dingaka* usually were at the center of any political intrigue, though often in a clandestine fashion.

Though rainmaking was the most specialized and elite of the healing arts, perhaps we can look to it for an example of the diversity of bush products a doctor might use. In 1931, Schapera observed Rapedi making rain; he used seven different vegetable substances gathered in the bush, each of which had its own metonymic value. He also used a variety of animal substances: the feathers, breastbone, and urine of the lightning bird (fish eagle); the skin from the chest and belly of the crocodile; the body of the *senanatswii* frog; the dried belly-skin of a "big sea fish"; pieces of the claw of the *kgwadira* bird (bateleur eagle); raw skin from the belly of the hippopotamus; the dried dung of the *korwe* bird (red-billed hornbill); a piece of ostrich shinbone with a few pieces of flesh still clinging to it; three scales of the Cape pangolin; whale fat; and the fat of the *phika* snake.[62] The great distance from Rapedi's home in the village of Mochudi to the habitats of many of these animals made maintenance of this type of pharmacopoeia a complex affair.

Though doctors collected the majority of their own medicines, a wider regional market already existed among *dingaka* for the acquisition of these substances at the turn of the century. Such medicines were expensive; Rapedi reported that a small quantity of the dried urine of the lightning bird was sold for £1, a hefty sum in those days.[63] Though a successful *ngaka,* especially one who made rain, would be compensated well by the chief, this suggests that people enjoyed uneven access to the potency of *bongaka* by virtue of their class status. In the southeastern *merafe,* where the hierarchies of class ran from cattle-wealthy aristocrat to servant and where medicine was an integral element of productive efforts in agriculture and herding as well as the bodily health of individuals, the therapeutic system served in part to reproduce the stratified social system.

Each *morafe* had many doctors, and the chief retained a select few on behalf of the community as a whole. His political position and the well-being of his *morafe* depended upon his ability to attract and maintain the services of the most powerful doctors in the territory. Most important, he retained rainmakers, but specialists were also required for various other public health activities including the cleansing of widows and land. Each year young boys were sent out to "peg" the boundaries of the reserve, and young girls were sent to "sprinkle" the fields with special medicines prepared by one of the chief's doctors. Ideally these actions served to protect the *morafe* as a whole from the polluting influences of the external world. Still, there was an inherent power (and danger) in both medicines and healers brought in from outside the *morafe*'s territory. The massive migration of populations, the settlement of immigrant communities in the southeastern *merafe,* and long-standing regional trade networks surely all added to the historical dynamism of local medical knowledge in the nineteenth century. In addition to the markets in medicinal substances described above, by the early twentieth century a new market had begun in European patent medicines. By the 1910s, European and Indian traders were hawking patent medicines in local shops[64] and local *dingaka* were incorporating the use of patent medicines imported from South Africa into their regular practice.[65]

Likewise, by the 1910s, the major *merafe* were seeking to acquire European doctors to work in their respective territories. At the time, western medicine was only partially separable from Tswana medicine, which included respect for the healing power of foreignness.[66] Imported medicines, be they whale fat or cough syrup, were potent because they were exotic, and so were imported healers. Basarwa and Bakgalagadi doctors were sought after for their specialized knowledge in treating disease, as were European healers. Likewise, most of the rainmakers working among the Bakgatla came from distant areas of Southern Africa that were more well watered; they were brought in by Tswana chiefs during times of drought.[67] Local Tswana doctors could also travel to learn their craft from a respected doctor from outside the Tswana *merafe*.[68] Conversely, Batswana living on the South African high veld coveted the healing power of Tswana doctors from the protectorate and might cross the border to seek medical training.[69] Just as a Bangwaketse chief might announce that a white doctor had come to the territory, he might also announce the arrival of a visiting foreign African doctor in the territory.[70] The difference was a question of payment. Batswana expected their chiefs to provide certain healing services on behalf of the *morafe* as a whole and for the most potent healers to be involved in public healing. After colonization, they expected the British queen and the European churches to do the same. For this reason, the people at a massive *letsholo* meeting rejected the offer of intermittent services by a private white doctor, renewing their demands for a permanent doctor paid by the British.[71]

While the people expected the chief and later the British to provide for public healing, they also hired doctors to meet the medical needs of individuals or families through a system of private practice. Families hired doctors to strengthen cattle kraals, fields, and compounds against the threat of sorcery or misfortune. They also hired them to strengthen the bodies of young men who were leaving to work in the South African mines, just as *dingaka* had historically strengthened the bodies of young men leaving for battle. Some doctors specialized in orthopedic practices such as setting broken bones, while others diagnosed and treated disease, infertility, and chronic pain. The patriarchy controlled access to these services by prohibiting women and youth from visiting *dingaka* without an adult male escort (father, husband, brother, or maternal uncle). Women and youth who visited *dingaka* unescorted were suspected of attempting to acquire the means for sorcery.[72] Payment, which varied depending on the service provided, was always due after a treatment, and then only upon a successful outcome.[73] As with political expression, in medicine there was a tension between the egalitarian and the hierarchical. Through his doctors, the chief provided for certain collective rituals designed to cool and strengthen on behalf of the whole community. This was balanced against the ongoing need for more localized family or individual medical needs. Treatment and strengthening often required the sacrifice of an ox or goat in addition to the doctor's payment, placing regular access to the most powerful medicines beyond the financial means of many families.[74]

Dingaka trained through intensive apprenticeships, often traveling to train with doctors of other *merafe*, including non-Tswana areas in South Africa. Though there were broad areas of consensus in terms of physiology, disease classification, and the like, Tswana medicine included a great deal of variation, and *dingaka* might disagree about certain therapies, diagnoses, or aspects of pharmacopoeia. No one doctor was expected to master all the areas of *bongaka*, so they often specialized (in bonesetting, in women's menstrual complaints, in widow purification, in protecting and strengthening fields and cattle, etc.) People also recognized that doctors had profit motives and might lie or deceive patients by offering a false diagnosis of witchcraft, since such diagnoses often encouraged patients to purchase costly strengthening and protective services. But chiefs who discovered such practices or who found doctors selling sorcery substances (another lucrative enterprise) would drive them from the *morafe*.[75]

Misfortune and *Boloi*

Illnesses presented occasions for analysis, and the moral imagination flourished. Any particular incident of misfortune could easily be understood as the outcome of natural processes or as part of the mysterious logic of *Modimo*. But serious instances of bodily misfortune might also suggest poor sociability revealed in unchecked negative emotions, toxins resulting from misbehavior, or witchcraft.[76] Despite the cooperation and respect demonstrated in caregiving, collective rituals, and the veneration of the elderly and the *badimo*, Tswana society was not without its underlying tensions. The wealth of some in cattle, children, crops, love, political power, and health brought on the jealousy of others. And likewise, the wealthy might not be satisfied with their share and might lust for more. Sorcery (*boloi*) was the mechanism for this type of competition, and its threat permeated political and social relations. The majority of witchcraft cases involved close kin.[77] Schapera explains:

> In our own [European] society such disputes, if they cannot be settled amicably or adjusted by processes of law, generally result in the separation of the persons concerned. But in tribal law people are not free to change their residence when and as they wish; they are expected to remain living among their kinsmen, and only in exceptional circumstances will the tribal authorities permit a man to move away from his own group. Consequently, the people on terms of hostility may find themselves forced to continue living in daily close contact, and unable to avoid one another; and it is in situations of this sort that they sometimes fall back on the traditional weapon of sorcery.[78]

As the century progressed, residence patterns changed, new domains of competition (work, school, etc.) opened, and sorcery was invoked and deployed in novel ways, including among non-kin. But in the early decades of the century these opportunities for mobility were not yet pervasive.

Most people who wished to bring misfortune on others did so through the use of poisonous substances (*sejeso*). These were usually made from bush medicines but perhaps were mixed with some substance taken from the intended victim—clothing, fingernails, footprints left in the sand—and could be employed through various methods, in the same ways healing or strengthening medicines could. They were procured from a *ngaka* and then either slipped into food or drink of a victim; placed in a fire to fumigate the victim; hidden in the compound, kraal, or fields of a victim (like *dibeela*); or hidden in the eaves of a hut. As trading shops opened in the protectorate in the early twentieth century, caustic soda and other such toxins were added to the array of *dijeso*.[79] In empirical terms, the ingestion of *sejeso*, just like the use of *setlhare* (medicines), which were indeed chemical agents by any modern estimation, could produce palpable physiological effects.

Sorcery was confirmed through divination performed by a *ngaka*. Compounds and kraals would be searched for any potential *sejeso/dibeela* (charms/ medicines/toxins) buried within them. If the injury caused was fatal, the victim's dying declaration accusing an individual of bewitching them was taken as strong evidence.[80] An array of evidence was presented to the chief, who would decide upon the case and severely punish those found guilty.

While women certainly were accused of witchcraft at this time, it appears that men, particularly seniors, were more often implicated in suspicious behavior.[81] This makes sense, given the restrictions on women and juniors who visited *dingaka* and the greater access by senior men to goods used to pay for such visits. In August 1912, Chief Seepapitso warned the whole community against seniors bewitching junior men: "There is also much dying of young men, but it is not warfare that is killing them. This practice must cease." These intergenerational machinations were apparently long-standing phenomena, as Schapera noted in the margins of this entry: "Seepapitso's grandfather, Gaseitsiwe (c. 1845–89), is said to have also once summoned a veld assembly, where he stated that too many young people were being killed by the witchcraft of their elders, and that if this did not cease he would hold the older members of a ward responsible whenever one of their young men died suddenly."[82] The most notorious examples of witchcraft were directed at chiefs and were an integral part of much political intrigue.[83]

Chiefs sought to limit sorcery in two ways: through control of *dingaka* and prosecution of witchcraft cases and as an extension of their promotion of the moral order. In each *morafe* there were some *dingaka* who were notorious for providing sorcery substances to laypersons. Chiefs tried to restrain these *dingaka* as a way to retard sorcery. To this end they attempted to publicly distinguish between *dingaka* of whom they approved and others. In this project, they were never as successful as they would have liked, as the degree of sorcery attempts directed against the chiefs showed. Seepapitso, for example, attempted to force the people to access their medical care through him as a means of eliminating untrustworthy *dingaka*. He introduced a new law into the Bangwaketse code: "Should a man want a doctor, he must come to the chief who will find a doctor to treat him. Any sick man who is found to have been doctored privately [without the chief's knowledge] will be [regarded] just like a thief." [84] The populace resisted this policy, which would have concentrated yet more power in the chiefship, and Seepapitso's calls for a registration of *dingaka* appears to have been ignored for the most part. Yet even without such laws, chiefs kept check on the medical profession by prosecuting *dingaka* who facilitated or practiced witchcraft.

Medicines, like *dingaka,* could be ambiguous. Thus, the chief also tried to control the procurement and use of the most powerful medicines through his tenuous hold over the *dingaka.* Everyone recognized that human tissue was a remarkably powerful medicine, though one that perhaps had the widest potential for malevolent misuse. Miscarried fetuses, placentas, and foreskins, even hearts, genitals, hands, and other parts cut from living human beings were all used by doctors in different ways to different ends, for the human body contained so much vitality that its life force could be converted into ritual power. [85] Usually these ingredients were burned to ash and then the ash was mixed with fat to make a paste. The medicine could then be stored in a horn and used in combination with other medicines for a variety of purposes. These body parts strengthened the power of other medicines and could be used for healing or for the personal gains of sorcery. While murder for the acquisition of human medicines was surely a rare event, in 1930 Rapedi was able to maintain a continual supply of miscarried fetuses, which he purchased from an old woman in Mochudi for £1 each. [86]

When body parts were used in the interest of the commonweal, the practice was considered necessary, and therefore benign, albeit requiring secrecy, but using body parts for the gain of an individual or faction was evidence of sorcery. Though the practice had most likely died out among the Bakgatla by the time Isang took power in 1920, several people, including Rapedi and Isang himself, reported how his predecessors would, if need be, send someone out in secret to kill a small boy at the cattle post, letting his people believe he had simply gotten lost in the veldt and perished. [87] The body was then given over to the rainmaker, who added it to his medicines. Accounts of the body parts used varied— "the flesh of the genitals and face," "the entrails such as the lungs and liver," the whole body was cut up and burned." [88] Willoughby's informants reported that in the past, in times of severe drought, the chief would send out a party of trusted men to sacrifice a man, woman, or child, depending on the rainmaker's divination. "They always sought a very black person, rather than one of lighter complexion, 'so that the clouds might become very black.' " [89] Reports of ritual murder in the early 1930s and later included as victims the mentally impaired, the blind, and the elderly as well as young children; it would have been easier to procure these bodies in secret. [90] However, the proverb *Mabele apheko yalesilo atsala thata* (Corn doctored with an idiot's flesh yields abundantly) suggests the possibility of deeper meanings behind the choice of victims.[91]

The British colonial administration was concerned about a broad array of practices they deemed witchcraft, and in 1927 it instituted a law against practices and accusations of *boloi*. A few years later, they further usurped the power of the chiefs to prosecute such cases by placing all of them under the jurisdiction of the district commissioners rather than the native tribunals.[92] The Witchcraft Proclamation Act of 1927 did not, of course, eliminate the practice of *boloi,* and not all cases of *boloi* wound up at the district rather than tribunal court.[93] Tswana chiefs might often attempt to subvert or ignore colonial policies, a greater possibility in Bechuanaland than in some other African colonies, given the sparseness of the colonial administration. But, as in other parts of Africa where the British implemented similar policies, the Witchcraft Proclamation Act undermined the indigenous therapeutic system by criminalizing practices that were at the heart of Tswana medicine. While individual practitioners and their patients could easily avoid colonial authorities and continue their healing practices, public healing (which was already undergoing significant changes in the face of Christian conversion) was more vulnerable. As limits on the ability to purge the community of witches joined a decline in the initiation of youth (discussed below), a long process was began that over time separated *bongaka* from public health.[94]

The British collapsed anything they thought smacked of the occult and the irrational—including the use of *sejeso* and the diagnostic practices of divination—into a single category they called witchcraft. Equally important, they threatened those who falsely accused others of *boloi* with stiff criminal penalties. Baseless accusations had long been criminal in Tswana law. But after the new law, divination (one of the key means by which accusations were developed) was redefined in law as *boloi,* cases were tried in front of colonial officers who did not believe in *boloi,* and new types of court proceedings were used where evidence was marshaled differently. It became increasingly difficult to cleanse *bongaka* and the *morafe* of the malignancies of witchcraft, and some practices of necessity were pushed underground.

The chiefs clearly recognized the serious problem this presented and the deep misunderstanding that lay at the heart of a colonial law that considered divination a form of *boloi,* and, in its failure to grasp the empirical power of *sejeso,* gave more credence to those accused of witchcraft than to the victims of malfeasance. The following joint letter by the chiefs of the Bakwena, Bangwato, and Bangwaketse *merafe,* who had previously traveled to Cape Town to discuss this issue with the high commissioner illustrates their understanding of the situation and the problems of translation involved. I quote it at length.

We understand . . . that although his Excellency would out of consideration allow our native doctors to practice, he at the same time could not in any way amend or repeal section 4 of Proc. #17 of 1927, which, enacts that any Native doctor discovered practising would be liable on conviction to a fine not exceeding £100, or to be imprisoned with or without hard labour for a period not exceeding 5 years. . . . We do not consider [that] the question of witchcraft Proclamation of 1927 has been carefully discussed and investigated with the object of either disproving to us that a belief in "Boloi" was foolish, *to see clearly our interpretation of the word "Boloi,"* or to consider to what effect this Proclamation is going to bring about amongst the Bechuana tribes ("Boloi" is the word his honour The Resident Commissioner, Col. Ellenberger has interpreted as witch craft). If this word, witch craft is the true equivalent of the word "Boloi," we would explain to our father that he should have no cause of anxiety about the ridicule towards us on this subject from the educated natives in the Union which our father has referred to. This question might seem and appear foolish in the eyes of some white men, but it is indeed not foolish to the black people.

We feel unable to discuss this subject on paper. It is a big subject and difficult to understand. . . . Our father has mentioned that "the Government has appointed medical officers and placed dispensaries in the Protectorate," but we wish to point out to our father that these are inadequate to meet the needs of the people, because they are of a very limited number, there is only one medical Officer in the country of Chief Sebele II, only one doctor in the vast country of Chief Tshekedi and one doctor and hospital in the major country of Chieftainess Ntebogan. Where, then will the majority of our people get white men's medicine? This is made more difficult by the fact that many of these people are beyond the reach of the Government Medical Officers. This being the case, therefore, there is no other alternative, but to seek the help of our native doctors, who will, of course treat as according to their own means of medical knowledge, for which section 4 of Proclamation #17 of 1927 provides a grievous penalty. Our fathers should, therefore in enforcing this rule expect grievous consequences arising there from.[95] (Emphasis and reparagraphing mine)

Many older people today remember the early twentieth century as a time of social harmony when the lack of money and commodities, clear sexual rules, and strong *dingaka* protected people from expressions of malice. Yet the degree of social tension and discord present was evidenced by the incredible efforts spent to prevent and defend against *boloi*. As Kago's sister, who we met in the previous chapter, commented to me on the naiveté of such nostalgia, there is nothing particularly new or "modern" about jealousy.

Body and Age

Here I describe key elements of the idealized Tswana life course in the early twentieth century. I do this for two reasons. First, because in all societies bodily well-being or deviance is perceived within age- and gender-based frameworks, we need to know what the specific southeastern Tswana life cycle looked like in order to understand how people experienced debility and aging (both their own and that of others). Second, human bodies are the final piece missing from our picture of local cosmology. Bodies, their parts, their capacities, and their qualities were all in some ways manifestations of the links between the world of the *badimo* and that of humans. The community, led by the chief and his doctors, geared much of its moral guidance toward control of bodies and their substances. Proper movement through the life course was a cornerstone of collective moral management, and improper aging (either too fast, too slow, or too short) threatened the long-term viability of the *morafe*. Disciplined aging converted bodies into productive value used on behalf of family, lineage, and community. The *morafe* and its physical and spiritual world formed a great chain extending from the ancestors to earth and back again. Through their vital essence, human bodies actually connected the life force of ancestors to living kin—it was no accident that kin were called *losika,* or people of the vein. This is not to imply, of course, that everyone's aging processes fit neatly within the idealized model. They did not. Some children did not survive to adulthood, some married women failed in their attempts to bear children, and some initiated men did not secure marriage partners.[96] But the ways in which individual experiences of aging did not match up with idealized models provided the fodder for the moral imagination to flourish; people struggled to make sense of their own confusing processes of maturation and senescence. I present this model because it contains the set of symbols and ideas with which people expressed and experienced the vagaries of growing up and growing old.[97]

Southeastern Tswana see the life course as a circle. The *badimo* bestowed infants on their human descendants, and the elderly moved through a final period of childhood before traveling to rejoin the ancestors.[98] The fetus was built through the combination of the menstrual blood (*madi*) of the woman with the semen (*madi*) of her male partner. The Setswana term for both was the same—*madi.* The father of the child continued to have intercourse with the mother during the first several months of her pregnancy so that his *madi* would contribute to fetal development in the womb. A few months after the birth, the parents would end the confinement period with intercourse, after which the father would rub some of his semen (*madi*) along the infant's back to "strengthen its spine."[99] The mother, meanwhile, continued to strengthen the baby with breast milk; ideally children were not weaned until close to two years old.

Prepubescent children performed vital roles in the annual public healing rituals of purification and pegging of the land. The chief would gather them and direct boys and girls to do separate tasks. The chief had regimental labor at his disposal yet specifically chose prepubescent children to sprinkle the land with strengthening and purifying medicines and peg the boundaries of the territory.[100] This was probably because of their cool bodies, which were not yet hot from the blood of menstruation or sex, and because of their proximity to the *badimo*. These rituals were vital to the maintenance of community health: they protected the *morafe* from outsiders who wished to harm or weaken the community with their sorcery and they purified the land of dangerous heat-producing elements.

At puberty, adults began to coax children's bodies into productivity. In the back of the compound, women regulated the physical maturation of their daughters. When a young girl first began to develop small, budding breasts, her mother would give her an old broom made from a bundle of grass that was worn from months of daily sweeping. She would then teach her daughter to rise each morning before anyone else in the compound and to go to the *segotlo*, where she should sweep off these new breasts, moderating the pace of their development. This way the girl would not become appealing to men and thus potentially pregnant before her body had developed the physical strength necessary for pregnancy, child birth, and breast-feeding. Without such regulation of the physical life cycle it was feared a young girl might squander her vitality at a young age.[101]

Boys did not need such daily regulation of physical maturation. Instead, they needed to demonstrate that they were fit for adulthood through public behavior. Boys who were to be initiated at the next *bogwera* were called *magwane* (sing. *legwane*). It was up to them to establish that they wanted *bogwera* through their dress and their actions. From the end of the formation of the previous regiment until their own initiation, the *magwane* enjoyed a special status. Schapera explains:

> Magwane while at home in the villages "could do just as they liked." They went about idly by day. At night, wearing their distinctive costumes, they gathered in small groups to dance and sing to the accompaniment of a girls' chorus. The words of their songs, which they composed themselves, were often "very insulting to people." Those whom they singled out by name or offended in other ways, had no legal redress. As the proverb says, *Legwane gaseleseke.* "A legwane does not go to court" i.e. he could not be sued for his

Magwane (boys waiting to be initiated into the next age set) in Gakgatla dressed in the distinctive clothing that marked their status. Photo by Isaac Schapera, c. 1929–1934. Courtesy of the Royal Anthropological Institute.

actions. But if he was particularly insolent, or disobedient towards older people, or made a girl pregnant, this would be remembered against him, and when he went through the *bogwera* he was treated more harshly than his fellows.[102]

Initiation was a crucial marker in the transition from adolescence to adulthood. Through education and community purification, it was also a cornerstone of public health. Through initiation rituals, seniors converted young men and women into productive community members. Each group of male initiates was formed into a regiment, which meant the beginning of regulated labor necessary for developing the community and maintaining public health. Beginning in the late nineteenth century (the date varies from *morafe* to *morafe*), the uninitiated, regardless of their age, were barred from marriage, and therefore ideally from procreation, and uninitiated men were prohibited from attending or speaking in the *kgotla* and from eating or sitting with other men at the fire.[103] Women could not marry and begin childbearing until they had completed *bojale*. The specifics of *bogwera* and *bojale* varied between *morafe* and are difficult to uncover since all initiates, male and female, took vows to preserve the secrecy of the initiation rites. Nonetheless, missionaries Brown and Willoughby and anthropologist Schapera all were able to gather some information from initiated informants about *bogwera* practices. The following is based on their accounts.[104]

Bogwera, which took three months to complete, was usually held every four to five years, when the chief had a close agnate who would undergo the rite. The boys, their heads newly shaven, were assembled. All aspects of the initiation process reinforced the social hierarchy. Initiates were made to kneel for hours in a single line, each staring at the back of their immediate superior, recreating the social pecking order of the *morafe*. The circumcision also proceeded in this same order; the chief's son, if he were among the initiates, underwent the operation first.[105] The rituals took place in a special camp built for the purpose out in the bush, where the initiates would reside for the duration. Afterward, the camp would be burned. The circumcision was performed in the first few days at the camp.[106] For the rest of their stay the initiates received instructions on Tswana law and knowledge, including the rules of sexual conduct. Schapera reported that the initiates were taught, often through song, not to sleep with menstruating women or with women who had recently miscarried, with much-older women, or with a woman carrying another man's child because "intercourse with any such woman would make them ill." They also were cautioned not to "throw away their seed" by sleeping with women of other wards, villages, or *merafe*.[107]

Men of various regiments taught skills and didactic songs to the initiates during their stay in the camp. But those of the previously initiated regiment were placed in special charge of the new initiates. These men were expected to remain celibate from the time of their own initiation until they played their role in the next *bogwera* ritual. They were directly questioned by the chief about their celibacy, and if a man had failed to maintain this restriction he was not allowed to fulfill his special role in the initiation, since his heat could kill the delicate *magwane* during this ritual of rebirth.[108]

A central aspect of *bogwera* was punishment, and this newest regiment was often in charge of meting out penalties. As the regent Isang described it, "*Bogwera* was a powerful disciplinary force."[109] The young men began their initiation by cutting canes from the *moretlwa* tree. This was followed by a formal beating in the *kgotla*, where they were thrashed with the canes they had cut for any disrespect they had committed in the past. Those who had been troublesome youths, who had broken many rules, were on occasion beaten so severely that they died from the wounds. In other cases, an elderly man could come forward and place his hat on a young man's head to suggest that he had been a particularly good boy and had shown proper respect and deference for his elders. That initiate would then be spared a beating.[110] After this initial punishment, the initiates were beaten daily in the circumcision camp.

Throughout the event, discipline was imposed on and through the body. The circumcision operation was the pinnacle of this practice. Initiates were first smeared on their forehead, temples, and chest with medicines made in part with the ash of the burnt foreskins of the previously initiated regiment.[111] Schapera was told that this was "so that he must no longer think of his home or mother or be afraid," and the initiate was expected to remain still and silent through the surgery.[112] But beyond circumcision, bodily discipline through prescribed postures was enforced throughout *bogwera*. Initiates had to eat with their left hand held up in the air. They could scrape porridge with the side of their right hand, but they were barred from using their fingers, as was customary in the village.[113] They were expected to kneel for long hours and were monitored to make sure that they did not rest on their buttocks. When they slept, they were required to lie on their backs and not to roll on to their sides.[114] Any breach of these rules was swiftly met with a thrashing. Part of the initiate's rebirth as an adult in society meant a new ability to control his body. Since initiation marked the socially sanctioned beginning of the adult practices of sexual activity, which opened the man up to the physical impurities and the potential social pitfalls of sexual intercourse, it was necessary that he gain and demonstrate physical mastery over his own body as a mediating influence. Aging did not just happen to Batswana, they performed it, through posture, gait, and countenance, and *bogwera* reinforced this broader fact.[115] Likewise *bogwera* marked the conversion of laboring male bodies into community robustness; thus, bodies had to be disciplined into subordinated vehicles for collective action.

There is much less detailed evidence about *bojale* than there is about *bogwera* and the ceremony was much less involved, but still a brief description is possible.[116] Girls who had already begun to menstruate were gathered into a regiment for initiation shortly after *bogwera* had ended. *Bojale* was led by senior women (often a widow was in charge) and was held in compounds in the village that were concealed from view. Each girl was cut on the inner thigh, and a burning hot stick was twisted in the cut.[117] As in other parts of Africa, where excision was part of initiation ceremonies, the pain of the operation was thought to prepare girls for the pain they would experience in childbirth, and they were expected to bear it with great fortitude.[118] Each girl was inspected to ensure she was a virgin, and then her hymen was pierced with a tuber.[119] When their wounds were healed, the girls began spending time each day in the bush. "Here they were instructed by the older women in matters concerning womanhood, domestic and agricultural activities, sex, and behavior towards men."[120] As with *bogwera,* discipline was applied through the body. Initiates were beaten daily, and in the second month of *bojale,* they "donned vests of damp stalks which when dried became so hard as to chafe and even cut the skin."[121] At the end of the two-month rites, the initiates were women and were ready for marriage, parenthood, and other aspects of adulthood.

As various chiefs converted to Christianity in the late nineteenth and early twentieth centuries, they abandoned the *bogwera* and *bojale* rites under pressure from missionaries. But they continued to form age-based regiments to access communal labor for the *morafe.*[122] The abandonment of initiation met with much popular protest, and for several decades many boys and girls from *merafe* that had ceased the practice were sent by their elders or ran off on their own to join the rites of a neighboring *morafe* that was initiating a new regiment. After all of the *merafe* in Botswana had officially abandoned *bogwera* and *bojale,* clandestine initiation camps continued in a few places, sometimes even held across the border in the South African high veld, which attracted initiates from a wide geographic area.[123]

Marriage and parenthood were the next steps in the life course. Without offspring one was never fully considered an adult, and in the early twentieth century premarital pregnancy was still rare, though by the 1930s it was already a significant trend.[124] Marriage rituals also involved bodily processes. A *ngaka* made cuts on the bodies of both the bride and the groom and rubbed medicine into the cuts.[125] This treatment strengthened and prepared the couple for their new roles and responsibilities. Through the sexual exchange of *madi,* men and women linked their (and their respective families') vital essence to one another. Through procreation and the raising of children, they ensured the continuation of the lineage and *morafe.* Through the instillation of proper conduct in their children, they helped knit together the moral fiber of the community so necessary for physical health, well-being, and peace with both neighbors and the *badimo.* Parents taught extreme deference to age and (male) gender as the cornerstone of Tswana ethics, a value siblings and cousins reinforced with one another.

Through rituals and avoidances (*meila*) people strove to align social, physical, and spiritual aging within individual persons. As parents aged and became grandparents and household heads and took on senior roles in their families and communities, they became elders (*bagolo*). Social elderhood, it was hoped, preceded physical decline. Physical markers such as debility and functional impairments in older adults often signaled the onset of *tsofetse* (senescence). Wrinkled skin, gray hair, bent posture, use of a cane or walking stick, failing eyesight, painful swollen joints, and paralysis were all associated with *tsofetse* and could signal transition into the final phase of the life cycle, when the elderly became children again, to some extent trading their social power for spiritual power. The level of personal knowledge and inner harmony ideally gained through a lifetime of experience and striving was matched by a growing proximity to the *badimo*. The physical maturation and decline embodied in the final phase of being *ngwana* (child) marked a return when the *mowa* (breath, spirit, essence) of a person would rejoin the ancestral spirits.[126]

At this point in the life cycle, the physical body was so imbued with spiritual power that the heart, which was the house of the spirit (*pelo ke ntlo ya mowa*) and the central organ of human experience, the very embodiment of personhood, came to directly take on the moral project of the *badimo*. If the *motsofe* (old person) felt sorrow or anger in his/her heart for the treatment received from a junior, this sorrow would manifest itself in the misfortune of the junior.[127] The *motsofe*'s heart, which was in a liminal phase between the human and metaphysical realms, began affecting the living in an enforcement of the larger moral order. This process, and the resulting misfortune, was called *dikgaba*. The cure for *dikgaba* entailed a realigning of the behavior of the victim with Tswana cultural ideals and a purification of sentiment through verbal forgiveness and healing, practiced in a ritual washing of the victim by the elder.[128] If this was not achieved before the death of the *motsofe*, ancestral propitiation and sacrifice, which could only be directed by lineage heads, would be required.

By contrast, the spiritually imbued heart of the *motsofe* could also bestow blessings upon juniors. Elderly Batswana today recall the blessings they received from grandparents with warmth and awe.[129] They continue to experience the power of these blessings as they navigate their way through the vagaries of life. In these final phases of the life cycle, juniors expressed their respect and love for their seniors through nurturance. Bathing, feeding, clothing, and gift-giving by juniors demonstrated respect to *batsofetse* (frail elderly) and *banna* (old children) and was not seen as patronizing or humiliating, despite the personal frustrations that accompanied physical decline. Rather, such nurturance was a reinforcement of the moral order.[130] These very acts of caregiving were blessings in themselves, as contact with the physical body of a *ngwana* could convey some of the spiritual force of the heart. Even in the 1990s, children in Botswana would be sent to the homes of extremely old villagers to touch the body of the *motsofe* and gain luck.

The community strove for the ideal, ritually regulating girls' movement through puberty and fostering a disciplined late-adolescent transition to manhood and womanhood. They attempted to control fertility through marriage and pervasive sanctions against premarital pregnancy. Finally, they strove to send elders to their graves in peace, without bitterness in their powerful hearts. These practices were all necessary elements of southeastern Tswana public health and well-being. This life course was only the ideal, though. Social discord and violation of or ambiguity within the moral guidelines of society, which was often realized through historical change, brought sorcery and the anger of the ancestors. Failed ambitions curtailed the ability of some to reach social elderhood. Disease, accident, and infertility hampered many people's physical progress through the stages of life.

Debility and Care

In this final section I want to suggest how the spatial, cosmological, and community logic of society affected local experiences of debility. Here again, we will see women, doctors, and chiefs as all specially positioned in the world of care and in the prevention of misfortune. Early-twentieth-century experiences of debility are very difficult to glean from the historical record, as are women's nursing practices. In places, I am left with recollections from the 1930s and 1940s projected backward to the 1910s and 1920s, an admittedly problematic strategy. Thus, what follows is meant to be suggestive rather than comprehensive or definite.

As we have seen, doctors took potent, if ambiguous, substances from the bush and brought them safely into the heart of the human, domesticated world. These substances were used for either healing (*go alafa*) or strengthening (*go thaya*), which were linked processes and were both necessary to stave off misfortune.[131] Jean Comaroff provides a wonderful analysis of the symbolic processes of heat and healing to which my own understanding is deeply indebted; she has described how the female body with its dangerous heat was antithetical to healing and strengthening in the Tswana symbolic imaginary.[132]

But while (male-dominated) Tswana cultural logic stresses the dangers of heat and emphasizes the role of male *dingaka* in health care, such formal accounts are challenged by both the historical evidence of female *dingaka* and by the crucial realm of palliative care. Women's bodies did produce heat, and adult women were expected to sit with their legs straight out and close together to protect their genitals from view but also to help contain their bodily essence. Menstruating women, widows, pregnant women, and women who had miscarried each had their own set of ritual observances meant to protect others from the heat they contained. But heat, while dangerous, also had nurturing qualities, manifested in wombs and womblike confinement huts. Women were the primary caregivers in Tswana society at the turn of the twentieth century, much as they are today. Motherly love, infused with the special qualities of a woman's heart, was a basic and essential attribute seen as necessary for life, health, and caregiving. Long after cemeteries had appeared in Tswana villages, young children were still buried in their mothers' courtyards, for they needed a mother's love to carry them safely into the afterlife.[133] Women continued to attend to their married daughters when they were sick, though they had moved out of their natal compound.[134] They even provided care to co-wives, perhaps out of concern, love, or reciprocity, but perhaps also out of the need to publicly demonstrate positive sentiment toward an enemy.[135] Not all women lived lives which embodied motherly love, but they might be judged against this ideal. Those who were seen as falling short of the mark would be met with suspicion, gossip, and rebuke or they might even be directly accused of witchcraft.

Women administered palliative care for the ill, the frail elderly, and newly delivered infants and their mothers in prescribed spaces in their compounds. Though in the early nineteenth century patients who had suffered battle wounds were treated in special shelters out in the bush and tended by selected aides, this practice was apparently limited to the wounded and was not applied to those who suffered other ailments.[136] By the second half of the nineteenth century, no further mention of this specific nursing practice appears in the archival record. Elderly Batswana today recall their mothers and grandmothers tending to the ill within their compounds in the early twentieth century. Elderly or seriously ill patients were often kept on blankets or skin mats in separate huts marked by a set of crossed poles placed at the opening.[137] The proverb "A visitor's arrival, like a doctor's, heals the sick" (*Moeng ngaka, o sidila babobodi*), which was already in circulation in the 1910s, suggests that visiting the sick was a regular and important occurrence.[138] It is hard to know if and when patients would be brought out into the more social spaces of the compound. For a bedridden patient, this would require a critical mass of woman power, however, as the patient would need to be moved several times a day in order to remain in the shade, though the deep, well-groomed sand in a compound enabled patients to be dragged on mats rather than picked up and carried. When the adult women of the compound were out, the doors of patients' huts would be kept closed, indicating to visitors and children that they should not be entered. The women feared that young children would be too rambunctious or mischievous and would disturb patients who required rest. Women might also assist frail or ill neighbors who lacked their own immediate kinswomen to care for them.[139]

Women massaged and bathed patients and washed their bedding. They emptied chamber pots, threw feces and vomit out into the bush, and whisked flies away from open mouths, eyes, and wounds. They fed those who could not do so for themselves. Mothers cleaned and disposed of the menstrual blood of daughters who could not. People were not supposed to view the naked bodies of their seniors, but when necessary this custom was put aside in the interest of nursing care, though it was preferable for a mother to nurse her children.[140] Though some people stressed that upon the death of a mother, a father might commit himself to and excel at child-rearing, gender-based conventions around the bodily care of adults were not as easily ignored.[141] When necessary, women directed junior men in the care of their seniors. It was considered inappropriate for a woman to bathe or to empty the chamber pot of her male seniors, and women would call upon young male relatives to assist in such cases.[142]

Senior women also provided midwifery and postnatal care.[143] For the time immediately after delivery, a period called *botsetse* (confinement), new mothers and their infants were to remain secluded in huts in their mothers' compounds. A stick or a broom (*mopakwana*) was placed across the threshold to signify that *motsetse* (a woman in confinement) was inside, the same sign used to indicate that a sick patient was being nursed inside a hut.[144] Pregnant women or women who had recently miscarried were not allowed in since it was feared that their heat would be too powerful within the already womblike confinement hut and might harm the new infant. Likewise, the father was the only man allowed to enter the hut. A *motsetse*'s mother would cook special dishes for her from her own fire; she was not to eat from the communal pot. Her female relatives would shave her head when the baby's umbilical cord fell out and they would regularly bathe her and rub her all over with a flat stone from the riverbed until her skin was smooth. They would massage oil into her skin and scalp until it shone, for "*motsetse* was the pride of the family."[145] *Botsetse* ended with a celebration, a ritual in which the mother's maternal uncles presented the new child to the world. For well-to-do women, *botsetse* lasted for two to three months, but poorer women and their infants could ill afford such lengthy periods of rest and rejuvenation; their confinement period was short of the ideal, often lasting only a month.[146]

The liminal state of the elderly and the newborn and the hot blood of postpartum women made them all potentially dangerous to visitors and visitors potentially dangerous to them. Confinement served a dual purpose, both protecting these most fragile and valued family members from the dangers of the outside world and protecting the rest of the family and its visitors from their bodies, which were so vulnerable to pollution that they could both fall ill and bring harm.[147] The special food prepared for *motsetse* protected the mother and her breastfed baby at the same time that it shielded male kin from the hot blood of a *motsetse,* which could infect cooking and eating utensils. Confinement also protected treasured *batsetse* and *batsofe* from the jealousies and malevolence of others who might try to poison or otherwise harm them. Only closely related women, particularly those who were linked by the womb, were able to pass between the public world and the confined bodies of the vulnerable to provide nurturance and maintain purity in times of life-course transition. The female attendant, who slept in the confinement hut, was expected to remain celibate and to avoid attending funerals and other spaces of death and pollution during her time as nurse.[148]

The prevalence of chronic illness, old age, and disability reinforced the importance of palliative care. In the 1910s and 1920s, the population of debilitated persons was relatively small compared to later decades, and an ethos of self-reliance, ad hoc coping, and stoicism characterized debilitating physical experiences for the Tswana. This spirit of self-determination for individuals was balanced by the doctrines of nurturance and caregiving embodied in women's nursing care. The combination of these sentiments was captured in the well-known proverb *Goo segole ga go lelwe* (At the home of the cripple there is no weeping), which was taken to mean both that family should continue to provide for a disabled member and not cry as if he or she were dead and that the disabled person should make every effort to keep on living, to become self-reliant to the best of his or her abilities.

It is impossible to provide even rough statistics on the prevalence of debilitating conditions in these early years of the twentieth century, but we can draw from both anecdotal evidence and the records of the early colonial medical service to make some general observations about cause and effect. Before discussing specific causes of debility in early colonial Botswana, it is worth reviewing some of the extreme physical challenges that impaired persons would have met, challenges that necessarily limited life-span prognosis. People who were bedridden for extensive periods would have easily developed bedsores. Unless they were able to be vigilant about frequently changing position, and there is no evidence to suggest that this was recognized as a necessity, the pressure of remaining in fixed positions for long periods of time (especially lying on mats on the hard earth floors) could easily have caused the skin and the underlying bone to begin to break down. A pressure sore might only appear as a small and seemingly unimportant wound on the skin's surface, belying a vast root system underneath the skin and into the flesh and bone. When the wound was washed, water would travel deep inside, and unless it was deliberately squeezed out it could cause severe infection, bone loss, and eventually death. Urine and feces could also break down skin and cause severe infections for the bedridden unless patients were vigilantly nursed. Likewise, people who experienced joint or limb pain or were incapacitated for whatever reason could easily develop stiff contractures of their joints. If joints are not used and moved regularly, they lose their suppleness and become fixed. Thus, an arthritic wrist and hand could easily develop into a clawed one over time.

The lack of eyeglasses meant that many who might have managed to see well with assistance were for all intents and purposes blind. After years in the strong sun, cataracts were common, and blindness was an expected, or at least accepted, aspect of old age and thus not a mark of disability (*bogole*) but rather of old age (*botsofe*).[149] It was only those who were born blind who were considered disabled. The same held true for walking "on a stick"; this type of frailty was a marker of old age, of seniority. Young children might be assigned to guide one of their blind seniors about the village, as Maphakela guided his *malome* (mother's brother) Sekgwa, who was a councilor in Chief Sechele's court, to the *kgotla* each day.[150]

Though elderly Tswana often carved their own canes or walking sticks, the lack of more elaborate technical aides such as prosthetic limbs and crutches provided challenges to those with limb impairments. Nomsa Rapela, whose leg was amputated in the early 1940s shortly before she was widowed, demonstrated for me how she would weed her fields on one leg by dragging a metal drum crushed to the appropriate height under her stump. She would hoe in a circle around the spot where she was standing and then move onward a few feet, holding the hoe in one hand and dragging the drum with another, a laborious maneuver added to an already laborious task.[151] Such customized methods of coping with physical impairments were common, though over time they were adapted to new tools that became available. By the 1940s, many people who could not walk were pushed to important events or appointments in wheelbarrows and others simply crawled, sometimes with pieces of motor tires strapped to their knees.[152]

Amputations such as Nomsa's were introduced by the handful of European doctors who came to work in the protectorate in the late nineteenth and early twentieth centuries. By this point the Tswana had some historical experience with the amputations of war; the Matabele regularly cut off the hands of Tswana victims during mid-nineteenth-century raids and battles.[153] And in the nineteenth century, Tswana laws against repeat offenders of certain crimes prescribed the mutilation or amputation of a hand as an extreme form of punishment, though this penalty ceased with colonization and conversion to Christianity.[154] But amputation as a part of a surgical cure was still a frightening colonial novelty in the early decades of the twentieth century that was performed at only the handful of locations in the country staffed with a European doctor. While the long-term survival rates for these amputees are not known, it is likely that many of the patients developed potentially fatal infections from such massive wounds in an environment where antisepsis and asepsis were difficult to achieve and where professional postoperative nursing care was practically nonexistent. In the town of Gaberones, surgery was performed outside under a tree on a piece of mackintosh sheeting laid on an iron bedstead.

A variety of wounds could potentially result in amputation. The principal medical officer described the impetus for surgery in his annual report in 1926:

The surgical work at Gaberones has been in the past, and is still, concerned with the results of violence mostly. These are due less to criminal than to accidental causes. When to the former, they are, as a rule, ordinary scalp or body wounds or bruises—seldom requiring more than out-door treatment. The accidental cases ranged from fractures of the skull, simple fractures of arms, thighs, and legs, to compound fractures of those extremities with every variety of complication, and, occasionally, abdominal wounds or penetration; and the operations, from trepanning of the skull to single or double amputations of arms legs, and thighs—with an abdominal section thrown in here and there. . . .

The accidental injuries were, and are, largely, the results of being run over by wagons, of goring by cattle or wild animals (rare), and, (more common) in the old days of well sinking than now falls into, or blasting operations in[,] shafts or wells, and gunshot wounds. As the subjects have to be conveyed considerable distances in native wagons, over rough roads, serious aggravations of their original condition have to be reckoned with on their arrival such as extreme weakness from loss of blood, continued and prolonged shock and varying in hot weather extreme—degrees of putrefaction [sic].[155]

Disabling industrial accidents and road accidents, which were to become major causes of disability in subsequent decades, were still relatively rare in the 1910s and 1920s. It was more common for accidents in the South African mines to have a fatal outcome, and the mines were already recognized as a particularly dangerous place.[156] But the trickle of repatriated disabled miners had already begun, a harbinger of the epidemic to come.

Trauma, of course was not the only cause of disability in early-twentieth-century Botswana. Congenital impairments also played a role in the array of bodily and mental differences people exhibited. Children with mental impairments were tolerated despite their behavioral differences. When such children wandered into neighbors' compounds, they would be welcomed, though if they broke crockery or caused other difficulties their parents might be expected to compensate the owner.[157] When a mentally impaired girl wandered out of Kanye in 1911, the chief alerted the whole village to her disappearance in a meeting at the kgotla in the hope of locating her and returning her to her home.[158]

Physical impairments were apparently also accepted, though depending on their nature and severity they may have foreclosed opportunities for self-making. Though I have no evidence about men with clubfoot, oral recollections suggest that women with clubfoot, though recognized as digole (disabled), were well integrated into society. For women, this was not a serious barrier to marriage or agricultural pursuits. Chum Sejabadila described how his mother, the senior wife of a wealthy cattle owner and an early Catholic, could not wear a shoe because of her congenital clubfoot.

> Well, she was used to her disability so it was causing her no problem. By then there were no white doctors so she couldn't have gotten any help like if it caused her some pain—she couldn't go to see a doctor—she would just cope with the pain. From the lands to the village about 25 kilometers walking I remember—but I was just a boy walking after this woman and mind you she was carrying this basket on her head.[159]

Some of the leading causes of disability and debility in later years were either lethal or not yet prevalent in the early twentieth century. Though few patients at this time would have made their way to European doctors, medical reports from this era provide at least a glimpse of the range and outcomes of infectious disease. For example, cerebrospinal meningitis, a leading factor in childhood impairments in later years, was still a very deadly disease. In 1929, the medical officer in the northern district of Ngamiland saw fourteen cases of the disease, thirteen of which were fatal.[160] Tuberculosis was not yet prevalent in the area in the early 1900s, though by the 1920s the incidence of both debilitating pulmonary TB and the potentially disabling TB of the bones, joints, or spine was steadily growing, adding new types of infirmity to the area.[161] Polio and leprosy, major causes of disfigurement in other parts of Africa, were not a major problem for the Tswana at this time, though cases of each could be found.[162]

Arthritic diseases, on the other hand, were a painful and debilitating hindrance to some.[163] It is difficult to state with absolute certainty that the causes of arthritic joints were interpreted the same way by Tswana medicine in the past as they are today, but the centrality of joints in Tswana medical knowledge and the reports of current *dingaka* who trained with their fathers in the 1940s and after suggest that there is a fair degree of historical consistency about joint pain. According to these doctors, blood which has been polluted (*madi a maswe*) has a hard time circulating through the body properly, so it builds up in joints, causing the swelling and pain characteristic of arthritis.[164] Blood could become polluted in a number of ways—through ingestion, inhalation, or passage over poisons (*sejeso*); through contact with hot blood during improper sexual conduct or promiscuous sexual activity in which the blood of several partners mix together; or through widowhood, during which the blood of one spouse "misses" the blood of the deceased and becomes overly hot, requiring ritual purification and cooling. In one of the regular practices of medical strengthening in Tswana medicine, the *ngaka* made small cuts over all the joints in the body and rubbed medicines into them; this was intended to protect against sorcery/poisoning by making it bounce back against its user.[165]

Oral sources suggest that people with physical impairments were considered full members of society, complete with all the responsibilities and opportunities prescribed by gender, status, and age. An elderly woman in Thamaga recalled how her cousin who was already a young man in 1916, when she was born, had the congenital debility and growth on his back that I think of as characteristic of spina bifida. He was unable to walk and instead got around by crawling, but still "he grew up, got married, had children."[166] Likewise, Wamona Wanguru remembered how two of his uncles each had a leg amputated yet still had many cattle and rode donkeys to the *kgotla* to attend important meetings there.[167] Some families apparently had severe congenital physical impairments running through them, and yet both their men and women were able to marry and have children.[168] Though it was difficult for disabled community members to attend *kgotla* and *letsholo* meetings as regularly as their able-bodied neighbors, they were at times publicly encouraged to attend these community meetings when crucial decisions were to be made.[169]

The exception to this was found in the special case of the chief. Chiefs who suffered disabling trauma or disease stepped down from office. Still, they might continue to wield political and/or cosmological power, as we saw in the case of Chief Lentswe, who abdicated after suffering a disabling stroke. Similarly, Livingstone noted in the 1850s how the Kwena chief stepped down: "The elder brother of Sechele's father, becoming blind, gave over the chieftainship to Sechele's father. The descendants of this man pay no tribute to Sechele, though he is the actual ruler, and superior to the head of that family; and Sechele, while in every other respect supreme, calls him Kosi, or chief."[170]

These were the outlines of health, physicality, community, and environment in southeastern Bechuanaland in the early twentieth century. Through public and personal efforts people strove to make the spatial, cosmological, and social aspects of life mirror one another and to unify them in a greater moral ethos that was directed by the chief but also depended on the specialized roles of able-bodied men, doctors, and women. Intergenerational tensions, political factionalism, the growth of new Christian cults, and the threat of female subversion of patriarchal authority in times of ecological or political crisis all indicated how elusive this model of public and private health could be. The strength of a particular chief proved crucial to the successful enforcement and maintenance of norms, which protected the health of people, land, and cattle and effected benevolent seasonal change. The *merafe* were on the crest of yet another sea change, which would soon come through massive labor migration and increased colonial and missionary presence beginning in the 1930s and 1940s. These transformations would strain the often-tenuous chiefly led systems of public and private health. Yet throughout these changes, the landscape of earlier decades provided the semantic and semiotic base for the morally imagined responses to community and family fissures and physical misfortune.

3   Male Migration and the Pluralization of Medicine

Mogopo wa segole ga go ribegwe.
    —Setswana proverb: The bowl of the cripple is not put upside down.

Motse o senang makolwane lo gora lwa one ga loo.
    —Setswana proverb: A village without young men has no outer walls.

This chapter describes two historical processes that transformed the experiences and meanings of debility in southeastern Tswana society from the late 1920s through the beginning of World War II: labor migration and the pluralization of medicine. Both processes had their roots in earlier decades, but in this period they intensified and came together to reinforce one another. Through labor migration and pluralization of medicine new meanings were assigned to able-bodiedness. Changes in the determination and value of that hazy entity lay at the heart of transformations in disability, debility, and aging.

The severe drought and economic depression of the first half of the 1930s brought great suffering and hardship to southeastern Bechuanaland, forcing thousands of men into the system of labor migration to the South African mines. Migration increased further during the 1940s; the economic upswing brought by World War II deepened the local value of wage labor instead of stemming the tide of migration. Meanwhile, the growth of missionary and government medical services in the region laid the foundations for the binary medical system of later decades. Labor migration drove men into the new western medical institutions for examination and treatment, and biomedicine established the local criteria for migration. Though the impact of these two changes, socioeconomic and medical, were not so radical at first, they created a series of fault lines running through Tswana society which decades later had tunneled far into daily life. Within these cracks, men and women opened new spaces to renegotiate identities and social institutions.

Labor migration and colonial medicine began to alter relations between community members in ways that undermined the moral basis and daily functioning of the southeastern Tswana system of public health. Through wage work, young people gained power and saw increased potential for autonomy from the gerontocracy. This transition threatened the institutional structures of family and generation through which society shaped behaviors designed to

SOUTH WEST AFRICA

SOUTHERN
RHODESIA

BATAWANA
• Maun

RAILWAY

BECHUANALAND

Francistown

Serowe
TSWAPONG
HILLS

BANGWATO

BAKWENA
BAKGATLA

Mochudi
Molepolole
BATLOKWA
BANGWAKETSE
Kanye
BAROLONG
BALETE
MINING AREA
TRANSVAAL

Mafeking

Johannesburg

SOUTH AFRICA

Molepolole
Mochudi
Thamaga Gabane
Sikwane
Gaberones
Ramotswa
Tlokweng
Kanye
Lobatse

LEGEND
BATAWANA = morafe
Maun = major town

Map of the Bechuanaland Protectorate before
1966 showing *merafe* and major towns mentioned
in the text

placate the *badimo*. The new regimes of labor and medicine caused a local re-valuation of various aspects of personhood, repositioning disabled, chronically ill, and elderly persons within communities and families. Disabled men found themselves marginalized in the emerging socioeconomic order just as the brutality of the mines generated a growing population of debilitated persons. At the core of some of these changes lay a shift in the meanings of key markers in the local imaginative landscape. Wealth, adulthood, and *bongaka,* like able-bodiedness, all took on new, often-contested meanings through these historical transformations.

The changing nature of community was, in part, experienced through the distribution of bodily misfortune and care. In southeastern Bechuanaland in the early 1930s, as in all places during lean and difficult times, the physically frail were the most vulnerable. Megan Vaughan's work on famine in Malawi suggests ways in which able-bodied men are the least exposed during periods of ecological and economic hardship because of their mobility and social capital. This was the case in Depression-era Bechuanaland. The elderly, the chronically ill, disabled children, and fragile infants succumbed to the vagaries of hunger and disease more quickly than their able-bodied relatives, and men enjoyed much more freedom to seek wage-earning opportunities than their wives or sisters.[1] Even for those hardy enough to ride out the drought, hunger and malnutrition had become seasonal and endemic, and access to a wage, which meant access to able-bodied male labor, was now critical for maintenance of basic nutrition.[2]

Mines were dangerous and unhealthy places where disabling or fatal accidents were frequent events, and life in the mining compounds and work in the deep mine shafts facilitated the spread of infectious diseases. Randall Packard has documented how miners brought home tuberculosis and spread it in their rural communities.[3] By the late 1930s, tuberculosis, which was unknown in the nineteenth century, had become endemic in southeastern Bechuanaland. Though pulmonary TB was the most common form among the Tswana, many people suffered from extrapulmonary TB, often in the bones, spine, joints, lymph nodes, or brain, each type with its own particularly disabling effects.[4] This debilitating disease left many bedridden and many more weakened and frail, straining the capacity of local households. Likewise, the changing sexual morality and the actual movement of bodies that accompanied labor migration fueled a rising rate of syphilis infection, which disfigured and debilitated many.[5]

Regional political economy and ecological collapse thrust Batswana into economic reliance on mine wages. But South African industry realized that not all labor was equal, and it sought to harvest the most robust labor from its Tswana neighbors through a system of local physical examination just as the general health of the populace was in decline. Southeastern Tswana ideas about able-bodiedness were suddenly being shaped in relation to European ideas about African labor. As chiefs and seniors competed with the mines for the resources of male able-bodiedness, that contested attribute became increasingly prized, albeit ever-more-hazily understood. The medical examination, which was performed at local recruiting centers by protectorate medical officers, many of them missionaries, became the context for a new encounter between two systems of physiology, Tswana and industrial. As able-bodiedness changed, so too did the meanings of debility and the place of debilitated persons in society. Debilitated men became men who couldn't earn wages, which threatened their economic and social success in a changing community. And women, as a group, were deemed unfit for work by the mine industry.

In addition, the elderly lost some of their hold over their juniors, since only young robust men could earn a wage. Young men with money in their pockets and lacking the transformative and disciplinary experience of *bogwera* subverted the power of their seniors. There was a decreased emphasis on the *badimo,* and the spiritual power of elderly men and women became less important than it had once been, though elders' ability to invoke the *badimo* through their hearts, dreams, and propitiations remained a key element of their identities. Despite these changes, most seniors continued to retain their privileged position in family and community life, and sanctions by senior uncles and ward and village courts (*dikgotla*) continued to provide for the care and respect of the elderly. Nonetheless, the writing was now on the wall: a social inversion of the age hierarchy was on its way.

Below I begin with a discussion of the Depression and drought and the effects of labor migration and then move to the role of colonial and missionary medicine in a changing therapeutic landscape. Much of this discussion will focus on male bodies and men's experiences, since in the 1930s and early 1940s it was primarily men who migrated for work and thus they were the first to enter the new system of medical care through its labor examinations. In the next chapter I will focus more on women's experiences by exploring changing ideas and practices around female sexuality and care through which people tried to manage bodily misfortune.

The Depression

The first half of the 1930s was a disastrous time in southeastern Bechuanaland, much as in many parts of the world. Massive drought plagued the Protectorate from 1927 to 1937.[6] This combined with locusts in the south in 1933 to further limit the harvests.[7] Meanwhile, foot-and-mouth disease came across the eastern borders from Southern Rhodesia and the southern border of the

Protectorate from South Africa to threaten already weakened livestock populations throughout the region. The infection was a mild strain with only a 1 percent fatality rate. Still, men were forced to look on as their cattle stood unwilling to eat with hanging heads, feverish eyes, and pustule-covered tongues and hooves.[8] Because of the epizootic, men couldn't sell their cattle for much-needed cash or grain.[9] For many who had lived through the devastating rinderpest epizootic of 1898, the specter of massive losses loomed large. Human starvation, evidenced by wasting and scurvy, was common and was felt most severely by the elderly and the frail.[10] The dust was everywhere, rising up in great clouds, with never enough rain to cool the earth into benevolence. When they dug at the well in the dry riverbed, people found the moisture receding ever deeper into the ground. Finally, six years into the drought the colonial government began distributing dynamite to help people deepen their wells.[11]

In addition to turning to chiefs and doctors to seek salvation through cooling rain from the *badimo,* or to praying for rain from the Christianized Modimo, both of which in any event were proving illusory, the people looked both to the colonial government for rations and to their sons to bring home wages from South Africa.[12] This is consistent with the trend John Iliffe describes for much of rural colonial Africa in which the "means of survival" through recurrent ecological crises shifted during the colonial period to an increased tendency to sell able-bodied labor.[13] This meant that contingent poverty and suffering would come to hinge in part on the definitions of able-bodiedness held by purchasers of labor.

The old system of public health failed to control the rise of misfortune in the *merafe* during the 1930s. In the previous decade, a method of addressing economic wants had begun to grow around the wage opportunities for migrant workers on the South African mines. Now, as more and more men embraced that option, seeking to solve or escape troubles at home, their absence created new sets of problems, which threw the system of public health and medicine into further disarray.

The public health system led by the chief and his *dingaka,* as we have seen, was based on local cosmology which divided the world spatially and which regularly ritually protected territorial boundaries from the polluting influences of the outside world. Now this system had to cope with a constant influx of men returning from abroad where they had been mixing with strangers. People returning from long journeys had always been thought hot-blooded, in need of ritual cooling like widows and recently miscarried women, lest they scorch the earth into heat and dust. But with so many men now regularly returning from abroad, too much polluting heat was entering the territories. The consequences of the increasing permeability of territorial boundaries and the cycle of migrants polluted through their experiences in the hot and dusty mines returning to homesteads and cattle kraals were devastating. The years of intense drought and human suffering underscored in the popular consciousness both the dangers of this new migrant system and the spiritual weakening of the chiefship and the *dingaka,* just as the absence and drain of able-bodiedness threatened the strength and the viability of the southeastern *merafe.*

At the same time, colonial involvement in local political and legal affairs altered chiefly power. As in other British colonies, chiefs in Bechuanaland gained or consolidated authority through the politically reifying policies of indirect rule. The chiefs, compensated with a 10 percent share of the tax receipts, took on the important function of politicolegal mediators between the *merafe* and the British state. However, the demise of *bogwera* and *bojale* was all but complete, the collective rainmaking ceremonies were at an end, and the power of local churches was increasing. In these circumstances, the chiefs lost or reoriented much of their role as cosmological mediators. The *badimo* too were fading to the background of spiritual life, losing their central role in Tswana ecological and social mediation, though they were by no means forgotten entirely. Christianity had long begun to vie with *bongaka* at the political power nexus, and successful chiefs might embrace and control the Christian cult to maintain their rule.[14] Christian practice offered the possibility of direct propitiation to Modimo without the intermediary influence of the ancestors. Meanwhile, the Depression drought and the economic hardships that accompanied it unglued the agro-pastoral system for a lengthy period, exposing and straining a shifting set of safety nets that underpinned communities.

The deepening presence of colonizers and the growth of Christian cults displaced *dingaka* as well. Rainmaking was replaced by mission-led annual Christian prayers for rain, and divination, a cornerstone of the Tswana therapeutic system, became a criminal offense. In the changing landscape of political and spiritual power in the southeastern *merafe, dingaka* became more diffuse in their work, still helping patients and strengthening homes, fields, and cattle but no longer the most powerful force in the public health system which had become a bricolage of Tswana, Christian, and "scientific" policies. Into this changing picture of local medical practice came an expansion of missionary and government medical services. European doctors' central role in labor recruitment and syphilis treatment drew thousands into their practices. As in countless other places in Africa, their dispensaries and hospitals became new sites for cultural encounters over the nature of physical control, health, and medicine.[15]

Men from the southeastern Protectorate had been working in the South African mines for several decades at this point. In the 1930s, both push and pull factors worked together to turn what had been a mere trickle of labor into a wider outpouring. Lean times at home forced many men to seek wages to pay tax, rebuild herds, and stave off family starvation.[16] Others desired the new goods traders hawked in the major villages or wished to leave what to many was an oppressive patriarchal system that relegated them to distant cattle posts in favor of the relative freedoms and adventure of life in South Africa.[17] With local industry almost nonexistent, work in South Africa, and more specifically on the mines, was one of the few opportunities available to Batswana who wished to earn a wage.

The discovery and development of significant gold and diamond deposits in late-nineteenth-century South Africa, sometimes termed the mineral revolution, led to the development of a tightly controlled migrant labor system, fueled British imperialism in the region, and helped spark the South African war. The mines drew large numbers of migrant workers into South Africa from all over the Southern African region, including places as far away as Malawi and Angola. Mining capital helped finance the development of secondary industry and urban development in South Africa and helped create South Africa's role as a major economic and political force in the region.

The Tswana always formed a small minority among South African miners, just as the sparse population of arid Bechuanaland was dwarfed in comparison to that in the major labor-sending colonies of Mozambique, Basutoland, or Nyasaland. However, their numbers grew fairly steadily between 1930 and 1960. In 1930 there were only 3,151 Tswana miners employed in South Africa, but by 1960 there were 21,404 Tswana men working in the South African mines.[18] More important, even though their numbers were small relative to men from surrounding colonies, they represented a significant portion of the male labor of the Protectorate as a whole, particularly in the southeastern districts. In 1942, Schapera found that 59.6 percent of the taxpayers from the eastern Protectorate were away from home at work at the time of his survey; the overwhelming majority of them would have been at the mines or in the army.[19] The war had certainly increased the number of men who were away, but even in 1938 and 1940 Schapera found 40.3 percent of the adult men in the southeastern zone of the country away at work.[20] These figures represent only those men absent on a given day. The total percentage of men who had ever gone abroad to work—83.9 percent—illustrates the true extent of the migrant experience.[21]

Like its fellow High Commission Territory Basutoland, Bechuanaland went from exporting surplus grain in the mid- to late nineteenth century to dependency on imports purchased through mining wages from the 1930s onward.[22] Bechuanaland had become an impoverished labor reserve, its economy static. In his 1933 survey of the economic situation in the territory commissioned by the colonial government, Sir Alan Pim had declared that "for the cultivation of maize the country is clearly unsuitable," yet the drain of labor and increasing importance of cash encouraged shifts from hardier, more drought-resistant millet and sorghum to maize cultivation, which required less labor and which in good years would bring a higher price at market.[23] Growing familiarity with European goods had turned some past luxuries, such as plows, cloth, sugar, sunshades, and cooking oil, into common household items.[24] Last, more efficient tax collection beginning in the 1930s pushed more and more men toward the mines to fulfill household tax obligations.[25]

Schapera published two letters written in Mochudi in 1933 at the height of the depression and ecological crisis which illustrated the new experience of hunger and highlighted local dependence on migrant husbands, sons, and brothers. Both letters were written to the same young man at work in Johannesburg. The first was from his widowed mother and the second from his younger sister. Schapera noted that these letters "may serve finally as an illustration of the straits to which even what is by Kgatla standards a moderately wealthy family was then reduced, and the reliance it placed on the menfolk in the towns":

> I greet you and ask how you are living. I am sick, my child, I have nothing to say except starvation. You have left me in loneliness. The starvation that is here is very, very serious. I beg you to send me just one bag of corn, so that I can help my child who is at the cattle-post. You must remember that M_____ [her eldest son, a loafer] refuses to let me use the cattle as you well know. The whole day, my child, we sit at the store hoping to get a little corn [as relief rations], but we come back empty, I don't know what to do, but you must know that I depend upon you, and put all my hopes in you. You must "carry" us as you usually do. Other men are striving for themselves, but M_____ does not care for anything; he looks to me, but I have nothing to give him. Do not let the eyes of the people look at me [with scorn]. You complain that I do not write to you, but you know that I have nothing with which to buy stamps. That is all I can tell you. Many greetings, my child. . . .

> The thing that troubles me very much over here is the starvation. I get up in the morning and go to bed at night without having eaten anything. When I wrote last time I had not eaten anything for about four days, not only myself, but we are all staying without eating anything. When I walk my breath gives out. I tie myself with a belt to hold in my stomach. I am wondering if we are going to live through this starvation. It is the first time I have ever slept without eating since I was borne by my mother. If you could see us you would cry. . . . Could you not send us just a little meal, just to keep ourselves going, or a little bit of corn? . . . This is mother's message: "Look after the orphans of your father and mother"; and myself I say, "To whom are you throwing us?" Even as I write I feel very sad, and my tears keep coming down.[26]

In these harsh times threatened families turned to their sons, brothers, and fathers working abroad to ameliorate their suffering. Those men who chose to stay at home in the territory rather than go abroad in search of a wage were clearly disparaged, as the references to M_____ highlight. Yet a tension existed here between resentment toward those young men with their wages, fear that they would desert their families and communities, and dependence on the money they brought home. Those young men who went off to work had un-precedented power over and responsibility for their families, as these letters pleading for corn from a son/brother suggest. By the late 1930s as the Depres-sion and drought subsided, the system of migration was firmly entrenched. South African industry rebounded from the economic slump, only to recruit ever-greater numbers of African men at meager wages.

Age, Strength, and Able-Bodiedness

It became increasingly easy to look for work. After several decades of disorganized recruiting in the protectorate, the mines began using their re-cruiting corporation to implement a more effective system of accessing labor in the southeastern *merafe* in the early 1930s. The establishment of several ma-jor recruiting stations not only facilitated the flow of labor but also provided a new means for families and miners to access remittances, deferred pay, tax ad-vances, and the like. Though recruitment was easier, however, the standards of physical fitness were raised as the mines enjoyed the glut of labor brought by drought and the Depression. It became easier to seek work just as it became more difficult to actually succeed in gaining a contract.

Migrants were not just pushed out by family need. They also were drawn in by the desire for material goods and new opportunities to accumulate wealth.[27] Migrancy in Gangwaketse was spurred by a law passed by Seepapitso in 1914. And the Bangwaketse *morafe*'s proximity to one of the earliest recruiting sites in Lobatse made it one of the vanguard areas of migration. Previously, young men could not own stock in their own name; all cattle belonged to the father. Then Seepapitso, appalled by young migrants squandering their earnings on fancy clothing, watches, and other impractical manufactured goods, passed a law of separate ownership that allowed young returned migrants to purchase cattle on their own behalf.[28] This new opportunity had some social costs, how-ever; shortly after its start, the chief was forced to caution older men against ensorcelling their sons.[29]

The wages young men brought back from South Africa generated a new type of conspicuous wealth in manufactured goods, breeding envy. The newfound economic power of these young men was a potential threat to Tswana values of economic prudence. The resources they commanded brought prestige and obligation within families because all could see who had contributed what—how much cash, what goods, and how many cattle—toward the family assets. This was a more direct relationship between labor and contribution than in the agricultural and cattle-keeping economies. Migrancy and wages also affected marriage. Because young men could use their wages to buy cattle, they could contribute financially to their bridewealth payments, and they often wanted a say in choosing a wife, a process previously arranged by senior relatives.

Ideally, families redistributed the money and goods earned through wage labor in ways that reinforced the primacy of key relations. Men who were migrants in this period report that as unmarried men, they were expected to turn over all of their earnings to their fathers, who would then "give them their share" and distribute the rest to various family members.[30] In the early years of labor migration, workers were expected to bring gifts to their chief, but this practice had begun to decline by the mid-1930s. Over time, some workers who remitted took greater control over directing the allocation of their wages. In the 1930s, though, the patriarchal hierarchy that controlled the dispersal of cattle and bridewealth maintained a tenuous hold over wages of returning migrants as well, though young men's economic importance was becoming ever more obvious.

Within families, fathers oversaw the redistribution of wages, apparently applying the familiar idiom of meat distribution during ritual slaughter as a guide. Fathers directed their sons to give their first paycheck and whatever goods they had purchased from it in their entirety to the worker's *malome* (mother's brother).[31] The *malome* would then take his share, called *ditlhogo* (heads), and distribute the rest among parents, siblings, and maternal relatives. This mimicked the division of meat at a wedding feast, when maternal uncles received the heads of beasts slaughtered.[32] Sons handed over subsequent pay and goods to their parents for redistribution. When they married, their wives began participating in the dispersal of goods, which the parents still directed. Again the interplay between wife and in-laws drew on preexisting local semantics of exchange, in this case from the practice of wedding negotiations in which future in-laws would give their sons' fiancées gifts of blankets, cloth, and ornaments to "seal the betrothal."[33] Mosito Makwapeng, who first went to the mines in the early 1930s, described the practice of wage reallocation:

> The money that I worked for I used to give it to my parents, but even after I was married I used to give it to my parents, and still while I was still at the mines I used to give it to my parents, send more money and my parents they will know that they have to give my wife something. When the money arrived my parents would call my wife and show her all the money, and from there my parents would give my wife her share, and even if I myself had

arrived my wife will be called at my parents' compound, they will sit there and they will share. I used to bring some clothes and blankets with me, so again my wife will be called from her parents' compound, she will be shown all of those things and from there they will be sharing all of those clothes and the blankets. My wife again, well, she will be the one in charge of those clothes and blankets. My parents will be saying "Okay," telling my wife "we are giving you these. These blankets they are yours," then my wife will say "No," then give them one blanket saying "No, this is yours."[34]

Throughout the 1930s and 1940s, wives needed to carefully exercise their redistributive options to maintain favor with their in-laws and brothers, who continued to control the bulk of migrant wages. But, as Barbara Cooper has shown for women in Niger, such gifts operated as visual reminders of the social ties and debts that made up the recipient's social world: "The giving of gifts creates not so much material wealth as social capital: the recognition of worth and value, dependency and patronage."[35] Gifts of blankets and crockery stood as markers of social wealth, material symbols of a woman's extensive web of people. A woman with gifts from her brothers could display these goods to remind her husband's family of the strength of her own nurturing connections or return one of the blankets given by her in-laws to reinforce her own place of worth and production within the patrilineage.

Though not all of the male migrants were at the mines, most were. Those who found work in factories or as domestic servants, the two largest secondary employment sectors, often had begun their working life as miners.[36] The tempo of mine migrancy set the tone for the expected schedules of all migrant workers. Miners worked on roughly nine-month contracts.[37] They were then expected to return home for several months to rejoin their families and help with agricultural and pastoral responsibilities. It seems that most men were still coming home at the end of their contracts in the 1910s and 1920s. By the 1930s and 1940s, however, many men were attempting to renew their contracts several times before returning home to the protectorate.[38] The mines encouraged this; they benefited from an experienced work force and decreased labor acquisition costs.

Though some of these men might still send wage remittances home, many lost contact with their people and failed to pay their taxes. There are of course many reasons why men might not have wanted to return to their homes. Some men had probably left amid disagreements to which they did not wish to return, others had established new lives with wives and children in South Africa, and still more may well have wanted to continue to control the entirety of their wages. This was more easily done in South Africa outside the locus of patriarchal and community sanction. These men were feared "lost" to families and communities, who called them *makgwelwa* (deserters). Batswana made their attitude toward these men powerfully evident in the use of that name *makgwelwa,* which literally meant "those who have been spat at." A Batlokwa councilor summed up the local view toward *makgwelwa*: "They left wives behind and when they got away they became married to others. They marry those women there [in South Africa], and when they want to come back they leave them there with the issue they have had after they become sufferers from tuberculosis."[39]

Senior men, including chiefs, feared the moral ramifications of youth leaving the territory unsupervised. Though this was not the norm, it was a growing problem of deep concern to seniors. Southeastern Tswana understood ablebodiedness to include fertility. The procreative and productive labor of persons were bound up in one another, and together they constituted the key assets of household, lineage, and community.[40] Concerned seniors relayed rumors of girls running away to the Union and going mad and of others becoming pregnant outside of the *morafe*.[41] Seniors also regularly complained about men of all ages fathering children in South Africa. This behavior violated one of the key teachings about sexual conduct imparted to initiates during *bogwera*: initiates had been taught not to "throw away their seed" by having sex with women of other villages.[42] Now they were fathering children of other *morafe*! The procreative capacity of young women and men were tied together as part of the wealth of the community as a whole, linking the living to the *badimo,* and thus was not something that individuals should "squander" outside of the boundaries of family, lineage, and *morafe.*

The ability of young men to find wage work in South Africa also challenged local conceptions of well-paced aging and the purpose and nature of work. The new opportunities for wage labor called into question the logic of a migrant labor situation that enabled young boys to contract as individuals rather than as junior family members. Martinus Seboni, a Mokwena councilor, complained to the Native Advisory Council in 1925 on his return from a trip to the Rand "about boys going to Johannesburg, I saw many Bakwena there who are lost. Some told me they had deserted from Natal and Koster, little boys not fit for work."[43] Anthropologists have observed that the Tswana distinguish between wage labor (*go bereka*: to work) and work within a kin-based mode of production (*go dira*: to do).[44] For the Tswana, *go dira* was determined not only by physical capacity and prowess but also by mental, emotional, and social development that nurtured a sense of responsibility and initiative not thought possible in young boys. When Seboni remarked that these young boys were "not fit for work," he was not necessarily suggesting that they were too young chronologically or too small physically to engage in arduous manual tasks (though his words implied this as well). Rather, he meant that they were too immature to handle the responsibilities and rewards of wage work (*go bereka*) that took them outside of the firm and immediate direction of their seniors. Surely boys who had abandoned their herds and their families to "run away" to the Union did not yet possess a level of responsibility and self-discipline necessary for wage work and successful reintegration into family and community.

The elderly expected to direct their same-sex juniors at tasks and to provide an integrative vision and direction to the economic projects of the household, thereby imbuing qualities of patience, diligence, and long-term planning in their juniors, who would inherit their wealth and perpetuate their blood. This provided for the continuation of lead economic and sociopolitical roles for even the frail elderly, reminding the young that physical strength and stamina were no replacement for the accumulated experiences of age. Pelonome Kebafetse remembered an old woman in her neighborhood from the 1930s who was blind. "So this old woman was farming. [J. L.: She was weeding and harvesting?] Okay, she was farming, but not herself exactly. Her children were doing the plowing because she couldn't move around so she was always seated. She was supervising because she couldn't move around so the children would do it."[45] Being "always seated" and being blind did not mean an end to "work" (*go dira*); Pelonome's elderly neighbor was farming. Nor could one separate the physical elements and material goals of "work" from the moral world in which they were realized.

Work (*go dira*) within the lineage-based mode of production inculcated values of social discipline and reinforced the authority of the sociopolitical hierarchy, something wage work (*go bereka*) threatened. Councilors complained to the resident commissioner about the social ramifications of the recruitment policies, which excluded older men from mine work.

> Councilor Sefako Pilane (Bakgatla): . . . We send men to go on contract
> if they are unable to pay their tax, and when they get to Gaberones the
> recruiter there does not accept them saying they are aged, and the reason
> I think contributes to the behavior of the young men who go to the mines
> is the fact that only young men are picked out to go to the mines and they
> are not mixed up with grown men. There are quite a lot of men who are gray
> headed who are able to lift up heavy things that I would not be able to lift.[46]

The resident commissioner refuted this claim. Drawing on his own work history, he instructed the councilor on the rigorous requirements of industry:

> One speaker made a complaint that only the young men were taken for the
> mines, and he seemed to think that there were some strong, able-bodied old
> men who could do a better day's work than the young ones who go. I am an
> old man myself, but I manage to do a fair day's work. On the other hand, I

recognise that work in a mine—and I have worked in a mine with pick and shovel—is a young man's job. I think we should not interfere with the choice of the recruiter who knows very well what is wanted.[47]

The resident commissioner's approach placed responsibility for male youth with their parents and restated the protectorate's policy of denying passes to cross into South Africa to boys under age 18 unless they possessed a letter from their chief.[48] This, of course, ignored the reality of the situation. It was difficult to document age with precision. Labor recruiters usually took boys at their word unless they were obviously so young that they would be rejected when they reached the mines. Many young boys sneaked across the border without ever procuring a pass yet were quickly able to find work. More important, such a policy ignored the local understandings of youth and adult. Eighteen was not a magical age in Tswana society when rights and duties were conferred. Until a boy had been incorporated into a regiment, he was still *legwane*, with all the doubt and ambiguity that implied. It was only by incorporation into the larger community through regimental membership that big boys (*magwane*) became robust young men (*makolwane*). As in many British colonies, however, the administration addressed the matter along gendered lines, placing more emphasis on restricting the movements of women than on the movements of young men or boys.[49] They agreed with the Bakwena Chief Sebele II, "A girl should not be allowed out of the Protectorate unless she is with her husband or father."[50] Railway passes were no longer issued to a woman unless she had a pass from a magistrate or was accompanied by her husband and was listed on his pass.[51]

Among the southeastern *merafe*, the ubiquitous experience of migrancy was becoming a new marker on the adult male life cycle. With the demise of *bogwera*, there was no longer a clear-cut process through which individual physical, spiritual, and social development were harnessed into benign vitality. Now the transition to adulthood was more atomized, more haphazard. For many young men, their first mine contract became an important step in the gateway to adulthood. It brought men into a new hierarchy of work and wealth and was a dangerous and transformative experience, both physically and socially. Some colonial observers likened the labor contract to initiation, describing it as a masculine rite of passage.[52] But however tempting that analogy might be, mining could not take the place of *bogwera*, with its collective rituals of discipline. In many ways it did quite the opposite: one converted physical vitality and spiritual growth into disciplined collective productivity, procreative potential, and hierarchically controlled wealth; the other converted able-bodiedness into money at a distance, community absence, and new forms of individual autonomy. It brought no guarantees of discipline, it left young men "squandering their seed in a distant land," and it would ultimately place the power of redistribution in the hands of young men.[53]

Though labor migration did not serve the same purpose for the *morafe* that *bogwera* did, it functioned as an important physically transformative process and thus became a marker of bodily as well as social life-cycle transition. The ability to pass a mine medical exam and bring home a wage were evidence that a body was maturing into adult productivity and thus the decision to become a labor migrant was still decided by an interplay between a young man and his seniors in a cultural language drawn from the historical experience of male initiation. In earlier times, when *bogwera* was still practiced, *magwane* who wanted to be initiated would come into the villages from the cattle posts wearing headdresses made from the hair of wildebeest tails and loincloths made from gemsbok skin. They would gather at night to dance and sing songs. They were "despised" and "insulted" to no end, but they would seek retribution through their songs and dances.[54] They would do this more and more, until the old men at the *kgotla* would begin to talk about forming them into a regiment. Then, after the first good rains, they would come and ask the chief to make them men. Before *bogwera* could be made, their fathers had to agree and then discuss the matter at *kgotla* with the chief and his advisors; also, the year had to be evaluated for suitability.[55] Even after the people had abandoned *bogwera*, *magwane* continued to follow this process to be formed into regiments by their chief.

Similarly, in the 1930s, most young men did not make the decision to migrate on their own; they needed to consult their parents (though some young men did run away). Likewise, fathers could not simply send their sons off to the mines the way they could to the cattle post. They had to wait for their sons to decide that they were ready to leave and to come and ask for permission. Returned miners from that period emphasized to me that their families could not make them go to the mines; it had to be their own choice.[56] Yet it was expected that sons would demonstrate their value, their ambition, and their readiness for adult responsibilities by asking for permission to migrate just as they had been expected to ask for *bogwera*. After the young man had gained his parents' permission, it was his father's responsibility to take his son to a *ngaka* for ritual doctoring to protect him from the dangers which lay ahead.[57] As with *bogwera*, this passage into adult labor necessitated physical strengthening, which was the responsibility of the father to ensure.

Though from the 1910s to the early 1930s some chiefs sent regiments of men to the mines to earn tax money, those were men already incorporated into adulthood by virtue of their membership in a regiment. By the later 1930s, young men were often going on contract before becoming regiment members. Thus, they were still *magwane* in the eyes of the community, though they were considered physical adults by the mining industry. They wielded economic power before they had taken on community-level responsibilities. More important, they were *magwane,* the despised and unruly youth who were socially disincorporated by the community during this liminal phase, and many left before reincorporation as adult regiment members smoothed the tensions and opened new spaces for personal accountability. This disjuncture of physical and social identity marked the beginnings of a shift in the life cycle that would be fully realized in later decades.

By the 1940s, the lure of wages had begun to undermine patriarchal authority, and many more young men were going to the labor recruiters against the wishes of their parents. When a father wished to keep his son at home to herd cattle and help with plowing, the young man would often sneak off to the recruiter in secret. Once he had passed the examination and signed the mining contract, there was little the father could do.[58]

Young laboring men did not gain the spiritual and social power that came from collective disciplined movement toward adulthood through participation in ritual. Yet the money they brought home augmented and empowered them in new ways. These miners saw themselves as physically strengthened through mining. They noted that men returning from the mines in the 1930s and 1940s were always the strongest, fittest men in their villages. Though they clearly acknowledged the dangers inherent in mining, these men described the mine as a place of rejuvenation, where one's strength was constantly replenished through a good diet, exercise, and the abundance of clean water.[59] Men also explain that at the mines they were given special tablets and injections by the mine doctors to make them stronger. These medicines were set aside for men whose work required exceptional physical power and were given only to soldiers, policemen, and miners.[60] More important, the new economic power and prestige gained through mining, despite the meager wages, was a crucial factor in the recognition of the mines as a place of self-development, a place where one could become "big and strong."

Money and its power linked physical and social vitality to one another. As one miner who worked at the Rand beginning in the 1930s explained, "The thing that made us strong when coming from the mines is that we were pleased with the money being given. So that money made us feel that we had something, so we just became strong."[61] Anthropologists have long noted that the Setswana term for money, *madi,* is the same as that for blood (and semen). Jean Comaroff has unpacked this local linguistic commentary on the oppressive regimes of wage labor in South Africa, suggesting that wage labor through its violence and control depleted or bled workers, unlike older lineage-based modes of production. She explores the dense web of symbolic connections between hot, polluted blood and industrially earned money, noting that "Tshidi perception of money would seem to imply a process of circulation which, from their point of view, is unregulated and uncontrollable." But she also suggests other, more benign associations, including the "life-giving motion of blood within the body."[62] While it makes sense that the Barolong boo Ratshidi in South Africa under the grip of an increasingly aggressive political regime emphasized the polluting, destructive nature of *madi*, it is clear that by the 1930s in southeastern Bechuanaland across the border, *madi* was taking on a different emphasis that able-bodied men sought to harness. Money had joined blood and semen as one of the vital substances necessary for life, procreation, and power. Workers did not separate the physical from the social strength that *madi* brought to able-bodied bodies laboring in South Africa. But *madi* and its power could not be gained without risk and heat, and bodies required strengthening in order to successfully quest for it.

Most migrants visited a *ngaka* before leaving for the mines and then again immediately upon their return, though some of the growing body of Christians eschewed this custom.[63] This practice drew from the older culture of public health in which people would be strengthened before going on a long journey and purified on their return home. Because of the various pollutants, possible *dibeela,* and powerful poisons a traveler would have encountered traversing the bush and entering the territory of other *merafe,* a person needed a strong body to fend off the effects of these substances. Despite this pre-journey strengthening, a returning traveler again needed to be cleansed of the dangerous heat that had built up in his or her body during the journey lest he or she burn the earth into drought and the local people and cattle into illness. Miners, therefore, needed these therapies in order to successfully leave and later reenter their *morafe.*

The distance of the miners' journey and the unique qualities of the mining environment reinforced the need for therapeutic intervention. *Dingaka* gave miners medicines designed to strengthen them for the arduous work that lay ahead. This meant a strong mind and a strong heart more than just a strong body. Strengthening medicines targeted three specific areas of industrial success: 1) access to higher-paying jobs; 2) peaceful relations with men of other ethnicities and races so that none "had problems with them as Batswana"; and 3) a strengthened "consciousness" so that if an accident were to occur, a man would be able to anticipate it and move to safety.[64]

Part of the danger of mining for the Tswana came from the mixing of so many ethnicities in one place. The mining companies exacerbated and perpetuated this notion in an attempt to divide the massive African workforce in order to make mine labor easier to control. They created various work and leisure sites of competition between men of different ethnicities to further the divisiveness. As Thabane and Guy have shown, some ethnic groups used this divi-

A group of men consulting a Ngwaketse *ngaka* (with bare head).
Photograph by Isaac Schapera, 1938. Courtesy of the Royal Anthropological

sion to their advantage. The Basuto, for example, promoted themselves as specialists in the higher-paying, though more dangerous, work of shaft-sinking.[65]

The southeastern Tswana, who were a distinct minority in South Africa and who never successfully cast themselves as experts in any particular mining niche, saw the bodily danger of interethnic mixing on two fronts. First, they feared the physical violence that was part of daily life in the mining compounds. This stood in stark contrast to the morally imagined emphasis on physical peace among men that pervaded the *merafe* of southeastern Bechuanaland. Though domestic abuse and corporal punishment appear to have been common and accepted in the Tswana *merafe,* assault and insult between men violated the local ethos and were met with corporal punishment and social sanction meted out in the *kgotla.* Though violent crime and drunken brawls were not unknown in southeastern Bechuanaland in the 1930s and 1940s, punishments were powerful deterrents that kept random and spontaneous physical violence relatively rare and much despised. Returned miners from this period explained to me that they wanted to get along with men of other ethnicities and to be seen as peaceful, not "always fighting" like their historic rivals the Ndebele, with whom they labored in South Africa.[66]

Second, workers recognized in empirical terms that the mines were dangerous places where rock bursts and rock falls occurred with alarming frequency. The men saw accidents as a zero-sum game in which someone was bound to get hurt and sought to have more powerful medicine than their co-workers so that they would not be the ones upon whom the table fell. Mololokane Makati, who first went to the mines in 1933, explained the rationale of visiting a *ngaka* before leaving for the mines:

> It seems that there are different people working on the mines, and these people they will bring different charms. A Zulu will bring this one, the other one will bring this one, so you'll find that all of these charms will wind up bringing bad luck on someone who is not protected. So you'll find that maybe you didn't go and strengthen yourself at the *ngaka*—well, you'll find that maybe you'll always be involved in accidents because you didn't strengthen yourself.[67]

Tshukudu Mokgele, who was initiated into the same regiment as Mololokane Makati, also thought it imperative to gain protection from a local *ngaka* before going to the mines. He was well aware of the physical dangers of mining; his father had died in the mines in the early 1920s. Thus, he took the highly unusual step of going on his own to the doctor, after consulting with his mother, since his father was dead, his brothers were off in the mines, and his uncles were away. He explained why:

> The doctor was just for protection and since there are many *merafe* there in the mines and maybe that one will be bringing his traditional medicine and then maybe that one will be bringing his, and then maybe if an accident occurs it won't be him involved in that accident. So even with us it was just like that, it was for protection. The name in Setswana is *go okama* [to hang over; to protect; to defend].[68]

Dingaka gave miners items for protection harvested from the local bush. These medicines brought the protection of Modimo through the inherent power of the *badimo* who had planted them. Ephraim Motlhalamme described the protection he received from his doctor and gave a startling testimony of its efficacy:

> Mining is something which is dangerous. So I went to this *ngaka* and he gave me a small bud, the outer cover of the tree, so I put it in my pocket. It was my shield. Then in the morning when I am going underground it should be in my pocket and it was just acting as a protector, the place where I was working there were many accidents there. So one day while I was working there in the mines the rocks fell on us, and it was darkened by that time and there was such a big rock, and well I was just under that rock so by the time

when the mines fell that rock it broke into two parts! The one, it fell in front and the other it fell to the back of me, so that time I was the only one who was left. Many people were screaming around me, screaming for help, and I was the only one left standing there! From there I just saw a light from a far distance, many people were coming to help us, and I was one of those people who were helping to rescue those who were involved in the accidents. So ever since I was working in those mines I was never involved in an accident, but I was a leader for those people who were working in those areas where many accidents occurred. Each and every time I was the one leading those people to those areas where there were many accidents. So I found that that *ngaka* has done the right thing in that Modimo helped me to never be involved in any accidents.[69]

After returning home from the mines, migrants would again visit the doctor who had strengthened them to report on the success of their treatment, to receive a ritual cleansing to cool their bodies, and "to be checked you didn't bring anything bad back from there."[70] If they had been involved in an accident or returned home ill, the doctor would use this knowledge to evaluate the efficacy of his medicine. Migrancy made the 1930s and 1940s a dynamic period in Tswana medicine, as doctors coped with new problems and learned new medications and techniques from the expanded contact that accompanied migration. Many *dingaka* worked as migrant laborers for extended periods of time and returned to southeastern Bechuanaland with new therapies and a developed understanding of the particularities of the mine environment—its challenges, its pollutants, and its dangers.[71] *Dingaka* from other *merafe* who visited among the Tswana and travels by local *dingaka* outside their territory had long contributed to the development of and innovations in the local therapeutic system. But during this period, interethnic mixing in the urban areas and the mining compounds of the Witwatersrand accelerated cross-germination among Southern African medical communities.

Dingaka began to adapt their "strengthening" medicines so that they would generate an industrially defined state of able-bodiedness in their patients. These medicines were specifically targeted at enabling men to pass the fitness tests given at the mines. Peter Mokwena, a *ngaka* who worked in the mines, explained the situation:

> The moment they got there they were checked by the doctors in the mines, and you find that only those who were strengthened, only those who went to their *dingaka* before going were surviving those tests, but those who didn't go, they had problems. The moment that their bosses find that they had problems they will see from them if that problem can be solved or not, but you find that most of the time they had bigger problems and they were always

sent back home. So it's like those who just met their *dingaka,* they were the ones who were surviving and they were the ones who were sent to work down in the mines.[72]

Dingaka did not limit their medical innovation to strengthening practices; they also adapted to face the changing burden of disease in their communities. The burgeoning epidemics of tuberculosis and accidents brought a new urgency to their local epidemiological observations and pharmacological innovations. Older disease categories were expanded or adapted to include new symptom schemes and new diseases were recognized and named.

Debility in a Changing Economy

Despite the efforts of recruits to strengthen themselves before leaving for the Rand, many suffered in accidents or from disease, which contributed to an expansion of physical misfortune and depletion in the southeastern *merafe.* Though *madi* made one "strong," it also depleted the bodies of the men who earned it over time. Men with whom I spoke would comment with great pride if they had been able to work in the mines until they decided to retire rather than "being sent home" or changing to factory or farm work after a decade or so of mining. The physical vitality of men's bodies, which the community recognized as a key asset, was not just being siphoned off into the mines, it was also being depleted there. One of the primary causes of this depletion was tuberculosis. From the available data, it is impossible to quantify with any accuracy the incidence of tuberculosis in the southeastern protectorate during the Depression era. However, impressions by colonial medical staff working in the region at the time match up with Packard's historical epidemiology to suggest that a new and pervasive type of suffering had moved into the foreground of community life and economic planning.

But how, we might ask, did expanded labor migration impact the local experience of debility other than contribute to a pervasive experience of general bodily misfortune? Debilitated men and women had always had to cope with various handicaps in their pursuit of a livelihood and social and political power in Bechuanaland. Most likely the emphasis placed on physical strength and the views people held toward those with impairments depended in part on the specific historical moment. For example, it is unclear how physical impairment affected the social roles of disabled young men during the period of warfare in the nineteenth century, but we might guess that those whose impairments precluded participation in battle had at least one key route to social prestige and manhood closed to them. At the same time, we know that many of the frail elderly and the more severely debilitated adults and children would have perished, unable to climb to the rocky hilltops where the people sought refuge when under attack.[73] We also saw in the last chapter how in the early decades of the twentieth century many disabled men and women were able to surmount their own physical limitations and achieve social, political, and economic success within the boundaries prescribed by gender, age, and social status. But beginning in the early 1930s, the new culture of wage employment emphasized physical "fitness," and success within that culture became ever-more important economically and socially.

Just as able-bodied young men returned from work "stronger" through their acquisition of *madi*, the "unfit," who were left behind, found themselves becoming weaker. Physical personhood for men was increasingly defined locally through reference to industrial labor. New interpretations were given to older Tswana knowledge, reinforcing the primacy of wage work in male identity, as the evolving significance of the proverb *Mogopu wa segole ga go ribegwe* (The bowl of the cripple is not put upside down) suggests. People who learned the proverb in the 1910s and 1920s explained its meaning as similar to that of other proverbs about disability discussed in the previous chapter, namely that disability is not death, so one should not turn one's back on a disabled person and fail to provide for them by metaphorically "turning their bowl upside down." But some who learned the proverb in the 1940s refute the earlier meaning, believing that the proverb refers to mining. They claim that a man's bowl would be turned upside down while he was away at the mines, just as basins were inverted for initiates away at *bogwera* or *bojale*. Since a *segole* (disabled person) wouldn't be working in the mines, his bowl would not be turned upside down.[74] Thus, for some, the proverb came to mean that disabled men couldn't go for work (*go bereka*).

Physical fitness became central to socioeconomic success, and the meanings of "fitness" were debated in a variety of ways and in a variety of spaces. The medical examinations for the mines formed one key arena where these debates took shape. Men who surmounted physical impairments in their agricultural-pastoral work found themselves rejected from the primary source of wage work: mining. Gabotlhaleshwe Morwane, who had been partially blind since birth, recalled his shock at being rejected during the medical exam in 1940:

> Long ago I wanted to go to the mines but I was cut because of some eye problems—but while I knew deep inside my heart that I could do it. . . . Yes, I went to Molepolole and Merriweather still was the person who was working there—and they just cut me there—they just looked at my eyes and said "No, you cannot do that."[75]

After that rejection Morwane found employment as a herdsman, but he still felt frustrated about being prevented from earning cash at the mines. He did not agree that he would not be able to work hard because of blindness, but he would never have the opportunity to demonstrate this in return for *madi*.

Those men who were not eligible for mining might find employment on white-owned farms. When they paid cash at all, white farmers paid even less than the already pitiful wages given to African miners; usually the worker received bags of maize after the harvest.[76] The jobs were often seasonal, yet they corresponded to the peak labor demands back home, thus making this work a much less attractive option. Nonetheless, in the 1930s and 1940s some men who were too young or too old to work at the mines or too debilitated (often from a previous history of mine service) went to work on the smattering of white-owned farms in southeastern Bechuanaland across the border in South Africa.[77]

Many others, perhaps deterred by their rejections from the mines and, by the early 1940s, even from the army, found local work as herdsmen for Batswana cattle owners, where, if all went well, they would receive a beast at the end of the year. Although this work allowed men to remain within the territory, they found it much less desirable than wage employment.[78] Not only did herding fail to generate *madi*, it was also the traditional occupation of boys and servants. Working as a herder in this new economy left young men (*makolwane*) trapped in the netherworld of the *magwane*. The cattle posts may have lacked the dangers of the mines, but work there wouldn't transform a hired man into a new status. As young disabled and debilitated men became husbands, they might find their economic status slipping ever farther behind that of their "able-bodied" brothers and friends, since one beast each year could hardly clothe and help to feed a worker, a wife, and their children, much less contribute to gifts exchanged within the wider kin network. The new economy marginalized debilitated men just at the time when families depended on male wages the most.[79]

Men who were prevented from mining by virtue of their physical condition had the same desire for material goods and economic pressures that had pushed so many into the quest for cash in the first place. Included among those pressures was the burden of taxation. The colonial government did not necessarily excuse sick or disabled men from their tax obligations. In some cases the chief intervened to promote the tax exemption of elderly men whose sons failed to support them.[80] In other cases, elderly men didn't know to apply for exemption until they had reached abject poverty and were facing imprisonment. In 1944, Mathe Kelatlhilwe of Ramotswa was tried for failing to pay his tax for 1943 and 1944. Though he had struggled and paid his tax up until that time, his only defense was his statement that "he has no more property to sell and is too old and ill to work." The district commissioner granted him an exemption.[81]

Younger men with physical impairments were often not as lucky as their

**A colonial official collecting hut tax in the *kgotla* in Molepolole.
Photographer unknown, n.d. Reproduced from London Missionary
Society/Council for World Mission Archives.**

grandfathers. The older system of regimentally based tribute labor had accom-
modated physical impairments by excusing debilitated regiment members from
certain tasks, but the new system of taxation did not do so without substantial
"proof." In 1942, Kalete Mokoleti, a 24-year-old epileptic man, was fined £6 or
six months' hard labor for failing to pay tax for the past six years. He described
his situation for the court:

> I went to Johannesburg about three months after my regiment was called. I
> was a kitchen boy for five months, then I came home. I stayed at home until
> now. I worked at a school in Johannesburg. The chief knows I have not been
> well. Everyone knows I am an invalid. I have never been to school.

He was nonetheless examined by Dr. Ludwin, the medical officer, who reported:

> I have today examined Kalete and apart from an old scar on the right tem-
> poral region found him clinically in a good state of health and fit. It is impos-
> sible for me to assess the degree of impairment of his capacity to work

caused by the wound which has resulted in the above scar. I think however, that it would be right to give him the benefit of the doubt and assume that the wound has affected him adversely.

As regards his fitness in the years preceding 1941 I regret being unable to state anything definite. I may, however, venture an opinion that most probably he was fit—he is well built and there are no signs of old disease.

The court ordered Mokoleti to contract himself as a laborer to avoid imprisonment. This proved impossible. He had then tried to enlist in the army during recruitments in Lobatse, but though military standards for fitness were noticeably lower than mining standards, Mokoleti was rejected after a few weeks' service. This forced his father to pay the back tax and fines to escape sending his epileptic son to jail.[82] Medical definitions of fitness could cut two ways, excluding those who thought themselves fit and including those who thought themselves unfit.

Furthermore, fitness for work and fitness for paying taxes were two quite different qualities. In 1938 in Molepolole, Ramatsimako Radipitsi, a 38-year-old man, found himself unable to pay his tax for the first time after he was rejected from the mine medical exam. He had recently lost the sight of his right eye and now found the left one sore too. Dr. Shepherd, the missionary doctor in Molepolole who had rejected him from mine work, nonetheless upheld his tax burden in his report for the court:

> I certify that I have this day medically examined this man Ramatsimako Radipitsi and find that his eye sight is such that he would be debarred from work at the mines. But he is, in my opinion, fit for manual labour, and I cannot recommend him for exemption from hut tax payment.

The court fined Radipitsi one pound or one month hard labor.[83]

Cases like Radipitsi's became more and more common. These men had once worked in the mines, perhaps earning their *bogadi* (bridewealth) and then remitting wages as a household head. Yet at relatively young ages they found themselves physically transformed into nonlaborers. Mining brought sudden impairments for some and gradual debility for many more. Many men found their physical status vis-à-vis employment and their economic future altered at some point during their work career.[84] Though some families, particularly those drawn from the aristocracy, succeeded in converting mining careers into robust herds, homes, and fields, most struggled to continue to succeed and survive in a changing local economy once the job and the money ran out. Middle-aged men (those in their late 30s, 40s, or 50s) found themselves at the end of work careers that typically had begun at the mines and often ended on white-owned farms or as herdsmen, with declining income accompanying each transition. Others were not so lucky, and the mines sent many men home to die, spreading tuberculosis among their families in the process.[85] A review of the tax cases that reached the district commissioner for Kweneng District in the 1920s and 1930s reveals an age distribution of defendants that is not surprising, given the nature of work and debility at the time. In the cases that listed defendants' ages, the majority of men were between their mid-30s and mid-50s.[86] These men would have reached the end of their potential mining careers but perhaps their sons were not yet adults who could contribute to their fathers' tax obligations. That a number of tax defaulters died while their cases were being reviewed suggests that tuberculosis or silicosis may have ended their work life before they could build herds and families to support themselves.[87]

Debility was of concern to the *morafe* as well as to the individual. Chiefs and elders expressed their anxiety over declining able-bodiedness and the increased power of individual miners in discussions of the waning strength of the territory—the able-bodiedness of men was a resource that belonged to the community and to the family as much as to the individual. They complained that this resource was being spent in a foreign place. Even when miners returned home, they were so undisciplined that they were no longer using their vitality to enhance the health of the commonweal.[88] At the height of the Depression in 1933, community leaders urged the colonial administration to make the mines take more Tswana. But within a few years, as many miners lost contact with their home communities and failed to send back wage remittances, they began to express concern about the drain on local able-bodiedness.[89]

Chief Kgari of the Bakwena explained the situation in a Native Advisory Council meeting in 1936. Reading from a document issued to the chiefs called "Notes on the Problem of Mine Recruits in Native Reserves," he estimated that in 1935, 1,500 "young men" from Gakwena had gone to the mines on nine-month contracts.

> With roughly 6000 tax payers in the Reserve about 2000 are unfit by reason of age, disease and various other causes to do any strenuous manual labor. This leaves 4000 fit men in the tribe. Of the total that is 37%. This number leave every year for the mines. It's a very great percentage and results in
> 1) Lack of man power in the reserve to cultivate the land and carry on tribal labor. 2) Lower food supply for the tribe, because old men and women who do the tilling haven't the power to plow it properly. 3) No doubt tuberculosis will become a very serious matter in the Reserve. 4) So many men are gone and it's bad for the health of the tribe because women are left behind and immorality takes place. 5) Young men from the mines, if they go every year and for long periods, lose contact with the tribe, and when they come home they do not care for the tribal work and they have no respect for their Chiefs,

Headman or their elders. If this is allowed to go on the tribe will gradually die because men who should build up the tribe are spending more and more time in mines.[90]

The Changing Medical Landscape

The new wave of occupational injuries and illnesses occurred in the context of a changing medical milieu. Elite *dingaka* (*dingaka tsa kgosing*) faced a public loss of power as chiefs curbed their principle public health activities of rainmaking and initiation in favor of mission-led rituals and as divination was criminalized. Despite this erosion of key collective rituals, in the 1930s and 1940s *dingaka* and their services were in high demand among individual households. They were also finding new footing through the steady growth of the migrant economy.[91] Strengthening migrants before their journeys and treating those injured or infected in the workplace buoyed the business of *bongaka*. Some of the new *madi* entering the protectorate was finding its way into the hands of local doctors. Into this changing landscape of *bongaka* marched a new cadre of missionary doctors.

The missions, who had been in Bechuanaland for a century, were expanding their presence in the territory. In one sense, Batswana had long seen the growing Christian cults as aspects of *bongaka* and missionaries as foreign *dingaka*, a perception that missionaries had reinforced since Livingstone's time with their provision of medical services.[92] But in another sense, these two different approaches to medicine also developed as a pair defined in opposition to one another by both *dingaka* and mission doctors.[93] This contrast grew more accentuated as missionary medicine became more "scientific" in its orientation. In the 1930s, several missions began enlarging their medical practices by building clinics and hospitals. This expansion joined a widening of government medical services to create a new terrain in which a larger number of people would be drawn into the biomedical realm for the first time.

Syphilis and tuberculosis in particular drew many people into the new sites of colonial medicine. Though western doctors could offer no efficacious treatment for either disease, they promoted their own therapies over indigenous therapies. Not all patients came voluntarily; some came because the district commissioner might suspend the fine on a tubercular or syphilitic tax defaulter provided he attend the local clinic regularly for treatment.[94]

Yet despite this expansion of services, western medical outlets in the southeast (and elsewhere in the protectorate) remained sparse, located mostly in the capital towns of the various *merafe*. Because of the great distances between dispensaries, western medicine remained outside most patients' reach, and it was not yet in direct competition with *dingaka* and women for care of the sick and the suffering. As headman Mupi observed in a meeting of his peers to ask for a dispensary in Gabane village, "It is a very bad thing to travel a long distance when you are sick."[95] But white doctors and their nurses specialized in a number of key services, including examinations for labor recruits, treatment for syphilis (which was provided free of charge), and surgery, thus making their presence more and more central to changing local experiences of medicine.[96] The medical exam to qualify for mine work became for many Batswana the first site of introduction into a foreign medical ethos, one in which the disparate yet overlapping concerns of industry, mission, and government melded into a singular experience.

Physical Fitness Exams

The medical exams given at recruiting stations established the outlines of the industrial definitions of able-bodiedness that were becoming so critical to the economic experiences of southeastern Tswana men. These exams became the first stop on the migrant pipeline. Biomedicine emerged from its tenuous hold as the practice of a handful of white doctors to become a larger system with a vital role to play in socioeconomic life. Its newfound power over the well-being of the local populace stemmed from the convergence of industrial, colonial, and Christian interests in local bodies and their physical capacities. Within the medical exams the mystifying and objectifying force of the biomedical gaze merged with colonial subjugation of workers and their bodies.[97]

From the earliest days of labor recruitment all prospective miners were medically examined when they reached the mines. Those who did not match required standards of physical fitness were returned home at the expense of the recruiters, who took risks when they sent marginal workers they hoped might get through. Prior to World War I, as Packard has documented, recruiters would often take a gamble on attesting marginally fit labor because the examination in South Africa was haphazardly administered. Between 1916 and 1930, however, at the recommendation of the Association of Mine Medical Officers and further spurred by the Miner's Phthisis Act of 1925, the mines gradually established compulsory medical examinations for all recruits. Mine management preferred to have migrants examined in their home area first to save the cost of repatriating the unfit. Besides, if many recruits traveled all the way to the Rand only to be sent back without any earnings, it might deter prospective recruits. Bechuanaland was one of the last labor recruitment areas to begin a local medical screening process. In its early decades, the protectorate had lacked the capacity for large-scale examinations, but by 1935, the colonial medical service had grown, primarily through the establishment of several mission hospitals, and the colonial government began to require a compulsory medical examination for all mine recruits.[98]

Exams were given on a large scale. Recruits were brought into the clinic or hospital, stripped naked, and weighed. They stood in a group and were made to raise their arms and turn so their bodies could be better viewed. Lungs were examined with a stethoscope for signs of phthisis (tuberculosis). The process emphasized efficiency, and little time could be given to individual men. But even this cursory exam was enough to weed out a substantial percentage of recruits. In 1933, at the height of the Depression, when the mines raised fitness standards to take advantage of the glut of labor, Dr. Shepherd of the United Free Church/London Missionary Society mission in the major recruiting center of Molepolole recorded the results of the examination of 500 men. He found only 250 "fit" for mine work. Of the remainder, he rejected 207 outright, while 43 men were deemed "doubtful or borderline cases."[99] This had been a drought year, so the general health of the men may have been lower than otherwise, but in Bechuanaland drought years were frequent events. Throughout the 1930s and 1940s Tswana men faced high rejection rates from labor recruiters on medical grounds.[100]

European scrutiny of African physiques in Bechuanaland was not new. But the compulsory examinations systematically read the bodies of the young men of the protectorate. Guided by the Chamber of Mines and interpreted by individual doctors, the process began to draw a line between the fit and the unfit. It was not a static line; it fluctuated with the labor needs of the mines, individual relations between doctors and recruiters, and the view of any particular local doctor.[101] Nevertheless, the process demonstrated that there *was* a line, and that line determined access to all-important wages, even if prospective miners were at a loss to understand how, where, and why that line existed.

Doctors used measurements such as weight to divide a large group of recruits into a hierarchy of smaller sections. Such measurements were then interpreted as indicators of individual capacity. Weight, however, was not viewed in combination with any other precise measurement such as height or age. General impressions, such as the evaluation that someone had a "poor physique," were converted into concrete statistical categories.[102] The structured formality of the examination and the report masked vague categories with an aura of precision. These categories were used to draw broad conclusions about the suitability of Tswana men to industrial employment. In 1928 and again in 1932 the Native Recruitment Corporation (NRC) sent out a list of "Suggestions Relating to Medical Examinations of Native Mine Labourers" that warned doctors of possible "defects" in their recruits.[103] Some of these suggestions were quite vague and open to an arbitrary interpretation, such as the category "defective development" which was described as "long, thin, young natives, who's [*sic*] chests and arms aren't developed in proportion to the legs" or the caution against "congenital deformities which interfere with proper performance of work." For other, more exacting criteria, such as "valvular lesions of the heart," the rapid nature of the examination was inappropriate for the accurate discovery of such defects.

Ultimately, it would seem, each doctor set his own examination criteria. Dr. Alfred Merriweather, who worked with Dr. Shepherd in Molepolole from the 1940s, examined recruits twice a week. He recalls that

> a lot, a lot of that examination depended on the individual doctor, some doctors were very strict, others were not so strict, others thought the weight was very important, others thought the weight wasn't so important, and so on. And there were no criteria laid down as to—apart from weight and oneself— the examination was really quite cursory.[104]

Industrially valued able-bodiedness was a transitory asset. It could change from examination center to examination center. It also diminished over the life of the worker. Age and ability had an inverse relationship. In the late 1970s, as the mines sought to develop a more stable workforce, they began to value seniority, skill, and experience in their workers. In the 1930s and early 1940s, however, this was not yet the case. Renewal of the workforce was the goal. Mine managers knew that work in the mines had a gradual debilitating effect for many and caused sudden disability for others. Thus, the NRC instructed doctors to pay special attention when examining returning miners to "defects" such as "old injuries to arms and legs, which interfere with function to any considerable extent." Yet these criteria were applied in an unpredictable and confusing manner. A returned miner from this period told me of an accident on the mines in the late 1940s that crushed his knee. It was treated in South Africa with a fixed joint, preventing him from bending it. This did not prevent him from reenlisting for mine work. When asked how he was able to pass the medical exam with a fixed joint he replied, "They didn't mind, it was up to you. You say that you can manage, so I was still underground after the accident."[105] This type of favoritism shown experienced miners with orthopedic problems in contrast to the extra scrutiny given experienced miners suspected of chest conditions, though not irrational from a medical point of view, further confused the picture of fitness presented to the Tswana.[106]

As examiners, doctors stood between two different sets of interest and interpretation; those of prospective workers and those of recruiters. Though one might expect divergent interests among labor and industry, between would-be workers and would-be employers, the gap was actually quite narrow. Recruits wanted to be accepted for mine work and its opportunities to accrue *madi,* and recruiters wanted as many men passed as possible because they were paid on a per capita basis. It was individual missionary doctors who appointed themselves as protectors of local interests. Mission doctors knew that mine work took a toll on men over time and understood that many miners contracted tuberculosis in the mines. Yet, like the colonial government, they also acknowledged the vital impact mine wage remittances had on local nutrition. They struggled against both recruiters and recruits to safeguard those bodies they found incompetent for work, even though they relied on the revenue the exams brought to their struggling hospitals.[107] This situation may have been unique to Bechuanaland, where medical examinations were given almost entirely by missionary doctors. Though their hospital budgets depended on the fees earned from the recruitment companies, these doctors still seem to have seen themselves in the paternalist, protector mode vis-à-vis the African communities in which they lived.

Individual doctors did not seek to personally benefit financially, but they gladly accepted grants for institutional development from a Deferred Pay Interest Fund. They did not question why they should receive this interest money rather than the miners from whose pay it was generated; they believed themselves able to put the money to better use than individual workers.[108] While examination fees were paid in relation to the number of recruits examined, grant amounts were determined in relation to the number of mine workers that originated from the mission hospital's district.[109] As the Depression subsided and the mines began to compete for labor with other industries, the NRC's financial assistance to mission hospitals and labor examination centers increased.[110] Dr. Shepherd's report to the London Missionary Society in 1939 illustrates that he was able to see this increased income as validation of his work as the medical protector of the Bakwena people.

> Then a great new opportunity was opened up to us in the desire of the Native Recruiting Corporation that all Mine Recruits from the Bakwena Reserve be medically examined by me. The result was that the number of recruits examined rose to 1426 as against 424 last year. The fees for the examinations reached £129:16:6 with an additional £26:15:6 for motor mileage. These figures will probably be augmented in the coming year as our services were sought two months after the year began, and January and February are the big months for men going off to the Mines, because they wait till the ploughing season is over and ploughing ceases at the end of the year. There is satisfaction in the extra receipts, more satisfaction in having our hand completely over those who are to be deemed physically fit for the occupation of mining, but perhaps the greatest satisfaction is in the knowledge that a

policy carried out for five years, and by which we had to accept loss, has been more than justified. That policy was to decline to pass medically those who were not quite fit or those who were too young.[111]

Medical exams fused a number of fractured vantage points through which industry, the Christian missions, and the British colonial government variously fought to exploit, enhance, and protect young male African bodies and their vitality. But what did examinees take from their introduction to western medical culture?[112] How did the group examination fit into these men's lay understanding of medicine and able-bodiedness?

To new labor recruits, medical examinations to test their "fitness" were a novel experience. Yet examinees brought their own ideas about doctors, diagnosis, and physiology to the new examination procedure, forging new understandings of the meanings of physical "fitness" and "unfitness" in the process. Former miners who were recruited in the 1930s and 1940s with whom I spoke agreed that work underground required a more fit body than farming or cattle-herding.[113] However, they perceived this "fitness" (Setswana: *itekanela*) as an internal quality and usually focused on the use of the stethoscope as the vehicle by which western doctors determined fitness.[114] The stethoscope was quite unlike any of the instruments local *dingaka* used. Yet laymen, who didn't expect to fully understand the inner workings or medical theories behind the *dingaka*'s use of diagnostic methods—visual examination, wrist palpation, or *ditaola* (divining bones)—trusted in the stethoscope as a diagnostic tool. They did not question the white doctors' examination methods any more than they did those of the *dingaka*. The ability of doctors to read bodies and discern their invisible inner workings and to extrapolate from that information to decode wellness or illness, which were complex socially and spiritually located states, was inherently mysterious, as was the process by which they gained that knowledge. Mololokane Makati, who first went to the mines in 1937, described the exam process for me. His description was typical of those given to me by men recruited in 1930s.

> The white doctors, they just put their machines on our bodies so they were just checking from my body to see if I was healthy [*itekanela*], but I don't know what diseases actually they were looking for. . . . They were checking all things but mostly the lungs to see whether my breath [*mowa*] was normal or what.

When I remarked that this sounded quite different from an exam given by a Setswana doctor (*ngaka*) and asked why the white doctor would have been concerned with breathing (*mowa*), he explained:

I'm not quite sure why they were doing that, the only thing I know is that these Setswana doctors check on the wrists not the chest, but I don't even know why they do that either.[115]

Konobule Kobue, who was made to wait in a holding camp for several weeks to be fattened up before he could be attested in 1937, also did not ask why he was on the margins of fitness or how precisely that was determined. He explained:

> They didn't tell us exactly what the disease was they were looking for, but they just checked us were we strong enough to work. They were just placing their machines on top of our bodies so that they could find out if we were fit [*itekanela*] enough to work. So those who were fit they were put on the one side and those who were not fit they were just put on the other side.[116]

Recruits didn't directly inquire about the doctor's standards or judgment despite the frustration men such as Rra Kobue must have felt at being kept for several weeks with no wage. This was as much because of local medical culture as because of the new power whites had in southeastern Tswana society. Mystification was an expected part of local medical encounters. As in contemporary British society, the efficacy of the local therapeutic system depended upon an imbalance of knowledge, with doctors as experts. *Dingaka* were intimidating authority figures whom patients suspected had the power to harm as much as to heal, and patients—particularly young ones—did not expect to be educated about their diagnosis or to ask questions about methods and theories. Though a man might be rejected for mine work by one doctor and then accepted by another a week later, this inconsistency did not call into question western diagnostic criteria. Standardized measurements as a basis for diagnosis were foreign medical concepts, but second opinions were not. Patients who could afford it commonly moved from *ngaka* to *ngaka* in search of satisfaction, and an evolving or layered diagnosis often emerged from each subsequent encounter. Mine medical exams were proving to be no different.[117] Some men who had been rejected by one doctor went for strengthening from a local *ngaka* before trying to attest again, perhaps traveling to a new recruiting center to do so. This might tip the balance for them, reinforcing the inherent power and veracity of both western and Tswana medicine in the process.

In any event, even if recruits had gleaned more about the specifics of the white doctors' methods and purposes, they would have understood this new information within a Tswana physiological system rather than a biomedical one. Any possible mediation of physiological concepts between the two systems was further confused by translation between Setswana and English. Thus, checking on a prospective recruit's "breath" would have been interpreted in a more complex sense than simply measuring lung function, something lost in my translation of Mr. Makati's words into English. *Mowa,* or breath, in Setswana was and is an entity that contains the soul or essence of a person. Thus, checking on *mowa* could be a way to gather a deeper understanding of personal inner strength and cosmological potency as much as it could be a screen for phthisis—which in the 1930s was just being recognized by the south-eastern Tswana as a discrete illness. This kind of talking past one another masked the level of confusion that permeated the new clinical encounters and contributed to the tendency by colonial medical personnel to make glib observations about a range of patient behaviors, from sharing medications to failure to return for follow-up care. Recruits saw physical examination as an attempt to judge fitness (*itekanela*) on a more holistic level, despite the mining industry's intentions to the contrary.

The objectification of recruits' bodies generated more than simple confusion, though. Examinees rejected elements of the colonial (including missionary) medical culture that violated local norms about bodily conduct and exposure. They reasserted the intimacy of human bodies—even black ones—to colonial medical practitioners. As Megan Vaughan shows, colonial medicine had begun to distinguish itself through its presentation of a new medical etiquette that objectified African bodies.[118] But patients continued to experience their bodies in extremely personal terms. In 1937, Chief Bathoen took a local missionary doctor to task for humiliating Bangwaketse mine recruits. He complained that the men were examined "in a nude condition by Seventh Day Adventist medical missionary Dr. Marcus—in a room in the presence of a European nurse." Dr. Marcus had explained that the nurse had her back to the men and was writing out reports, but Bathoen was firm. He told Dr. Marcus that "natives had a rooted objection to be exposed *in their persons* at any time and that under the circumstances described there was a grave objection to the practice and further that his Mission was being damaged as a consequence" (emphasis mine).[119] Dr. Marcus promised it wouldn't happen again.

Two historical processes—labor migration and colonial medicine—intersected and shaped one another in the 1930s and 1940s in southeastern Bechuanaland. Together they determined a new context in which local meanings of able-bodiedness were shaped by external standards, both industrial and medical. Changing definitions of able-bodiedness sowed the seeds of a new socioeconomic hierarchy that was only just beginning to emerge, one in which youthful vigor, extra weight, and deep breathing could be converted into *madi* in ways that the wisdom and experience of age could not. Accessing mine work either personally or through young male relatives became a central economic strategy for most southeastern Tswana, who were struggling to survive in a depressed ecological and economic climate. Work in the mines had the potential to "strengthen" miners through the acquisition of *madi,* but it was both dangerous and depleting over the long term, and the strength young men acquired was elusive or short lived for many. Fragments of the vitality of Southeastern Tswana communities (in both productive and procreative terms) were siphoned off to the Rand and replaced by a growing local community of suffering. This experience underscored the disarray the local systems of public health experienced in the face of expanded colonial, capitalist, and missionary penetration. Processes begun in the early decades of the twentieth century crystallized in the 1930s. The spiritual weakening of the chiefship and the dispersal and disaggregation of *bongaka* from the core of community cosmology into a diffuse system of therapeutics necessarily altered the spiritual basis of community wellness and together with the outmigration of able-bodied men compromised the system of public health.

4   Increasing Autonomy, Entangled Therapeutics, and Hidden Wombs

Pelo e ntle ke leswalo la motho.
> —Setswana proverb: A good heart is the medicine of a person.

Matlo ke mabipa.
> —Setswana proverb: Houses are covers for secrets.

From the late 1940s until Independence in 1966, people in southeastern Bechuanaland struggled to manage the effects of colonization, Christian conversion, and labor migration on family and community institutions in the context of widespread experiences of bodily misfortune. The end of the war brought economic advancement for a few but a further decline for most. Some aristocratic men (and a notable handful of commoners) were able to take advantage of agricultural improvement schemes, borehole technology, and the 1954 reopening of the Lobatse abattoir to increase their wealth. But the majority saw access to wealth in cattle slipping by as borehole syndicates arose—groups of wealthy men who paid to sink and maintain private sources for watering their cattle. This gave them de facto control over large stretches of grazing land, crowding the smallholders who lacked access to boreholes onto increasingly depleted land. The *mafisa* system by which men had farmed out cattle to be herded by poorer relatives or neighbors, which often was the last economic refuge for debilitated men, also began to decline. It no longer made sense for the wealthy to spread their cattle over a larger geographic area under the control of many dependents; now it was better to cluster the herd near the borehole.[1] In these difficult economic times, labor migration continued to pick up pace, and ever-larger numbers of men and now women crossed the border for work. Agriculture, which was increasingly performed by children, seniors, and the debilitated, also suffered, periodic droughts continued, and the southern protectorate produced less food per capita than ever before.[2]

Within the protectorate, unease with the colonial government was increased by the tense popular struggles against an increasingly repressive state across the border in South Africa. The *bogosi* (chiefship) was weakened as its inability to maintain morality and collective well-being grew more evident and as individual *merafe* faced succession crises or increasingly autocratic and extractive policies. The establishment and growth of independent churches, the efforts of neoconservatives who promoted the illicit continuation of *bogwera* and *bojale* in dissident villages, and the rising cadre of newly technologized elites were all evidence of the internal fracturing and reconfiguring of communities, and various groups sought to regain control over health and well-being in the context of what looked like an absence of chiefly efficacy.

Labor migration and the war caused marriage, parenthood, and other processes of affiliation to continue to undergo significant changes. Absent husbands, brothers, and fathers also meant an increase in female autonomy and growing labor burdens for women involved in local agriculture and domestic production. But heightened autonomy for women came with a heavy price. Many soldiers returned from the war to find that their wives had borne children with other men in their absence.[3] This pervasive experience was already on the rise in a country where labor migration had long been the norm. In some areas polygyny began to sharply decline, while in other *merafe* its demise was already complete.[4] As in other parts of the wider Southern African region, many young men achieved control over the choice of marriage partners through the social power of their wages, and emotional desires emerged more strongly to mix with political and economic motives in forging affinal ties. Premarital pregnancy, long on the rise, became commonplace, and many couples incorporated parenthood into the early stages of their marriage processes.[5] By the mid-1960s, both women and men were delaying the age of marriage, and many women did not necessarily expect to marry at all. The ambiguities of the marriage process, which took years to complete, also engendered disputes between partners and their respective relatives over the nature of particular unions and their accompanying obligations.[6] Instead of marriage, many people entered informal (*bonyatsi*) relationships in which men provided gifts and other forms of support for their girlfriends but did not commit themselves to the legal and familial obligations of marriage.

Struggles over marriage, sexuality, and parenthood during the war revealed the variety of alliances and tensions possible in this protean socioeconomic climate. Wartime letters from Bangwato soldiers who were stationed abroad to their chief asking for help in managing domestic affairs while the men were away illustrate the incredible fluidity of the social landscape at the beginning of the period we will explore. Some husbands acted to protect their wives from their agnates (be they siblings, fathers, or uncles), as in the case of a man who, "alarmed to hear that my wife goes about in poor clothing," appealed to the chief to prevent his uncle from collecting the paychecks he sent home to the protectorate.[7] Others, either independently or in alliance with their fathers, challenged their in-laws about a wife's desertion or infidelity.[8] Some men felt abandoned by their wives, parents, uncles, and in-laws simultaneously. Others questioned their mothers, sisters, wives, or daughters-in-law from a distance, troubled by their long silences. A father might even inquire about his daughter's behavior on behalf of his son-in-law who was stationed nearby.[9] Collectively, these letters remind us that as processes of affiliation shifted, generational and gendered, affinal and agnatic axes combined in multiple ways in wartime and postwar social relationships. Since our focus is on bodily misfortune here, the social and legal intricacies of these changes will remain in the background of this chapter. But it is worth bearing in mind Lynn Thomas's apt description of similar processes in Kenya, where "the problem of premarital pregnancies emerged as much from attempts to create something new as from the collapse of something old."[10]

Throughout this period, all four of the systems designed to promote health and manage misfortune that we have come to know—public health, colonial medicine, *bongaka,* and lay nursing care—reflected and reshaped the social, cultural, political, and moral transformations that gripped local society. Meanwhile, a new force in health and welfare—independent healing churches—entered the mix. Through this array of health-related domains individuals, families, and the wider society explained and managed the experiences and meanings of debility and misfortune that so many Batswana encountered and underwent in the postwar period. One trend in particular was central to the new climate of health care and bodily misfortune that emerged: a narrowing of the scale of personal obligations. The roots of this growing autonomy lay decades earlier in the prewar period: it was born of industrial labor migration, *madi* production, and the resulting weakening of the gerontocracy.

One of the central effects of this highly contested development was a heightened concern about sexual behavior, particularly women's. "The possibility of a person making individual sexual choices and then evading the consequences," as Diana Jeater has phrased it, had deep moral implications that were experienced physically. Sex meant the mixing of *madi*—the vital, shared substance that tied lineage members together bodily. In addition, a sexual relationship often meant the movement of cattle between families as either bridewealth or pregnancy compensation. Thus, sex was the concern of the lineage as much as the individual.[11] Extramarital and premarital affairs were not new in the postwar period, but the restrictions on their timing and conduct were weakening, as evidenced in escalating experiences of bodily misfortune. People had long thought that women needed to remain faithful to husbands who were out hunting, at war, "or engaged in some other enterprise of a dangerous nature," as mining surely was. Schapera, writing in the late 1930s explained, "It is held that if she commits adultery at this time he will meet with some serious misfortune or accident. Formerly this taboo was applied also to women whose husbands were away working in the towns, but it is certainly not observed today."[12] But even as the simple equation of female adultery and male accident declined, ideas persisted about the dangers of women's unchecked sexuality in a context of male absence. In the 1930s, the rise of male migrancy meant public worries about men fathering children outside the *morafe*. Now the continuing absence of men merged with gradually increasing possibilities for female mobility and a steadily increasing rate of extramarital and premarital pregnancies to focus attention on women's sexual agency. One of the central health-related ramifications of this focus on the loss of social control over female sexuality was an increased pathologization of the womb.

Over this period, a new epidemiological reality crystallized in the public consciousness and the moral imagination took root and flourished in an array of new health-related ideas and practices. Bodies themselves were changing as new patterns of debility emerged in the context of a shifting local ecology of industrial migrancy, tenuous agriculture, and increasingly skewed access to cattle. This new ecology of misfortune produced wasted men who returned home to cough blood, women with collapsed spines who crawled about their fields while hoeing, raving madmen and madwomen wandering village paths, and sickly and impaired children hidden at the back of their mothers' compounds. All these patients were diagnosed and cared for in ways that spoke of women's dangerous sexuality gone unchecked and the perils of burgeoning individualism and that portended the ensuing demise and reconfiguration of community-based cooperation and redistribution. These experiences suggest that caregiving (in its broadest sense) was becoming an increasingly contested and uncertain domain.

Autonomy and Public Health

The average number of Tswana men working on the mines doubled between 1946 and 1960, moving from roughly 10,000 to 20,000.[13] To these figures we should add the uncounted, but growing, number of Tswana women working in seasonal agriculture and domestic service in South Africa and the men who secured work in non-mining occupations. The tensions in intergenerational relationships intensified as a nascent ethos of individualism began to pull at the edges of the Tswana moral economy. This is not to argue that people in earlier times had no sense of the particularities of their own interests and motivations, simply to suggest that the permeability and interconnectedness of people and their environment—as evidenced in the public health system, in fundamental institutions controlled by the gerontocracy, and in the implicit community surveillance that was part of village life—located individual interests in a complex web of overlapping relations; it was very difficult for any one person to successfully extricate his/her own wants and actions from the life he/she would take on in the wider group.[14]

By the 1950s, local chiefs faced resistance to their attempts to organize labor for public health activities, including weeding and sprinkling the land. The rigid timing of work contracts meant that many men simply couldn't make themselves available to perform regimental labor, and the potential for self-determination born out of earning wages encouraged other "physically fit" men to challenge the chief's control by asserting that wage work trumped collective labor obligations. Such instances of resistance to regimental tasks started at different times in different villages, probably owing to the strength and views of particular chiefs and *dingaka,* but it seems likely that by Independence most southeastern Tswana chiefs lacked the power to control the necessary labor for public health.

Oral sources confirm that resistance to collective public health activities became a widespread problem between the 1950s and mid-1960s. They suggest that local people perceived the decay of community and chiefly power as evidence of the rising tide of individualism and jealousy (*lefufa*) and its negative effects on health. Some people specifically linked this erosion of public health to migrant labor and the rise of western education and blamed the chiefs for their impotence.[15] The following is a Diphaleng resident's description:

> The chiefs these days they are from school, and it's that they have broken the law, they are no longer doing as their fathers did in the olden days. . . . But maybe now you hear that people are being called from the *kgotla* they should go and pray for rain, but then you find that people don't come to the *kgotla,* the chief will stay there with people please do come, pray for the rain. So nobody, they will not come. They will be told bring *mokgalo* tree at the *kgotla.* Nobody will go. Nowadays each and every one is very busy on his own. . . . I think men going to the mines and children going to school may have contributed to that because many people and more especially men were going to mines, so very few were left, so maybe it's because men were not enough to go and do such things.[16]

This woman could not recall exactly when such public health rituals ceased, but three elderly people from the chief's ward, including the widow of the previous chief and a councilor from the *kgotla,* confirm that in Diphaleng, people began to abandon these practices in the 1950s.[17] In a neighboring village, Andrew Mmanthe, a *ngaka* and prophet healer, remembers that parents began refusing to send their children for collective ritual in the mid-1960s.[18]

Chiefs punished men who failed to attend important *kgotla* meetings and refused to participate in key public health activities.[19] In January 1961, the appeals court upheld the verdict of the Bamalete court in Ramotswa in a case against Mmoko Maotonyane, who was found guilty of refusing the chief's order to weed and was sentenced to a total of four months in jail with hard labor.

Rra Maotonyane was on his way back to the railway station to report for a mining contract when the chief gave the order. Though he lost his case and his appeal, the following two excerpts from his testimony reflect a recognition of the commodification of labor (even the chief's labor!) underlying a growing sense of autonomy.

> I am a Molete. I know the law governing my people here. I can obey the orders of the Chief *provided that I have time*. It is for those who are present in the village to obey the Chief's order not those who are outside. Even those working in the office here [the clerks] they cannot do Regimental work if the Chief calls them. (Emphasis mine)

> I eat where I am working and I even pay my tax there. If I am here at home I cannot eat. As I am here I was supposed to be at work now all this has spoiled. I am now complaining that the Chief should give me some job which I will work and get some food because he has caused me to lose my work which I was able to get some food, like himself getting food from his job.[20]

These changes did not signify a rejection of Tswana medical and environmental epistemology in favor of the growing paradigms of Christianity and western medicine. Nor did they reflect a period of ecological balance and harmony in which such practices were thought unnecessary—periodic drought and bouts of epizootic and epidemic disease continued to plague southeastern Bechuanaland throughout the postwar period.[21] Rather, resistance to collective labor in public health was part of a larger conceptual shift in how local people defined their interests and understood the relevant parameters of the social body. In Britain, the expansion of organized public health activities and social welfare policies in the first half of the nineteenth century signaled the rise of class-linking notions of a diseased social body. In the southeastern *merafe*, the demise of organized public health activities and social welfare practices signaled the reverse: the erosion of a village- or *morafe*-level sense of community interest in the face of the opposing force of individual identity. In the postwar period, families continued to strengthen and purify the boundaries of *their own* compounds, fields, and cattle kraals to protect against *boloi* and the harmful effects of the *dibeela* and pollution brought by returning migrants. Miners continued to visit *dingaka* for their own benefit before and after their trips to the Rand. It was only community-wide attempts at purification and strengthening that villagers resisted, preferring to invest themselves in the escalating realm of personal deterrents and protection in an increasingly toxic world.

People also continued to see *dingaka* for curative purposes. In fact, from the late 1940s onward, new opportunities opened for women to visit *dingaka*. Remember that a woman needed a male relative to accompany her when seeking medical care. A woman who attempted to see a *ngaka* on her own would be suspected of seeking poison or some other substance of sorcery.[22] This does not mean that men were unconcerned about the health of their wives or children or mothers—many were quite worried about them, especially if they left someone with an ongoing illness.[23] But many husbands began to realize the dangers of this restriction—What would happen if their wife or child became seriously ill while they were away at work in the mines?[24] Some husbands began introducing their wives to *dingaka* and setting up a financial relationship whereby the doctor would treat the miner's wife and children while he was away on contract. When the husband returned home, both wife and doctor would report on what services the wife had received and the husband would pay the outstanding bill.[25] Women still did not enjoy free (and private) access to the powers of *bongaka,* but this period provided a means for some women to publicly access *bongaka* unaccompanied. Though the increasingly popular missionary and government medical services provided alternatives for women who lived near these scattered institutions (and the medical statistics suggest higher rates of attendance for women than men), even the nominal cash fee meant that many women still needed male sponsorship for such visits.[26]

The decline of chiefly led public health and the atomization of health interests also stemmed from the ramifications of the colonial witchcraft laws put in place in the 1920s that prohibited both accusations and practices of witchcraft. Without the ability to publicly accuse untrustworthy doctors of witchcraft, it became increasingly difficult for chiefs to prevent perceived charlatans or those trafficking in witchcraft substances from profiting from people's misfortune.[27] Barriers to the medical marketplace were lowering just as the increasing mobility of people and the influx of *madi* created new entrepreneurial opportunities in healing.

Community and Care

If the scope of personal obligation was narrowing in some domains, it was also broadening in others as women, in particular, continued to pursue new forms of community and domesticity through their churches. Christian cults had already become more effective sites for women's political and cosmological activity.[28] In the 1950s, and picking up pace in the 1960s Zionist, Apostolic, and other, often tiny, "churches of the spirit" began to proliferate in the protectorate, as chiefs eased in their opposition to these new forms of Christianity.[29] As in other parts of the region and indeed the continent, women formed the backbone of membership, and often took on important leadership positions in these new churches. These churches were more egalitarian than their European-controlled counterparts, and encouraged freer religious expression by congregants. In rhetoric, ritual, and organization, they undercut and challenged the entwined chiefly and colonial authority in ways quite unlike the more established mission churches, and some "alleged that these church women 'refused to obey their husbands.'"[30] But women who were caught up in the changing sexual norms may have found these new churches particularly appealing. The established churches, unlike the new "independent" ones, had major sanctions against premarital pregnancy.[31] Unmarried pregnant women might be excommunicated (at least temporarily), and their mothers scrutinized as well. In the LMS church in Molepolole, church deacons questioned the mothers of such girls, to ascertain any possible role they might have in their daughters' moral lapses.[32]

Women's participation in local churches played key roles in public health in the postwar period. First, women reflected and reshaped the growing communities of suffering that emerged in the face of male absence and persistent material uncertainty. Church members organized regular visits to the sick and the suffering in hospital and in their homes. Both LMS missionaries, whose activities included teaching TB patients in hospital to play chess, and African church leaders embraced these opportunities. In Lobatse, women congregants were well organized in their visiting work "There are those who are to visit the hospital twice a week. Moreover the secretary always comes with a list of those who are sick in the village, for whom we pray; then groups of three are deputed to visit and pray with each sick person immediately after the meeting. We are also learning other ways in which we may help the sick."[33]

Second, within the new churches, some women began to heal directly, harnessing their traditional spiritual and caregiving powers to new syncretic forms of Christian medicine. Tracing the history of ideas and practices in these churches is a complex and challenging project that is outside the scope of this book but the subject of many excellent studies.[34] It is, however, important to note how central healing was to these new forms of Christianity which women in particular found so appealing. As Sundkler noted about South African Zionism, "prayer for the sick is not just a detail of Zionist church services, but is their most important feature."[35]

Through church visits to the sick of whatever denomination, and through these new healing practices, women combined the new power of the Christian cults, in which individual women were armed with potentially healing prayers, with the Tswana practice of visiting and its all-important affirmations of community and personhood. In the process, they perpetuated women's historical roles in harnessing spiritual power to collective moral projects (roles that the demise of rain-making had set aside), by forging new types of community, and new modes of kinship and care amidst the ongoing social dislocations of the postwar era.[36] These church women also began to provide a language that validated suffering. The book of Job and the book of Revelation in particular, suggested possibilities for a total reorientation of physical misery and pain into a new scheme of righteousness and redemption.[37] In later decades this would take root and flourish. A number of the women we met in chapter one—Lorato, the grandmother of Nanki; Mrs. Ditaba the mother of my friend Frances; Lesego Dinare; and the mother of Kago—were all young church women at this time.

The changes in the nature of community underlined by resistance to collective labor and chiefly authority, however, partially extended to cooperation and sharing among neighbors. As B. C. Thema points out, as the household need for cash increased, so did efforts at entrepreneurship, which resulted in a decrease in the sharing of food. Previously any surplus milk, greens, melons, and other farm products that the household could not consume were given freely to neighbors or passersby, and old cows were slaughtered in the winter to share among members of a ward. But now increasingly they were sold for cash.[38] But people continued to bring gifts of food and even clothing to destitute neighbors and family, the disabled and the elderly among them.[39] Women would assist or send their children to provide domestic labor for such neighbors as well helping to draw water, carry firewood, wash clothes, cook food, and run errands.[40] Those who lived alone, once unthinkable but now increasingly possible, received particular help from neighbors.[41]

Nor did such resistance to chiefly authority mean an end to the chief's role in public health. Instead, it signaled a change in scope and tone, with chiefs still assisting commoners in paternalistic ways, though with a waning of the chief's central role in cosmology and the quest for ecological harmony. Though they could not prevent destitution and physical suffering by providing cooling rains and safe public spaces cleansed of the toxins of *dibeela* and *boloi*, Chiefs provided care for many of their poor, sick, disabled, and elderly people by helping them navigate their way through the bureaucracies of pension, hospital, and tax relief programs.[42] Occasionally a wealthy chief might even provide a large group of people with a set of welfare services.[43] Most of the care such people received came from relatives and neighbors.[44] Relatives were most often expected to help fellow kin, but in situations in which a person lacked nearby relatives, nursing care, food, and domestic help might come from women neighbors.[45] Nomsa Rapela, a below-the-knee amputee whose husband died during the mid-1940s, struggled to care for herself and her young daughter in the following years. She relied heavily on gifts of food from neighbors, though her own brother, who in later decades would accuse her of witchcraft, often refused to plow her field.

> Long time ago people were taking care of *digole,* because many people
> were plowing, many, many people were plowing so the morning they will
> just come with a watermelon or maybe some soft porridge saying How are
> you? . . . In the olden days they would come by with some food and say
> Ah! Take and eat, just take and eat, we just wanted to check on you . . . and
> those older people (adults), those in that compound over there (immediately
> across from hers) would be visiting me, giving me some food, clothes, dresses
> almost everything.[46]

Though it is tempting to see such gift-giving as evidence of a harmonious community and generous public spirit, in fact, these types of cooperation were part
of a more complicated social and moral world. Life was precarious for most
people, as the high infant mortality rates, rising numbers of returned tubercular miners, and the recurrent and brutal droughts suggested.[47] Cooperation and
gift-giving were, at least in part, a way of redistributing the risk of destitution.
If one cared for neighbors and relatives in their times of trouble, one might
reasonably expect similar consideration in return. This is not to suggest that
Batswana in the postwar period were making simple actuarial calculations in
deciding to give gifts of food and clothing nor that they didn't truly feel sympathy, concern, or pity for those in need. Yet receipt of such gifts, particularly
in the case of disabled or ill widows or other female household heads, who were
those most often in need, should be viewed in tandem with ideas about the
underlying causes of misfortune. Stories about such gifts, in fact, seem para-
doxical given that many of these debilitated persons suspected that the jealous
malevolence of others lay at the root of their troubles, as the following account
by Alita Seati suggests. In telling her story Alita separated out the various types
of help given to those in need from her own odyssey of misfortune. She first
explained about general practices of sharing with disabled persons in the 1950s
and 1960s.

> Well the [disabled] ones we used to see or to know, they were getting help
> from other people like when walking in the streets seeing somebody with
> some disability would either give that person some money or some food or
> some clothes.

Then she described her own life in which her husband passed away in 1941 leaving her with small children (her youngest was born in 1944). She eventually left
to find work as a maid in South Africa, sending money home to relatives (older
sisters) who were caring for her children. But after a few years she was forced
to return home permanently because she had gone blind. Though she con-

tinued to farm her fields she found herself dependent on cooperation with others, though she expressed this time as one of "struggling on her own."

> So then well, I had to struggle on my own because when my husband passed away we didn't even have any cattle. So coming back [from South Africa], for me to have some plowing I had to go help others with plowing, then in turn they would pay me by plowing in my field.

Yet despite such opportunities for cooperation in labor and such public instances of caring for others through gift-giving, Alita suspected her neighbors were ultimately responsible for her blindness,

> [The reason neighbors bewitched me] was because of jealousy because people had thought the time when my husband passed away—we were really very poor—so they were looking forward to seeing us as destitutes—but then I managed to raise up my children and I was able to try to find my own way so that we had a better or moderate living. So they got jealous of me.[48]

In certain instances gifts of food might even be quietly dispensed with as the recipient feared possible poisoning by a seemingly well-meaning relative or neighbor. Children might be told not to eat at the home of this or that person, as parents feared a jealous woman might purposely feed *sejeso* (poison) to an unsuspecting child.[49] Bouts of diarrhea and vomiting, common particularly in the summertime, might generate silent suspicions, whispered accusations, or even open hostilities. Likewise, those people who suffered the misfortunes of debility (including epilepsy and mental illness) might themselves be suspected of foul play gone awry, as the moral unease settling over the nascent individualism and reorienting female roles became entangled with the pervasive realities of physical misfortune.[50] It is quite possible that Alita's neighbors (and/or Nomsa's) actually feared she might be a witch, and thus gave gifts to placate her. The chief's declining power to affect public health was set against the unpredictability of *madi* production and redistribution, which generated wealth for some and poverty and debility for many others. This created an uncertain moral environment in which people suspected that the *lefufa* (jealousy) they observed and felt might more easily find secret outlet in the practices of *boloi* (witchcraft).

Diagnosis as History

Postwar reorientations in local public health and safety nets occurred within a shifting epidemiological context. In this period, the burden of debility in the southeastern *merafe* grew, as the ranks of the frail and debilitated swelled with people at all stages of the life course suffering a variety of impairing and/or debilitating illnesses. The diagnostic frameworks through which medical practitioners define, describe, and explain disease are one of the key sites through which these popular experiences and understandings of illness (both subjective and observed) are defined and made sense of historically. Medical meaning-making, in turn, expresses as much about current sociocultural realities, and biases, therapeutic technologies and the power of medical epistemologies as it does about any objective organic state.[51] This is why it was possible for biomedical practitioners and *dingaka* to perceive and publicly define elements of postwar epidemiology in very different, though at times mutually reinforcing ways. Diagnosis, then, becomes a historical index of its own as well as a powerful force shaping contemporary understandings of history. Through the changing diagnostics of postwar Bechuanaland, we can witness how the shifting moral universe with its escalating ethos of personal autonomy, increased female sexual agency, weakening gerontocracy, and rampant migrancy —was experienced physically. When people in the postwar period felt that "culture is breaking," they saw evidence of how that was happening inscribed in the physical and mental suffering of relatives, neighbors, and friends.

In what follows I will attempt to sketch some of the salient features of the burden of debility in southeastern Bechuanaland from the mid-1940s to Independence in 1966 to suggest how the sociocultural and the physical came together in the local moral imagination. My aim is not to provide a comprehensive discussion or statistical analysis of debilitating illness in this period, which would be impossible given the available source material, but rather to indicate contemporary perceptions of trends in some (not all) of the primary causes of debility. Doing so requires that I first draw two very different historical/epidemiological maps, one biomedical and one Tswana, and then suggest some of the ways that they were enmeshed with one another. The comparison is slightly skewed. My analysis actually juxtaposes a doctor-based biomedical epidemiology with a patient-centered Tswana epidemiology. I am not only comparing knowledge systems here, but also highlighting the differences between lay and professional understandings of disease burdens.

It is tempting for readers/researchers, such as myself, of non-western medical histories and ethnographies to see local knowledge as "beliefs" or culture messily grafted on top of primary natural experience expressed best in modern scientific models, and to silently ask "Yes but what was *really* going on here?" when faced with the foreign framing of disease. This happened to me countless times during my research as I found myself involuntarily "code-switching" into biomedical frameworks in the back of my mind, each time I met or read about a patient. This approach, however, is a barrier to our ability to engage our historical imagination, and to discern what *was* really going on here in

.multiple registers.[52] Therefore, what follows is an attempt to provide competing epidemiological models, each located in their own sets of local conversations, and then to illustrate their confused interactions. In the end, these interactions always seem to reinforce each other's point of view in unintended ways, much the way we saw in Chapter 3 that mine medical examinations reinforced local ideas about "strength" (*itekanela*) and "breath" *(mowa)* as well as biomedical notions about lung capacity, weight, and fitness, even as both sets of concepts changed in historically contingent ways.

Biomedical Epidemiology and Diagnosis

Though biomedical diagnostics and epidemiology reflect already-well-known European assumptions about black bodies, African sexuality, "tropical" environments (even in the desert), and the like, they also help ground the reader oriented to biomedicine or western thought by providing us with a version of health posited through familiar forms of knowledge. For the purpose of clarity, I will initially set up an overly determined separation between biomedical knowledge and Tswana understandings of illness and healing. By the postwar period, through vaccination campaigns, medical exams for mining companies, and the growing prominence of local biomedical personnel and institutions, medical knowledge was being generated in a complex epistemological milieu, and neither body of knowledge could be fully extricated from the other.

In mapping the major illnesses and impairments of Tswana in southeastern Bechuanaland during the postwar period, the historian faces a number of difficulties. Mission and government hospitals and clinics kept careful tallies of all patients they saw, but the sparseness and novelty of western medical services leave us with an incomplete picture. Most people didn't live within easy range of western medical services. Moreover, these institutions, though they were growing significantly in popularity, were still struggling to establish their pre-eminence in their local communities, so it is hard to know what percentage of cases of a given condition would have made their way into the clinic/hospital and onto the tally sheet. We also do not know how local people decided that a western medical intervention was likely to be effective. Were families more likely to take a patient with arthritis than a patient with measles to a western doctor? Did selective choices introduce bias into the western doctors' morbidity charts?

There were also issues about which aspect of any given case should count as the ultimate diagnosis of the problem. The Bechuanaland Annual Medical Report of 1950 noted this problem as it related to "deficiency diseases," the contemporary term for malnutrition. "There was no apparent increase in the incidence though accurate figures are difficult to obtain in view of the signs of such diseases merging into the varying clinical pictures presented by some of the more common diseases."[53] The problem of differential diagnosis was further complicated by financial pressures and the low level of technological equipment available for diagnostic tests.

In the face of these difficulties we can use anecdotal evidence (both oral and that found in pension records and applications for tax exemption) combined with our admittedly problematic statistics to make a few cautious observations about local biomedical epidemiology from 1945 to 1963.[54] Below I will draw together the available evidence to make some rough conclusions about several of the primary causes of debility in this period as perceived by western medical practitioners: tuberculosis, polio, trachoma, malnutrition, and mental illness. This list is meant to be illustrative rather than exhaustive.[55]

A large amount of evidence for the postwar period describes the high prevalence of tuberculosis in the southeastern *merafe*. The disease was still relatively uncommon in the 1920s, but it had become the subject of much comment by medical officers and chiefs in the 1930s. As the troops started coming home in the mid-1940s, a new degree of urgency about and recognition of the expanding scope of the problem and the total inefficacy of current medical solutions within Bechuanaland could be heard.

> One almost feels that it is useless to discuss this subject because it is such a vast and growing problem. While the number of cases per thousand may not surpass that of European communities of equal size, yet the absolute lack of any kind of facilities for their care, the entire absence of any semblance of control, the lack of even the most fundamental knowledge concerning the hygiene of the disease and many other factors, serve to cause one to feel almost frustrated.
>
> The practice, for instance, of discharging from the army open dying cases of far advanced pulmonary and intestinal TB, who return to their homes their wives, mothers, children, sisters, brothers—literally scores of relatives and friends—come into close daily intimate contact with the patients, their clothing, and utensils their excreta, etc, is nothing short of deplorable. What the harvest will be within a few years makes one shiver in contemplation. The control and treatment of TB in Bechuanaland is one of the most important and pressing medical problems at this time![56]

Many tubercular soldiers returned home without adequate diagnosis of their condition, since the British government feared the potential burden of compensation claims.[57] Even those who were diagnosed received minimal treatment, and many were repatriated near death.[58] This only exacerbated a situation begun in the mines in the previous three decades.[59] A survey conducted in

1952 found a prevalence of 13 per 1,000 tubercular individuals in the population, and talks had begun with the World Health Organization about the potential for organizing a mass vaccination campaign.[60] By 1955, tuberculosis had become "the main medical problem of the territory" for the government medical service.[61]

Tuberculosis was evident among men and women, adults and children. Extrapulmonary infections accounted for nearly one-third of the 2,079 reported cases in 1955, yet the medical service continued to characterize the disease as a pulmonary problem.[62] Both the mines and military concerned themselves primarily with pulmonary tuberculosis, and the introduction of sputum culture and X-ray technology in Southern Africa only furthered medical depictions of the disease as primarily a lung affliction.[63] The rise of international health as a domain of expert knowledge and policymaking, with its focus on the prevention of transmission of infectious disease, also contributed.[64] This doesn't mean that individual doctors failed to recognize the burden of nonpulmonary TB;[65] it simple means that for the colonial government and the health service (as well as the mining industry), the term "tuberculosis" continued to evoke images of the persistent bloody cough and wasting typical of pulmonary infection. There was a brief moment in 1950 when the colonial medical officers noted with alarm that "the incidence of bone, joint, and glandular tuberculosis more than quadrupled itself from 215 to 918." They hypothesized that this new statistic was partly the result of the extension of medical services to new populations and hoped to undertake a survey of the problem. However, this proved impossible.[66] After this fleeting interest, collapsed spines, seizures, numbness, wasting bones, and the debilitating aftermath of TB meningitis failed to garner direct attention in the medical reports, masking the extent of a serious local problem.[67]

Children typically suffer disproportionately from extrapulmonary tuberculosis, particularly from TB meningitis, and we might guess that this was the case in Bechuanaland at the time, though statistics were not broken down by age and we know little about how patients' ages affected local choices to seek therapy. Dr. Merriweather, however, also recalls a number of adults with such problems.

> I remember several women who had the TB spine—they'd get paralysis of the legs because the spine—when the bones collapse they would trap the spinal cord—they used to have—they used to put part of a tire, a motor tire on both knees and they would go crawling the rest of their lives. Quite a number of them—I remember quite a number of them. . . . Even now there's one or two around. Far out at the lands you'd see them and they would go and actually work in the fields—weeding or even harvesting.[68]

There were also a number of sporadic outbreaks of polio during the late 1940s and early 1950s. From existing materials we can only glimpse the barest bit of the polio outbreaks; most cases would not have been identified by clinic staff.[69] Since polio would first appear as a more routine viral infection with fever and aches but only days later distinguish itself in some instances with paralysis, many cases that did make their way to the mobile dispensaries or mission hospitals would have gone undetected. It was only later when the child could not move an arm or leg that the doctor might find out that the disease had been polio.[70] Even then such cases were rarely brought to western doctors *because* of such paralysis; rather, the doctor might hear of them or meet such patients for other reasons long after the initial illness. This contrasted with how people reacted to clubfoot; patients with the malformation were brought into the hospitals for straightening with plaster casts in the 1950s:

> Others who perhaps had polio when they were a child and they were paralyzed then they would come with other things and you would discover the disability. . . . I think they knew that—I think they must have known that we could help the clubfoot—or clubfoot wasn't such a catastrophic thing and sometimes they used to come in the acute stages of polio and then we couldn't do much and I think they realized that once polio had set in that there wasn't much that we could do, we didn't have orthopedic services—but they thought that clubfoot could maybe be helped.[71]

Even today one regularly meets adults who were afflicted by these outbreaks in the second half of the 1950s, suggesting a much wider impact than the dozen or so cases that might be reported in a given year.[72] The sporadic outbreaks of polio were extensions of much larger epidemics in the Transvaal and were usually traceable back to Johannesburg as the primary site of infection.[73] As in South Africa, most of the polio patients doctors identified were European, reflecting both the peculiar etiology of polio and the racial divergences in therapy-seeking.[74] The threat to the tiny population of white children contributed to the forceful response by the government, which closed schools in affected areas, quarantined confirmed cases, and passed legislation requiring notice of all cases of suspected polio.[75] As in the United States and South Africa, though the disease hit hardest among the children of middle-class whites, often that population would pathologize their poorer immigrant (in the United States) or African (in South Africa) neighbors, drawing on the science of domestic hygiene.[76] By 1957, the government had begun to give polio vaccinations on request, and within five years 3,216 oral doses of polio vaccine had been handed out.[77] But we know little about how many of these patients actually received the necessary follow-up doses or how well doctors in Bechuanaland could maintain the vaccine, which needed to be kept chilled. Polio continued to disable Tswana children well into the post-Independence period.[78]

Blindness was a more general problem that concerned the colonial administration and the medical missionaries who worked under the auspices of both church and colonial government. Spurred by intermittent offers for assistance to the blind from British charitable organizations and local medical practitioners, the government made sporadic attempts in the 1940s and 1950s to ascertain the prevalence of blindness in the protectorate.[79] The 1946 census found 1,881 fully blind Batswana (and a further 2,714 persons who were blind in one eye) out of a total estimated population of 217,906 persons.[80] The rate varied considerably from district to district, suggesting serious reporting errors, but the overall prevalence of 750 per 100,000 was comparable to rates in parts of the Transvaal and Central Africa. Nonetheless, the figures were "disturbingly high" when compared to those for Europeans elsewhere. For example, the rate for whites in Canada was 71 per 100,000; in the United States, it was 51.8 per 100,000; and in South Africa, it was 81.06 per 100,000.[81]

It is hard to know how accurate such statistics might be. On the one hand, as the director of the British Empire Society for the Blind explained, "Some doubt has been cast on their reliability but, in our experience, they are unlikely to be an over-estimate. An enumerator may miss many blind people, but it is unlikely to count as blind someone who can see. No attempt has made to count people who, though not actually sightless, have such poor vision that they must be regarded as blind for the purposes of education and economic life; these are likely to out-number the totally blind."[82] This makes sense. The more nagging question in my mind is the overall population figure. With so many men and women regularly crossing the border for work, it is likely that the total population figure for the territory was an underestimate.[83] Because blind people would not have been able to secure work contracts and would have had extreme difficulty even in accessing a temporary pass to leave the protectorate, the statistics reflect the political and economic realities that trapped blind people within the territory while allowing the "able-bodied" (in this case the sighted) increased opportunities for migration.

The colonial medical service focused most of its efforts around blindness on preventing trachoma infections. There are several reasons why the government focused on trachoma. Though cataracts and glaucoma, for example, were important causes of blindness, there was little that local doctors could do to intervene in these problems aside from the occasional referral to Johannesburg for cataract surgery.[84] This couldn't be the entire reason, however, given one doctor's quite revealing position on refractive errors, which could have been easily corrected with eyeglasses. Dr. Jokl, a South African ophthalmologist who advised the Bechuanaland government on local eye problems, felt that the number of Batswana with refractive errors would be small, though he did not suggest a reason for this. He did, however, explain why he failed to carry out any systematic refraction tests during his tours of the protectorate. Dr. Jokl felt that such testing would be "slow and difficult" because the

> [Native] mind is not experienced like the minds of white persons to distinguish rapidly, and assess the differences of small details (in white persons this faculty has been developed since centuries before by the art of reading). . . . From this point of view, the efforts of traveling opticians who examine Natives, and supply them with spectacles, should not be encouraged. The more educated Native has a nearly morbid desire to wear spectacles, firstly because he imagines they give him an air of importance, and secondly because he very often suffers from eye strain. This eye strain, however, is not due to an uncorrected refractive error, but to the lack of familiarity with the art of reading and writing.[85]

Despite Dr. Jokl's feelings on the matter, some people in the postwar period did access eyeglasses, though they would not become commonplace until after Independence. Still, more important than the ease of correction or the toll it took in lost sight, trachoma was contagious and was thought to be perhaps preventable through education about proper hygiene. In this approach, as with the almost exclusive focus on pulmonary TB, we find what was to become a key aspect of postwar colonial medical paternalism laid bare: the combination of limited resources, racist prejudices about African behavior and African bodies, and a nascent developmentalist ethos in colonial health care. These three factors combined to place a primacy on available technological fixes for infectious disease, marginalizing issues of palliative care, rhetoric from Christian missionaries about the alleviation of suffering notwithstanding.[86] "Controlling disease" was the agenda of the day. This does not mean that individual doctors and nurses felt no compassion for their patients. But they held a variety of ideas about a higher threshold for pain among Africans—such as the one that "children with severe trachoma infections have so little discomfort from the disease." Observations like this in Bechuanaland dated back to at least Livingstone's time. They also had particular beliefs about the appropriate roles and tasks African bodies should perform; these jobs did not apparently include reading and close handwork that required sharp eyesight. Finally, individual doctors had to make difficult decisions in the context of extremely limited budgets. All of these factors merged with the economic interests of the administration to set a tone and an agenda for local medical care.[87]

There were two key exceptions to the trend that emphasized control of infectious disease: treatments for malnutrition and mental illness.[88] Since the Depression era, malnutrition had been a major health problem in the southeastern

"A trained and capable domestic servant" wearing eyeglasses and reading a letter. Photo by A. S. Sandilands, n.d. Reproduced from London Missionary Society/Council for World Mission Archives.

protectorate. But in the postwar era, new ways of counting, thinking, and talking about malnutrition (including the shift in terminology from "malnutrition" to "deficiency diseases") developed. Many cases of scurvy, pellagra, beriberi, and "general nutritional deficiencies" appeared on the yearly clinic tally sheets as political and economic changes brought by colonization and regional industrialization limited diets and weakened bodies.[89] But colonial medical concern about diet and malnutrition in Bechuanaland left these larger political issues untouched for the most part. As Michael Worboys explains, studies of colonial health and nutrition in the 1930s blamed poor nutrition on social and economic factors associated with colonial development. One might expect that this somewhat radical linking of colonial development with ill health might lead to social or economic reforms. Instead, colonial medical frameworks for understanding malnutrition were refocused on nutritional science, which transformed hunger into malnutrition measured in terms of the absence of specific micronutrients. In the postwar protectorate, this made it possible to blame individuals for poor dietary choices and agricultural practices, shifting the focus away from patterns of colonial appropriation and control.[90] It also opened the way for the growing developmentalist approach we have seen evidenced above in the focus on infectious disease. In the developmentalist paradigm that dominated health efforts after the war, colonial governments promoted narrow technological solutions and knowledge transfers to complex politically, economically, and socially embedded phenomena. Agricultural betterment schemes and health education programs thus became the new solutions to a purported African dietary backwardness parsed in terms of specific micronutrients.[91]

Unlike the long-standing but shifting concerns around malnutrition, mental illness, which was hardly mentioned in prewar medical correspondence, became a pressing problem in the protectorate's postwar colonial medical agenda. Until the 1940s, the protectorate government sent the most "dangerous" and intransigent cases of mental illness to South African asylums, footing the bill for their stays there.[92] A handful of other mental patients were confined in local jails in Bechuanaland. Treatment within jail appears to have been spotty and haphazardly administered. In the 1910s and 1920s, the jails provided no treatment for these mental patients, who might be confined for years at a time, though there are scattered references to hydrotherapy in the colonial record.[93] By the 1940s, however, many jailed "lunatics" were given sedatives to bring them "under control" and then released.[94]

By the middle of World War II, the problem had grown in scale, and local district officers and paramount chiefs alike began to complain about the increasing numbers of "uncontrollable lunatics or semi-lunatics" in the territories. During this same period, the overcrowded South African asylums refused to take any more protectorate patients.[95] Local doctors, who felt that jail provided an inadequate context for treatment and yet whose hospitals were not equipped to cope with the mentally ill, further pressed the issue with repeated complaints to the colonial administration.[96] The repatriated troops in 1945 included a number of men "suffering from mental derangement," prompting the colonial administration to begin construction of a lunatic asylum in Lobatse in the southeastern protectorate to treat these veterans and other mentally ill Batswana.[97]

The colonial and missionary medical services both embraced the general impression that mental illness posed a problem in the postwar protectorate, and the opening of the mental hospital meant new work in diagnosing and evaluating potential patients for confinement. But for the most part, the medical service never systematically discussed or researched the underlying causes of mental illness or why it appeared to be on the rise. Doctors lacked more than basic training in psychiatry and were busy at any rate with the pressing problems of infectious disease, trauma, and rising clinic and hospital attendance. Individual case reports might make mention of manic depression, schizophrenia, or "feeble-mindedness," but there was no overarching policy that broke general impressions and conversations about mental illness into discrete diagnostic categories.

This unexacting approach was mirrored in certification and treatment practices. Committal to the asylum required certification by two doctors that the patient was both "insane and dangerous." Doctors struggled to diagnose patients brought in by distraught family members, police officers, and the chief's officials. Doctors asked patients a series of questions to discern if they were oriented in time and space. Often a patient who had been violent and uncontrollable for some time would be quite passive during his/her interview with the doctor, leaving the doctor unable to certify the patient.[98] Other times one doctor would certify and then a second doctor, perhaps some days later, couldn't concur, and again the patient would be returned to familial care.[99] Diagnostic outcomes were haphazard, and treatment was limited. In the first two decades following the construction of the mental hospital, differential diagnoses and treatment became more precise. While in the late 1940s a diagnosis of potential manic depression meant little in terms of specific treatment and outcomes, by the 1960s it was treated differently than a case of suspected schizophrenia.

All these trends in the identification and characterization of debilitating disease by the colonial medical service tell us only fragments about changes in Tswana epidemiology and the changing picture of illness that shaped people's lives. There is no easy one-to-one correlation between Tswana and biomedical nosologies; each is anchored in radically different ontological (and diagnostic) regimes.[100] We cannot and should not simply say that a rise in tuberculosis meant a rise in *sefuba* (chest conditions) any more than we might say that a rise in *pelo-mpe* (bad feelings/dirty heart—associated with witchcraft) signified a rise in "heart disease." Nor are we interested in juxtaposing "what really happened" (i.e., biomedical epidemiology) with "what they thought happened" (Tswana epidemiology). Though it is tempting for biomedically minded readers to think in such a way, this deceptively "rational" mode simply can't capture the reality of somatic experience and the geography of misfortune that linked bodies and body parts and environments in ways that biomedicine failed to witness. Yet, as we saw in the previous chapter, biomedicine, with its novel technologies and accompanying translations provided a language for local people to comprehend and infuse new meanings into bodies caught up in wider historical transformations. Indeed, each framework captures different and interlocking aspects of "what really happened." By combining these two epidemiological understandings and their entanglements with one another, we can begin to grasp a fuller sense of history.

Tswana Epidemiology and Diagnosis

"Traditional" medical knowledge is often erroneously perceived and portrayed by westerners as static and ahistorical. Yet African therapeutic systems certainly evolve, as all therapeutic systems do, through empirical knowledge, debate, and paradigmatic shifts, despite local claims to authority based on tropes of ancient or traditional legacies. Tswana medicine was no exception, and in the postwar period locally defined epidemiology changed in ways that reflected not only conversation and overlap with western disease frames but also the social, biological, and cultural changes that were reordering society. Tswana framing of disease entailed a historical fluidity of diagnostic categories and a layering of disease etiology.[101] This enabled local medical epistemology to incorporate novel ideas and events within a larger framework that reinforced the overarching unity of the natural, cosmological, and social realms—all of which were in flux. Through the following exploration of Tswana diagnostics and epidemiology in the postwar period, we will see how the increasingly pervasive experiences of bodily misfortune merged with trends in women's extramarital and premarital sexual activity, male migration, intergenerational struggles over *madi*, and collapsing public health to became understood in terms of evolving local disease etiologies.

Capturing this kind of dynamism, however, is a difficult task. The available source material (mostly oral recollections) allows us only to infer or glimpse certain aspects of this diagnostic fluidity. Even with a rich source base, comprehending the processes and priorities of Tswana diagnosis are difficult for the western reader (and researcher). Much that *dingaka* did may seem familiar at first glance: diagnostically analyzing constellations of physically manifested symptoms; using some techniques which appear similar to biomedical ones, such as visual examination and palpation; and prescribing "herbal remedies" which looked much like western "medicines," albeit manufactured in a different way. But these techniques were employed by doctors who viewed the very substances of the human body and the material elements of personhood quite differently than their western counterparts. As Shigehisa Kuriyama so elegantly illustrates in his work on the divergences between ancient Greek and Chinese medicine, even something as deceptively simple and seemingly universal as the human pulse could be felt, understood, and perceived quite differently in ways that were rooted in cultural understandings of cosmology and the fundamentals of what it meant to be a person.[102] These divergences affected the experience of having a pulse for the patients themselves. So if we take medical knowledge and techniques to be not just socially constructed but deeply embedded in and reflective of historically determined understandings of personhood and cosmology, then how are we to make sense of Tswana diagnostic fluidity and its relationship to a changing epidemiology in the 1950s and 1960s?

A good place to begin is with a brief discussion of what it meant to be a person in postwar Tswana society. Essential understandings of personhood and cosmology continually change as certain social and cultural values and principles are reinterpreted and reapplied within shifting historical contexts. Tamara Giles Vernick has recently demonstrated the utility for historians of the concept of "the person as a category of experience," illustrating how Mpiemu speakers in equatorial Africa managed the ecological ramifications of colonial and postcolonial conservation initiatives by "grafting new notions of the person onto older ones." Her work further reminds us that many of the central idioms through which persons are publicly constituted persist even as the underlying meanings of such idioms reference change.[103] We can see similar transformations among the Tswana. One example is the changing meanings of and potential scope for human relations and communication with *Modimo*, who moved from original ancestor to Christian-influenced God over the twentieth century.[104] Likewise, we can see that the shifting personal responsibilities and opportunities for men and women, old and young that accompanied wider socioeconomic changes entailed ongoing redefinitions of selfhood. But in this case we can also juxtapose observations on this topic gathered by Isaac Schapera in the late 1920s and early 1930s with those gathered by Hoyt Alverson in the mid-1970s and still find some consistency over the intermediate time period (the postwar era) of certain basic features of Tswana personhood that affected experiences of health and illness. Both of these anthropologists, however, worked mostly (though by no means exclusively) with male informants when gathering the specific material presented here, and we are left with an implicitly gendered perspective. Nonetheless, many of the comments and descriptions were again echoed in my conversations with Tswana women in the late 1990s, suggesting the validity of such concepts for both men and women.

Here we will focus on the objective aspects of personhood, since medical epistemology focused on locating the person within wider social and cosmological realms. Subjective personhood is central to the illness experience.[105] The concept might be defined as the inner life of persons that includes complex changes in perspective, multivalent and contradictory consciousnesses, and changes over the life course. However, though Tswana diagnosis lacks the specific causal agents and universalistic human body of post-bacteriological western medicine, *dingaka* still look to the external sociocosmological context (or to the objective) to understand the inner person whose qualities are to some extent understood to be unknowable or hidden.

The essential character of each Tswana person is unique; his or her own thoughts and feelings and way of approaching life are specific to him or her, just as each person has a unique appearance all his or her own. This essential nature is determined and bestowed by the ancestors and centered in the heart (*pelo*) of the individual.[106] This uniqueness means that a person's inner life, his or her thoughts and feelings (his heart), may never be fully known by another. As two of Alverson's informants explained,

> An individual's nature is inborn. Even habits you cannot count on, because they are always influenced by a person's inner human nature (*botho-motho*). You can never know what is inside another person. We say in Setswana, "unlike a field [which you can come to know every part of], you can never know a man." The way people act is no reliable guide to what they are really intending.

> A person can act one way and be thinking something entirely undiscernible. For example we say, "smiling teeth can kill." A person's actions can harbor any number of intentions. You can never know what a person is planning by looking at what he does.[107]

This opacity is potentially dangerous; the jealous, angry, bitter, or envious feelings in one person's heart might be potentially toxic to another whether through purposeful action or simply by their very existence.[108] On the other hand, as two elderly men told Alverson, this essential unique human nature is what enables people to cope with adversity and suffering without compromising their humanity, individuality, and sense of self. It is stronger than circumstance.

> No matter how the body is handled by others, the thoughts cannot be controlled. While one's circumstances may control one's actions, the suffering body will cause a man to make plans to decide to run away and look for better prospects elsewhere. No kind of ill-treatment can cause you to lose your inner self [bo-wena].

> Someone can misuse your body by using coercion [patikanyo], but this cannot affect or change your thoughts.

> Reasoning ability is not removed by suffering. . . . In any circumstance people experience the same things differently. We say, "When I am bitter, everything will be bitterness to me; when I am kindly everything will be kindness to me."[109]

But there is a perpetual tension in Tswana thought between the individuality of each person, which is a defining feature of his or her humanity, and the interconnectedness of people and their hearts as reflected in procreation, language, law, and morality. This social character is the other basic element of personhood and the one to be healed through bongaka.

> A person's strength does not lie in the body; it lies in his ability to speak his thoughts. "I am not strong in and of myself [ke le nosi]; I am strong in virtue of the word [ka lentswe]." Thinking and reasoning make us different from animals. We live by rules and by law. That separates us from [wild] animals; every person is made [created] differently. Yet a person, we say, is a person by virtue of people. To be utterly alone is unthinkable. We are human because of the way we are brought up and live together with others. Our relations [botsalano] with others shape our behavior. But our thoughts are our own. They can never be known by looking at actions or by knowing the people of [one's] home.[110]

These aspects of Tswana personhood will not sound unfamiliar to the western reader (nor perhaps to readers from other parts of Africa or beyond), despite the migration of personhood from heart to brain in modern western physiology.[111] Indeed, they are not. As many have argued, models that stress a contrast between the individualism of Euro-Americans and the communalism of Africans (and others) are highly overdetermined. But as we explore the Tswana relationships between personhood, biology, and medicine, some differences become apparent. In bongaka, tensions between the social person and the inner/individual self are reflected in physiology and medical diagnosis: the heart is the center of individuality, the *madi* (blood, semen) is the substance of relationships and social life, and the *mowa* (breath or soul) constantly moves between the person and the environment. The material and social aspects of health are not separate in the embodied experiences of patients or the therapeutic strategies of healers; nor are western dichotomies between body and mind or emotion and intellect.[112] Instead, the interconnectedness of people and the individuality of hearts are triangulated through the ancestors, who bestow inner nature yet concern themselves with social harmony and who created the ecological world in which people, their cattle, and their fields are located. *Madi* is the substance that flows through relationships (as semen, blood, and money), and the sharing of *madi* by relatives generates responsibilities among people as well as the potential for discord to manifest itself in illness.[113] Furthermore, *madi* is not just confined in the body of the individual; even after it is shed, it continues to contain some of the essential qualities of the person and the lineage. Thus, the *madi* of one person can be used by another to injure, and each generation must be concerned with the *madi* of the succeeding generation.[114]

Bodies, like persons, are also gendered (sexed?). Wombs (*dipopelo*) were central to the exchange of *madi* because they provided a site for the *madi* of two lineages to congeal into new persons. It is significant that the root of the word for womb (*popelo*) is the collective noun for heart (*bopelo*); it is the womb that nurtures and heats new persons and their developing qualities. Wombs were and are the essential organ of femininity. Historically, through symbolic exchanges of cattle (bridewealth), seniors appropriated uteruses within individual women on behalf of the lineage, just as in *bojale* senior women tamed the wombs of their juniors on behalf of the commonweal. Uteruses, like hearts, were hidden and unknowable, and ambiguity had long characterized the womb. But in this period, because communities had less social control over reproduction, Tswana medical diagnoses began to place an increasing stress on the hidden nature of the womb—of the womb as a space where one never quite knew what kind of toxins and trouble might be brewing. At the same time, gerontocratic and masculine control over women's labor and sexuality became more tentative.[115] As we have seen, adultery (if improperly timed) and other forms of sexuality had long been connected to disease. But what I am suggesting here is that whereas previously this pathology had been linked to ancestral displeasure at particular behaviors, increasingly the *badimo* were dropping out of the picture and in their place attention was focused on the uterus as a site female behavior. The *pelo* was a somewhat different entity than the biomedically understood blood pump; similarly, the *popelo* (uterus) was a broader domain than the small organ envisioned by postwar biomedicine. Women extended its work into the domestic realm through the construction, maintenance, and use of uterine architectural forms.

This all means that physical symptoms and somatic experience were embedded in deeper social and cosmological realms. But physical symptoms in and of themselves were only ever starting points for negotiated diagnostic and therapeutic inquiry. For example, as Schapera's research assistant, Sofonia, explained to him in 1932, the death of a stillborn child was sometimes attributed to God (because he alone knows what is happening in the womb), sometimes to *boloi* (witchcraft), sometimes to *dikgaba* (ancestral anger), sometimes to *pelo dibotlhoko* (bitterness of the heart) of the girl's parents or the boy's parents, and sometimes to relatives of either parent.[116] Likewise, even interpretations of physical symptoms read in combination with sociomoral evaluations were highly subjective and open to renegotiation over time, reflecting the coexistence of socialized and individual notions of persons. Tswana diagnosis was and is diachronic, flexible, and fluid by nature.

Steven Feierman has explained a similar diagnostic epistemology among the Shambaa in northeastern Tanzania. He contrasts the additive or layered understanding of cause to the deductive or subtractive nature of biomedical diagnosis, which attempts to locate a singular cause. In Ghaambo, as he describes, "illnesses had more than one cause and the causes were entwined with one another."

> Questions about the personal context of the disease, and about the patient's experience of illness, were at the center of the process in Ghaambo. Patients there worked in the opposite direction, by a process of addition: they explored the social and moral circumstances of an illness in ever-widening circles. Ghaambo's illness narratives were extended reflections on the sick individual's personal nature and social position.[117]

Because of this complex layered nature of disease, changes in the social world altered the meanings and interpretations of symptoms and could even generate new symptoms; ruptures in the web of social, cosmological/ecological, and moral relationships might manifest themselves in the bodies of people or their cattle. Usually disease and disability were associated with the heat and dryness of the blood, limbs, or organs. Their logic was the same as those of fields and the sky, which could also become dry (rainless, dusty) or hot (lightening filled, scorched). Health and well-being was further associated with a proper balance of these vital forces: a light steady rain (rain that goes pitter pat) was good, while a torrential downpour might ruin crops and wash away rondavels. *Madi* needed to be present in the right amounts in the body; too much *madi* was dangerous, too little signaled weakness.

Diagnostic technology was multilayered and complex. In addition to the seemingly familiar, though radically reoriented practices of viewing and palpating the body and taking case histories, *dingaka* also used divining bones (*ditaola*) to perceive the causal web of relationships and circumstances manifested in the ailing body. A deep discussion of divination is beyond the scope of this book, but the interested reader should certainly read Richard Werbner's excellent chapter on divination as the recreation and reading of a microcosmic universe among the Tswapong of northeastern Botswana.[118]

Understandings of prevalence based on numbers and statistics that have been so central to western (and colonial) public health and medical knowledge since the mid-nineteenth century are for the most part missing from this Tswana epidemiology. Patients, family members, neighbors, *dingaka,* and even headmen and chiefs continued to experience and observe illness mostly through anecdote in the mid-twentieth century. Despite the fetishes of the colonial administration, formal statistical analysis was not part of their understandings of public health, though people may have "kept count" of the scale of misfortune unfolding in their midst. Perhaps this undermines my use of the term "epidemiology" for some readers, so let me clarify. Though we are unable to quantify, we are nonetheless able to explore which illnesses were of greatest concern to local people, which felt more pervasive and virulent in their effects, and how such perceptions suggested associations between cause and effect (even in cases where disease etiology or pathogenesis remained unclear to many). Keeping in mind the difficulties inherent in the statistics generated by the colonial medical service, I hope that the reader will not find the Tswana any less "scientific" in their reckonings of illness in society, only differently so.

Migrant labor necessarily affected Tswana epidemiology as much as it did biomedical epidemiology, which linked mobility to tuberculosis and polio. Tswana bodies were connected to one another through shared *madi* and to the local environment through consanguinity with the *badimo,* who embedded the human world in the natural world. Potentially debilitating pollutants were transmitted between persons and the wider world in ways that might not make sense in post–germ theory biomedicine but which nonetheless painfully expressed the moral ruptures and social changes wrought by the forced movement of people and the growing atomization of interests in individual bodies, cattle, and fields. During the postwar period, Batswana experienced a rise in several debilitating conditions which reflected changes in sexual and emotional life as well as the crumbling of collective public health and the increasing dominance of individualized therapeutics.

Here I will focus on three disease categories, each of which expressed transitions in illness experiences in terms of wider historical transformations: *thibamo, mopakwane,* and *botsenwa.* Each of these diagnostic categories expanded in the postwar period to link various social and cultural changes in sexual behavior, intergenerational struggles over *madi,* and the recent experiences of the war to the perceived rise in debility. I will resist translating these

Setswana terms here until the reader has gained an understanding of local meanings of each category. Then in the final section, I will turn to how these categories and overlapping biomedical meanings were forced into an uneasy correlation and became entangled in one another, reshaping and reinforcing both therapeutic systems in the process. This entanglement was partially accomplished through translation from Setswana to English.

I should also note here that other important etiological elements most likely underwent changes in this period: particularly *boloi* (witchcraft—including the use of *sejeso*, or poisons), the results of local *dibeela* (toxic abominations such as unpurified abortions and decomposing corpses) that were previously identified and cleansed through the local public health system, and *dikgaba*, in which the (often unconscious) anger or intense sorrow of a scorned elder poisons the body of a junior, causing disease and/or debility, which then requires healing through forgiveness and the cleansing of the elder's heart. These were diagnostic layers and not discrete illness categories in their own right. Thus, they were not associated with specific symptom constellations but might instead underlie a range of disease outcomes. For example, *dibeela* could both burst rocks deep underground on the Rand, severing limbs and breaking spines, and scorch the earth at home into dust and drought. *Boloi*, if well made, could imitate or cause the symptoms of a range of diseases. In Nanki's case, debates over the cause of her illness ranged from *boloi* to *mopakwane*.

I would guess from a look at a range of factors that *boloi*, *dikgaba*, and *dibeela* were diagnosed more often in the postwar period, facilitated in part by the erosion of public health practices, but I lack the data necessary to map out transitions in any of these categories. Though the occasional reference to any of these etiological elements might appear in the colonial record (particularly in court cases), such references represent too small a sample to determine rates of increase or decrease. These were also very difficult topics to ask people to discuss with me in anything but the most evasive terms. I also found myself consistently running up against constructions of a nostalgic past in which juniors respected their elders, people obeyed "the rules," and such glaring examples of moral decay were fewer.

Still, we might imagine that the range of social, economic, and political transitions brought an increase in each of these causal categories. For example, with *dibeela* (toxic abominations), the waning of the local systems of public health which would have cleansed the land of these toxins coincided with what appears to be an increase in illicit abortions, most likely caused by the rise in premarital and extramarital pregnancy, to create a dangerous situation which particularly affected those traveling across the boundaries of the *morafe*, the migrants.[119] But we know that women were procuring abortions before this period[120] and cannot say with certainty that the frequency or even the perceived frequency of abortion was on the rise. Though as women found themselves pregnant and their male partners reneging on marriage promises made to secure sex, a number of cases concerning abortion or infanticide began to appear in the court records, and the court in one such case noted that "offences of this nature [infanticide], and abortions, are becoming prevalent amongst young women."[121] Likewise, cases in which decomposing bodies of infants and dismembered adults who were victims of ritual murder also appeared in some areas, but again it was difficult to know whether the incidence of court cases reflected a change in the number of such cases brought to the courts or in the number of such incidents altogether.[122] Nonetheless, over this period, older systems by which chiefs harnessed collective labor to mitigate the effects of these toxins began to crumble.

Similarly, we know that many elders in this period may have felt scorned or neglected by their juniors, who were wresting control of key decisions and resources. The anguish (*botlhoko jo bo gamolang pelo*—pain that squeezes the heart) they felt was dangerous, particularly to the most vulnerable of their juniors. *Dikgaba* was often displaced onto infants and small children, even though they were not the original source of the ill feelings. As Solway and Lambek explain, *dikgaba* plays on the emotional ambiguity of nurturing matrilateral relations (especially with one's sisters, mothers, and aunts), in which love (*lorato*) is expected to dominate but where quarrel or disappointment of course also occur.[123] In such relationships, elders worry that their feelings may provoke *dikgaba* in their juniors and juniors worry about disappointing their elders. In the context of the shifting and contested norms of personal responsibility, hurt feelings, even within the context of love, surely arose.

Boloi, which, unlike *dikgaba,* is purposeful, is more common in competitive relationships (particularly agnatic ones). In the postwar period, struggles over *madi,* which were common, created toxic fields of envy (*lefufa*) among kin and neighbors that could spur malice. Similarly, changing patterns of sexuality fostered *lefufa* (and sometimes violent retribution) among those who suspected or found that their spouse or *nyatsi* (boyfriend/girlfriend) had taken another lover.[124] But though the written and oral source material allows us to glimpse occasional references to these tensions and to specific instances of malevolent behavior, it is difficult to make a clear case for an increase in these factors. The three diseases discussed below were diagnosed and experienced within a larger set of potentially overlapping layers of causation which made each illness experience (or illness narrative) negotiated, processual, and unique and which combined emotional, ecological, social, and physical elements.

Thibamo, the first disease we will consider, emerged and evolved during the mid-twentieth century to explain linkages between two novel and increasingly pervasive phenomena: male migrancy and an illness marked by persistent and often bloody cough, weight loss, and weakness. The word *thibamo* comes from the verb *thiba*, meaning to turn or obstruct. *Thibamo* begins or is first noticed when an infant is born in an abnormal position—rotated face down, breech, or perhaps with the cord wrapped around its neck. If the baby and the parents are not treated (and treatments vary from doctor to doctor), then the baby might die and/or one of the parents could develop the persistent cough and wasting characteristic of the disease. *Thibamo* is highly contagious and can be transmitted from either of the parents to a third party through the violation of a variety of sexual rules that triangulate through potentially toxic uteruses—the nexus linking babies, mothers, fathers, and other sex partners. For example, if a man sleeps with a woman who has had a recent miscarriage or who has recently lost a child, he can contract *thibamo* from her. Likewise, if he sleeps with another woman while his wife is pregnant, the wife or child can develop *thibamo*.

Thibamo provided a flexible umbrella under which any number of behaviors were potentially implicated, and its diagnosis might overlap with several other diseases. Sexual contact with anyone whose blood is hot or impure for a variety of reasons might potentially cause *thibamo*, even though such behavior might also be associated with other specific diseases. For example, sexual relations with widows usually manifested itself as *boswagadi* but could also be *thibamo*, and jumping the *mopakwana*, usually associated with illness or disability in the child (discussed in more detail below), could also cause *thibamo* manifested in the parents.[125] Observations about the postwar period explicitly linked the sexual secrecy thought available to women to the rise in *thibamo*. "[During the time of mines, 1940s, 1950s] yes there was a lot of *thibamo* in those days because the men were working far and they couldn't see what was happening in their absence."[126]

I have not found any references to "*thibamo*" (or "*tibamo*") in any of the written records before the 1940s (though I cannot claim to have made an exhaustive search). In their book on traditional Tswana midwifery, Sandra Anderson and Frants Staugart refer to a number of their own informants (both *dingaka* and patients) who claimed that *thibamo* was a relatively recent disease that began in the 1920s and 1930s.[127] It seems likely that *thibamo* emerged as a key diagnostic category in the 1940s to merge an increasingly pervasive constellation of symptoms (persistent bloody cough and wasting) with a loosening in sexual surveillance in the context of migrant labor, the demise of initiation, and the weakening of the gerontocracy. Alternatively, an older disease which was much less pervasive and associated with obstructed or abnormal birth may have been expanded to incorporate cough and wasting in the parents in the context of the changes in regular purification rituals, sexual behavior, and birth practices migrant labor brought. One thing is clear; in the decades following the end of the war, *thibamo* became quite prevalent and was of major concern to *dingaka* and their patients. This makes sense; many men returned from the war wasted and coughing to whispered rumors or glaring evidence that their wives had been unfaithful in their absence. The aftermath of the war and the ever-rising tide of male and female migrancy increased the incidence of the disease, and by the 1950s *thibamo* was everywhere, a grim reminder of the perils of decreased sexual surveillance, the loss of collective control over individual wombs, and the difficulties inherent in disciplining a migrant workforce empowered by their production of *madi*.

Mopakwane also indicated dangerous sexual behavior that went unpurified, but its symptoms were solely manifested in the infant or child whose parent had broken important sexual taboos regarding postpartum confinement. After the birth of an infant, the mother was to remain with her newborn in a special hut that was marked by a stick or broom (a *mopakwana*) placed across the threshold. During the months of confinement, both parents were to refrain from sexual contact with one another and with outsiders (in earlier times this had included co-wives) until they ended the confinement period with ritual intercourse. With so many men absent during this period, parents needed to continue postpartum abstinence until they met again, which in some cases meant many months or even years. If either had sexual relations with another during the confinement, they were said to have "jumped the *mopakwana*." Both parents then needed to be purified with medicines before they could meet, or the mixing of the blood of a third party which "would not agree" in the woman created dangerous pollution and heat which the mother then passed on to the infant through her breast milk. Symptoms might appear immediately or at any point for several years hence. Like *thibamo, mopakwane* reflected a fluidity in diagnosis over time; the constellation of symptoms that indicated the disease expanded beginning in the 1940s and then contracted in the 1980s and 1990s. The expansion of potentially identifiable symptomatology in the postwar period divided the crude diagnoses of *mopakwane* into a number of closely read variations, each of which indicated specific causal chains of behavior.

Schapera's field notes from the mid-1930s indicate that a child whose parent broke these rules would become "stupid" (*boso*) or suddenly "die with its mouth open."[128] The child might "grow up weak, stupid, or deformed."[129] His informants suggested that there had already been a slackening of the strict surveillance and constraints on behavior associated with *mopakwane* in recent decades. They reported that if either parent had the hot blood arising from postpartum adultery, the mere entry into the confinement hut by the father would be enough to seriously harm the child, or senior wife in a polygynous household. "Even Christians" took this prohibition seriously.

By the 1940s it seems that *mopakwane* was explicitly tied to polluted uteruses and no longer directly linked to the movement of fathers. Elderly Batswana with whom I spoke about *mopakwane* in the 1950s flatly denied its potential to harm adults.[130] Nor was the father's mere entry into the confinement hut enough to pollute the child. *Mopakwane* was now solely generated through polluted wombs and breast-feeding. Symptoms had moved beyond the vague descriptions of "stupid" or "weak" given to Schapera. Though people continued to say that *boso* and *mopakwane* were linked, they also added drooling saliva; floppy limbs; the inability to sit, crawl, or walk at the appropriate ages; muscle wasting; distended bellies; and muscle contractures to the list of possible indicators of *mopakwane*. Diagnosis thus combined the interpretation of specific symptoms with divination and case histories to gender the causal etiology of various types of *mopakwane*.

> The signs would be like for on the father's side [if the father was the one who jumped the *mopakwana*]—the child would be disabled not being able to roll, not being able to move, but the body would be just normal still growing. But if it is on the mother's side—the child will start having muscle wasting—especially on the thighs, the arms, and the tummy will be big. The child would be eating, the tummy would be big—but the food doesn't get used to build up the body.[131]

Others added that a child with floppy limbs would also be a sign of the mother's violation of the rules of confinement. No one could speak definitively on the meanings of high tone (tight muscle contractures) versus the meaning of floppiness, and in the 1990s this symptom was indicative of *mopakwane* but potentially attributed to either parent.

In the late 1990s, "weight loss, severe diarrhea, lack of appetite and failure to thrive" in children in Lesotho (though no longer in Botswana for the most part) indicated sexual promiscuity on the part of their mothers and were termed *senyega*.[132] In the early 1960s in Bechuanaland, *senyega* was a term used to refer to illegitimate births.[133] It is possible that the new interpretation of those symptoms beginning in the late 1940s was learned by Tswana men (including *dingaka*) from Basotho men (or by both from a third group) in the mining compounds of the Rand. Or perhaps both emerged simultaneously as men (again including *dingaka*) in multiethnic conversation with one another struggled to understand this increasingly prevalent set of symptoms among their children. In either scenario, diagnostic fluidity absorbed new symptoms and new social circumstances simultaneously.

With *thibamo* and *mopakwane*, though the illness models potentially pathologized both male and female illicit sexual behavior, actual diagnosis and the experience of illness occurred in a context in which men exercised political, juridical, and economic power over women and in which men still controlled access to *dingaka* and the production of core medical knowledge. Though women played central roles in forging illness narratives, which included moral negotiations over diagnoses, they did so within a paradigm in which men's sexual urges and acts were interpreted differently than women's. Over the first half of the twentieth century, normal restrictions eased on male sexual activity for ritual, social, and physical reasons and a new model took its place, which placed more emphasis on how men required regular sexual activity for good health.[134] Generational and social differences also meant that individual women understood each case of illness in particular terms rather than developing a primarily gendered perspective on diagnoses. Thus, both men and women regularly blamed women rather than men for individual instances of illness and debility that stemmed from illicit sexual behavior, as one astute elderly *ngaka* bemoaned.[135]

> Why are women always being accused of this *mopakwane*? Well, they are not the ones causing this because you will find that a woman will not go and sleep with another woman's husband while she is pregnant. She's already kept in the house while she has a small child, she can't go and sleep in another man's bed. While men are the very ones who go to other men's houses during the men's absence, going to their wives. So, well, it's only that men only like to accuse women of almost everything. . . . Many times you'll find that they [men] are the ones who are bringing all these problems in their homes, they are the only ones who are bringing all these kinds of diseases in their homes—but still blaming women.

But for women, *mopakwane* and *thibamo* were about motherhood as well as sexuality. It was women who labored to nurse and care for patients (husbands and children) with these debilitating conditions. Even pathologies that might physically displace dangerous behavior into the bodies of others (husbands and babies) soon came home to roost. These diseases and their subsequent nursing burdens reminded women of the perils of violating their twin moral ties to their menfolk and their children manifested through wombs, blood, and milk. Families and the wider community could hardly afford to have their young women exhibit the same individualism that enabled young men to renounce their obligations to community and elders. As female labor migration picked up pace, women became primary producers and distributors of *madi*, *mopakwane*, and *thibamo*. These diseases served as public idioms that warned women against severing their own interests from those of family.

Diagnoses and observed prevalence of the third disease category that experienced a great increase in the postwar period were likewise embedded in contemporary historical transformations: the recent experiences of battle, intergenerational struggles over *madi,* and in some cases referred to polluted uteruses. The disease was indicated by the interchangeable terms: *botsenwa, bolwetsi ba tlhaloganyo* (illnesses of the mind), and *bogole ba tlhaloganyo* (disability of the mind).[136] The term *botsenwa* comes from the passive construction of the verb *go tsena,* meaning "to enter." A *setsenwa* (a person suffering from *botsenwa*) was someone whose *madi* had been entered either by a spirit or a poison. It was possible for *botsenwa* to be hereditary, because sometimes the tainted blood was carried over generations.[137] All of the symptoms of *botsenwa* were anti-social behaviors and ran a wide range: from taking off one's clothes in public or other lewd acts to incessant and incoherent speech to uncontrollable bouts of violence or crying to failure to comprehend familiar situations to withdrawal from social life.

There had always been some people who were *ditsenwa* within local communities, though in the early twentieth century it seems that their numbers were few. During the latter period of World War II in April 1944, however, Bangwato regent Tshekedi Khama began to complain to the government about the *ditsenwa* who were disrupting village life in the Gammangwato capital, Serowe. Women were removing their clothing and walking around the village naked. Some were setting fire to huts and damaging property. Tshekedi complained of four such cases in the previous year.[138] His testimony noted the increasing lack of family members necessary to cope with chronically ill persons. Though southeastern chiefs did not echo his complaint at the time, within another two years, when the soldiers started coming home, the problem of *botsenwa* grew.[139]

Causes of the rise in *botsenwa* were debated locally. The disease was attributed to a number of disparate causes (including the possible migration of the womb to the head), which were combined into a phenomenon in which the heart became overfull with *madi* and sent too much into the head. As the madi rose into the head it could flood it with memories and overwhelm the thoughts. The person could become introverted and speak to their heart (*bua ka pelo*) or with their heart rather than through their head. Since the heart housed the unique qualities of the individual, speaking through the heart or with the heart confused inner and outer life in a range of dangerous ways. The potential for suicide and unknowable acts would intensify. Though the reasons for the rise of *madi* into the head and the causes of too much *madi* in the heart were debated, all agreed that *botsenwa* was a disease of the blood.[140] In fact, the Setswana terms for the English word "mind" included both *tlhaloganyo* (understanding) and *pelo* (heart), but not *boboko* (brain).[141]

Certain pressures in life could bring on the illness. The experiences of the war were a key reason why returning soldiers began exhibiting signs of *botsenwa.*

Pacifistic qualities were a central trope in local ethnic identity. Batswana who went to the mines often compared themselves to men of other ethnicities by referring to themselves as "men of peace." They doctored themselves so that "none would have problems with us as Batswana."[142] Many had resisted fighting in the war, and stories abounded of both successful and failed ploys to evade conscription into the army.[143] It was no surprise to many when veterans began acting strangely or even violently, requiring serious medical attention. Modise Thebe fought in the war; he also began his practice as a *ngaka* (which he learned from his father) in the immediate postwar period. When I asked him about *bolwetsi ba tlhaloganyo* at this time he explained. "Yes. It went up, up, up. Those things went up after the war. Yes, if you keep on killing people that will affect your mind [*pelo*]. And if you keep on, the sounds from all these guns and canons will affect you. . . . Yes, fighting destroys the mind [*tlhaloganyo*]."[144]

Purposeful malevolence was also at the root of much mental illness in this period (and well into the postcolonial era as well). A certain type of *boloi* was used to cause *botsenwa* among individuals, and the shifting emphasis on individualized preventive health measures in a climate of generalized envy and potential mistrust which came from the nascent culture of individualism, the weakening gerontocracy, and the uneven accumulation and circulation of vital *madi* provided a new context in which this *boloi* could flourish.[145] Male household heads would hire *dingaka* to strengthen their cattle kraals and compounds in an attempt to prevent disease and misfortune in an increasingly toxic world. After strengthening the boundaries of beasts, kraals, fields, and homes, the *ngaka* then gave all resident family members a special treatment that enabled them to enter these places safely. Outsiders who crossed these boundaries with ill will and intentions of *boloi* would find that their medicines would "bounce back" on them, bringing harm to the perpetrator rather than the intended victims. This had been a common practice for those who could afford it for many decades.[146]

But now people were strengthening home places in their sons' absences. With so many juniors off at work, the challenge became to ensure that they were doctored upon reaching home before they entered the newly strengthened boundaries of house or kraal. Those juniors who were not warned and treated in time suffered grave harm and often became *ditsenwa*.

> Well, it was caused by people. Let me say for example my husband may have cattle, and he had those cattle and he wanted some to be fat so he would call a *ngaka* to come and put medicine on the kraal. And then let me say the elder son is not here, the other children are not here, but you still go on with

the *ngaka* taking herbs and strengthening the kraal, and then if this one comes if he comes and he go into the kraal he will go *setsenwa,* he is *bolwetsi ba tlhaloganyo.* The other things were done really by *dingaka* when they come and heal the place here while the others are not here and then they come, well, they are going to be affected, you see. . . . Yes, everybody must be here. If he is not here he is in trouble, or the *ngaka* will tell you when he comes you must meet him, meet him before he goes in. But now what happens if he comes when you are not here? Perhaps he comes in the night, what can happen then? And there were all these things, that's why so many people got *setsenwa.*[147]

This practice took advantage of the precautions migrants already used to minimize the dangers of their return. Migrants who returned to their village by day laden with *madi* would wait in the bush across from their village until nightfall, lest those jealous of their earnings bewitch their footprints before they had time to return to their *ngaka* for purification and strengthening.[148]

Some seniors (particularly fathers) who struggled to control the earnings and labor of recalcitrant juniors began using the ruse of protective strengthening to extract the wealth and labor they thought were owed to them.[149] One notorious woman in Diphaleng who was *setsenwa* had fallen victim to such a ploy in the early 1950s. She was a particularly hard worker ("that one can work, hey!"), and her parents sought to control her labor, preventing her marriage and possible labor migration by strengthening the compound in her absence and "accidentally" failing to inform her. She became *setsenwa* but was still able to farm for them and upon their death for her older brother, her labor safely ensured.[150]

Regardless of the specific route an individual case of *botsenwa* followed, all seemed to agree that there was a seasonal aspect to the disease. When the early spring rains came and the flowers started exploding into bloom, when shoots and leaves appeared everywhere, then the *ditsenwa* would start acting up. As the leaves, flowers, and branches became stronger, the illness would again die down. The end of the moon and the very beginnings of the new moon could also exaggerate the problem, much the way the full moon does to westerners. No one I met in the late 1990s could clearly articulate for me why the flowering of trees and plants would cause *botsenwa* to start acting up. Perhaps the deep understanding of this concept died long ago with other pieces of medical knowledge or, and this is more likely, I simply did not understand enough of Tswana ecological cosmology to ask the right questions and grasp the underlying logic of their explanations beyond their linking of trees to medicines and the *badimo.* The question remains for someone else to explore.

The virulence of *botsenwa* appears to have grown in the postwar period.

Healers remember many patients brought to them with the illness.[151] Correspondence between local chiefs, medical officers, and the mental hospital at Lobatse reveal many more who, unable to find cure from *dingaka* or the growing group of prophet healers who emerged as an alternative therapeutic option in the 1950s, turned to the government for assistance.[152] Cure proved elusive for many. Many patients who seemed fine after some time in treatment (of any kind) would later, after several months or years, begin suffering from the illness again.[153] Observers noted that this recrudescence usually came with the flowering trees.[154] The public spectacle of the occasional *setsenwa* wandering the village, talking to himself or herself, interrupting dancing and beer drinking or even church services or simply sitting quietly dressed in an overcoat in the heat of the summer or hardly clothed against the cold winter winds became a familiar one in many villages.

More Translations: The Further Entanglement of *Bongaka* and Biomedicine

The Tswana and western diagnostic categories outlined above were often grafted onto one another in a range of ways. Missionary doctors educated patients about "*thibamo*" (using the Setswana word), and some Tswana began referring to certain people as "mad" (using the English word), perhaps gesturing with a rotating index finger pointing the side of their head to indicate as much. But what overlapped in these two medical lexicons were only partial symptoms, expressed through radically different physiological systems. These symptoms, in turn, were generated by behaviors that meant very different things in different moral universes. Translation between these two ways of understanding the world and the human body occurred through the already-limited vehicle of language. That bridge between Setswana and English could not fully accommodate the radical differences between the two systems of thought that underlay medical language, and encounters between the representatives of the two medical systems were too brief and too loaded to convey the meanings either party intended. Instead, choppy conversations consisting of partial meanings were absorbed into the internal discourse of either culture, shaping medicine and its meanings but in ways neither side perhaps intended.[155]

Diagnoses of TB and *thibamo* were mutually reinforcing. Yet they were based on different etiologies and had different moral consequences. TB was caused by exposure to infection, often in the context of mine work, and carried no moral weight. *Thibamo*, on the other hand, implied sexual misconduct. Conversations about TB/*thibamo* that crossed between therapeutic systems reinforced and entangled therapeutic options as well as moral meanings.

By the late 1940s colonial doctors had begun to translate "TB" into "*thibamo*" when speaking to Tswana patients, and certainly some patients had learned to do the same.[156] Perhaps "*thibamo*" became associated with the new symptomatology in the 1930s and 1940s because of how similar it sounded to the "TB" the white doctors spoke of at their hospitals. Or perhaps that is simply a coincidence—it is hard to know. In any event, the partial merging of the two diseases during their mutual rise in prevalence affected patients in a variety of ways. By 1986, Anderson and Staugart were able to claim, "The symptoms of *tibamo* [sic] are identical with those of tuberculosis."[157] But were they? Tswana patients, their relatives, and *dingaka* recognized only the pulmonary form of TB as *thibamo*.[158] The focus of colonial medical personnel on pulmonary TB further contributed to the growing overlap between the two illnesses. Yet despite medical lectures on "germs," which were translated as "*moghari wa bolwetse*" ("illness worms"), the presence of the tubercule bacilli in other organs or tissue of the body did not indicate *thibamo* any more than an unusual birth position indicated the potential for TB.[159] To the colonial medical service, the characterization of TB as the greatest medical problem facing the territory meant a desire for screening facilities, antibiotics, and the construction of tuberculosis shelters to house infected patients during treatment. To *dingaka* and their patients, it meant a need for better uterine purity managed through greater constraints on and monitoring of sexual activity, preventive strengthening of bodies, and regular ritual cleansing of many types of hot-blooded women and men.

In the late 1950s and early 1960s the government began erecting tuberculosis shelters in hospitals where patients could be housed for many weeks or even months while receiving antibiotic treatment.[160] This project would continue in the early postcolonial period, when TB shelters were added to some village clinics. But before that time, colonial doctors, who lacked the necessary antibiotics to treat TB, regularly dispensed behavioral advice to tubercular patients.

> Imagine in the late 1940s and 1950s when we diagnosed a case here. When Dr. Shepherd diagnosed a case of TB, he always would say to the parents "Take them"—'cause there weren't streptomycin then—"take them to the cattle post and give them lots of milk and porridge and meat and look after them there." And they used to do that and some of them actually recovered, although most of the TB cases didn't. But there they were looked after by their own people. . . . That's the other point. Spread was less. Less people, more open air and so on.[161]

Patients were further instructed to collect all their sputum in a cup and burn it each night and to take care not to let others share their clothing, utensils, and bedding.[162] Such advice also made sense in Tswana medical terms, though for different reasons. Movement to the cattle post isolated patients in areas where sexual contact would most likely be at a minimum. It also removed patients from the social world of the village, where witchcraft and other dangers were present. Proximity to the bush meant increased consumption of gathered foods, which were seen as "body protective and body building" since they had been planted by Modimo and were unsullied by human pollution.[163] Collecting and burning bloody sputum also further protected patients from potential harm because it prevented enemies from procuring vital bodily substances. Moreover, saliva historically was thought to contain some of the negative essence of the heart. Thus, spitting was an integral part of certain rituals because it expelled ill feelings or resentment, healing relations and bodies in the process.[164] Perhaps burning sputum also had some special healing potential.

Many patients with TB and/or *thibamo* could not follow through with this isolation program.[165] Either they or their caretakers needed to remain in the village or at the agricultural lands for other reasons, and patients were brought where those nursing them most needed to be.[166] But the logic of biomedicine, when brought to the logic of Tswana medicine, enabled the merging of these two illnesses into a somewhat awkward coexistence. It also reinforced the veracity and power of each diagnostic system; many patients were first told by the *ngaka* that they had *thibamo* only to later have this diagnosis confirmed at the hospital/clinic, and vice versa.

The burgeoning but hidden epidemic of *mopakwane* did not become entangled with biomedical concerns in the same way that *thibamo* did. In part, this was because *mopakwane* did not correlate to a single western diagnostic category but might indicate polio, malnutrition, cerebral palsy, post-meningitis cerebral palsy (often brought on by TB-meningitis), spina bifida, Down's syndrome, tertiary syphilis, and/or a host of other potential conditions, many of which were on the rise at the time. Furthermore, mothers were much less likely to take children with *mopakwane* into public spaces such as the waiting verandas at hospitals for fear of ridicule.[167] Therefore, western medical practitioners had few interactions that would bring the term "*mopakwane*" into their vocabulary and the meaning of the term was not shaped through a slightly altered usage, as happened with *thibamo*.[168] Likewise, they had little opportunity to offer advice on treatment and nursing care of children with *mopakwane*. Though generalized nutrition information was often dispensed and outbreaks of polio brought specific responses about quarantine from western medical institutions and personnel, these conversations were not specifically targeted at the children with wasted limbs and protruding bellies or the children who only after an initial fever and generalized sickness later could not move an arm or leg. These children were increasingly hidden from view and thus from the efforts of biomedical discourse to treat the illness as an event that happened to an individual.

Botsenwa and mental illness, however, both shared a broad, flexible character that was readily diagnosable that identified patients through their behavior. Even some of the causal chains of etiology which could lead to mental illness/ *botsenwa* seemed to overlap. Both therapeutic systems accepted the possibility of links between stress and neurasthenia, between the horrors of war and mental breakdowns, between scorned love and suicide, and the potential for a person to inherit mental illness/*botsenwa*. Both allowed for periodic episodes of mania followed by periods of relative quiet in individual patients. As a result, they merged easily, if messily, as parallel epidemics of mental illness and *botsenwa* occurred.

Though neither therapeutic system had clear-cut solutions to the growing problem of *botsenwa,* western doctors, administrators, and even chiefs often struggled to convince relatives to bring mental patients to them for evaluation and possible committal rather than to the *dingaka.*[169] Friction appeared most often between the two diagnostic systems over the certification of particular patients as deserving of government care. The size and budget of the local mental hospital meant that the government could treat only those patients who were determined to be "insane and dangerous" by two separate colonial doctors. Each component was, of course, subjective. In addition, many of the symptoms of the illness were erratic; a patient who had been violent the day before might be quite calm and collected during his medical examination. This was the case with Pitoro Sebobi in 1956, as the contrast in the following two pieces of correspondence suggest. The first is excerpted from a letter sent by Chief Bathoen of the Bangwaketse to the district commissioner in Kanye, requesting on behalf of Pitoro's family that he be committed to the asylum. The second is from Dr. Manson, the doctor at the United Free Church Moffat Hospital in Kanye, denying the request.

> Pitoro Sebobi I understand has been most violent attempting to strangulate his wife, picking up dangerous weapons such as a knife or an axe and throws away his clothing to remain nude. He has been under the care of the family for about two months but his abnormal condition and behavior do not improve hence his removal to Kanye.[170]

> Pitoro speaks coherently and during conversation appears to be emotionally stable. He is completely oriented in time and space, he has no obvious delusions and from my examination I can find no reason to regard him as being insane.[171]

The fact that family testimony was not enough evidence to warrant committal did not necessarily prevent family members from appealing to the government for help via their chief. But it may well have cast western diagnostic abilities into a poor light. We can only imagine how family members interpreted the rejection of an application for the confinement of someone who to them was obviously both sick and dangerous. But committal at the mental hospital was not the only mode of confinement in the postwar period. Struggles over the care of *ditsenwa* were only one aspect of a larger set of transformations in the history of local confinement in the 1950s and 1960s.

By anyone's estimation, the population of debilitated persons grew in the postwar period. But the contours of the epidemiological scheme and its underlying map of associations and causation looked different through different epistemological lenses. These two systems, *bongaka* and biomedicine, overlapped and merged—as they continue to do today—but translation in Bechuanaland between two sets of medical lexicons was not as easy and obvious as we might want it to be.[172] Diagnosis was and is a key element of illness narratives and illness experiences. But diagnostics must be historically situated, and diagnostic trends provide one means for understanding how physical experience and historical transformations reflected and shaped one another in powerful ways. In the postwar period, Tswana diagnostics imprinted the realities of changing sexual behavior, labor migrancy, and struggles over labor and *madi* on the bodies and minds of patients.

Colonial medical thought also had tremendous power in shaping people's lives and in dictating terms in the local marriage between bodily experience and sociocultural history. But that power was not coherent and cogent in its messages and manifestations. Biomedical diagnostics indexed a different set of concerns, rooted in postwar metropolitan laboratories, colonial labor and administrative agendas, and racialized constructs of human bodies and their capacities and purposes.[173] Biomedicine did not speak to certain illness (*mopakwane*), reinforced others (*thibamo*), and conflicted with still others (*botsenwa*). People realized as much, translating overlapping biomedical terms into Tswana medical logic and ignoring the rest. How could disease categories and epidemiology that referred back to metropolitan and global agendas make sense of bodily experiences in Bechuanaland? Though in the post-Independence period some people who suffered the stigma of certain Tswana diagnoses found succor and redemption in biomedical epistemology, it was Tswana diagnoses and local epidemiology that spoke to the daily experiences of people during the postwar period, and it was locally made diagnoses and local epidemiology that dictated nursing behaviors through which women reaped the uncertain rewards of postwar responsibilities and opportunities. It is to those nursing practices, the final element of the four-pronged systems of health and welfare, that we now turn.

Inside the Uterine Wall: Motherly Care in a Changing Moral Landscape

In the postwar period, women in southeastern Botswana, as we have seen, were stretched thin by their competing sets of obligations in the absence of male labor. Families depended heavily upon women's knowledge and work in agriculture, but those without dependable access to *madi,* especially those living in female-headed households, sometimes needed to send their womenfolk off to seek wages. Other women, interested in new opportunities for self-making and increased autonomy, crossed the border to earn their own *madi,* either with spousal or parental encouragement or despite parental or spousal disapproval. All this was taking place at the same time that postwar epidemiological realities were placing greater demands on women's time as nurses. Assistance with nursing burdens from female kin (mostly from mothers and sisters) reinforced women's intergenerational and sibling connections in the face of the atomization of interests evident in the changes in men's intergenerational relations and within the wider community.

Yet nursing practices in this context of increasing personal autonomy, sexual suspicion, *lefufa,* labor shortages, shifting marriage patterns, and growing populations of chronically ill and debilitated persons underwent critical changes that are still evidenced in the moral imagination of Batswana today. The rising incidence of *mopakwane* and *botsenwa* were key elements in the transformation of long-term nursing care. The changes were evidenced through shifts in the physical spaces utilized for confinement and nursing of patients suffering from *thibamo, mopakwane,* and *botsenwa*: the cattle posts and agricultural lands, the back of the compound, and the mental hospital. The most important of these changes took place in the domestic area behind the low arc of the uterine wall—the back of the compound (*segotlo*). In this postwar period, this symbolically uterine space took on new meanings. Changing nursing practices transformed the back of the compound from the historical site of female nurturance and intimacy to a repository of private shame, the place where *digole* and *ditsenwa* were hidden from public scrutiny.

In this sense, one of the many ways we can pursue how changes in diagnostics outlined above combined with the new modes of caregiving outlined below is to follow the uterus into the domestic realm.[174] In southeastern Botswana, as we have already begun to see, uteruses have historically been ambiguous spaces, embodying both the promise of productive, generative power and the perils of secrecy, autonomy, and pollution. The literal wombs within the bodies of actual women were increasingly imbued with this doubled nature, as evidenced above through shifts in Tswana diagnostics. But so too were the socioarchitectural spaces within domestic compounds that drew their meaning and their shape from the uterus, whose qualities and purpose they extended into the social realm. This essential organ of femininity and reproduction loomed quite large in the overlapping social and medical imaginaries of postwar Bechuanaland—to the extent that ideas, talk, and practices about and around uteruses as organs and uteruses as architectural spaces reflected and shaped ideas about women as social actors.

But it was not only through spatial practices that nursing engaged uterine symbolism. Fred Klaits reminds us of the powerful role of sentiment in shaping experiences of nursing care.

> [A]ccording to some, the emotional demands of nursing the ill mirror those involved in childbearing. Mma Maipelo often compared the experience of caring for her sick husband with being pregnant. "When you are pregnant, you don't know how the baby will turn out—will he be crippled [*segole*], will he be sick? Will your labor be hard? You have to resign yourself to God's will. In the same way, you don't know if the sick person you are nursing will get better or when. You must not lose patience." . . . The parallel between childbearing and caring for the sick reflects how sentiments of "care" influence the well-being of those who are comparatively helpless in their immobility—the sick, the very elderly, and infants, all of whom lack the "joints" necessary to rise.[175]

In this final section we continue our foray into the modern social history of southeastern Tswana uteruses by describing how changes in the talk and practices within and around material wombs fostered related changes in the talk and practices in and around symbolic, architectural wombs in the two decades following World War II.

Southeastern Batswana had long confined certain types of patients as an integral part of their care. The very frail elderly and postpartum mothers and infants in particular were confined in womblike huts whose productive heat sheltered them from the toxins of the social world. This sequestration reinforced the value and prestige of these individuals within the family as well as the perils of their liminal locations in the life course. Through confinement practices, caretakers demonstrated love and respect for these physically fragile relatives who were so near to the *badimo* buried in the compound. But in the 1950s and 1960s, within the shifting epidemiological and diagnostic context, the types of persons confined and the modes and meanings of confinement began to change. Many of the elderly and the *batsetse* (postpartum mothers) continued to receive special care and treatment, though some elderly suffered from the neglect of daughters-in-law who may have felt crumbling allegiance to affines during the absences of husbands and the tensions of domestic life in a time of great poverty.[176] But certain disabled children, mentally ill persons, and tubercular patients gradually joined the ranks of the confined in different ways and for different reasons. Together, these new modes of nursing care remade public and private experiences of debility, even as they reflected changing epidemiological and social realities.

Researching such changes in confinement practices was a confusing process at first. Many Batswana compared disability "long ago" (*bogologolo*) to disability "today" (*gompieno*) in one of two ways: either by denying that there were any disabled persons in the past[177] or by contrasting the implicitly primitive past when all the *digole* were hidden with the enlightened present when hiding no longer occurs.[178] A third group argued explicitly against either of these two approaches, stating categorically that there were *digole* in the past and that they weren't hidden: "One would meet them about the village," "I grew up next door to a girl with a dropped wrist and limp, we played together often," "My mother had a club foot and she certainly wasn't hidden anywhere."[179] Anthropologist Benedicte Ingstad has argued that the practice of hiding disabled persons, often held up by both expatriates and Batswana as an example of the primitivism of the African past, was in fact a myth. She found in the late 1980s that most disabled people were not hidden, though some, given their particular physical or mental circumstances, might be limited in their mobility and under the close care of family members.[180]

Ingstad's work is convincing, but historical questions remain. What do we make of the people who claimed to have had a hidden disabled resident in their own home or those who peered over walls or in windows to illicitly glimpse the hidden *digole*? What do we make of those early postcolonial health care workers who insisted upon entering homes and unearthing the hidden? The way to make sense of all this confusion is in terms of both historical change and terminology. In this case, basic comparisons of past (*bogologolo*) and present (*gompieno*) make little sense. It seems that in the early twentieth century few, if any, *digole* were confined. Yet there came a time, beginning in the late 1940s, when *mopakwane, botsenwa,* and *thibamo* were on the rise and women were both overburdened and suspected of illicit sexual behavior, when some debilitated people were, in fact, hidden from public life. This practice was reversed in the post-Independence period, so that by the time of Ingstad's study, hiding rarely occurred, though it had become a key practice in the collective moral imagination.

But even in the period between the end of World War II and Independence in 1966—the peak period of this type of clandestine confinement—it was never the case that all *digole* were confined. *Bogole* is far too broad a category for such an assertion to make much sense. Or, as one of the slogans at the Botswana Ministry of Health reads, "There is ability in dis-ability" (*bokgoni bo teng mo bogoleng*). This was a period of labor shortage in southeastern Bechuanaland; many vital men were laboring in the mines and many women were working in the fields and kitchens of the Transvaal. It was hardly a time to begin to confine productive, if impaired, members of society. It would be difficult to suddenly confine a vital adult who had recently suffered a debilitating accident but who could communicate and/or move about on his or her own. Many of the men who returned from the mines missing an arm or leg remained household heads with all the authority and responsibilities that implied. Confinement for these men was clearly out of the question. Likewise, remember Nomsa Rapela, who crushed a metal drum to support the remains of her thigh while hoeing her fields, or Alita Seati, who farmed though she had lost her sight, and the polio survivors Dr. Merriweather saw in Molepolole, who went about weeding their fields with pieces of tire strapped to their knees. These very able women continued to work despite their physical impairments. So the answer, then, is that some debilitated people were hidden for some period in the recent history of southeastern Bechuanaland. The question becomes one of figuring out which people were confined, how they were confined, and why they were confined. Let us return to our three growing illness categories—*thibamo, mopakwane*, and *botsenwa*—for an illustration of some of the changing modes of confinement in the late colonial period.

In what follows I should note explicitly that I was unable to glean much through my research about the *subjective* experience of being hidden/confined. Most of the people who were hidden in the 1950s and 1960s have since passed away. The few individuals I met who had been hidden in years past (or who I suspected had been hidden) either did not willingly speak about that experience or were unable to do so because of an impairment in their ability to communicate or because of their mental state. Thus, what follows can only partially explore the experiences of hidden *digole.*

Some families followed the advice of colonial doctors and took their family member to the cattle posts, and many more were taken to the lands during the growing season to be nursed there by womenfolk who had to continue to feed their families even though they were nursing a relative.[181] Because of the high prevalence of TB/*thibamo*, one can imagine that many households had at least one such patient in their care. The colonial medical service also attempted to hospitalize some of these patients to provide long-term care. But patients and their families resisted such attempts for the most part, and in 1950, Dr. Merriweather wrote to the director of medical services to ask if he could convert the tuberculosis shelter the government had donated to the mission hospital in Molepolole three years earlier to a maternity ward. There were not enough pa-

Poster on the wall of a *kgotla* meeting to celebrate the Day of the Disabled.
It reads, "*Bokgoni bo teng mo Bogoleng:* There is Ability in Dis-ability."
Photo by Stephanie Cohen, 1998.

tients to necessitate overflow to a special shelter.[182] But wherever such patients
might have stayed, they were not hidden, though they may have been confined
to bed during the final stages of their illness. Tubercular/*thibamo* patients
moved about freely, traveling between the cattle post or lands and the village.
They visited with neighbors and attended important social and political events
if they were able to do so.[183] Nonetheless, the care they required as they pro-
gressively weakened taxed their women relatives, who already struggled to farm
their fields and maintain their households in a world deprived of male and
some female labor. One can only imagine the emotional dynamics of a situation where wives cared for husbands who suspected marital infidelity as the
source of a *thibamo* illness or where mothers nursed sons who had been absent
for years without sending money, returning home only when they needed care
and mother love.

This type of long term nursing care contrasted sharply with the growing secrecy surrounding *mopakwane.* The flexibility of the symptoms of *mopakwane*
meant that the growing incidence of various illnesses, including outbreaks of
polio, serious malnutrition, and tubercular and viral meningitis, all indicated
an increase in the disease. As the disability of children became embedded in

public analysis of women's changing sexual behavior, mothers began hiding children with *mopakwane* behind the low arc of the uterine wall of their compounds. Such children were known to immediate family members and other close kin (who may well have encouraged their sequestration), but when neighbors or more distant relatives would visit, these children would be kept either in the back of the compound or locked inside a hut.[184] The following narrative by Esther, an elderly woman who is now herself a diabetic amputee, illustrates the general practice of children's confinement.

> I have my one brother—the father to the one disabled girl. That girl was born in 1953, she was just all right. After a year she was ill—I don't know what what's wrong with her but she was admitted to the hospital. When she was admitted, she couldn't move, the legs were what do you call it—polio—that's what. Ever since she was admitted, anyway, I don't know what was wrong with her—let's say it was polio—even now she is like that.

> J. L.: So then when she came out of hospital, what happened then? Were people saying this *boloi, kana mopakwane*?

> So she wasn't able to walk anymore. *Kana* they can just say *boloi*, when I was just all right, from hospital she became not walking just crawling. *Gore* we never expected a person to be crippled like that one—*kana* most of the cripples they were put behind at home—but even to the back of the compound, *ko* back of the compound. She was kept to the back.

> J. L.: So then if neighbors came to visit back then?

> She would be kept indoors, indoors. . . . It's because that they thought "No, they are just coming to peep and see. They have heard that our daughter is not walking. They want to come and see her and laugh at us." Yes that's why—guilty conscience, guilty conscience—that's why she was always kept indoors so that whoever comes—they just visited the parents, he or she must not [see her]. Yes, if the relatives come and then they say "Where is so and so?" yes—a relative can be allowed to see her—only just neighbors, no they were not allowed.[185]

Not all children with *mopakwane* or with particular western diagnoses, such as polio or Down's syndrome, were confined. Though some people explicitly linked "*boso*" (feeble-mindedness/mental retardation) and drooling saliva to *mopakwane* confinement, there were others whose mothers resisted the current diagnostic trends and maintained that such differences were "just nature" and brought their children out in public. With the support of in-laws, parents, and/or spouses in embracing these causal understandings, such things were possible.[186] Other children with polio might be confined, while many simply suffered the restrictions that limited mobility brought but were welcome to interact with visitors of all kinds.[187] In both cases, the laboriousness of constantly carrying children who couldn't walk on their own merged with the new trend toward hiding, so that some children who remained at home for such practical reasons might be whispered about as hidden when both they and their parents did not consider this to be the case.[188]

Reasons for purposefully sequestering such children were manifold and depended on the particular nature of the impairment as much as the personal predilections of those involved. On the one hand there was the stigma that these children brought on their mothers. Public display of such a child inevitably led to gossip and rumor, even when grandmothers and aunts defended a woman against accusations of "breaking the rules."[189] Some women friends who gave birth to disabled children in a slightly later period recalled that they did not know the word "*mopakwane*" until they first heard it directed at them while they were drawing water or at some other site where women gathered, and they remarked on how painful and frustrating it was to get their mother or auntie to explain what the word meant. Because the sexual education that had previously been conveyed during *bojale* was missing, we can imagine that this may also have been the case during the immediate postwar period. Related to this was the desire of many women to protect their children from malicious gossip and teasing that they knew would be hurtful.[190] Even those mothers who knew that they had not jumped the *mopakwana* "were thinking that they have been bewitched by the neighbors and might be injured more if they see them [the disabled children] outside."[191]

On the other hand, many feared that such children would "misbehave" in front of visitors, thus embarrassing everyone present.[192] Mpho Lekile remembers that her uncle and her older brother's son were confined with *mopakwane* at that time.

> They were many that time. They were there, and it's like their relatives were just looking for them, but not taking care of them as such. It's only that they didn't want people to see them. They were afraid they will misbehave maybe while they have some visitors. They were always put somewhere, maybe at the back of the compound, so that when the visitors come they shouldn't see because they were always misbehaving, some of them. So the reason why their relatives didn't want them to be seen, they thought that people will laugh at them.[193]

Misbehaving in this case usually meant a violation of the norms of bodily control.

Maybe someone would be coming, a visitor, and that one would be sitting another leg there and another leg there [indicating far apart] in front of them, just like that.[194]

Actually it wasn't people who were disabled as such [who were hidden], only those who had some kinds of strange behaviors, which prevented them to be with others. Then that person might pee in front of others or some something. Because they are like ashamed of what is going to happen in front of others so they hide that one so that others won't see, when there are visitors. But anyone who had physical disabilities but was fine otherwise, you would see them around. . . . So when they were like talking on their own, they were still being kept inside because parents were worried that maybe they will say something embarrassing, people will laugh or what but within the family it was okay. So those ones also they were kept aside . . . it was like they were thinking if they [guests] were given food and then they are in front of others like drooling saliva it will not be nice.[195]

Despite this woman's assertions, some people with physical impairments were indeed kept hidden, as was the case with some children with polio.[196] In his autobiography, Dr. Merriweather recalled meeting adults in the mid-1950s whose severe facial deformities resulted in their sequestration, though one cannot be sure at what age the spatial restrictions on these men began.

I was taken to a hut on the outskirts of Bokspits to see two men who were hidden away from public view. Both had extensive syphilitic ulceration of their faces, with one of them all that was left of the face was a hole where the mouth was, surrounded by scar tissue which had replaced the face muscles. The eyes had also been affected and were scarred over. This was an awful sight which I saw on several occasions on my travels, one of the worst being at Sesung in Kweneng; at that stage of disease of course, one could do nothing for the patient.[197]

In contemporary Botswana, many people in speaking about *mopakwane* (including in the course of some of the interviews quoted here) would contort their faces into a grotesque imitation of such children. These "aesthetic impairments" that such speakers sought to mimic often became a dense signifier, a mnemonic for a range of other moral concerns that congealed in affective responses. But beyond deformities as signs of moral transgressions, the aesthetics of such bodily configurations also had the power to move the observer through affect. Batswana were not alone in the severity of their reactions to such children. In many contexts, aesthetically challenging bodies, particularly faces, pose problems for some people, parents especially, who experience deep negative feelings toward their children, for whom they are expected to experience unconditional love. Thus, they seek to dispose of, shun, sequester, or abandon them. Such reactions occur cross-culturally and in a range of historical contexts (with attendant variation in aesthetic norms) independent of underlying ideas about causation or the prognosis for improvement. Anthropologist Meira Weiss argues that many such parents make sense of these affective reactions they have to their children's appearance by categorizing them through word and deed as nonpersons.[198] Long-term sequestration for "aesthetically impaired" Batswana children certainly accomplished this, as did a focus on drooling, posture, and incontinence, since maturing persons were expected to maintain control over their bodies and the processes of sitting, swallowing, urination, and defecation. Social interaction was and is such a fundamental part of becoming and being a Tswana person that severe restrictions in socialization and a lack of public acknowledgment of the existence of certain family members evidenced a powerful combination of aesthetic and moral judgments.

But in Botswana, affect, sentiment, and feeling were not just inner experiences; they were also powerful social forces that impacted the bodily, emotional, and material well-being of others and thus had to be kept in check. Sentiments of care and love had the power to nurture, and sentiments of jealousy, anger, sorrow, and disgust had the power to harm. Deborah Durham and Frederick Klaits, writing about funerals in contemporary Botswana, expand on Habermas's notion of the public sphere as a site shaped by "rational-critical discourse" to argue that for Batswana, "linkages between self and other are not imagined as relations between discrete, independent and rational thinkers, under the influence of socio-political currents; rather, people find themselves connected in their very physical well-being through emotional states and sentimental connections recognized and forged in public space."[199] Though Durham and Klaits focus on funerals in the late twentieth century as distinct public spaces, their analysis helps us understand another dimension of the sequestration of people with aesthetically challenging bodies. In the context of the jealousies, resentments, and uncertainties of postwar society, the capacity for certain bodies to generate deep and spontaneous negative feelings in onlookers threatened the delicate sociability of public space. The privacy of the *segotlo* (backyard) offered one means to manage the material, emotional, and bodily effects of toxic feelings.

The back of the compound had transformed in the moral imagination from the special site of female intimacy and motherly love to a place where stigma and shame were hidden from prying eyes, a place where the rules of public society did not fully reach. As cemeteries gradually became the main burial sites (a process that began for early Christians in the 1890s in some villages but spread to other groups over time), the *segotlo* was no longer protected by the female ancestors buried beneath the floor.[200] Those kept behind the uterine wall, both *mopakwane* children and *ditsenwa*, became the fodder for gossip and rumor. Many people (especially children) found the whole situation titillating. When a family with a confined patient was away at church or out visiting, they would go to peer over compound walls and through fences in the hopes of getting a glimpse of the hidden *segole*.[201]

Those "to the back" also lived outside the normal rules of caregiving enforced by the community. Parents who did not provide proper medical and nursing care or food for their children were called to the *kgotla* and asked to explain their actions. This might result in a fine or reprimand; in severe cases, the child would be taken away and put in the care of relatives. But hidden children existed outside the system, and their parents would not be brought to the chief and headmen for questioning; they were left alone.[202] Some people assumed that these children were not well cared for. Because of the overwhelming labor burdens that women faced in the absence of so many men, perhaps mothers did not always shift them out of the strong sun and into the forever-moving shade. In the context of pervasive poverty, maybe some mothers stinted these children, especially those who could not feed themselves.[203] This assumption was not necessarily true: Ruth's niece lived to adulthood, when she became a successful seamstress. But most likely there were cases—given the nature and degree of a particular child's impairments—in which women took advantage of the privacy of the back of the compound and hastened death.

Relatives also confined some *ditsenwa*, though for different reasons and in different ways and places. Temporary confinement was often a part of Tswana medical treatment for *botsenwa*. *Dingaka* regularly had to restrain those patients who were difficult to control during the lengthy therapy, which might last for several weeks. Such patients would be taken to live in the *ngaka*'s compound, where they were kept in a hut or tied to a tree for much of the time if they exhibited signs of violence or attempted escape from the doctor's care.[204] Western doctors also confined and/or physically restrained mental patients. At the Lobatse Mental Hospital (which was constructed in 1947), patients were kept in locked wards and, as with mental patients kept in the regular mission hospitals, strapped to beds or straitjacketed if necessary.[205] Overflow patients might be kept in local jail cells.[206] So it seemed that all agreed that restraint and confinement were at times a necessary part of both biomedical and Tswana treatment for *botsenwa*/mental illness.

By the time the mental hospital was completed, it was already obvious that its capacity of twelve patients was not enough to accommodate all the persons needing treatment.[207] The demand for space should not have caught the administration by surprise, In 1944, before the repatriation of troops, Bangwato Native Authorities alone reported a population of fifty "lunatics."[208] This population, combined with the large numbers of veterans requiring care, over-taxed the new facility from the moment it opened.[209] Though the mental hospital was subsequently expanded in 1959 to house thirty patients, the shortage of space remained a perpetual problem. Family members and doctors might vigorously disagree about the threat posed by a particular patient. As a result, some of the patients whose families faced serious difficulty in controlling them were kept "to the back of the compound," in some cases tethered to a stationary object such as a tree or the center pole to a hut or locked inside a rondavel.[210] Others were taken far out to the cattle post, where they remained under the permanent care of a male relative.[211] Western observers saw such practices as emblematic of Tswana barbarity, but in many such cases, relatives had exhausted all other options and cared very much for the welfare of their loved ones.[212]

The gap between those who were certified insane and dangerous and those who were mentally ill/*botsenwa* and in need of help but not certifiable meant that many families struggled to care for their ill relatives while also trying to perform their regular domestic and agricultural-pastoral tasks. Some of those patients might be enough of a "nuisance"—stealing and damaging property, running away repeatedly, acting inappropriately, threatening people they encountered—that they risked beatings from fellow villagers whom they angered. Some families suffered serious physical harm and damage to or even complete destruction of their own property before they secured committal for their sick relative.[213]

The colonial government repeatedly voiced fears that the local population would take advantage of the new mental hospital to shift the burden of caring for unwanted relatives to the state, and it maintained its strict certification rules.[214] But the reality was that in the postwar period, as the scale of personal responsibility shrank, there were more and more patients who simply lacked such family altogether.[215] Those *ditsenwa* who lacked family but were not dangerous except perhaps to themselves had few options in this new social climate. This was the case with Setanke Ketlaaren, who attempted suicide in 1948 and was brought to Athlone Hospital in Lobatse. Though Chief Bathoen himself visited Setanke in the hospital, he found no clear solution for this man's situation.

> This man is not married and his two adult brothers are both in the Union. His paternal uncle is not alive upon whom he chiefly depended.
>
> When I was in Lobatse yesterday I made a special point of calling on him in Hospital with a view to ascertaining from him where he would wish to be removed to, but even then I get nothing helpful.[216]

Setanke Ketlaaren's case is a poignant example of how the fracturing of local families and familial responsibility and the narrow scope of colonial welfare policy left some people with few options.

Amid the constraints on care that were developing in the postwar period, independent healing churches presented a new alternative site and mode of care, one that would grow in importance in the postwar period. Within independent churches, women in particular created new forms of family and community in domestic spaces that they now imbued with Christian spiritual power. Some mentally ill and otherwise debilitated people found care in these new spaces. Just as the scope of care was narrowing for many Batswana and as the uterine wall was closing off private spaces to the prying eyes of outsiders, some women opened their compounds to non-kin as spiritual houses of healing and sought to reincorporate neighbors and even strangers into new communities of caring.

Through nursing and confinement practices, the larger changes in public health, epidemiology, and diagnostics took root in the lives of individual patients and their families. Women in particular, as mothers and wives and as neighbors, grandmothers and visitors, experienced the dialectical relationship between the sociocultural trends in migrancy, sexuality, and individualism and the health-related changes in diagnostics, epidemiology, and public health through the process of nursing. Nursing crises in caring for and controlling *ditsenwa* made evident the dearth of menfolk and the instability of substitute safety nets offered by the colonial government. The shifting meanings of the key nursing site at the back of the compound to a place of hiding referred to the dangers of the new sexuality and of women's attempts to gain their own foothold in the new climate of individualism. Sequestration linked architectural and anatomical, symbolic and material wombs in a larger logic of secrecy and danger. The change also highlighted the toxic climate of *lefufa* and *boloi* left in the wake of collapsing public health. And the ubiquitous burdens of caring for and witnessing the decline of those with *thibamo* at the lands, at the cattle posts, and in the villages were daily reminders of the brutality of the cycle of migrancy and all that it entailed.

5 Postcolonial Development and Constrained Care

Mma-ngwana ke yo o tswarang thipa ka bogale.
>—Setswana proverb: The mother of the child is the one who seizes the knife by the blade.

O re go lemoga ngaka le bolwetse o bo lemoge.
>—Setswana proverb: If you are too smart to pay the doctor, you had better be too smart to get sick.

The end of colonial rule in 1966 meant a decline in the power of local chiefs and a corresponding increase in the centralization and bureaucratization of authority and welfare at the national level. International aid agencies soon combined with a very liberal-minded postcolonial state to provide new mechanisms for charity and health care, and the rhetoric and impact of internationally modeled "development" accelerated in southeastern Botswana. The discovery of diamonds and the resulting mineral boom beginning in the 1970s brought unprecedented wealth into the newly independent nation and enabled the government to begin providing clean water, primary health care, education, and modern infrastructure.[1] These transformations engendered bodily changes as rates of infectious disease and malnutrition fell and rates of debility rose.

Bechuanaland had no cities, but a new capital was established in Gaborone after Independence that grew rapidly, as did a number of towns. By the 1980s, the booming city of Gaborone and the major towns throughout eastern Botswana had begun drawing large numbers of men and women seeking economic opportunities as jobs gradually proliferated in urban and town centers. Migration for work was now reoriented in country, especially in the wake of large-scale retrenchments of Tswana miners on the Rand when the South African mines began a major effort to localize their workforce in the mid-1970s.[2] Those who migrated for work in country maintained homes in their natal villages, just as previous generations of labor migrants had done. And just as before, those adults who suffered a debilitating injury or illness were brought back to their home communities by family members. They returned to villages already disproportionately populated by children and the elderly. These rural residents enjoyed visits and possible financial help but not daily domestic assistance from their working kin.[3] In fact, those working "in town" usually relied on their unemployed female relatives, often elderly women, to raise children and care for the family's chronically debilitated members.

New money brought new jealousies and stark socioeconomic ruptures within communities. Opportunities for upward mobility through education, entrepreneurship, and work, which intensified over the course of the 1980s and 1990s, fractured families and generated struggles and debate over new forms of liberal individualism. As always, this individualism existed in tension with the priorities of gerontocratic and social hierarchies and the obligations and responsibilities of kin and community, but increasingly such tensions were played out on a national (rather than *morafe*) as well as household or family scale. Even though the postcolonial state promoted self-reliance and productivity for its citizens, leaders also referred to "traditional" Tswana civic values of familial and community caregiving and cooperation. Changes that began in the colonial period that narrowed the scale of personal obligations accelerated in the post-Independence period in the context of national and international programs that provided assistance to the destitute, the feeble, and the frail.

This chapter explores how people imagined and weighed the opportunities and the misfortunes possible for themselves and others amid these changes through a focus on care. By care here I mean bodily care in the more narrow sense of the palliation that people provide daily to debilitated persons but also in the broader sense of activities that contribute to the well-being of others. As suggested in the introduction, attending funerals and weddings; visiting neighbors and friends; giving blankets, money, or food; bathing children; sharing resources; fetching water or wood; and cooking for others are all acts of care. Care is important for Batswana in part because it is through these acts that people mobilize positive sentiments such as love that strengthen or heal relationships and build up persons.[4] Care is where responsibilities, actions, and sentiment combine. In the postcolonial period, caregiving shifted in important ways as *merafe* and villages ceded control over public healing to regional, national, and international authorities; as access to biomedicine and its ideas and practices increased steadily; and as self-making continued to change amid greater possibilities for new forms and expressions of personal autonomy. These changes fostered epidemiological shifts and new forms of able-bodiedness. They also spawned intergenerational and other struggles over the meanings and responsibilities of certain key relationships enacted through care. The identities of mothers, daughters, friends, neighbors, church members, doctors, nurses, employers, and government and civic leaders (and many others) were all, in part, understood and made sense of in terms of a reconfiguring politics of care.

Changing Bodies

The British left Botswana poorer than they had found it. Their decades of taxation policies had long depleted the protectorate of its surplus and then some. Bechuanaland had been transformed through colonial rule from a net exporter of food (albeit with recurrent droughts and accompanying lean years) to an impoverished labor reserve. Even with the promise of foreign aid, the path to development looked long and arduous at best. But in the late 1960s and early 1970s, a series of mineral discoveries boosted Botswana's economic prospects and set in motion a decades-long period of rapid development that is still under way at the beginning of the twenty-first century.[5]

As diamond earnings began flowing into the country, the government used the new revenues prudently, rapidly building a network of roads, telecommunications, educational infrastructure, hospitals and clinics, and boreholes and dams where previously there had been next to none. Even as some people reaped individual rewards in the new economy, more enjoyed the benefits of clean water, accessible primary health care, western education, and roads. As in other post-Independence countries, government-led health and development programs relied on international expertise and labor as they gradually built human resources in the country. A fixation with technological solutions existed in tension with discussions of "appropriate" technology, and Botswana, like so many other "third world" countries, began developing tertiary hospital care in its capital city in tandem with a burgeoning network of primary health care clinics and the handful of primary hospitals in its villages and towns.

Independence in Botswana did not mean a return to Tswana modes of public healing or the incorporation of *dingaka* into the center of medical services. Though in the late 1960s and 1970s some *dingaka* made attempts to form professional associations, the Ministry of Health and its international partners considered biomedicine and western-style public health to be the route to development. For the most part, *bongaka,* which was cast as traditional, was more often portrayed as an impediment to health than as a national resource.[6] Though only a fraction of the total range of development programs were designed to address the specific concerns of the debilitated, the new climate of welfare and development brought wide-ranging changes to the picture of debility we saw for the postwar period.

Developments in public health and health care service initiatives improved overall health but also inadvertently added to the growing incidence of chronic illness and debility. The rise in the general standard of living, the success of vaccination and other public health campaigns, and the provision of regular food aid and clean water in every village had a collective positive impact on the general health of the population, even though after two decades of rapid development over half the population of Botswana continued to live in relative poverty. Mortality rates for infants plummeted from 98 per 1,000 live births in 1971 to 37 per 1,000 live births in 1994,[7] while life expectancy in Botswana rose from 48 years in 1966 to 65.3 years in 1991.[8] The census figures also showed that the population of persons over age 60 doubled between 1971 and 1991.[9]

However, the declining mortality from infectious disease and malnutrition and the increase in life expectancy meant that chronic illnesses and other forms of debility became more prevalent. In 1987 and again in 1991 the Ministry of Health reported that cardiovascular disease was the third leading cause of death in the country.[10] The incidence of hypertension, stroke, cancer, diabetes, and other chronic conditions continued to rise as the population underwent a rapid epidemiological transition resulting from new changes in diet and life-style and the decline of infectious disease. As a network of tarred highways was built and more Batswana were able to purchase cars and bus and taxi rides, a sharp rise in the incidence of motor accidents became another unfortunate by-product of development. By 1991, road accidents had become the sixth leading cause of death and certainly a major contributor to the rise in debility.[11]

Improvements in obstetrics and primary health care reduced maternal and infant mortality, but they also fostered a growing population of disabled children. In the post-Independence period the percentage of medically supervised deliveries increased dramatically. While statistics are not available on the percentage of such deliveries in the mid-1960s, all agree that the incidence of medically supervised labor then was very low. By 1993, however, fully 77 percent of women delivered with medical supervision.[12] Children who were born premature or during difficult or obstructed labor in hospital and clinic settings often survived into infancy with disabling conditions that might have proved fatal had their mothers lacked access to such services. Likewise, though the mortality rates from infectious diseases such as meningitis declined, many children survived such illnesses with some form of residual impairment.[13] And the improvement in secondary and tertiary care meant that more people survived episodes of what would have been potentially fatal trauma or illness only decades before, and they became debilitated in the process.

Some of the new health care programs targeted key diseases directly, and some of these programs produced remarkable successes. These included World Health Organization programs to eradicate smallpox and tuberculosis.[14] Through a concerted and well-orchestrated national campaign that combined vaccination of children, antibiotic therapy for patients, and stays in the recently built network of TB wards, the rates of illness and death from tuberculosis dropped substantially.[15] The rate of new cases was halved between 1975 and 1985, falling from 506 per 100,000 to 255 per 100,000.[16] By the first half of the 1990s, tuberculosis shelters were no longer full, and eventually many were converted to other uses. In the mid-1990s the Diphaleng TB shelter was given over for part-time use to the community-based rehabilitation team, its changing uses mirroring the ongoing epidemiological transitions. Sadly, the disappearance of TB was to prove only a temporary reprieve. Tuberculosis rates started slowly rising again in the late 1990s and early 2000s. The HIV/AIDS epidemic brought bloody coughs, night sweats, wasted bones, collapsed spines, and seizures back into bodies, beds, clinics, and homes.

Improvements in local nutrition, primary health care, and infectious disease control also affected the demographic makeup of society and began to alter the meanings of age. The gerontocracy, already threatened by decades of migrant labor and the collapse of the public health system previously controlled by seniors, was further weakened. Elderhood was losing its cultural and spiritual capital through the demise of ancestor cults and the entrenchment of the wage labor economy just as more of the population began to survive into old age. A rise in chronic diseases such as diabetes and hypertension meant that many older persons were leaving adulthood and entering *botsofe* at much younger chronological ages than in earlier times, as stroke, crippling arthritis, certain types of cancer, diabetic amputations and the like marked otherwise middle-aged bodies as senescent in the popular imagination.[17] These new diseases splintered the meanings of old age by separating spiritual development from physical decrepitude.

The epidemiological transition has not gone unnoticed. As one elderly woman commented, "Long ago we old people were not sick as we are today. We didn't know about stroke and sugar diabetes, and heart attack."[18] Many others expressed similar sentiments about a seeming rise in the prevalence of disability.[19] Nongovernmental organizations and government health care institutions began offering rehabilitation services as local health care workers began a slow process of unearthing the hidden population of disabled persons. Disabled children, frail elderly, and chronically ill adults became increasingly visible in public spaces, and it seemed to some that there had been a sudden surge in the number of disabled people in their villages. The new context of improved local economic opportunity alongside a growing community of suffering generated a philosophical rethinking of recent history and the meanings of "development" and "progress" among many people, particularly the elderly. For Nanki's grandmother, whom we met in Chapter 1, the rising tide of physical misfortune—which no doubt included the generalized climate of the AIDS epidemic as well as the rise in disabilities such as her granddaughter's post-meningitis cerebral palsy—was a sign of much greater things. When I asked her in 1997 to explain why she thought there was so much more *bogole* in the late 1990s than in earlier times, she turned to her Bible: "It has been said that it will be the time when we know that the world will be coming to the end—we will see things happening around us, changes and so sudden—so I don't know exactly what to do—but I am thinking that maybe the world is coming to an end."[20]

Welfare and Rehabilitation

In this shifting epidemiological landscape, two new developments in particular had a profound impact on the lives of debilitated persons and the public meanings of debility: the extension of welfare and rehabilitation services (considered here) and increased access to education (considered in the next section). The promise of welfare services and payments, rehabilitation and technical aides, and a new rhetoric of development, modernity, and human rights repositioned the disabled population as potential recipients of special care and attention.[21]

By the early 1970s, the final collapse of the indigenous Tswana public health system, the fracturing of families during the years of migrant labor, and the emerging ethos of the individual meant that a growing population of destitute persons, often elderly or disabled or both, became visible in the major villages of the southeastern region. "Crippled beggars" were frequently seen in the main mall in the newly built capital city of Gaborone.[22] The Botswana government did not yet in the 1970s command the resources necessary to address stark instances of destitution, but it would later build upon initiatives begun and sustained by nongovernmental organizations. The newly constituted Botswana Red Cross, led by the British-born First Lady, Ruth Khama, responded to what had become large gaps in the local welfare systems with sporadic gifts of food, clothing, and blankets (particularly at Christmas) to the destitute elderly in a few areas near its center in Tlokweng or through its regional branches in various districts of the country.

By 1980, there were many people who regularly depended on the monthly rations of food the organization dispensed to the destitute population. Many of their recipients were sick, blind, or both. In 1977, for example, its list of twenty-nine "Old and Poor People" whom they assisted in Old Naledi, the earliest squatter settlement in Gaborone, included "Mosimanewatlala: old and thin. No place of his own"; "Jungle Moeketsi: Just had an eye transplant done by Dr Winther waiting for results"; "John Matlapeng and his wife: Old and poor couple, eye troubles. Wife is at Lobatse Hospital, were given roofing in August"; "Thomas Thlobe: Has relatives at Mochudi whom he left many years ago"; "John Modimoeng: Old t.b. case—was taken to hospital recently because of heavy bleeding. Lives alone."; "Keipetle Molebatse, Mantloane, Puleng: Three women old and poor stay near each other, [Mantloane] has no place of her own"; "Hilda: No place of her own stays with different people"; "Maria: No place of her own stays with different people"; and "Ngwanyana Pula: Blind, might be two with the same name."[23] The picture was similar in villages outside the city. In 1972, volunteers at the new Red Cross chapter in Thamaga had already identified 200 destitute residents desperately in need of winter clothing and twenty-two disabled villagers who could benefit from the new Red Cross clinics held in Gaborone.[24]

The relationship between debility and poverty was not lost on Red Cross planners. Soon the organization, overwhelmed with requests for assistance in procuring wheelchairs, crutches, and the like, began the first programs in Botswana to specifically target disabled persons. Starting in 1973, their traveling clinics identified and attempted to provide artificial limbs, calipers, braces, and other technical aides for those in need.[25] Red Cross workers, some of whom would become the first cadre of family welfare educators—the community health workers in the new national health service—began a long, slow process of identifying the disabled, signaling an end to the brief era of intensified confinement.

The Red Cross was emblematic of a new form of care that emerged in the postcolonial milieu. Nongovernmental organizations (NGOs) such as the Red Cross sprang up in the 1970s and 1980s and included a handful of rehabilitation centers and other groups that provided services to disabled and destitute persons. Their work built upon the colonial-era precedents for paternalism set by chiefs and missionaries but also regularized the paternalist mood of Christian charity in crucial ways by explicitly linking care to local capitalist development. The Red Cross fostered new, very public forms of philanthropy among local elites and the business community through its fund-raising and publicity efforts. The debilitated and the poor became important targets of NGO activity in the context of the growing national rhetoric of liberal individualism and the flurry of development. As American Peace Corps workers, Danish medical students, European doctors, engineers, hydrologists, and other international public service personnel entered Botswana to contribute to its development, local actors took center stage in news reports and community meetings that publicly acknowledged who gave what to whom. In contrast to the daily caregiving efforts of mothers, daughters, neighbors, and friends, such donations often made the front page of the *Botswana Daily News,* where the gifts by General Motors (South Africa), Mobil Oil (Botswana), Botswana Grain and Milling, the Lobatse and Gaborone Lions Clubs, the Gaborone Hotel, the Mine Labor Organization, prominent local businessmen, student groups at the university, church groups such as Trinity Ladies, and even neighboring African elites such as Chief Lobone of Pietersberg, South Africa, were all acknowledged, often in front-page articles.[26] Debilitated people thus became vehicles through which new forms of leadership, citizenship, charity, and care were publicly enacted. Those "made whole again" through artificial limbs stood as a testament to the promise of trickle-down capital and technology.[27]

Unlike direct gifts of blankets and food, rehabilitation activities within NGOs or orchestrated by the Ministry of Health were part of a larger trend toward health initiatives in Botswana modeled on those of international organizations. For example, the community-based rehabilitation program that Dikeledi worked for in the cases described in Chapter 1 followed a global initiative led by the World Health Organization. International health care practitioners and planners (including those working within ministries of health) saw health as a crucial element in a long-term strategy of western-modeled economic and social development. Bodily well-being via biomedical care was increasingly promoted as a universal right, and the presence of such care became a key indicator of a country's level of development, though the strategies by which health was sought changed over time as programs went in and out of fashion.

Programs for disabled persons centered on a set of practices termed "rehabilitation" that incorporated the development of physical, emotional, cognitive, and socioeconomic skills into a single paradigm aimed to make disabled persons more independent.[28] Simultaneously, a growing international disability rights movement included a handful of Tswana activists and pointed to the need to empower disabled persons to access rights and opportunities by removing social, political, and economic barriers. Rehabilitation programs promote this goal of individual autonomy as both universally desirable and a necessary foundation for citizenship and personhood. This autonomous self is, in turn, predicated upon an unquestioned biological model of an individually bounded body. As we saw in the previous chapter, the desirability of autonomous selfhood was highly contested within families and communities and Tswana notions of *madi, mowa, pelo,* and *popelo* (among other concepts and entities) pointed to the interconnectedness of bodies rather than their individuation. Thus, rehabilitation, which was embraced by many and resisted by many others, entered into a more complex intellectual, moral, and social world than its proponents (or even its recipients) might have wished.[29]

The Ministry of Health and NGOs such as the Red Cross—whose personnel often overlapped when NGO trainees eventually gained employment in government programs—encouraged movement away from the era of hidden disability with a new and overdetermined language of "modernity," "development," and "civilization." "Traditional practices" such as hiding disabled persons at the back of the compound, though they were only a few decades old at most, were held up as symbols of Tswana backwardness and primitivism.[30] International health care experts and agencies, including the World Health Or-

Community-based rehabilitation worker with a girl who is wearing a plaster cast after "straightening" surgery, in front of her house. Photo by Stephanie Cohen, 1998.

ganization, promoted the ethnocentric and unsubtantiated notion that disabled persons in less developed countries suffered greater abuse and neglect than their counterparts in developed countries. Development included the adoption of new forms of human rights discourse brought by international funders and expatriate health and social workers or brought home by Batswana on their return from training abroad.[31] This language merged with the old Christian paternalism to collapse and confuse the recent and ancient into the "traditional" and to condemn certain practices. The FWEs, social workers, teachers, and other community workers were then enlisted to bring the new models of progressive behavior to the people.

Mma Mosala, who later became an FWE in her home village of Mogoditshane, started volunteering for the Red Cross in 1970. Already active in her church, she began her work as a Setswana translator for a British Red Cross worker. "Mrs. Wilson was a member of the Red Cross and I was also a member of the Red Cross. Mrs. Wilson she didn't know Setswana so I was just interpreting for her. After that I decided that no, I have to help her because she has nobody to help her." The Red Cross and the Danish Medical aid agency Denmed subsequently trained Mma Mosala in 1971, and she soon became a regular employee, weighing children, giving lectures to parents, and so forth. It wasn't until 1973 that the Kweneng District government employed her as one of the first FWEs in the district. She remembered that soon after, in 1975, the government, prodded by a few key local activists, began sending workers to identify and attempt to help the disabled specifically.

> It seemed [at first glance] that disabilities at that time were not many—but they were many!! They were hiding them. Even if you go to a woman asking—she will say "I've got only 2 or 3 children—Then anyhow there's another one." Then you enquire—"Where is she? Why do you say there is another one but not finishing your sentence?" And she says "Well, this one is disabled." Then you go and report statistics—"I've got three children, but this one is disabled she needs something like clothes, food, but the other three, they are quite well." . . .
>
> But myself I would just go—I visited those who were disabled at that time. I didn't have any *mathata* [problem] with their parent.
>
> There was a president for the disabled, a man called Monageng. He was really pressing the government on the aid which they give to them, because there were no wheelchairs that time. They were not going to the *kgotla* meetings—disabled were not going to school. Now they are mixing in with the other people, they are pressing the government about this. He was also encouraging the people not to hide their *digole*, but to tell social workers and even the FWEs about them and their disabilities.[32]

By the mid-1970s, the Red Cross also offered vocational training to some disabled persons at their residential center in Tlokweng. Training and technical aides, however, offered possibilities that were still in many ways shaped by individual circumstances, as the contrast between the experiences of two women whom the Red Cross trained in dressmaking suggests. Matshediso, one of the most successful seamstresses in Diphaleng despite her congenital rickets and hearing problems, learned to sew at Tlokweng in the mid-1970s and received a government grant to purchase her first sewing machine.[33] By 1997, when I first met her, she was head of her own household, living in a nice cement house with electricity and television and training her own daughter, who also had rickets, to work in her sewing business, which was now equipped with multiple sewing machines and sergers. Matshediso was from an aristocratic family, had attended a few years of school, and was a regular at public events such as weddings, funerals, and parties. Perhaps her extensive social capital helped her negotiate the most lucrative sewing contracts—those for large orders of school uniforms, track suits, and wedding outfits.

She also tried to leverage Dikeledi's visits into economic assistance by asking her to purchase fabric and other supplies in town on her behalf. On more than one occasion she was quite irritated and standoffish when Dikeledi refused, suggesting that as a successful businesswoman, Matshediso should hire someone to do this work. Matshediso was not alone in such requests—many clients tried to draw social workers, rehabilitation technicians, FWEs, and other professional community workers into kinlike relations that implied certain obligations. These workers walked a fine line; they needed to generate some of the intimacy and authority of kin so that they could intervene in social relationships, but they wanted to promote the "independence" that contrasted with the weblike connections and obligations that consanguinity implied. So they honored some but denied many other requests their clients made—requests that kin, unlike friends, might be expected to honor.[34] These new forms of professionalized care depended in part on the ability of workers such as Dikeledi to open up and maintain a new social space for novel forms of caregiving.[35]

Matshediso's situation contrasted with that of Thuso Odirilwe, who lived in a neighboring ward and had post-polio paralysis in her legs. Thuso first met Matshediso at the sewing class at Tlokweng, despite the fact that the two women had grown up in the same village and were of similar age. Though Matshediso had attended school, visited friends and relatives, and attended social events, Thuso had been semi-confined or sheltered by her parents and brothers ever since her original illness. She was brought to the Red Cross clinic in 1974 with contractures in her legs, referred for surgery, and subsequently fitted with leg calipers and special shoes. She was able to walk for the first time since childhood (albeit with a walking frame, crutch, or other supports), and she was soon enrolled in the same dressmaking class as Matshediso. Thuso was not a household head and had no children to care for her.[36] In the second half of the 1980s, Thuso sold her dresses at a stall in the Gaborone marketplace. But she was forced to close shop when her stall was moved as the market expanded. The new location forced her to use several sets of steps, which she could not navigate. When her parents died in the early 1990s, her options for opening a dressmaking business in her own compound were limited by her brothers, who inherited the compound and resisted all of their sister's efforts attempts to be independent. Her business collapsed, leaving her reliant on government rations and occasional gifts from family (including a telephone paid for by her sister's children, who love her dearly), though she continues to make a little money doing mending and other odd sewing jobs.

The promise of food, clothing, and employment training encouraged many disabled adults and frail elderly persons to register with their local clinic or social welfare office as potential beneficiaries. The newly accessible medical care offered at village clinics and health care posts also brought debilitated villagers into public medical settings. Postnatal clinics began identifying disabled infants just as their impairments became apparent to their caregivers and followed up with home visits if the infant was not brought back for subsequent clinic trips. At the same time, the provision of technical aids such as wheelchairs, prosthetic limbs, walking frames, calipers, eyeglasses, and leg braces enabled many persons to lead a more active public life. Though many had never been "hidden at the back," their impairments had hindered their ability to move about their communities. Though the deep sand of Tswana villages impeded the easy movement of wheelchairs, such tools nonetheless enabled many to visit with neighbors, to sit in the *lolwapa* with the rest of the family, and to attend bars and parties and meetings.

Registration at local clinics and social welfare offices identified those disabled persons who qualified for destitute rations. The Botswana government divides destitute citizens into two types, those who were temporarily destitute (i.e., the able-bodied) are Type B, and those who were considered permanently destitute are Type A—the frail elderly and the permanently debilitated. For much of the 1980s, Botswana suffered a severe drought. The government responded with direct food transfers to groups they determined to be particularly vulnerable, including school-going children and pregnant and nursing women. These programs operated in addition to public-works programs, which employed many rural men and women. Ideally they "pay a wage that is comparable with agricultural incomes in a year of adequate rainfall and are aimed at maintaining rural household incomes as well as improving rural roads and infrastructure."[37] These programs have continued in the post-drought years and in 1995 were supplemented with an old-age pension scheme, which provides a monthly stipend of 100 pula (about US$22) to all Batswana age 65 and older.[38]

Since these new safety nets were put in place, older forms of sharing, including gifts of food, clothing, and labor to frail or debilitated neighbors, have continued to wane considerably.[39] Expectations within even immediate families have also shifted. While many younger Batswana continue to "build" for their parents before they do so for themselves and to regularly give struggling siblings gifts of food, cash, housing, and material goods, the norms for redistribution are changing. The days of returned migrants presenting parents with all of their wages and gifts for seniors to redistribute are clearly over. Rural relatives often complain bitterly of urban kin who do not visit enough or share their wages with less fortunate family members. These complaints persist even though many kin earn wages that barely enable subsistence in expensive urban locations. Some adults feel that the new old-age pension scheme releases them from their obligations to provide regular food, clothing, and monetary gifts to elderly parents, claiming that seniors now have their own money. Many elderly, in turn, complain of having to "beg from our children" for food and pocket change since their small pension inevitably runs out before the month's end.[40]

As some expectations have shifted away from older modes of sharing among neighbors and kin, a new questioning of governmental priorities has arisen as the state's role in caregiving has grown in the collective moral imagination. New possibilities have opened for care and community within the independent churches that have proliferated across the national landscape since the 1970s. Within these churches many people, particularly women, who feel scorned by relatives or geographically distanced from kin have forged new sites for community, cooperation, and love.[41] But such new efforts and opportunities do not negate the caring people expect from the state, expectations that have grown as the state has become increasingly wealthy from the diamonds that people understand to be collective national wealth. In a study of attitudes toward disability in the large central district village of Mahalapye in the late 1980s, Isaac Mazonde found that the majority of people surveyed (including able-bodied persons, disabled persons, and their relatives) believed that "the disabled should be the responsibility of *both* the government and their families."[42] Popular complaints about state welfare regularly discount the value of egalitarian programs that provide water, roads, and other public goods; usually, they concern equity in the distribution of rations or pensions as individual people or families worry that "we are not being given our share." This attitude is increasingly visible among some caretakers of disabled kin who suffer loss of harvest or wages to provide daily care, since if they hold assets such as livestock or have wage-earners in their immediate family (regardless of whether or not those wage-earners share with them) they do not qualify for rations given to Type A destitutes. Welfare programs in Botswana exist in tension with self-help opportunities. Microcredit schemes for sewing machines, food-for-work programs, vocational training, and other such programs are intended to create new pathways to self-development. Of these opportunities for self-making, education is clearly the most important nationally. Yet, education, like mining labor several decades earlier, has begun to forge new forms of fitness and achievement and, in the process, new types of disability.

Body, Mind, and Self-Making

In the post-Independence period, a new and growing emphasis on the benefits of education reconfigured the social meanings of various impairments. Though some key employers such as the military continued to evaluate physiques as the mines had long done, a new and growing emphasis on education in some ways has eclipsed "physical fitness" as a necessary route to economic opportunity and autonomous selfhood. Thus, some physically disabled persons saw newfound opportunities through education in the rapidly developing and entrepreneurial post-Independence society even as others with cognitive impairments found themselves with fewer options in an economic culture that prized literacy and Cambridge School Certificates. The former was the case with Isaac Mokwena, who went on to become both a university student and a leader in national disability advocate organizations. He is an incredibly dynamic and vibrant man who was willing and able to discuss his experiences with unusual clarity and depth. For this reason I will quote him at length below. Isaac was born in 1971 with a congenital malformation of one of his arms and grew up with only one functioning hand. His mother did not completely confine Isaac, but she shunned him and did not allow him to socialize with non-family members.

> Anyway if I can just see someone I know I can just dodge inside the house—if my mother can see me greeting I can be in trouble. So I mean I have to be [discrete], sometimes when the visitors come—cause, well maybe it's because my disability was bringing shame to them. So it's like I should be at the—well behind the homestead—behind the homestead—you know—at the back. So then no one should see me moving up and down and you know others would see me it should bring some shame on them. I mean I think that sometimes looking after the goats it was to keep someone from seeing me—from bringing shame on them. That I should not meet potential friends and that I should be there—that I should not be seen around. Because they used

to ask her and she would not like to answer—people can ask "What hap-pened to this guy's hand?" She will not like to answer that one—because she didn't know—she didn't like to spend time with me.

Despite her restrictions on his social activities, Isaac's mother nonetheless made sure her son contributed to the household maintenance. He weeded the com-pound and fetched water like his siblings, even though it meant he had to tie the wheelbarrow to his impaired hand with a leather cord to hold it steady. Isaac felt the frustrations of his life at that time acutely.

> I used to have to look after the goats and you know. Life was not that fair because even in the village some of the children were passing remarks on me and it was one of the things I didn't like—I was kind of an outcast, you see. Yeah, and I mean even my mother always rebuked me of my disability as if I was one kind of guy who decided to make myself like that. And I mean some of the complicated things that she asked me to do hey! There were so many things that she used to ask me to do—and then other people in the village used to sympathize with me and say "Hey! What kind of woman is this—can't she see that this guy is disabled?" And whenever someone would try to complain, instead of talking to that person she will end up thinking that I am the one who complained to that person, and she'll end up giving a spanking for no good reason.
>
> And so I used to take refuge behind the goats in the bush—it's like I was bored—and home was being in the village, so the best was just to spend time in the bush. But sometimes when I would be at school the other guys would be killing me. It would be less hateful compared with how it was at home—because at home it was a higher degree so that one was very worst and now it felt like it was better outside the home than inside the home. And I saw to cry even to the extent of trying to commit suicide one time. I mean I went out looking for a rope one time but then something told me that it would be difficult for me—What if your mother can find you still struggling to die there? . . . Yeah, and I even went looking for these herbs. These herbs they used to say that the sun will not go down before you when you eat it—but I didn't know it—I was out there hunting for it—eating every grass that I saw thinking that it was the one. I ate one grass and I looked at the sun happy saying, oh God here I come—I was so very disappointed seeing the sun go down while I was still breathing in and out.

But his mother, prodded by his older sister, did allow him to enroll in pri-mary school, where he excelled. Isaac was the only one in his village to earn a place in junior secondary school and so moved to a neighboring village to attend school there for two years. After that, however, his mother brought him back home.

> So I came back home and so I think my mother thought that I had done well at school—two terms were enough—it was a good qualification for me to look after the goats. So yes, I began now to be employed, unpaid, to look after goats—two years 1985 from 85 to 86, 87. Those two years I had to wake every morning to look after the goats and we were prosperous from them, they began to multiply with someone looking after them. And you know sometimes when I would be in the bush I would be thinking of my future. What is it that I am going to do? Sometimes I would think of being a soldier—just run away and go be a soldier—because those days they [the Botswana Defense Force] were taking Standard 7 graduates. So I understand that they needed people that are physically fit—so I am using one hand so it won't be allowed. Police, I should also forget—yeah, those were the potential employers by then—there was nothing I could do.

But his older sister eventually wore down his mother and convinced her to allow Isaac to return to school, though it meant starting again at Standard 7 because two years had elapsed.

> After those two years I was taken back to school by my sister—convinced her [my mother] I think she did. I started to go back to primary school—back 5 kilometers—so I had to wake up very early every morning to rush to school and it was good. I mean, I have come to my refuge—it was an exile. I mean school was an exile for me—it was very good—meeting students and realizing that particular potential of passing. . . . And now I began to have new friends and my character began to change again to take another shift. Because I had been so quiet at home—without talking to anybody—and so in the village they even are so shocked to see me talking. Because I mean they knew me as someone who was very quiet and now they knew me as someone able to greet somebody passing by.

After excelling in his Junior Certificate exams, Isaac won a coveted place in a senior secondary school up north, where he became a student leader and began to be interested in social work and community activism.

> Now talking not about my disability—they started to talk more about my capabilities now—saying "This guy, you know, he's a politician, you know." They didn't concentrate on who I am and how I look—they started to see a politician, you know, a guy who is not afraid to take chances. And I was so surprised—that most of the guys now when they talk about me—when they talk about me—they started to talk about how—forward, inquisitive, loqua-

cious I am. They don't talk about how disabled I am—how docile I am, they didn't see that—but it was because of the boredom I had and it was now. . . . Yes it was just like rebirth. And I could see that guys who are capable they are just sitting there. And then I think I was influenced by where I come from and then I learned later about guys who are studying social work. Most of the guys who are studying social work are the guys who you know their background it was horrible. And they begin to be—there's this aloneness that they have and they need someone to talk to, someone to share with, you know.[43]

Isaac's story, as he tells it, is perhaps exceptional in its extremes, but he was certainly not alone in finding new avenues for social and economic success through education. However, as a new emphasis on education became more central in the local meritocracy, other children who were "physically fit" but mentally impaired found themselves failing in the new academic climate. Connie Diphuti, who has five children with microcephalus, explained how school had remade her children's difference into disability.

Okay, well I noticed [their disability] with the heads, I noticed that immediately after birth, but at school I really noticed it because their minds are not like that of other students. Their performance is very, very, very, very bad, so I just noticed it at school. But it's like ah! they are not like other people. . . . I don't think I could have noticed it if it was in the olden days, because I think they could be plowing well, herding cattle like others are doing. So I don't think I could have noticed that they were disabled long ago.[44]

Between kids such as Isaac and the Diphuti boys, there were also children who had great cognitive skills but who had communicative impairments. Though special education classes became more prevalent in the 1990s, most schools lack them altogether and those facilities that do offer special education do not extend beyond early primary grades. In the late 1990s I met children with communicative problems, often the result of cerebral palsy, who, despite the ease with which they learned basic spelling and numeracy, would never have the opportunity to go farther with their studies. Needless to say, many were extremely frustrated by this fact.

Government and NGO programs that provided new opportunities for self-making shifted meanings of fitness and normality and repositioned disabled and destitute persons in a reconfiguring national politics of care. At the family and household level, however, opportunities for self-making among young women further strained the female economy of caregiving, fostering intergenerational struggles among women and making motherhood a central and contested trope in the moral imagination.

Motherhood and Mopakwane

The efforts of village workers such as Mma Mosala to identify disabled individuals and the new promise of biomedical care and welfare assistance for disabled children made *mopakwane* increasingly visible, at the same time that the expansion of education contributed to setting such children apart. The process of returning disabled children and other confined persons to public life was a gradual one that began in the major villages and large towns and spread outward from there. In the late 1980s, Isaac Mazonde found that many of the disabled children who lived in a small rural village in the central district (unlike, apparently, those in the large urban village of Mahalapye) were still shunned and kept in the *digotlo*. Young mothers in this village were still scorned for delivering babies with obvious impairments.[45] In roughly the same period, Benedicte Ingstad saw so little hiding in the large urban village of Molepolole that she was able to characterize the whole process of hiding as a myth.[46] The growing visibility of *mopakwane* coincided with continuing changes in women's social and economic lives, and *mopakwane* continued to be an important, though protean trope in the public evaluation of women.

While attention to female sexuality and polluted wombs continued (reinvigorated in the late 1990s by the AIDS epidemic), here I want to focus more on the dynamics between several generations of women who provided care for such children in the post-Independence period.[47] The study of cases of *mopakwane* in the 1980s and 1990s provides a window on women's intergenerational relationships in the new socioeconomic context of development. Since the debilitated subjects in these cases are children, we might reasonably expect that preexisting tensions between mothers-in-law and daughters-in-law would bear much of the brunt of stresses and contestation engendered by negotiations over responsibilities for disabled children, and indeed they often do. But here I am interested in focusing attention on mother-daughter relationships more than on relationships between in-laws, which are notoriously challenging. *Mopakwane* cases highlight a broader trend of ongoing reconfigurations in mother-daughter dynamics in an increasingly stressed postcolonial economy of daily care. This historically nurturing relationship has become a site where the tensions between the possibilities for autonomous selfhood and the responsibilities of social connectivity are played out as conflicts about care.

Marriage rates continued to decline in the post-Independence period, and many women now delay marriage until the second half of their 30s even though they have already become mothers. As a result, the centrality of mother-daughter relationships to the well-being of both parties have begun to extend much farther into the life course.[48] But these relationships are now absorbing some of the tensions over control of resources that historically characterized father/son and mother-in-law/daughter-in-law dynamics.

The dominance of the cash economy, especially following the massive drought of the 1980s, from which the agricultural sector never fully recovered, further shifted the balance between men and women and parents and children as contributors to the household economy. By 1991, migrant women outnumbered their male counterparts.[49] Though they were often employed in lower-paying occupations such as domestic service and drought relief,[50] younger working women were now able to exercise much more power in their relationships with mothers, grandmothers, and aunts (who by and large were farming, perhaps after having spent time themselves as labor migrants). Their wages were now central to household viability and growth, and young women were expected to regularly contribute money and gifts to their mothers. But many women lived in towns, where the temptations of growing consumerism and the high cost of living strained their low wages, and redistribution did not always occur as older women would have liked.

As daughters (and daughters-in-law) entered the wage economy en masse and began to play a central role in household income, they also entered increasing struggles about authority, expectations, and responsibilities within families and communities. As a result, older women's authority within the family has lessened, despite the fact that many more of these older women are household heads. These changes have combined to release older women somewhat from public responsibility for the moral behavior of their daughters. Instead, many older women have responded to their loss of status and power through attempts to exercise moral authority in a new way, through the image of the patient, tireless, and giving mother. By the early 1990s, diagnoses of *mopakwane* had become new arenas in which to express this moral authority because they contrasted the mothering practices of younger women and older women.[51]

Women who migrate to work in town often leave one or more of their children behind in their mothers' compounds. This arrangement is ideally mutually beneficial. Grandmothers provide care and direction which working mothers might not have time to offer, and the village where cousins, aunts, and uncles as well as grandparents live or visit is often seen as a preferable and safer setting for childhood than the city. Children provide company for the elderly and domestic assistance to older women, helping draw water and carry wood, performing small chores and errands, and perhaps looking after goats and other animals. Such relationships can be quite loving, with positive sentiment moving in both directions between grandchild and grandmother. Customarily, working mothers are expected to provide at least enough grain for their own children to eat and any cash required for school fees or the purchase of school uniforms and incidentals.

Unfortunately, the ideal does not always match the real. Very young children can provide little domestic help, and many older children are either overwhelmed with schoolwork and other responsibilities or simply try to shirk domestic obligations. Adults often discount the work children do perform by characterizing it as play.[52] In the late 1990s, it was not uncommon to see elderly women laboring to wash their own clothing—the clothing of any working children residing or visiting at home and the clothing of resident grandchildren—an exceedingly arduous task. Some working mothers provided irregular material support or failed to provide any. Given the very low wages that some of these women earn, this is understandable. In fact, it seems many urban employers in Botswana are reaping the rewards of grandmotherly labor; they are shifting the economic burden of the reproduction of the labor force back onto rural kin, just as the South African mining companies had done in earlier generations.

Many urban women forge relations of community and care in independent churches, relationships that sustain them in time of illness or unemployment. But when it comes to the kind of long-term care needed by a child with *mopakwane*, grandmothers are often the only possible refuge. Though they can provide a tremendous amount of love and companionship for their grandmothers, children with *mopakwane* are often unable to provide any domestic assistance, and many require near-constant care. Their status also reminds observers of all they imagine is wrong with "modern" youth, including disregard for Setswana customs such as postpartum sexual fidelity and responsible parenting.[53] From the perspective of many grandmothers, the situation of such children has become emblematic of all that is wrong with post-Independence society and the new economy.

As discussed in the previous chapter, any constellation of symptoms is open to interpretation in diagnosis. Diagnostic patterns tell us not only about the epidemiology of combinations of various symptoms but also about how history is made meaningful. In the late 1990s most Batswana, when asked, noted that beginning in the early 1980s the incidence of *mopakwane* began to rise sharply. This may be partially accounted for by an increase in the overall population and by the new obstetric and other biomedical services that allowed many children to survive disabling birth trauma and diseases such as meningitis. The reversal of confinement practices by the new cadre of primary health care workers such as Mma Mosala no doubt also contributed to local impressions of the rising incidence of the disease. But why is *mopakwane* assumed to be the cause of debilitating childhood impairments, and by whom, rather than other possible explanations such as "God's will," "just nature," "meningitis," or "oxygen deprivation during delivery"? I argue that many older women have promoted the diagnosis of *mopakwane* as part of a larger critique of post-

Independence social, cultural, and economic change, a critique these women direct against their juniors. Many younger women have responded to the critiques leveled against them with stories that deny the possibility of *mopakwane* and invoke biomedical explanations brought by rehabilitation workers or shift blame either to hospital and clinic staff or back onto older women with accusations of witchcraft. These opposing perspectives on causation are derived from redefinitions of what it means to be a responsible woman in Tswana society. There is very little overlap in these two sets of explanations, which points to the fractured and competing notions of morality in a world where acquisition of *madi* competes with mothering and nursing care for women's time.

Mopakwane has become a primary metaphor for older women in friction with their juniors and a way of analyzing broader social, cultural, and economic changes. Older women as a group concede that they have little power over their children's conduct any longer. It used to be that a daughter's behavior was a reflection of her mother's capacities to educate and discipline her children, thus linking the public moral images of mothers and daughters. Now, however, many older women react to a substantial loss of control over their daughters by attempting to invert public symbols so that a daughter's bad behavior is a sign of her mother's suffering and virtue. Older women in the 1990s regularly expressed their powerlessness to prevent what they saw as the chaotic unraveling of the social order. For example, older women's explanations of the breakdown of family hierarchies inevitably referred to that cornerstone of development, the expansion of western education. One person's self-making is another's loss of status.

> It is like since many children were sent to schools, because they thought that now they are more intelligent that their parents, so even when their parents would tell them—well, in traditional Setswana we are not supposed to do this. But maybe the child will say "But ah! at school we've been taught that you do this and this and you maybe you didn't go to school and this and me, well, I've gone to school, I know much more than you." They don't believe them [their parents] yet, it's just like that.[54]

> You try and speak to them [younger people] and they think you're mad. They are not listening. Yes, with my grandmother I'd be listening, but nowadays, ooh, they know too much. As soon as you tell them this, they say "Where did you see that? That is not written in the book." You cannot say anything to them. They are clever, you are stupid. Or when you live longer they think you are [a] *moloi* [witch]. They don't think that God is protecting you, they only think that you are a *moloi*. It's real, it's there. Many people are talking about each other that they are bewitching, but it's not direct, it's gossip, it's gossip.[55]

Caring for a disabled child can be a sign of a grandmother's moral strength. Many older women draw on Christianity to elevate themselves morally by describing their disabled charges as "gifts from God" (*mpho ya Modimo*). They position themselves as especially nurturing people, chosen by God to protect these "special children."

> They are a gift from God! I don't know exactly why it is like that, because no one really understands where a child is coming from, but only God knows, so I don't know if maybe God is [saying] 'Ah! But this one is patient, she will be patient enough to take care of this child."[56]

In each woman's view, God has chosen them specifically to save such children from the scorn and neglect of their parents, as Nanki's grandmother explained. God has recognized them as particularly patient (*pelotelele*, long-hearted) and righteous women and has bestowed special charges on them. This perspective is reinforced by that of their fellow church members, who come regularly to pray for the child and surround the child and her grandmother with love.

If the flip side of the immorality of mothers is the righteousness of grandmothers, this idiom also plays itself out in actions as well as words. Most grandmothers, even when they have help at their disposal, insist on caring for disabled children themselves, even though it might mean considerable personal sacrifice.[57] They state quite emphatically that they cannot leave the child in someone else's care because they can never be sure that another woman will really take care of the child properly, as they themselves would. Proper care, in this case, means not only bodily care but also loving sentiment and *bopelotelele* (patience), something that hired caregivers who might have negative aesthetic reactions to the physical manifestations of *mopakwane* might not have to offer. Sentiment and bodily well-being are deeply connected here. As Fred Klaits writes about nursing in the context of AIDS illnesses, "The feelings and actions of people who are 'caregivers' or 'nurses' to the sick have an immediate bearing on their welfare."[58] Grandmotherly love, in this case, is seen as the necessary corrective to a mother's scorn.

Many grandmothers support this view with stories of the poor care their grandchild received from its own mother. Their daughter's bad behavior may have begun with sexual license, but it soon reached into poor mothering and nursing. As we have seen, mothering of young children and nursing the sick are key elements of Tswana womanhood, and responsible, selfless, loving, patient, and compassionate handling of both roles are ideals woman are expected to strive toward. Thus, stories about *mopakwane* concern both a woman's sexuality and her lack of maternal sacrifice. Grandmothers who bring their disabled grandchildren for the new rehabilitation and medical services in health care facilities share stories about their daughters and their lack of responsibility.

Mma Phofuetsile, who cares for her granddaughter Maitseo, who suffers from *mopakwane,* explained the situation to me:

> My biggest problem is that I am not able to go see relatives as I used to do or even like if there are some funerals going on I can't go because of Maitseo. I can't leave Maitseo with some other people on their own—they won't do exactly what is supposed to be done. They won't take care of her as I could. . . . For this disability I am really convinced that it is because of you new generation not obeying the rules. I've been to Ramotswa [to the Bamalete Lutheran Hospital] and I have seen many of these children—some were even worse than this one and all they were grannies taking care of them—not with the moms. The moms were busy in town working, having fun! So I am really, well, I am saying when the condition gets worse like when we started seeing Maitseo she couldn't sit. You mothers you tend to get shy to be seen holding such a child—then you dump them with the grannies. Those other grannies in Ramotswa, they were actually saying to me that "Mine is better she will walk," but some were saying "Mine won't walk, it's worse," so we were discussing problems. I'm also thinking that if we hadn't collected the child to see me and maybe just left the child in Lobatse [where her mother lives] then maybe Maitseo would be dead. Because she was always lying—nobody taking care of her—flies all over—drooling saliva—and she didn't even have hair on the side and at the back because she was always lying on the side.[59]

Mma Selema's daughter no longer comes home. When one encounters her in the village or in town she says she cannot come home as she has no money to give to her son or to her mother. Yet her mother and sisters all agree that even visiting them would be a sign of responsibility, though she should be contributing money as well. Mma Selema's description of her daughter's behavior laments her daughter's refusal to care for her son with her mother.

> Ever since Botswana gained its Independence, it was in 1966, ever since then, well, it's like culture has changed. . . . You'll find that there are many disabled people these days unlike in the olden days because you'll find that unlike in the olden days at school children are taught about this sexuality. They are being taught that they can prevent themselves from being pregnant while they are still young, so you'll find that these children since they are taught at school they are just told that they are responsible enough to have children. So you'll find that a girl will have many boyfriends, which will end up causing problems. Because then maybe later on you'll find that those children can be disabled, like getting disabled from too many fathers. Like *mopakwane.* . . . With [my grandson] Wampona, well, the mother, while the mother was still pregnant she used to meet many men, so that was the

cause. . . . We don't share, the mother is not here, she just left the child with me the grandmother, she just left, so I am the one taking care of him. . . . In the olden days if there was a patient in the compound, the mother of that patient was the one what was taking care of that patient, and being assisted by the grandmothers and the sisters, unlike today, where you'll find that my daughter has left her child with me. My daughter could be taking care of the child with me assisting her.[60]

Occasionally daughters redeem themselves in their mother's eyes by taking exceptional care of a disabled child. Through such loving care, women can demonstrate to their mothers not only that they accept responsibility for their actions but also that they excel in the virtuous pursuits of mothering and nursing. In such instances, good care might suggest the kind of generosity of sentiment and conduct by a mother that can lead her own mother to doubt a *mopakwane* diagnosis. So not all older women blame their daughters' moral lapses for their grandchildren's disabilities. But those who do not must still construct narratives for active and repeated telling to protect their daughters from the gossip and scorn of neighbors, relatives, and fellow grandmothers they encounter in health care settings. They must respond in relation to the idiom of *mopakwane* by both providing another cause for the child's impairments and demonstrating how well their daughter cares for her child, since such care is evidence of benign sentiment and moral actions. Often these goals are intertwined in a single narrative. Thus, some women have heartbreaking stories about the failures of local clinic and hospital staff to provide proper care or the severe illness of a child, which surely caused his or her disability. They contrast this tragedy with evidence of their daughter's unusual sense of responsibility to her child, demonstrated in both economic and mothering behavior. Bantle's grandmother (the aunt of my friend Frances), who grew increasingly upset as she spoke about this, recounted the following story,

> They say to us, they say, "Hey your child, that child of yours must have slept with a man, that is why this child is like that," which is not true. She was born like that in the hospital, and I still believe it was the irresponsibility of the hospital that made her like that. Yes, it was problems when she was being born. The problem was we left here with, we took my daughter, she started labor pains so we went to the clinic, I think that they should have taken the temperature or done something to say that if we are going to the hospital right there, because instead of taking the temperature or doing anything like that, they said why do you come here? Why don't you just go straight to the hospital? We even said, "Why straight to the hospital, don't you need to check her first, then write something on the [patient's health] card so that I can give those people in Princess Marina [the hospital] your card?" They

said "No. Go." When we got there, it wasn't just normal, the temperature was so high, the blood pressure was like ooh! So they never took any care to take the blood pressure here. Then again at the hospital, the hospital was full, she was just put there to lie on the bed with a high temperature, nobody knew that she had a high temperature until she started having problems, then they started running around taking the blood pressure and it was ooh! They couldn't do anything, couldn't do the operation, couldn't do anything. The doctors even phoned and said either the child dies or the mother dies, so he didn't know which to die. So we kept praying with my mother here, just praying until the phone came and said no both the child and her are all right, but you know the child is supposed to cry when it comes out, but she couldn't cry you know she was being pulled out, the mother was like dead, she was being pulled there and the head, poor Bantle didn't even cry she only cried after five days. You know it's the fault of the hospital I tell you, the clinic and the hospital. . . . Sometimes she goes with the mother on weekends, to take her to Gaborone to see things like other normal children do. We try to treat her like other normal children. And the mother likes her so much. Some other kids they get ashamed of their children being like that, but with the mother here, Cindy, she likes Bantle so much, she takes her to town, goes with her everybody seeing her carrying her, other people don't do that, they are ashamed, but this one no.[61]

By contrast, among the poorest women, I found that grandmothers might accommodate a *mopakwane* diagnosis while still not condemning their daughters. One destitute grandmother who cared for her daughter's three children, including the middle child who had *mopakwane,* explained the tragedy of their circumstances. She and her daughter both understood that the younger woman's postnatal sexual activity might bring about a disability in the infant, but they had little choice because the father of the child would not accept the pregnancy and, unable to secure work, the mother needed to find a boyfriend to bring food into the house. They felt that the baby girl's *mopakwane* was the price they paid to eat.

Intergenerational tensions over *madi* and sexuality have also generated a new wave of post-Independence witchcraft accusations, primarily within families and directed against older women. As one friend commented cynically, "When you are a child your auntie is your best friend, but when you grow up, your auntie is a witch." Witchcraft accusations pervade society and are not limited to cases of disability, but they are the principle defense by younger women against seniors. They contest diagnoses of *mopakwane* with accusations of witchcraft. Peter Delius has described an explosion of witchcraft accusations directed against older women in Sekhukhuneland, South Africa, in the 1980s in the context of a similar historical background of crumbling local authority, intergenerational tensions and outright inversions of the generations, absent men, unruly women, and female-headed households, set in motion by the brutality of the South African political economy.[62] But in South Africa it was young men who accused older women, while in Botswana witchcraft accusations, embedded in conflict about the diagnosis of illness, were matters between women; they concerned nursing care and illness narratives that intertwined motherhood and children's health. Daughters seldom accuse their own mothers of witchcraft either directly or through innuendo and gossip. But their aunts, older women neighbors, the mothers of their boyfriends, and mothers-in-law are all potentially implicated in the climate of suspicion. In cases where accusations of *boloi* are used to counter diagnoses of *mopakwane*, the maternal grandmother is sometimes the instigator; she directs the accusation against the child's paternal grandmother (whether or not the parents are married) in an attempt to protect her own daughter, as was the case with Nanki and Lorato. Such accusations are often used to fend off rumors or outright accusations of *mopakwane*. In the cases where the maternal grandmother blames her own daughter for the child's disability, the mother usually deflects such counteraccusations onto other older women. This is understandable; the maternal grandmother is providing the child's daily care.

Older women describe these witchcraft allegations with great cynicism. They see them as part of a more generalized increase in suspicion of witchcraft directed against them as a group. In their descriptions of this environment of suspicion, they link accusations to the collapse of the previous system of collective dispute settlement and economic cooperation. Mma Mosala, the former FWE, described the situation of many of her friends who lack the expected economic support from daughters and the inability of paternal grandmothers and aunts to intervene in family disputes.

> Most of them [when trying to settle a family dispute] they go to, some do not even go to the small chief [headman]—they just go straight to the chief. Some see the social workers, some just ask their friends to help, but it is not the same as it was before. Then the chief was the only one, but he was doing well, because he called me and called my brother and called my sister and put us together and asked questions—and told us to go and live in peace, do not do that again. But it is not working now. It's not the same thing at all. If I am alone there I am just alone, and if the other one is there I am just alone. If I am rich and she is not, I don't care about her. No—I can just help myself and my rich friends. . . . These things changed after Independence, you see. Because even if I try to say to your child you are not being good by this, I not being not the mother, yeah—well if the child then tells the mother that

woman there was talking to me about this and this and this, the mother will call them here and she doesn't want me to help her child in any way . . . The witch doctor is going to say "No, that lady has done something to your baby—that's why your child is sick." Hey, I don't know, things are going up and down. . . . I don't know how today—what is happening these days. They just go—if they are in town—not even to their parents to go and see them. It changed after Independence. If you see these big houses and I think at my home there is only this thatched huts [not nice cement buildings]—no not even to see my parents.[63]

With their social and economic capital waning in the face of large-scale transformations around work and marriage, older women draw on and attempt to strengthen themselves morally as mothers in the new landscape of care. Through motherhood, they demonstrate their nurturing qualities of *bopelotelele* (long-heartedness, patience) and self-sacrifice. They compare these qualities with those of their daughters, who are renegotiating their own position in the female economy of care. The situations engendered by a diagnosis of *mopakwane* and women's descriptions of them provide a window onto older women's sense of the moral chaos that has accompanied the new socioeconomic order and onto younger women's predicaments as they balanced the need to earn cash and the need to provide care. They help us call into question the basic assumptions of "development" planners about women's cooperation and caring within families. They also remind us that as migrant labor has expanded to encompass both genders, intergenerational tensions, long recognized among fathers and sons, have now emerged in the historically nurturing relationships of mothers and daughters.

Longing for the Queen of England: Postcolonial Care and the Epidemiological Transition

In this final section we will explore how people make sense of recent changes in the culture and perceived efficacy of professional biomedicine and *bongaka*. It is an irony that, in part, the successes of postcolonial development have thrown the nature of care into doubt by fostering epidemiological transitions. As infectious disease and malnutrition declined, debility became more and more a central problem of bodily and social life, exposing the limits of both biomedicine and *bongaka* and calling into question the nature of recent changes in both therapeutic systems. In the post-Independence period, government medicine expanded and eclipsed mission medicine at the same time that it became increasingly impersonal and bureaucratized, while *bongaka* and the work of the growing body of prophet healers became more commodified. Many

Three generations: grandmother, daughter, grandchild. Photographer unknown, n.d. Reproduced from London Missionary Society/Council for World Mission Archives.

people in Botswana discuss both of these developments in terms of a decline in the efficacy and ethos of care. This too is ironic; the national health care system is one of the best on the African continent. Equally ironic is the historical periodization deployed in popular critiques. Many Batswana with whom I spoke in the late 1990s dated the decline in medical care as starting with Independence, when biomedicine was just beginning to expand coverage and services and when the practice of *bongaka* was no longer forced underground.[64]

During the late 1950s, the critiques of older people of this stated decline in medical care were often expressed through the construction of a nostalgic past in which people long for the days of Mma Mosadinyana, or the Queen of England, an interesting rhetorical move. While older people were more given to nostalgia and critique of "modern" ways in general, their complaints were strongly echoed by many younger people, whose criticisms coexisted with a rhetoric of progress. I heard no one challenge these claims about the changing ethos and culture of professional care made by their seniors. Even many lower-level health workers (who are trained in the rudiments of biomedicine) did not refute these criticisms as they tried to cajole older patients into a visit to the clinic or hospital. Let me emphasize that Batswana, whose country is surrounded by what were until recently notoriously racist and repressive colonial states, and who take great pride in their self-governance, wax nostalgic about the colonial era as a rhetorical device—one that encompasses shifts in civic life, in the locus of governance (from ward, village, and *morafe* to district and nation), and in the culture of social interactions. It is, perhaps, because of the clear consolidation of their self-rule that people are able to refer to colonialism in such a positive way.

Popular critiques shadow much international praise of the Botswana health service. Throughout the late 1980s and early 1990s international health experts viewed Botswana's health care system as a model of development success in Africa.[65] Progress in basic health indicators such as the infant mortality rate and life expectancy accompanied a tremendous improvement in access to biomedical care. This was evidenced by such factors as a change in nurse-to-patient ratios from 1 nurse per 2,564 persons in 1968 to 1 nurse per 462 patients in 1996 and an expansion of the number of clinics from 16 in 1968 to 209 in 1996.[66] The situation in the late 1990s represented a great departure from conditions in Botswana at Independence in 1966.

Despite the statistically proven efficacy and the rational modeling of the new health care and welfare systems, many Batswana with whom I spoke consistently expressed a diametrically opposite view of the historical trajectory of health care development than their international and government counterparts. Part of the reason for this contrasting perspective was certainly the AIDS epidemic, which has thrown this recent history into a new light. But this is not the entire reason. In many ways, the epidemic has highlighted and intensified a set of changes in the ethos and performance of care that people with debilitated bodies and their loved ones were already experiencing in their quest for therapy and palliation.[67] Situating these critiques historically helps illuminate how questions of efficacy, cost, and culture feed into one another in contemporary experiences of both biomedical and Tswana medical care.

Though complaints have plagued postcolonial biomedical care from the outset, they were previously tempered by the spirit of self-help and community-based development that characterized the international primary health care initiative of the 1970s and by enthusiasm for the expansion of biomedicine into areas that had previously lacked such services. In the early 1970s, construction of clinics, sanitation programs, and vaccination programs, and Red Cross health education campaigns were relatively novel endeavors, and they produced palpable results. Former health care workers from this period report a pervasive feeling of optimism about the prospects for health care in an independent Botswana, though it was difficult to pin laypersons down about possible changes in their perspectives on postcolonial development.[68]

Some of the complaints about professional biomedical care at the time centered on ensuring equity of access as the national health care system expanded; it was difficult for the government to build clinics fast enough to keep pace with community desires.[69] Similarly, shortages of nurses and doctors in the early 1970s contributed to vigorous critiques about the culture of care. Letters to the newspaper echoed complaints voiced in community meetings and even in Parliament about the length of waiting times at clinics and hospitals and questioned why doctors would not see patients in the evenings or on holidays.[70] The permanent secretary in the Ministry of Health "cautioned doctors in Botswana against taking a 'don't care' attitude towards the public." The Kanye district commissioner told graduating nursing students that they "should exercise a big amount of tolerance, patience, and sympathy in discharging their duties."[71] As the number of clinics and hospitals expanded over time, such complaints began to ease. Though many people retained the sense that many of the newly hired biomedical doctors and nurses were detached or haughty (a stereotype of service workers in businesses or government offices), improvements in general health ameliorated the virulence of such critiques.

Family welfare educators became the local face of the health care system, buffering the divide between patients and doctors or patients and nurses and connecting members of the local community to the clinic. Beginning in 1969 the Botswana government, supported by funds from UNICEF and the International Planned Parenthood Association, began training women with primary school education to become family welfare educators. After completing an eleven-week training course (which was supplemented annually with a three-week refresher program), these newly trained women dressed in government uniforms began providing basic nursing services, first aid, health education, and clinic referrals to people through home visits in villages where clinics were established.[72] As we have seen, visiting was and is a central aspect of village culture and part of the continual reaffirmation of personhood and community cohesion. Home nursing visits build on popular images of lay nursing as an extension of women's essential nurturing character and on the decades-long initiatives of church women who brought Christian love to the sick and the frail through their visits. So these services packaged new types of knowledge in familiar ways and were well received and easily fit into the broader social life of neighborhoods. As Mma Mosala remembers:

> In the beginning people were listening, you see. People were—when we held talks people were listening—they were trying to listen. We were asking them to clean up their compound and dig a hole and put the rubbish inside. We helped them, going into the village to clean up their children, to give them nutrition. Now things are going back again—you see the trash is scattered

everywhere, I don't know—things are going back now—but now at least some know that if the child is having diarrhea [the mother] knows how to mix some water with salt and sugar—and if they've got a fever—knows how to reduce the fever by using a warm rag—some are still doing it. Some goes to the witch-doctors and puts something on the head.[73]

By the 1990s, things had changed. Though family welfare educators still made as many home visits as they could manage, many clinics had become too busy to allow for as much home visiting as previously. Instead, the family welfare educators and nursing staff were more and more busy staffing the clinics, performing bureaucratic tasks, and organizing community events such as Sanitation Day, TB Awareness Day, or the Day of the Disabled.[74] The new clinic-based medical culture had become more public but less social. Home visits incorporated key family members in nursing care. But relatives who have work to do at home are often unable to accompany patients to the clinic, who now have to walk there and wait their turn for care.[75] Health workers at the clinic spend less time exchanging greetings and news with patients than when they visit them at home; they also spend less time praying and singing religious songs—a common practice among family welfare educators since patients and their relatives are often fellow church members. The clinic is more efficient, but without such cultural expressions of community and personhood and in such an obviously public setting, it is harder for health care workers to ask about difficult social and physical circumstances that a visit to a compound might make obvious.

Most people understood and talked about the culture of hospital- and clinic-based nursing as a set of practices distinct from the kinds of care female relatives provided. But as I discussed in the cases of Matshediso the dressmaker and Dikeledi the rehabilitation technician, as community-based health workers left institutions and entered homes, they blurred the lines between family and health professional. This is especially true of family welfare educators, since they are working in their home communities. Visiting helps establish their services as genuine care. In most visits I went on with a family welfare educator, the patient and their relatives would either already know the educator or as part of the process of greetings would begin to locate the educator in an ever-expanding web of kin until she was made familiar, perhaps even having been identified as a relative of some sort. This was brought home to me one day when Dikeledi, myself, and Lady and Bome, two family welfare educators we worked with, were visiting a home to help with an elderly woman in the family who was becoming increasingly frail. It was a household to which we had been several times, as there were other debilitated persons there who also benefited from Dikeledi's assistance. Since they had not been following the advice of our health team, Dikeledi began joking with the woman who headed the house, asking her, "Do you know why we come here to visit you?" She replied in all seriousness, "Well, with you and the white lady [me] we are not sure, though we do appreciate your visits, especially coming all the way from Mogoditshane, but Bome and Lady, they come because they are our relatives and they care about us."

Sedipe, one of the oldest women in Diphaleng, linked the expansion of institutions with the decline in efficacy and visits from family welfare educators (often called nurses by villagers).

> Long ago . . . we didn't have hospitals. But after Independence, hospitals were built and now they are no longer working, because the daily treatment we are getting from the hospitals is not offering any help. Nurses are no longer visiting us in our compounds.[76]

As the clinics and particularly the referral hospitals began to serve ever-larger numbers of people, they became more impersonal and bureaucratic in their culture. People talked about them as anonymous institutions that were less localized and therefore less participatory and interactive; this discourse was very similar to what people said about the changes in politics since Independence. Thus people invoked the trope of Mma Mosadinyana (the Queen of England), who reigned during a time of strong local politics, to contrast an older culture of medical care with the current one.

Peter Mokwena, an 81-year-old man, explained how medical care reflected the new post-Independence culture:

> In my opinion, since this country gained its independence things are messed up. Ever since this country gained its independence they didn't want to rule the country the way that Mma Mosadinyana [the queen] did. This country Botswana they didn't want to follow Mmamosadinyana's leadership, they wanted to follow their own since they got independence. From there you'll find that all this politics they are the ones which are leading to the extent that—okay, many schools are being built, hospitals are being built, but those hospitals they are just buildings just standing there, but what are they standing for? Only that people can go and be put inside. Batswana are spending much money building, trying to do all kinds of building, but without taking care of themselves, not caring for other people, without taking care of those who are poor and who are in need, they are just building all these things, but I think that *Modimo* doesn't like these things. That's why many of these buildings—the hospitals and the schools—but more especially the hospitals, they are just there for people to go inside, they are not there for anything else. . . . So what is the cause behind those things we will never know, but

according to me it's just that these politics they have broken culture here. People they are no longer following culture. . . . But ah, with these hospitals they were just like schools because you find that they will be a building just standing there. But that hospital it has no mouth to say something or to communicate with Modimo, nor no ears, it's just a building standing there. And these people they are using a lot of money to build all these things.[77]

As Rra Mokwena's critique shows, people saw spiritual contextualization as essential to the ability to accurately diagnose and treat their illnesses. Hospitals had no ears to hear and no mouth to speak or communicate with God. This contrasted sharply with *bongaka,* where doctors spoke to their patients and then to ancestors (*badimo*) and *Modimo* when diagnosing illness.[78] In Tswana therapeutics, the actual organic substances doctors used for medicines were empowered for healing through processes that both physically and spiritually transformed medicines through communication with *Modimo* and the ancestors. In the colonial period, people carried these fundamental understandings of medicine with them to encounters with medical missionaries, where they were transformed somewhat by the new semantics of missionary medicine but nonetheless made sense in terms of basic Tswana medical ontology. Missionary doctors and nurses regularly prayed with their patients, "communicated with *Modimo*" during treatment. Patients with whom I spoke perceived this as an equally (if not more) significant aspect of the treatment they received from missionaries than the actual medicines and surgical techniques doctors employed.[79] But some of the missions, under financial pressure, began handing over their hospitals and clinics to the government in the 1970s and 1980s and others were forced to staff their institutions with non-missionary doctors, and Christianity increasingly took a back seat to science.[80]

Rra Mokwena's critique also suggests that the ethos of care is very much in doubt. The government health service was no longer building up persons through care, it was now just building warehouses for the sick. Complaints about inconsiderate and uncaring nursing staff dominated talk in the late 1990s and proved to be great disincentives for many who refused to go to the hospital, no matter how much pain and discomfort they felt. As the AIDS epidemic and the rate of chronic illnesses have merged, hospitals have become overwhelmed and palliative care has suffered. The sentiments of community-based caregivers have a direct relationship with how patients perceive the efficacy of care and the abilities of patients to heal, but to many people, hospitals seemed like places devoid of healing sentiment and practice.

As chronic and debilitating illnesses became central problems, the issues of efficacy and care became intertwined. More and more people found that biomedical practitioners could not cure them of their illnesses, which threw the ultimate strength of the therapeutic system into question. Patients with cancer or diabetes or hypertension or arthritis or multiple sclerosis or a host of other problems questioned biomedical efficacy in terms of diagnosis and cure, as did their family members. They felt that biomedical practitioners were unable to determine or fix the root causes of ill health. Yet many also recognized that biomedicine could alleviate symptoms, and biomedicine became more important in the domain of palliative care, where the ethos and culture of caring was paramount.

The growing dominance of chronic illnesses and the desire for palliation lie behind the statistics of such "successes" as greater attendance at clinics and hospitals. For many people in Botswana, the diagnostic and curative capacity of biomedicine is sharply in doubt, and they argue that they attend clinics because they can no longer afford the escalating fees that Tswana doctors charge.[81] Their decision to go to the clinic or even the hospital is essentially a decision to seek palliation, though they may still hope for cure. When they try to describe the inefficacy of biomedicine, many people refer to the mental hospital, the cycle of confinement, and the failure to cure that they witness among relatives and neighbors.[82] Here is a typical description.

> I don't think that these people who are mentally sick, they are not offered enough help at the mental hospital, because you'll find someone will be going to mental hospital in January, then February, March, April he or she will be coming back, then after two months he or she will be going back to hospital again. So these people they are only being given tablets. They are not being helped. Okay, the only thing they are being given there is some tablets just for temporary, and that one, okay, fine, it's true, they are just going and coming back, and going and coming back, so I don't think that these people they are getting enough care from those hospitals.[83]

Batswana, of course, are not alone in these critiques. Many people in developed countries express similar frustrations with biomedical management of chronic illnesses. But in Botswana, the situation is further exacerbated by the vertical structure of the national health system in which great disparities in knowledge, technology, and supplies exist between institutional tiers. The cycle of managing symptoms through biomedical care is laborious and inconsistent in this system. The uneven supply of pharmaceuticals and other necessary goods in clinics shape popular experiences of sophisticated biomedical procedures. For example, a person who has been given a colostomy at the central hospital during emergency surgery after a serious accident might find that the disposable supplies they need to manage their condition are unavailable at their local clinic for weeks at a time, confining them to their home and causing infections. Diabetics might struggle to maintain a steady supply of insulin and syringes, and diabetic amputees might wait for a year or more for a prosthesis, only to find that it doesn't fit properly.[84] A poorly fitted prosthesis might cause sores on the patient's stump that leads to infection and another amputation.

Such difficulties often cause people to try a middle path in which they move back and forth between the biomedical and Tswana health systems, so that they become trapped between competing disease interpretations. For example, Boitumelo Kereke began having seizures when she was two and a half. Her grandmother, Mma Lekile, took her through the clinic system in Diphaleng until she was referred to the central hospital in Gaborone, where she was diagnosed with epilepsy. The doctor there prescribed Phenobarbital. Mma Lekile began giving it to Boitumelo but noticed that she was getting extremely sluggish, not acting like the child she knew. She had to work her way back through the clinic system to the referral hospital to have the dose adjusted. The medication controls Boitumelo's seizures but has not cured her of the disease. After several years' experience with biomedical management of her granddaughter's epilepsy, Mma Lekile stopped giving Boitumelo the Phenobarbital. She explained her decision to me this way:

> I even took her to the clinic so they are giving her some pills, but the reason why I took her to the *ngaka* is that sometimes we would take her to the clinic and find that there were no pills there, then I would take her to Mogoditshane and even Gaborone and still sometimes find that there were no pills there. So then I thought maybe if I can take her to the *ngaka* maybe it can help me somehow. . . . The *ngaka* was saying that Boitumelo should not be injected, because the moment she would be injected the blood would run throughout the body to the head. Boitumelo used to be very, very, very fat. I don't really know why she has lost it but I thought that maybe the pills we were getting her from the clinic maybe they were making her to lose her body.[85]

Tswana medical practitioners in these cases often directly pathologize foreign medical technologies. As the technologies become increasingly complex (a benefit of the steady modernization of health services), they also become increasingly mysterious. Mmamosweu Koloi, a woman from a very poor household in Diphaleng, took her 1-year-old grandchild, who was failing to thrive, to a *ngaka*. He could only point to a topical problem of skin lesions but did not diagnose any primary cause for the child's impairments. Since she could not accept that his difficulties were "just nature"—meaning that there was no identifiable disease or culprit—she deduced that the equipment to assist with premature births at the hospital must be to blame.

The problem was just at the hospital. We took the child to the *dingaka,* but there was just nothing so it means that the problem was just at the hospital. Well, I will try to explain how this came about. We took the child to the *dingaka,* only the *dingaka,* not the prophets. So they just told us that this— they diagnosed these sores on the chest. During the time of birth they were using something to remove him from the mother's womb and they were saying that at the time of birth he was like that [she points to an empty can of beans with a jet-black label]. Then his color changed. So the nurses took him and put him in a container with a light inside.[86]

So why do so many sick people go to biomedical institutions at all? Why don't they visit only *dingaka* and prophet healers? Palliation, as I suggested, is one key reason. Analgesics, clean bandages, anti-itch creams, antacids, and the like are appreciated by those who leave the clinic with such items. For caregivers with very sick relatives, a very scary and emotionally fraught situation, even help that temporarily calms symptoms rather than cures problems is valuable. Another key reason is cost. Clinic visits, medications, and hospital stays are free for many people (including registered destitutes and children), and others incur only a nominal charge. By contrast, *bongaka* can be tremendously expensive. Since Independence, *dingaka* and many healing prophets have steadily increased their rates. *Dingaka* have also changed the payment schedule. Where previously doctors had been paid at the end of each set of practices—divination, protective strengthening of property and persons, and *successful* cure—after Independence, they began demanding payment before services were rendered and medicines were dispensed.[87] This makes *bongaka* particularly difficult for the chronically ill to access. As they move from *ngaka* to *ngaka* seeking a cure or a diagnosis they have confidence in, they can accrue enormous medical bills. For example, Nanki's parents accepted that their daughter was *bogole* only after their assets were exhausted and they were deeply in debt to relatives. Many other people can't afford *bongaka* at all.[88] Those who incur debt to *dingaka* live with the persistent fear that the doctor will tire of waiting for his money and turn to sorcery or other means of retribution.

Rising prices and changes in payment schemes have also cast doubt on the efficacy of *bongaka.* *Dignaka* were already ambiguous figures, but the money now at stake has further drawn charlatans and other people with questionable motives into the profession.[89] As Rra Mokwena did, many often discuss rising prices and weakening care as evidence of a post-Independence capitalism in which many people strive for money at the expense of other values that stress community, family, and spiritual cooperation and respect.[90] Because people doubt the efficacy of both *bongaka* and biomedicine, they often try to hedge their bets by visiting both *dingaka* and clinics.[91] Kago's mother, who we met in Chapter 1, explained why she sought both types of medical services as well as healing prophecy for Kago, even though in her youth she relied exclusively on *bongaka*.

> Today we are using both of them, the *dingaka* and the prophets as well as going to the clinics. The *dingaka* these days they are not as strong like those of the olden days. . . . The reason they are not strong is maybe because they like *madi*. Because those in the olden days they were using maybe 50 thebe, maybe 1 pula so those [prices] but nowadays those *dingaka* they are just looking for money.[92]

That Batswana unite biomedicine and *bongaka* to some extent within a discourse that expresses dissatisfaction with the possibilities for care in the context of post-Independence capitalism and "development" is evidence of the continuing entanglement of these two systems with one another. There have long been people who sought both *bongaka* and biomedical services; one example is the miners of the twentieth century who visited *dingaka* to strengthen them to pass the medical exams of the mining company. But now there is also a two-way street; some people who express distrust in Tswana medicine nonetheless seek *bongaka* because they are fed up with clinic system, and some people who are staunch believers in *bongaka* and are cynical about biomedicine wind up at clinics because of rising prices and a growing distrust of modern *dingaka*. In the end, both clinics and *dingaka* are flourishing, with patients lining up to wait for care. Yet high attendance is not a testimony to increased faith in either therapeutic system; rather, it is evidence of people's lowered expectations for the possibilities of professional care in the plural medical climate of contemporary Botswana.

The period of rapid postcolonial development impacted both the incidence and the experiences of debility in southeastern Botswana. It was a period when many people began to see debility itself, both in terms of disability per se and chronic illness, as emblematic of deeper historical changes in community and personhood. "This land of disability" as Dikeledi once called it, is in popular reckoning the by-product of a series of closely linked transformations in social and economic life that have left many reeling and disoriented as explanatory models, welfare systems, and social discourse (both behavioral and verbal) become increasingly fragmented, plural, and divergent. In the end, the moral imagination and the historical imagination in Botswana have much overlap. *Gompieno* (today) is a time of physical and emotional peril, where debility has become commonplace and overwhelming and where bodies, persons, environments, and communities demonstrate both national promise and cultural disarray. The simultaneous celebration of development and mourning for the loss of older institutions and relationships are both evidence in the reconfiguring dynamics of debility and care. Local historical analysis found in critiques of both lay and professional health care has given us one means for glimpsing the impact of development and social change, epidemiology and misfortune, and the collective loss of locally determined health and well-being.

We also see in the postcolonial period the converging of the various systems whose history we have traced—the community-based public health system, *bongaka*, biomedicine, and lay nursing care—into a larger discursive rubric of a shifting politics of care. To some, new possibilities for care by the state, civic leaders, NGOs, and local churches open opportunities for self-making and the experience of healing sentiment. To many others, all of these systems (public healing, *bongaka*, biomedicine, lay nursing) seem to be in simultaneous disarray. The world appears to be overwhelmed with *madi* that no longer flows properly through the social arteries and capillaries of family and community. Instead, it collects in toxic quantities in narrowly defined persons, leading to pollution of the social body and the individuals who constitute it.

Conclusion

O se tshege o oleng, mareledi a sale pele.
> —Setswana proverb: Do not laugh at the fallen; there are slippery places ahead.

Lorato lo roba ditokololo.
> —Setswana proverb: Love paralyzes the joints.

This history of debility has drawn together changes in human bodies with shifting ideas and practices of care and personhood. Debility illuminates how fundamental social, moral, and biological dynamics are grounded in experience as people struggle to marshal care and rework meanings and lives within and around bodies that are somehow impaired or different. The relationships between bodies and persons, history and meaning-making are highlighted and transformed in the context of debility.

I have tried to show how processes that began decades earlier both congealed and shifted in southeastern Bechuanaland from the 1930s onward. During and after the Depression, labor migration and colonial medicine combined to remake the meanings of aging and able-bodiedness. Changing definitions of fitness forged by industry and mission doctors fostered intergenerational tensions as fathers became increasingly reliant on their sons for access to powerful *madi,* while the demise of initiation and labor migration empowered young men's moves toward autonomy. For southeastern Batswana, the priorities of industrial capital drained the productive and procreative strength of their communities and replaced physical vitality with polluted *madi,* disordered aging, and increasing poverty.

By the postwar period, the ways in which people cared for one another underwent significant changes. The spiritual weakening of the chiefship, the movement of *bongaka* from the core of public health into a diffuse system of individualized therapeutics, and an emerging ethos of individualism undermined the public health system and spurred transformations in family and community institutions. Tswana diagnostic categories expanded or shifted to incorporate new epidemiological realities, and *bongaka* and biomedicine became further entangled with one another, a process facilitated by the difficulties of translating between Setswana and English. In a climate of increasing autonomy and sexual suspicion and amid deep gender differences in access to political and economic capital, the pathologization of wombs in the popular imagination linked changes in the diagnosis of illness to transformations in women's caregiving and domestic spaces. In the context of these societal pressures, some women and their families began hiding debilitated persons in their compounds, infusing secrecy and shame into impaired bodies and relationships and contributing to the image of uteruses as ambiguous entities. Other women crafted new forms of caregiving through their Christian activities.

After Independence, as young women began migrating for work in large numbers, local welfare systems became strained beyond their capacity. The decline and delay in marriage and young women's new opportunities for self-making and *madi* production promoted new intergenerational tensions between women over the ethos and practices of motherhood and care. Into the shifting arena of care came new relationships and institutions, including those whose international programs unearthed the hidden and offered limited assistance and opportunities to some of the people caught in fraying systems of care and cooperation. During this time of rapid postcolonial development, many people saw debility as evidence of deeper historical changes in social life and personhood. Experiences of debility were profoundly shaped by intrafamilial debate and negotiation as people struggled to make sense of new forms of care and suffering.

By focusing on debility, we have learned about key issues in African health and medicine that are not well understood. First, the tremendous importance of familial caregiving becomes clear. While most historical scholarship on African health focuses on some form of professional medicine or spirit-possession cults or other organized forms of healing, most people receive the bulk of their care at home from their wives, mothers, sisters, and daughters. Familial care needs to be better historicized and acknowledged as operating within the shifting politics of gender, age, family, and community. Similarly, we are reminded yet again that even "traditional" medicine has a complex intellectual, political, and economic history, one that bears closer examination. In short, we need to do the legwork necessary to grant African therapeutics the intellectual, economic, and political dynamism of other, better understood healing traditions.[1] This history has tried to contribute a small piece to that larger project.

Through debility we can also see the centrality of bodily experience to the moral imagination. Communities which continually fractured and reconfigured over the course of the twentieth century in the context of broader historical transformations struggled to cope with increasingly chronic experiences of physical misfortune and suffering and to provide the redemptive possibilities of care. At the same time, instances of debility and care both publicly and privately crystallized as tropes in the Tswana collective moral imagination, serving as stark reminders of the physical dangers of moral uncertainty and reaffirming the long-recognized fact that the human body does not exist as somehow separate or abstracted from the complex lives of persons.

The moral imagination brought historical analysis and memories to the experiential crises of patients and caregivers in southeastern Botswana as chronic suffering exposed the relationship between ongoing changes in personhood and in the plural medical system. *Bongaka* probed the inner person and exposed links between self and the greater world, but *bongaka* became increasingly dysfunctional as colonial policies drove it underground and as postcolonial capital infused the Tswana medical profession with profit motives. Public healing drew on the socially hierarchical aspects of personhood to try to tame the seasons, heal the land, and strengthen and protect the community, but public healing too was undermined by conversions to Christianity, the outmigration of male (and later female) laborers, and the atomization of individual interests. It would be replaced by a western-derived but internationally framed public health, whose focus on technological fixes and trickle-down philanthropy fostered changes in bodies and new public relationships of caregiving that reinforced the tensions between the autonomous self and the social self. Women's nursing care nurtured and healed the patient in the maternal world of home and hearth, yet those womblike homes became suspect in the context of new forms of sexuality and personal autonomy. At the same time, the female economy of caregiving grew increasingly stressed as epidemiological changes merged with the rise of female labor migration. Many people created new opportunities for care and community through their churches, yet changes in healing and personhood in the face of larger historical transformations manifested themselves in the fraught experiences of many patients. They and their families and friends and neighbors attempted to make sense of the contradictions of health and disease, pain and suffering, fate and promise by morally imagining a different set of possibilities. These possibilities drew on historical memory as they reknit unraveling communities, families, and persons into a nostalgic wholeness.

Meanwhile, the biomedical system, which slowly penetrated the local landscape, provided an unsatisfactory or only partial solution to the dilemmas of changing illness experiences even as biomedicine was embroiled in a larger system which generated some of these very changes. Biomedicine commodified robust, male Tswana bodies and economically marginalized older people, women, and the debilitated. It posited an individual self whose interior could be known, probed, quantified, and exposed. It also constructed a social self that did not match up with broader realities, positing a person who was embedded in the community by virtue of his or her individual body as a carrier of disease. The relatively rigid boundaries of the self that underpinned first colonial and later postcolonial medicine prevented that therapeutic system from fully addressing the needs of Tswana patients, whose selves were socially permeable, even as the hard-won successes of postcolonial biomedicine helped spawn a rapid epidemiological transition.

HIV/AIDS

Today, debility and seemingly everything else related to health and bodies in Southern Africa is overshadowed by HIV/AIDS. What we have learned here may help us to better understand some aspects of the current AIDS epidemic. Indeed, the epidemic of HIV/AIDS in Botswana is not separable from this history of debility. Instead, it is an integral part of this story of entangled therapeutics, evolving diagnostic frameworks, negotiated illness experiences and meanings, intergenerational tensions, cyclical migrations, shifting public health paradigms, polluted *madi,* pathologized and ambiguous wombs, an increasingly stressed domestic economy of care, and a flourishing moral imagination.

I came to this work, like many people, thinking of HIV as a sexually transmitted infection and of AIDS as a deadly disease. I was, of course, correct. The rhetoric in the newspapers, on the radio, on the billboards in Gaborone, and among AIDS-industry personnel in Botswana only reinforced my sense of things. So did the growing number of funerals and absent persons. The epidemic escalated during the years of my research. I would return to work after several months away to learn from Dikeledi or other friends that the waitress in the cafe where we sometimes took lunch was "late" or that a co-worker or friend was now in the hospital struggling for her life or that another friend now was caring for her late sister's children and was worried about her brother's repeated illnesses. And as I accompanied Dikeledi on her work, we saw more and more people whose circumstances belied the dominant model of the epidemic: men with unexplained bouts of dementia, bedridden women with diarrhea who grew steadily thinner, young men who returned from the mines or the city no longer able to work, women with tuberculosis, which has begun to make a stunning reappearance. AIDS was indeed a deadly disease—and the premature loss of life was truly devastating—but in southeastern Botswana, where nutrition was relatively good and where treatment for some opportunistic infections was available, many AIDS patients, like all debilitated people, did a lot of living before they died. In focusing on mortality and transmission, I, like many (though by no means all) in the international health community, was overlooking a significant part of the epidemic.

AIDS has further stressed the domestic economy of care in Botswana, adding pressure to the tensions between women caregivers as they struggle to accommodate a growing population of debilitated kin, migrating daughters, and the return of sick and wasted adult children seeking care and mother love. The emotional, economic, social, and moral strains around care are visible in the homes where young adults lay shivering next to elderly stroke patients or where disabled children sit with orphaned cousins and with uncles or aunts who have returned home sick and tired, no longer able to stay in the city to work. And those women who care for such people know all too well that their suffering children may never again send a wage home or survive to provide them care when their own aging bodies begin to fail. The generational inversions first witnessed through the *madi* production of migrant laborers are now saturating the life course as the elderly attend the funerals of the youthful and middle-aged and face increasing uncertainties about their own futures.

In the previous chapter, we saw how new forms of debility (including AIDS) and changing health care services have combined to throw the efficacy and ethos of professional biomedicine into question. Unlike most of Southern Africa, hope is on the horizon for those Batswana with HIV (currently 38.5 percent of the adult population) as the national medical service and with its international partners begins to provide anti-retroviral therapy.[2] Perhaps this will change popular impressions of the efficacy of biomedical care. But most likely, anti-retroviral therapy will reinforce preexisting ideas about the limitations of biomedicine. These medications, doctors rightly stress, do not cure the disease, they only calm it, though patients, prospective patients, and their loved ones (in short everyone) will surely appreciate this powerful and much-needed form of palliation. Provision of anti-retroviral therapy only reinforces the need to accommodate a model of debility in international health, as patients taking complex drug regimens will join Batswana with diabetes, epilepsy, and hypertension who are living with a serious illness transmuted by biomedical management.[3]

The ethos of professional care, however, is another matter. As the hospitals and clinics struggle to accommodate a growing patient population—one that requires increasingly complex care regimens—professional nursing care is very much at the center of public debate. As heart patients, diabetics, and cancer patients join persons with AIDS or resurgent TB in the hospitals, the overloading and burnout of hospital staff has become acute and concerns about the relationship between positive healing sentiment and efficacious care are very much at the center of the moral imagination. In November 2003, the newspapers were reporting shocking stories about callous nursing staff and serious cases of patient neglect at Princess Marina Hospital in Gaborone.[4] An editorial in one paper made an urgent call for reform, reminding readers of the centrality of care to personhood: "Even if they cannot heal them, the least that hospital staff can do for patients is to handle them with love and care. . . . The type of rudeness, incompetence and haughty attitude reportedly exhibited by certain sectors of Marina staff have no place in a modern society that prides itself with *botho* [humanity]."[5] In July 2004, Joyce Tamocha, the president of the Botswana Nurses Association, "expressed concern about the declining commitment of nurses towards patients," saying that "most nurses do not carry out some of their prescribed tasks like feeding and cleaning patients. . . . Nurses, she said, must be compassionate, caring, and committed to their jobs, as they are the pillars of strength for the nation."[6] Meanwhile, opportunities in Europe and the United States continue to draw emotionally exhausted nurses out of the country in search of better pay and working conditions. Palliation and caring sentiment are rarely at the center of overloaded international health agendas, but they continue to structure popular evaluations of care and community and thus to shape impressions of biomedicine and choices in health-seeking behavior.

As this history of debility has demonstrated, the relationship between sexuality, blood, and disease in Botswana is more complicated than a biomedical model of sexually transmitted microbial pathogens would allow. Biomedical messages translated into Setswana are entangled with ideas based on the layered and historically embedded diagnostics of *bongaka*. The AIDS epidemic is coming at a time when social control over *madi* and sexuality is already very much at issue after a century of migrant labor, the demise of initiation, and the decline and delay of marriage. And it builds upon a history of pathologized wombs and unevenly gendered power relations. Popular interpretations of AIDS illnesses run a range—all of which bring biomedical messages about blood, sex, and condoms into conversation with historical ideas and understandings of *madi* and *popelo*.

Some Batswana stress the role of transmission of polluted *madi* in the epidemic. They see many of the illnesses in their midst as brought on by the anonymous sexuality of women who conceal their status as widows or carried in the hidden wombs of *madi*-seeking women. Such ideas are sometimes countered by those who assert that men's lack of bodily self-control threatens female health. Other interpretations stress the social pathologies of negative emotion and lack of self-restraint, pointing to witchcraft or heathenism as underlying causes. Still others wonder about new technologies, like those who debate the nature of the visible spermicide in the ubiquitous condoms colored like white flesh. Perhaps, some wonder aloud, the spermicide, these *megare* (germs, illness worms), are the virus in question. So the entanglement of biomedicine and *bongaka* continues, as does the embedding of diagnostic frameworks in broader socioeconomic and cultural contexts.

Parting Snapshots and New Directions

In 1999, I drove to work one morning through Mogoditshane to the spectacle of young men with large packs on their backs running up the road to the Botswana Defense Force barracks. They were only a fraction of the hordes of young men trying out for the annual recruitment drive. Securing enlistment, and therefore steady work, was the goal of many young men, even though the work could take them far from home. Most wouldn't make it, even if they successfully completed the many-kilometer run proving their fitness. So many young men had come to apply in recent years that the Botswana Defense Force now had the luxury of requiring secondary school certificates as a condition of enlistment. During the annual recruitment campaigns, the prospective soldiers are lined up and medically examined for fitness. One young man who had tried three times unsuccessfully to enlist told me, "They just check your eyes. Why are they looking at each and every one? It is so they can identify their relatives and secure them a position." In popular perceptions, the group medical exam was still a barrier to employment, but its meanings had shifted yet again—now it was a mechanism for nepotism.

In 1999, Mpule Kwelagobe, the pride of Botswana, was crowned Miss Universe in an internationally televised contest. For months afterward, readers submitted poems singing her praises to local newspapers, her face emblazoned T-shirts and posters, and her name was on everyone's lips. She came to Diphaleng, where she subsequently became a sponsor of the home-based care program for AIDS patients and was almost ripped from the car she rode in as the crowd surged forward and seemingly half the village tried to touch her arm, her hair, her body. She was tall, she was thin, her skin glowed, and her body had become symbolic of the nation. Teenage girls who subsequently attempted to enroll in the system of local beauty pageants that culminated in the Miss Botswana title soon found that the white couple who ran the pageants had set strict guidelines about weight. One young woman I knew, who held her own village-level beauty title, returned home from her pageant tryouts reporting that she was sent away—pageant organizers had determined she was too fat for competition. International "beauty" standards, already evident in glossy magazines and on western soap operas broadcast in Tswana homes, had become entangled in "official" local evaluations of girls' bodies. The human body remained a plastic site for both cultural continuity and change.

The people I have introduced to readers are only a few of those who continue to occupy my own moral imagination. Frances, my friend whom we met in Chapter 1, sent me and my husband a greeting card she had made in late 2000 that we still have on our refrigerator door. It was to be our last communication. Frances had received a grant several years earlier to pay for an operation at Baragwanath Hospital in South Africa which placed metal pins and plates in her hips. She never found such funds again for the scheduled replacement of these artificial parts. We got news in spring 2001 that her whole lower body had swelled enormously and then she was dead. To me, her death is a grim reminder of the pain entailed in the simultaneous transitions of epidemiological realities and health care systems. Messages such as the ones about Frances's death come in fits and starts from friends in Botswana, and most mail brings news of building plans and activities as well as human loss. I will leave you with an excerpt from one such letter, written by Dikeledi shortly after the devastating floods of early 2000—a year when rain came, but in too great an amount and in storms that were too lightening filled and violent. The letter included news about some of the people you met in Chapter 1, and I quote from it to remind you and me both that their experiences and those of others continue to unfold.

> Kago is still struggling but no improvement. I haven't seen Onkaetse since the day of the interview. Obakeng is now learning to walk with a walker, this morning I saw him walk to and from the dining hall, I don't know how his family survived the flood. Mogae is fine, they [his activist group for the disabled] managed to write their constitution which has been sent for approval at the Ministry of Home Affairs. Obusitswe is still in the day care and I should say making no progress, but his family is doing fine. David is as tiny as before and still not walking. Remember Lesego Dinare? She lost her son, who was building Tshepo's house. He was struck by lightning. We've started on Tebogo's toilet, Tiny's brother is the builder, only that he has been stopped by the rains.

Glossary of Setswana Terms

badimo: ancestors

bagolo: elders

banna (sing. *ngwana*): children

baprofiti: see *moprofiti*

batlhanka: servants

batsete: see *motsetse*

batsofe (sing. *motsofe*): elderly people

Batswana (sing. Motswana): Tswana people

boaga: building

boboko: brain

bogadi: bridewealth payments

bogole: disability

bogologolo: the past; a long time ago

bogosi: chiefship

bogwera: male initiation

bojale: female initiation

boloi: witchcraft

bongaka: medicine; the Tswana therapeutic system

bonyatsi: long-term amorous relationship

bopelotelele: patience; forbearance; lit. long-heartedness

boswagadi: disease caused by unpurified widows; purification rites for widows

botho: humanity; personhood

botsenwa: mental illness

botsofe: old age; senescence

dibeela: toxic abominations; some substances of sorcery; traps or pitfalls

digole (sing. *segole*): disabled persons

digotlo: see *segotlo*

dikgaba: misfortune brought by the sorrowful or bitter heart of a scorned elder

dikgosana: headmen; diminutive of *dikgosi*

dikgosi (sing. *kgosi*): chiefs

dingaka: see *ngaka*

ditlhare: see *setlhare*

ditlhogo (sing. *tlhogo*): heads; portion of meat given to maternal uncle

ditsenwa: see *setsenwa*

ditshika: nerves; veins

go alafa: to heal

go bereka: to work for a wage

go dira: to do; to make

go swa mogama: stroke; hemiplegia, lit. to be half-dead

go thaya: to strengthen

gompieno: today

itekanela: healthy; fit; well; self sufficient

kgosi: see *dikgosi*

kgotla: village meeting site; political assembly; customary court

lefufa: jealousy, envy

legwane: see *magwane*

lekolwane: see *makolwane*

leswafi: see *maswafi*

letsholo: public assembly

lolwapa: compound courtyard

lorato: love

losika: vein; artery; relative; family

madi: blood; semen; money

mafisa: system by which cattle are loaned to an individual for herding to the benefit of that individual and the cattle owner

magwane (sing. *legwane*): big boys; pre-initiation unruly youth

makgwelwa: deserters

makolwane (sing. *lekolwane*): young men

malome: maternal uncle

mashi: milk

maswafi (sing. *leswafi*): persons with albinism

mephato: see *mophato*

merafe (sing. *morafe*): nations; chiefdoms; tribes

meraka (sing. *moraka*): cattle post

Modimo: God

molwetsi: patient

mopakwane: disease caused by breaking of sexual taboo after the birth of a child, causing impairments in the child

mophato (pl. *mephato*): age-based regiment

moprofiti (pl. *baprofiti*): healing prophet

morafe: see *merafe*

moraka: see *meraka*

motho (pl. *batho*): person

motsetse (pl. *batsete*): postpartum mother still in confinement

motsofe: see *batsofe*

mowa: breath; spirit; soul

naga: bush

ngaka (pl. *dingaka*): doctor

ngwana: see *banna*

nyatsi: lover (see *bonyatsi*)

pelo: heart

popelo: womb

sefuba: chest

segole: see *digole*

segotlo (pl. *digotlo*): backyard

sejeso: poison; sorcery substance

sethunya: pain; gun; flower

setlhare (pl. *ditlhare*): tree; medicine

setsenwa (pl. *ditsenwa*): person with mental illness

thibamo: disease whose onset begins in a child in an unusual birth position (breech, face down), resulting in symptoms in the parents similar to those of pulmonary tuberculosis

tlhaloganyo: mind; understanding

tlhogo: see *ditlhogo*

tsofetse: has become old; aged

Tswana: noun root used as shorthand for things persons associated with the place, culture, language, and norms of the Batswana

Notes

Introduction

1. Author's interview with Malau Alita Seati.

2. In approaching the history of disability from this perspective I am indebted to Margaret Lock's model of "local biology" and Caroline Bledsoe's work on bodily "contingency." Lock, *Encounters with Aging*; Bledsoe, *Contingent Lives: Fertility, Time, and Aging in West Africa*.

3. Setswana, like all Bantu languages, utilizes a system of prefixes to classify nouns. Thus, Botswana is the country (or the collective noun of all Tswana), Motswana is a single Tswana person, Batswana more than one person, Setswana the language and the ways and customs of the Batswana, and Tswana the root. "Tswana" is often used in place of "Setswana" or "Batswana." In addition, the reader will sometimes encounter the prefix "Ga," which indicates that the word is a location: for example, "Gakwena" for the place of the Bakwena. Throughout the book I use the term "community" in both geographic and identity-based ways. The meanings should be apparent from the context.

4. I consider disfigurement (or "aesthetic impairments") to be a form of impairment because it can impair one's self-presentation. The impairment is driven by others and speaks to the nature of our physical bodies as sites and vehicles of social interaction. The term "aesthetic impairments" is from Weiss, *Conditional Love*; see also Dreger on "unusual anatomies" in *One of Us*.

5. Scheper-Hughes and Lock, "The Mindful Body"; Jean Comaroff, *Body of Power*.

6. Livingston, "Reconfiguring Old Age"; Livingston, "Maintaining Local Dependencies."

7. Karp, "Persons, Notions of," 392. See also Jackson and Karp, eds., *Personhood and Agency*; Riseman, "The Person and the Life-Cycle in African Social Life and Thought"; John L. and Jean Comaroff, "On Personhood: An Anthropological Perspective from Africa."

8. See Cassell, "The Nature of Suffering and the Goals of Medicine."

9. See Comaroff and Roberts, *Rules and Processes*; see also Kuper, *Kalahari Village Politics*.

10. Durham, "Soliciting Gifts and Negotiating Agency"; Durham, "Civil Lives: Leadership and Accomplishment in Botswana." See also the discussion by the Comaroffs, who make the distinction between "individuality" and "individualism," in Comaroff and Comaroff, "On Personhood."

11. See also Durham, "Empowering Youth: Making Youth Citizens in Botswana"; and Livingston, "Maintaining Local Dependencies."

12. Fred Klaits calls these "housed relationships" in "Care and Kinship in an Apostolic Church during Botswana's Time of AIDS."

13. Cf. Ferguson, *Expectations of Modernity*.

14. Thomas, *The Politics of the Womb*, 18–19.

15. Lamb, *White Saris and Sweet Mangoes*.

16. Rapp, "Extra Chromosomes and Blue Tulips." See also Dreger, *One of Us*; Frank, *Venus on Wheels*.

17. Baynton, "Disability and the Justification of Inequality in American History"; Kudlick, "Disability History."

18. I am grateful to Simi Linton for helping me think/phrase this in such clear terms.

19. Activists and their supporters in Botswana, including myself, often use the term *batho ba ba nang le bogole* (persons with disabilities), but *digole* was the term used by most people in the late 1990s. I translate "*digole*" as "disabled persons," but in certain contexts (for example, in some of the proverbs I will refer to in this book) I use "cripples" as the more accurate or appropriate translation.

20. Contemporary experiences of debility often trigger memories and conversations about various aspects of the past. Cole, *Forget Colonialism?*

21. See the discussion in Sadowsky, *Imperial Bedlam*.

22. I am borrowing this term and the framework of therapy as a diachronic and hetero-dox process from Janzen, *The Quest for Therapy in Lower Zaire*.

23. Kleinmann, *The Illness Narratives*.

24. Rapp and Ginsburg, "Enabling Disability."

25. See Davis, *Enforcing Normalcy*; Thomson, *Extraordinary Bodies*; Linton, *Claiming Disability*; Longmore and Umansky, eds., *The New Disability History*; Davis, ed., *The Disability Studies Reader*. For an overview, see Kudlick, "Disability History."

26. This Euro-American emphasis is an effect of the current trends in scholarship. Most disability studies scholars appear open to and enthusiastic about broadening their field geographically and culturally. Cf. Kudlick, "Disability History." Although four-fifths of the world's disabled persons live in developing countries, there is a relative dearth of humanities and social science scholarship exploring disability in non-western contexts. Important exceptions include Silla, *People Are Not the Same*; Kohrman, "Motorcycles for the Disabled"; Kohrman, "Why Am I Not Disabled?"; Ingstad and Whyte, eds., *Disability and Culture*; Holzer, Vreede, and Weigt, eds., *Disability in Different Cultures*; Das and Addlakha, "Disability and Domestic Citizenship."

27. Rapp and Ginsburg, "Enabling Disability"; see also Jean Comaroff, *Body of Power*, 9.

28. I have discussed these issues in greater depth in Livingston, "Maintaining Local Dependencies."

29. Geurts, *Culture and the Senses*; on emotions, see Lutz, *Unnatural Emotions*.

30. Author's interview with Oagile Tabola.

31. Klaits, "Care and Kinship"; see also Schapera, "Kgatla Notions of Ritual Impurity"; Lambek and Solway, "Just Anger"; Durham, "Love and Jealousy in the Space of Death"; Durham and Klaits, "Funerals and the Public Space of Sentiment in Botswana."

32. Goffman, *Stigma: Notes on the Management of a Spoiled Identity*.

33. Motzafi-Haller, *Fragmented Worlds, Coherent Lives: The Politics of Difference in Botswana*; Werbner and Gaitskell, eds., *Minorities and Citizenship in Botswana*.

34. "Stop Buying from Zimbabwean Hawkers, Says Phumaphi," *Botswana Daily News*, February 26, 2002 (despite the headline, this article is actually about popular demand for medical care for diabetes and other chronic illnesses); "Government Does Not Focus Only on HIV/AIDS, Says Hospital Chief," *Botswana Daily News*, March 11, 2002.

35. This norm is increasingly challenging for youth in a changing economy. Durham, "Empowering Youth: Making Youth Citizens in Botswana"; Burke, "Life at the Margins in Botswana."

36. This is a common pattern in many parts of Africa. For the best discussion of inversion of generational roles in the wake of capitalist growth and the significance of "building" in natal communities, see Berry, *Fathers Work for Their Sons*.

37. Livingston, "Reconfiguring Old Age."

38. A tuck shop is a small makeshift shop that sells basic commodities, usually in the yard of a house.

39. Alverson, *Mind in the Heart of Darkness.*

40. These domains shaped one another, and their boundaries are blurrier than the current rhetorical opposition between "traditional" and "modern" medicine or between "lay" and "professional" perspectives would imply. I am separating them for clarity of analysis. Given the central role of science in Euro-American notions of modernity, categories and practices of "tradition" and "modernity" arise together, each reliant on the other for its meaning. Pigg, "The Credible and the Credulous"; Pigg, "Inventing Social Categories through Place"; Pigg, "'Found in Most Traditional Societies.'"

41. Porter, *Health, Civilization and the State;* Rosenberg, *The Cholera Years;* Hamlin, *Public Health and Social Justice in the Age of Chadwick;* Leavitt, *The Healthiest City.*

42. This study builds on important work in African medicine and public healing by drawing together a range of historical approaches other scholars have pursued. Some works relate public health primarily to political ecology and cosmology; others locate biomedicine in the broader nexus of colonial thought and power. More recently, Nancy Hunt and Jonathon Sadowsky have each shown the need to better decipher complex historical experiences of patients and communities to make sense of hybrid meanings generated through colonial-era medical encounters, while Luise White's innovative work on rumor has helped locate biomedicine in the social imaginary. See White, *Speaking with Vampires;* Vaughan, *Curing Their Ills;* Taylor, *Milk, Honey, and Money;* Sadowsky, *Imperial Bedlam;* Packard, *White Plague, Black Labor;* Packard, "The 'Healthy Reserve' and the 'Dressed Native'"; Packard, *Chiefship and Cosmology;* Lyons, *The Colonial Disease;* Silla, *People Are Not the Same;* Janzen, *The Quest for Therapy in Lower Zaire;* Janzen, *Ngoma: Discourses of Healing in Central and Southern Africa;* Hunt, *A Colonial Lexicon;* Feierman, "Struggles for Control"; Feierman, *Peasant Intellectuals;* Feierman, *The Shambaa Kingdom;* Echenberg, *Black Death, White Medicine;* Callahan, "'Veni, VD, Vici?'"; Jean Comaroff, "The Diseased Heart of Africa"; Bell, *Frontiers of Medicine in the Anglo-Egyptian Sudan.* While there is some work on professional nursing (albeit limited despite the central role of nurses in African biomedical care), African histories, like many other medical histories, have mainly ignored lay nursing care, the major medical context in which people define and manage illness experiences on a daily basis. Or they have lumped such practices with "traditional" medicine, obscuring the unique position of women (the primary caregivers) in illness experiences and failing to account for differences in power and knowledge between laypersons and medical specialists. This book, I hope, broadens our understanding by documenting the relationships between changes within Tswana medicine, public health, and lay nursing. On professional nursing, see Marks, *Divided Sisterhood;* Burns, "'A Man Is a Clumsy Thing Who Does Not Know How to Handle a Sick Person.'" Nancy Hunt's work is an important exception in this regard. Though centered on an institution, her work draws together public healing, biomedicine, African medicine, and lay nursing care in a single, very rich narrative. Hunt, *A Colonial Lexicon.*

43. Mairs, *Waist-High in the World,* 58.

44. Whyte and Ingstad, "Disability and Culture: An Overview," 4.

45. Livingston, "Reconfiguring Old Age."

46. Klaits, "Care and Kinship in an Apostolic Church During Botswana's Time of AIDS." See also Durham, "Love and Jealousy in the Space of Death"; Durham and Klaits, "Funerals and the Public Space of Sentiment in Botswana."

47. Durham, "Love and Jealousy in the Space of Death."

48. I take this term from Beidelman, *Moral Imagination.*

49. Mutongi, " 'Worries of the Heart.' "

50. Jean Comaroff, *Body of Power.*

51. Malkki, *Purity and Exile;* Cole, *Forget Colonialism?;* Fabian, *Remembering the Present;* Hunt, *A Colonial Lexicon.*

52. Beidelman, *Moral Imagination;* Heald, *Manhood and Morality.* See also Lutz, *Unnatural Emotions.* For the different notions of morality of European colonizers and Southern Africans, see Jeater, *Marriage, Perversion, and Power.*

53. For more on the relationship between posture and gait and the performance of morality, see Geurts, *Culture and the Senses;* Durham, "The Predicament of Dress." For gift-giving in Botswana, see Durham, "Soliciting Gifts and Negotiating Agency."

54. This has been the case in many different places and at many different times. For contrasting cases, see Risse, *Mending Bodies, Saving Souls;* Goffman, *Stigma;* La Berge, "The Early Nineteenth-Century Public Health Movement"; Tomes, "The Private Side of Public Health."

55. Briggs and Mantini-Briggs, *Stories in the Time of Cholera;* Scheper-Hughes, *Death without Weeping.*

56. See Crais, *The Politics of Evil.*

57. See Ferguson, *Expectations of Modernity.*

58. Nonetheless, even the oblique references and bold denials which some people made in reference to such topics proved interesting in and of themselves. First, they indicated the degree of secrecy, stigma, and shame surrounding certain practices and behaviors; people continued to guard memories of events some four and five decades past. Second, such secrecy inspired others to be more forthcoming in their replies; they reacted with irritation and shock at what they considered to be the dishonesty of some. Telling an already frank interviewee that others (who remained anonymous) had suggested that hiding, sorcery, or extramarital affairs had not existed in earlier times often generated greater earnestness and detailed recollections as some sought to "set the record straight."

59. Kratz, " 'We've Always Done It Like This . . . Except for a Few Details.' " Here anthropologist Isaac Schapera's field notes and published texts from the 1930s and 1940s and secondary research on *bongaka* published in the 1970s and 1980s provide clues that help periodize transitions and changes in the local therapeutic system.

1. Family Matters and Money Matters

1. To preserve the privacy of those people whose lives I discuss here, I have changed the names of the villages in question. Pseudonyms are used for most contemporary actors throughout the book except for public figures. Real names are used in citing material from oral historical interviews that are used primarily as historical sources.

2. I was not in Botswana consistently throughout this period; I was in country for three and a half months in 1997 and then again for twelve months from 1998 to 1999.

3. I accompanied another technician, Mary Letswiti, to two other villages during a short trip to Botswana in 1996.

4. Deep Setswana is the use of elaborate references to proverbs, praise poems, and other types of culturally coded knowledge; the use of doubled or even tripled meanings; puns; and the like in speech. It is a high art form that distinguishes the speaker and is most often commanded by the elderly.

5. When I interviewed people without Dikeledi I was assisted by either Tshepiso Moremi or Condril Mosala.

6. Experience in pilot employment schemes in the developing world (including Botswana) as well as in western countries demonstrates that disabled persons are able to perform jobs as well as their able-bodied counterparts and that overall they tend to make more conscientious employees.

7. Siwawa-Ndai, "Employment Opportunities and Their Impact on the Quality of Life in Botswana." The 2004 unemployment rate is listed by the United Nations at www.unbotswana.org.bw/about_b.html (accessed July 26, 2004).

8. Siwawa-Ndai, "Employment Opportunities and Their Impact on the Quality of Life in Botswana," 138.

9. Mugabe, "Social Welfare Issues and the Quality of Life in Botswana," 181.

10. Festus Mogae, "Opening Speech," in Nteta, Hermans, and Jeskova, *Poverty and Plenty*, 11.

11. Ibid.

12. In 1998, official estimates stated that 6,887 people were injured and 453 people were killed in road accidents in Botswana. *The Botswana Gazette,* July 21, 1999, 12.

13. Though the foundation sees itself as a "disabled" persons' organization, Cheshire Foundation workers provide services to a wider range of debilitated persons, including the frail elderly and those with debilitating chronic illnesses.

14. See Janzen, *The Quest for Therapy in Lower Zaire*; Feierman, "Explanation and Uncertainty in the Medical World of Ghaambo"; Last, "The Importance of Knowing about Not-Knowing."

15. Evans-Pritchard, *Witchcraft, Oracles, and Magic among the Azande.*

16. Kohrman, "Why Am I Not Disabled?"

17. Ingstad, "The Myth of the Hidden Disabled," 26.

18. Botswana Ministry of Health Rehabilitation Services Division, Annual Report 1995, 69. Consulted at the Botswana Collection, University of Botswana Library, Gaborone.

19. In 1956, the Bangwaketse Tribal Administration did a census of *diphofhu* (blind persons) in their territory after the protectorate welfare officer had suggested the possibility of establishing an institute for the blind in Kanye to train young blind Batswana for work. The Bangwaketse census (though clearly incomplete) found that out of 199 blind people, only fourteen were under 48 years of age, and plans for the institute were abandoned. Treatment of Blind Africans in the Bechuanaland Protectorate, Secretariat Series 548/5, BNA.

20. Cohen, "Community Based Rehabilitation in Botswana," 39.

21. I got this figure directly from Cohen, though it is not specifically cited in her paper. Cohen, personal communication, September 1999. The national census in 1995 found that 10.5 percent of households had at least one disabled resident. Because the majority of these households would be in villages rather than in urban centers, we can cautiously accept Cohen's figure as a rough estimate. Republic of Botswana, Central Statistics Office, *Living Conditions in Botswana, 1986–1994,* 55.

22. In what follows here I am using western medical characterizations for the benefit of the reader and to convey how these webs of disability appeared to an American outsider. This same descriptive map would look quite different if I were to frame the various conditions in Tswana diagnostic terms.

23. This is not to suggest that impairments run in families, though in certain cases they might. Rather, I am saying that the experience of disability is more ubiquitous than actual numbers might suggest.

24. Most Batswana maintain two or three homes: one in the village, a more rustic one at their agricultural fields (usually called "the lands"), and another, still rougher, one at their cattle post.

25. Ingstad and Bruun, "Elderly People as Care Providers and Care Receivers," 71.

26. For more on the importance of greetings and "face work" in the local construction of personhood, see Alverson, *Mind in the Heart of Darkness*, 139–141.

27. Schapera, *Handbook of Tswana Law and Custom*, 176–179.

28. The AIDS epidemic, however, seems to be pushing the reality of overburdened caregivers to the foreground of contemporary debate.

2. Public Health and Developing Persons

1. This discussion focuses on the *merafe* of the southeastern region of the Bechuanaland Protectorate: Bakwena, Barolong, Bakgatla (Kgafela), Batlokwa, Balete, and Bangwaketse. This is a somewhat artificial geographic distinction. In several places throughout, however, I will supplement my discussion with evidence drawn from groups living in the central and northern regions of the country, especially the Bangwato and the Batawana. (When I refer to their geographic areas, I use the corresponding prefix "Ga." So "Bakwena" becomes "Gakwena," "Bakgatla" becomes "Gakgatla," and so forth.) Though all the *merafe* share a great deal in common culturally, politically, and historically, and though people moved between them and intermarried across such subethnic categories, there were and still are significant cultural distinctions between them. Furthermore, each *morafe* contains a number of groups who originally arrived seeking political refuge, and some contain branches that still reside in South Africa. These groups have further influenced the heterodox nature of cultural practice in a place often characterized as ethnically homogenous. I will try to note such variation where possible, but for the most part I will bracket the question of subethnicity in the interest of synthetic analysis. Other continuities can, of course, be found with Tswana groups residing across the border with South Africa (which was still new in the period in question), and I will use some sources from that area when discussing precolonial developments. In particular, I draw on Jean and John Comaroff's rich work on the Barolong Boo Ratshidi.

2. Schapera and Comaroff, *The Tswana*, 39.

3. This particularly apt description comes from Ingstad, Bruun, Sandberg, and Tlou, "Care for the Elderly, Care by the Elderly," 380.

4. See Comaroff and Comaroff, *Of Revelation and Revolution*, vols. 1 and 2; Landau, *The Realm of the Word*; Ramsay, "The Rise and Fall of the Bakwena Dynasty of South-Central Botswana, 1820–1940"; Schapera, *Tribal Innovators*.

5. For more on the role of the nostalgic or normative past in "tradition" and the canonization of practice and memory, see Kratz, "'We've Always Done it Like This . . . Except for a Few Details.'" On elision and slippages in the use of the past as a comment on the present, see Malkki, *Purity and Exile*. The best account of how collective and personal memories operate at times to suppress and at times to invoke recollections of negative experiences (and thus shape nostalgic reckonings) is Cole, *Forget Colonialism?*

6. Jean Comaroff, *Body of Power*, 54–60; see also Packard, "Social Change and the History of Misfortune among the Bashu of Eastern Zaire."

7. It is hard to know if this phrasing is new or old. A photo from 1989 shows a health poster hung as decoration in a home picturing an array of foods with the slogan at the top "Body Building Foods." Whether the ministry of health coopted an older phrase or whether

its language infiltrated common parlance is unclear. Grant and Grant, *Decorated Homes in Botswana*, 96. Author's interviews with Peter Mokwena (March 12, 1999); Lesego Moremi; Rra Seleka; and Neo Moamogwe (who remembers gathering wild foods and selling them in the early 1930s).

8. Author's interviews with Peter Mokwena (March 12, 1999); Lesego Moremi; Rra Seleka; and Neo Moamogwe. Pulane Tshwene put it well in her interview: "Now life has changed because in the olden days they used to eat wild fruits, but today someone will be told, ah! don't do that you can get sick, or maybe if someone is to eat those wild fruits they can get sick. There is a lot of wind and never any rain." Mmamontsho Segwatse touched on the same issues in her interview: "We used to eat wild fruits but today if a child can eat that same wild fruit he also might die and the nurses will say that child ate poison from that wild fruit." See also Mmasetadile Tshukudu's interview.

9. See van Onselen, *The Seed Is Mine*, 73; and Schapera, *Rainmaking Rites*, 47–48.

10. Schapera, *Rainmaking Rites*, 54. Translation from English to Setswana minimizes differences between the current explanation and the one from Rapedi in 1931. The word for tree or plant (*setlhare*; pl. *ditlhare*) is the same as the word for medicine; thus, a suggestion that the plants themselves were sown by the *badimo* could mean the same thing as the statement that the *ditlhare* were those of the *badimo*.

11. Author's interviews with Sebete Phatshwana and Ntene Moilwa.

12. For a more extensive discussion of the symbolic qualities of these spaces, see Jean Comaroff, *Body of Power*, 54–60, 62–74.

13. For an extended discussion of the role of cattle in social reproduction and ritual in Southern Africa, see Kuper, *Wives for Cattle*.

14. Willoughby, *The Soul of the Bantu*, 187.

15. On intestines, see Schapera, "Kgatla Notions of Ritual Impurity."

16. Cousins, ed., *The Chronicle of the London Missionary Society*, 146.

17. Carton, *Blood from Your Children*, 48–86.

18. Willoughby, *The Soul of the Bantu*, 200.

19. Jean Comaroff, *Body of Power*, 54–56 (quote on 56). See also Boddy, *Wombs and Alien Spirits* for a comparative discussion of the relationship between spatial and womb-based bodily symbolism.

20. The deep degree of nostalgia for such homes among today's elderly suggests something of the sentiments of comfort and succor that patients may have found in the home. On the impact of bourgeois notions of domesticity, see Comaroff and Comaroff, *Of Revelation and Revolution*, vol. 2, Chapter 6.

21. As Jean and John Comaroff suggest, architectural forms underwent various changes from the nineteenth century onward as some people began to appreciate the western architecture promoted by missionaries. They argue that architectural changes were a key site through which Tswana consciousness changed as people developed a consumerist desire for European-style goods. Some who had the means started to build western-style square or rectangular buildings. Comaroff and Comaroff, *Of Revelation and Revolution*, vol. 2, Chapter 6. That various chiefs focused attention on these architectural changes adds weight to the Comaroffs' sense of the centrality of architecture to consciousness. Some chiefs (Bakgatla) encouraged these innovations; others (Bangwaketse) actively discouraged it. Grant and Grant, *Decorated Homes in Botswana*, 36.

22. The Comaroffs describe how nineteenth-century missionaries were "put out" "by the Tswana . . . propensity to make uninvited calls." *Of Revelation and Revolution*, vol. 2, 286.

23. Schapera, ed., *The Political Annals of a Tswana Tribe*, January 31, 1912.

24. Grant and Grant, *Decorated Homes in Botswana*, 43.

25. Jean Comaroff, *Body of Power*, 58.

26. Ibid.

27. Willoughby, *The Soul of the Bantu*, 211; see also Schapera, *Rainmaking Rites*, 106.

28. Author's interviews with Norah Kgosietsile and Peter Mokwena (March 12, 1999).

29. Jean Comaroff, *Body of Power*, 47–52.

30. Packard, *Chiefship and Cosmology*, 6; Feierman, *The Shambaa Kingdom*; Feierman, *Peasant Intellectuals*. There is an extensive literature on chiefs as mediators; see Beidelman, "Swazi Royal Ritual"; Crais, *The Politics of Evil*.

31. Comaroff and Roberts, *Rules and Processes*, 62–69.

32. Much has been written on the history of Tswana chiefship. This description draws on several secondary sources, including Morton and Ramsay, eds., *The Birth of Botswana*; and Schapera, *The Political Annals of a Tswana Tribe* and *Tribal Innovators*. For more detail and analysis of chiefship in this period (1900–1930), see J. L. Comaroff, "Competition for Office and Political Processes among the Barolong Boo Ratshidi"; J. L. Comaroff, "Rules and Rulers"; Morton, "Chiefs and Ethnic Unity in Two Colonial Worlds"; Molefi, Morton, and Ngcongco, "The Modernists: Seepapitso, Ntebogang and Isang"; Ramsay, "The Neo-Traditionalist: Sebele II of the Bakwena"; Parsons, "Khama III, the Bamangwato, and the British"; Ramsay, "The Rise and Fall of the Bakwena Dynasty of South-Central Botswana, 1820–1940."

33. Schapera, *The Political Annals of a Tswana Tribe*, 16.

34. Schapera, ed., *Livingstone's Private Journals, 1851–1853*, 29.

35. Gagoangwe was the daughter of Bakwena chief Sechele I and wed Chief Pilane of the Mmanaana Kgatla, an immigrant Tswana group from the Transvaal who resided in Moshupa, the second major village of Gangwaketse. She then deserted him to wed Bathoen, chief of the Bangwaketse and father of Seepapitso. She was called the "one-eyed queen" because as a child she had put out the eye of a family servant. As Ramsay, Morton, and Morton describe it, "Her father used this occasion to invoke the biblical judgment of 'an eye for an eye, a tooth for a tooth' by allowing the injured servant to blind his own daughter, establishing thereby as well a degree of legal equanimity among his subjects." Ramsay, Morton, and Morton, *Historical Dictionary of Botswana*, 80.

36. Confidential District Commissioner's Report, 1934: Bakgatla Affairs: Domestic Relations between Isang's Family and Chief Molefi's Family, in Secretariat Series 305/19, BNA. See also the discussion in Schapera, *Rainmaking Rites*, 26–31.

37. Though little has been written about Tswana women's roles in politics in the precolonial and/or early colonial periods, it is quite likely that, as with the royal women of Dahomey, colonial rule usurped or displaced royal women's political power as the chiefship responded to the political orientations/machinations of the colonial government. Bay, *Wives of the Leopard*.

38. Landau, *The Realm of the Word*, Chapter 4. Dorothy Hodgson's work among Maasai women suggests a continuity here—that women's historic roles as spiritual mediators facilitated the gendered processes of Christian conversion, which produced more women congregants than men. Hodgson, *The Church of Women*.

39. Schapera, *Rainmaking Rites*, 92–97.

40. Willoughby, *The Soul of the Bantu*, 211; Schapera, *Rainmaking Rites*, 106. *Dibeela* could be purposefully planted as a form of sorcery or result from less-purposeful circumstances.

41. Schapera, *Rainmaking Rites*, 95.

42. Willoughby, *The Soul of the Bantu,* 207–208.

43. Schapera, *Married Life in an African Tribe,* 197.

44. The Minutes of Public Assemblies held in the major southern *morafe* of Gang-waketse from 1910–1917, which were later translated and edited by Schapera, provide a glimpse into the role of the chief in the moral direction of the populace. Chief Seepapitso, though clearly a reformer, took advantage of the 1911 British census of cattle in the various reserves to chastise the people and remind them of Tswana values of economic prudence and the centrality of cattle. Though the Bangwaketse were actually determined to have the most cattle of all the *merafe* in the southern protectorate, Seepapitso misrepresented the tallies to make a larger point about the need for proper economic choices in a widening marketplace, "You really make one ashamed, you are a nation without cattle. [At the last census] the number of your cattle was the least in the whole country. If you amass clothes in this way, will your children [be able to] eat them? What is the use of a man if he has clothes but no cattle? Or again, if he has cattle but goes about in rags?" Schapera, ed., *The Political Annals of a Tswana Tribe,* June 20, 1911.

45. This is evidenced by the ongoing admonitions about alcohol abuse, including repeated calls for the cessation of beer parties at night, the reiteration of the 1904 law against *kgadi* (an intoxicating drink which had become addictive to the point where some men were selling off their cattle to acquire it), and the rhetorical questioning of uninitiated youth, who, according to custom, were prohibited from drinking beer but who nonetheless seemed apt to indulge in it. "The other day there were feasts in the village of the Lower Flank that deprived us of sleep, because of the dances that were kept up all night; and yet I said long ago that there must be no more dancing at night. You also know well that I said beer must not be drunk at night when people are sleeping. Surely you realize that if this practice does not cease you will be wasting your food, as well as giving reason for other tribes to say that the Ngwaketse are drunkards." Ibid., October 23, 1911.

46. Schapera suggests that insults were pursued in the *kgotla* if they had been directed by a junior against anyone senior in age or rank. Schapera, *Handbook of Tswana Law and Custom,* 257–258.

47. Paul Landau, personal communication. Missionaries encouraged a new and direct propitiation to Modimo, while historically Modimo could only be approached through an ancestral medium. In the early decades of the twentieth century, despite the growing power of Christian doctrine and ritual, exemplified in the introduction of the annual church-led *thapelo ya pula,* or prayer for rain, older rainmaking practices persisted and continued to be part of the symbolic embodiment of the chiefship.

48. Schapera, *Rainmaking Rites,* 101.

49. Ibid., 98–99.

50. For more on women's songs as a particular idiom of subversive protest, see Vaughan, *Story of an African Famine;* Vail and White, *Power and the Praise Poem,* 198–277.

51. Schapera, *Rainmaking Rites,* 100–101. The word for "heaven," *legodimong,* is the same as that for sky. Thus, the explanation does not necessarily suggest Christian connotations.

52. The southeastern Tswana *merafe* were not the only African societies where women enjoyed a unique cosmological position and important roles in ritual. See Packard, "The Arudy of Historical Processes in African Traditions of Genesis."

53. Willoughby, *The Soul of the Bantu,* 291.

54. Author's interviews with Rra Molatlhwa and Rra (Kenalemang) Motlake. As Rra Motlake explained it, elderly regiments were excused because their children were now doing the work of the community on their behalf. Though I repeatedly asked people, it was very

difficult to establish whether boys who were considered *bogole* were initiated. I would guess that because of the tremendous physical variation subsumed under the label *bogole* that there were a variety of experiences. Perhaps some of these *magwane* whose impairments prevented them from dancing and participating in other crucial aspects of *bogwera* were circumcised in their homes in private ceremonies—it is impossible to say with any certainty.

55. These projects included building dams and wells, collecting stray cattle, and sending out search parties for missing persons. Schapera, ed., *The Political Annals of a Tswana Tribe*, February 14, 1912; July 8, 1912; July 8, 1913; August 17, 1914; November 10, 1914; July 5, 1915.

56. On February 9, 1912, when Seepapitso, chief of the Bangwaketse, wanted to eradicate the prickly pear growing in the capital village during the busy farming season, he first asked the men in the *kgotla* if they had time to do the task. "Have you time to do some [tribal] work?" The reply came: "We have no time we are busy building." Apparently this was acceptable to the chief, who then approached the men again five days later with a new plan that utilized ward-based rather than regimental labor. "There is a plant in your town known as 'prickly pear.' I had intended to summon regiments to [deal with] it, but this is difficult because you are at work; however, eradicate it according to [your] wards and by cooperation between neighboring wards." Ibid., February 12, 1912.

57. Schapera, ed., *The Political Annals of a Tswana Tribe*, October, 23, 1911 (editor's note).

58. Author's interviews with Mma Mosala; Peter Mokwena; Lekololwane Molefe; and Kenalemang Motlake and family.

59. For the period 1914 to 1929, the number of Batswana men working in the South African gold mines ranged from a high of 4,015 in 1922 to a low of 1,911 in 1927. Native Recruitment Corporation, Bechuanas Employed by Gold Mines, Secretariat Series 437/1/1, BNA. Most of the migrants at this time were still coming from the southern *merafe*, whose population (excluding the miners, who were not counted in the census) was counted at 57,520 in 1911. Census 1911, Native Administration Series 2/10, BNA.

60. Dennis, "The Role of Dingaka tsa Setswana from the 19th Century to the Present," 54.

61. Schapera, *Rainmaking Rites*, 47.

62. Ibid., 54–59.

63. Ibid. 59.

64. Schapera, ed., *The Political Annals of a Tswana Tribe*, March 15, 1913; July 18, 1913; April 18, 1916.

65. Author's interview with Mma Mantshadi (midwife). Schapera notes that by this time a number of European patent medicines were already in common use; Schapera, ed., *The Political Annals of a Tswana Tribe*, June 26, 1912 (editor's note).

66. Comaroff and Comaroff, *Of Revelation and Revolution*, vol. 2, Chapter 7, especially 345.

67. Schapera, *Rainmaking Rites*, 44.

68. Ibid., 47.

69. van Onselen, *The Seed Is Mine*, 73.

70. Schapera, ed., *The Political Annals of a Tswana Tribe*, August 14, 1912; August 23, 1912.

71. Ibid., August 14, 1912. Since the Bangwaketse did not separate veterinary doctors from human doctors (or rain doctors, etc.), instead seeing veterinary services as part of the larger project of public health, the British provision of veterinary services may well have reinforced the notion that British overrule would necessarily include the maintenance of a range of healers.

72. Author's interview with Neo Moamogwe; Seeley, "The Reaction of the Batswana to the Practice of Western Medicine," 52.

73. Schapera, *Handbook of Tswana Law and Custom*, 256.

74. Willoughby, *The Soul of the Bantu*, 192–193.

75. M. Rapoo, 1930; Sofonia, 1931 (July); Isang, 1932 (October); Schapera, field notebook 2/3, "Compiled Notes on Boloi," LSE. See also Schapera, ed., *The Political Annals of a Tswana Tribe*, April 7, 1914.

76. Paralysis might suggest witchcraft. Schapera, "Sorcery and Witchcraft in Bechuanaland," 45.

77. Ibid., 49.

78. Ibid.

79. Ibid., 46.

80. *The King versus Selaleco*, April 14, 1908, District Commissioner Gaberones Series 23/1, BNA.

81. I found only one court case in which a woman was accused of witchcraft in this period. See *The King versus Selaleco*. There is also a mention of two women accused of witchcraft by their husbands at Molepolole: Letter to the High Commissioner from Knutsford, February 26, 1889, High Commissioner Series 44/14, BNA. I imagine there were others, but given the paucity of surviving court records from this time it is difficult to make the case with absolute certainty.

82. Schapera, ed., *The Political Annals of a Tswana Tribe*, August 15, 1912.

83. See the examples of Isang and Kgabyana in Confidential District Commissioner's Report, 1934: Bakgatla Affairs: Domestic Relations between Isang's Family and Chief Molefi's Family, Secretariat Series 305/19, BNA; the planting of *dibeela* in Seepapitso's compound is in Schapera, ed., *The Political Annals of a Tswana Tribe*, December 15, 1911 (editor's note). Kwena Chief Sebele's accusation against two of his councilors is in "Chief Sebele II: Charged against His Councilors Kebohula and Moiteelasilo," 1927, Secretariat Series 25/3, BNA. Similar royal intrigue in the major northern *morafe* of Bangwato is recounted in "Chief Sekgoma vs. Phetu, Ketlalokile, etc.," December 21, 1923, Secretariat Series 3/6, BNA.

84. Schapera, ed., *The Political Annals of a Tswana Tribe*, April 7, 1914 (editor's note). See also statements made on September 15, 1911 and January 31, 1912.

85. Schapera, *Bogwera*, 7; Schapera, *Rainmaking Rites*, 49–50; "Witchcraft in the Bechuanaland Protectorate," Nettleton Resident Magistrate Serowe to Resident Commissioner 16/2/34, Secretariat Series 345/7, BNA.

86. Schapera, *Rainmaking Rites*, 49–50.

87. Though this data comes from the Bakgatla, there is no reason to believe that it was specific to this *morafe*. Rapedi himself told Schapera that they had learned the practice from the Bakwena, and in later decades, ritual murder and/or rumors of it appeared now and again in various *morafe* throughout the protectorate. See investigations in "Witchcraft in the Bechuanaland Protectorate," Secretariat Series 345/7, BNA.

88. Ibid.

89. Willoughby, *The Soul of the Bantu*, 211–212.

90. Ibid.; Schapera, *Rainmaking Rites*, 104–105.

91. Schapera, *Rainmaking Rites*, 104.

92. Schapera, "Sorcery and Witchcraft in Bechuanaland," 42.

93. Ibid.

94. For a discussion of similar processes in East Africa and the subsequent difficulties of writing about public healing as an alternative political and creative force over longer-term

history in the context of this colonial rupture, see Feierman, "Colonizers, Scholars, and the Creation of Invisible Histories."

95. "Record of the Proceedings of an Interview Granted by His Excellency the H. C. to Certain Bechuana Chiefs at Government House, Capetown, on the 21 and 22 Nov. 1927," Chiefs Tshekedi K., Sebele II and Chieftainess Ntebogang: Complaint Regarding Impositions of Control: Witchcraft, Tribal Labour, Hereditary Servants, Secretariat Series 6/1, BNA.

96. The social implications of married men's infertility were more easily solved by the wife's clandestine acts of adultery, often with the husband's tacit encouragement. See Schapera, *Married Life in an African Tribe,* 209.

97. Aging combines the social and the biological in crucial ways, and this brief discussion focuses on these intersections. In the interests of space I will not detail many important primarily social aspects of aging (such as building one's own homestead, to give one example) unless there is an attendant bodily component.

98. This model is based on the ethnographic research of anthropologists over several decades beginning in the 1930s and continues to resonate as an ideal in contemporary Botswana. People with whom I spoke presented this as the normative model of the life cycle they witnessed during their childhood and young adulthood (the 1910s–1960s). In recent decades, many aging experiences have begun to deviate from this normative model, and thus the entire life cycle is in a state of flux. They read these changes against the idealized model presented here. Schapera, "Premarital Pregnancy and Native Opinion"; Schapera, *Married Life in an African Tribe,* esp. Chapters 2, 7, 9, and 11; Alverson, *Mind in the Heart of Darkness,* Chapters 6 and 7; Guillette, "Finding the Good Life"; Ingstad, Bruun, Sandberg, and Tlou, "Care for the Elderly, Care by the Elderly," 379–398. For a more extensive discussion of some of these themes, see Livingston, "Reconfiguring Old Age"; Livingston, "Pregnant Children and Half-Dead Adults."

99. Schapera, *Married Life in an African Tribe,* 236.

100. Schapera, *Rainmaking Rites,* 84–85. *Magwane* were sent to guide them, as they knew the village and lands better, but the children were the ones who did the sprinkling.

101. Author's interviews with Rra Seleka; Ditirwa Mooki; Modise Thebe; and Sebete Phatswana.

102. Schapera, *Bogwera,* 2.

103. Ibid., 1.

104. Willoughby, "Notes on the Initiation Ceremonies of the Becwana"; Brown, "Circumcision Rites of the Becwana Tribes"; Schapera, *Bogwera.*

105. Willoughby, "Notes on the Initiation Ceremonies of the Becwana," 233.

106. Ibid., 233.

107. Schapera, *Bogwera,* 14.

108. Willoughby, "Notes on the Initiation Ceremonies of the Becwana," 232.

109. Schapera, *Bogwera,* 2.

110. Ibid., 4.

111. Ibid., 7.

112. Ibid.

113. Ibid., 10; Willoughby, "Notes on the Initiation Ceremonies of the Becwana," 235.

114. Schapera, *Bogwera,* 14.

115. Durham, "The Predicament of Dress."

116. Those interested in a longer, more detailed analysis of *bojale* in the nineteenth century should consult Jean Comaroff, *Body of Power,* 115–118.

117. Schapera, *Married Life in an African Tribe,* 259.

118. Kinsman, "Beasts of Burden," 49. See Thomas, *The Politics of the Womb*, for a comparative case.

119. Kinsman, "Beasts of Burden," 49.

120. Schapera, *Married Life in an African Tribe*, 259.

121. Kinsman, "Beasts of Burden," 49; Schapera, *Married Life in an African Tribe*, 259.

122. In at least one case (which raises the possibility of others), Christianity provided a pretext for what was really a politically motivated ban. Chief Lentswe of the Bakgatla was well aware of the trend by which chiefs never seemed to live more than five years past the initiation of their senior sons (a pattern which had held true for at least three generations). He feared one of his political rivals would somehow get hold of his eldest son's foreskin after circumcision and so, professing Christianity, he banned initiation. After much popular protest he allowed the regiment to be initiated but held his son back. Then in great secrecy with a powerful and trusted doctor, he had his son circumcised and told no one. Several boys died in the initiation camp that year, which led many to argue that an initiation without the chief's blessing or son was ill fated, so that was the last *bogwera* in the *morafe*. Confidential District Commissioner's Report, 1934: Bakgatla Affairs: Domestic Relations between Isang's Family and Chief Moelfi's Family, Secretariat Series 305/19, BNA.

123. Schapera, ed., *The Political Annals of a Tswana Tribe*, August 3, 1911 and December 14, 1911; author's interviews with Andrew Mmanthe (March 6, 1999); Mosito Makwapeng; and Tshukudu Mokgele and Mma Mokgele.

124. Schapera, "Premarital Pregnancy and Native Opinion."

125. Schapera, field notebook 2/3, "Compiled Notes on Boloi," Manyama Poonyane, August 24, 1934; Rapedi, May 11, 1931; Natale, January 23, 1934, LSE.

126. Jean Comaroff, *Body of Power*, 82.

127. Schapera, *Tswana Law and Custom*, 181–182; Willoughby, *The Soul of the Bantu*, 193–194; Schapera, field notebook 2/3, "Compiled Notes on Boloi," Rapedi, July 11, 1931; Lesaane, January 12, 1931; Sofonia, June 11, 1931; Rapedi, July 25, 1932, LSE.

128. Willoughby, *The Soul of the Bantu*, 176. Schapera, *Tswana Law and Custom*, 182; author's interview with Mma Pule, Rra Molathwa, and friend.

129. See author's interview with Mma Mosala.

130. Guillette, "Finding the Good Life," 115.

131. Jean Comaroff, *Body of Power*; Jean Comaroff, "Healing and Cultural Transformation."

132. Jean Comaroff, *Body of Power*, 80–82.

133. Author's interview with Esther Kenalemang.

134. Schapera, *Handbook of Tswana Law and Custom*, 178.

135. Miss Partridge, "Bechuana Women," *The Chronicle of the London Missionary Society* XII (1903): 38.

136. Moffat, *Missionary Labors and Scenes in Southern Africa*, 309.

137. Seeley, "The Reaction of the Batswana to the Practice of Western Medicine," 44; Mackenzie, *Ten Years North of the Orange River*, 393.

138. Plaatje, *Sechuana Proverbs*.

139. Author's interviews with Nomsa Rapela and family of Kenalemang Motlake; author's fieldnotes on casual conversation with Mma Moloi, Easter weekend, 1999, in Shashe Mookae.

140. See author's interview with family of Kenalemang Motlake.

141. Author's interview with Mma Bantle Segokgo.

142. It was also taboo for a male junior to do so for a female senior, but since women provided the palliative care, this was not a problem. Author's interview with Esther Gopane.

143. Schapera, *Married Life in an African Tribe,* 232; Evelyn Haile, "Ninth Annual Report of Maternity Work, Serowe, Bechuanaland Protectorate, 1941," Africa Odds, Box 17, London Missionary Society Papers (hereafter LMSP), Council for World Mission (hereafter CWM). In this report, Nurse Haile is reflecting back on the beginnings of her work in the very early 1930s, so we can guess that the situation she found then had existed for some time previous.

144. Schapera, *Married Life in an African Tribe,* 234.

145. Author's interview with Modise Thebe; author's field notes on casual conversation with Mma Moloi, Easter weekend, 1999 in Shashe Mookae.

146. Mackenzie, *Ten Years North of the Orange River,* 393; Schapera, *Married Life in an African Tribe,* 234.

147. Schapera, *Married Life in an African Tribe,* 234. See also Ngubane, *Body and Mind in Zulu Medicine,* 78–79.

148. Schapera, *Married Life in an African Tribe,* 234.

149. Author's interviews with Malau Alita Seati and Mma Bantle Segokgo.

150. Jennings, "Maphakela: The Witch-Doctor's Son."

151. Author's interview with Nomsa Rapela.

152. Author's interviews with Dr. Alfred Merriweather and Dr. Karl Seligmann. See also Gaye, *Better than Light,* 83.

153. Moffat, *Missionary Labors and Scenes in Southern Africa,* 248–249, 289; Hepburn, *Twenty Years in Khama's Country,* 246–247.

154. Mackenzie, *Ten Years North of the Orange River,* 375.

155. Bechuanaland Protectorate Annual Medical and Sanitary Report, 1925–1926. All of the protectorate's medical and sanitary reports are in the BNA.

156. Author's interviews with Tsukudu Mokgele and Mma Mokgele, Mololokane Makati, and Ephraim Motlhalamme.

157. Author's interview with Neo Moamogwe.

158. Schapera, ed., *The Political Annals of a Tswana Tribe,* June 3, 1911.

159. Author's interview with Chum Sejabadila.

160. Medical Officer [of] Ngamiland, "Annual Report," Secretariat Series 88/8, BNA.

161. Bechuanaland Annual Medical and Sanitary Report, 1929; Schapera, *Migrant Labour and Tribal Life,* 176. For comparative regional data, see Packard, *White Plague, Black Labor,* Chapter 4.

162. Leprosy affected only a handful of people in the country at any given time and never seemed to generate any type of large-scale outbreak. See Bechuanaland Protectorate Annual Medical and Sanitary Reports, 1926–1955.

163. Bechuanaland Protectorate Annual Medical and Sanitary Reports, 1926 and 1929; MacRae, "The Bechuanaland Protectorate," 35.

164. Author's interviews with Modise Thebe and Ntene Moilwa.

165. Seeley, "The Reaction of the Batswana to the Practice of Western Medicine." Joints were also cut and rubbed during the ceremony performed on a male child born outside the territory to welcome the infant into the lineage; see Brown, *Among the Bantu Nomads,* 54.

166. Author's interview with Neo Moamogwe.

167. Author's interview with Wamona Arona Anguru. Wamona's recollections were from his childhood in the 1930s, but he hypothesized that this had been typical of his uncles' situation before this point, since he "was born finding them this way."

168. Author's interview with Norah Kgosietsile.

169. Schapera, ed., *The Political Annals of a Tswana Tribe*, July 2, 1915.

170. Livingstone, *Missionary Travels and Researches in South Africa*, 51.

3. Male Migration and the Pluralization of Medicine

1. For more on the distribution of risk under extreme circumstances of hunger and how it maps onto uneven gender- and age-based opportunities for mobility and resource control, see Vaughan, *Story of an African Famine*; and Iliffe, *The African Poor*.

2. Wylie, "The Changing Face of Hunger in Southern African History." See also Principle Medical Officer to Dr. Shepherd, May 4, 1931, Secretariat Series 179/4, BNA; Bechuanaland Annual Medical Reports, 1933–1934 and 1935; Molepolole Annual Report, 1941, Box AF/45, LMSP, CWM.

3. Packard, *White Plague, Black Labor*.

4. For example, in 1931 the colonial medical service treated 180 cases of pulmonary and laryngeal tuberculosis and 51 cases of TB of the bones, joints, and vertebral column. The proportion of debilitating extrapulmonary TB seen at western medical sites had increased slightly by 1935, when 290 cases of pulmonary TB and 93 cases of TB of the vertebral column, bones, and bones and joints were reported. Here I am using these figures only to support my suggestion of high proportions of extrapulmonary TB; I am not claiming that these figures represent actual prevalence. Only a small fraction of the sick and debilitated would have entered the smattering of colonial medical dispensaries and hospitals by this date. Bechuanaland Annual Medical and Sanitary Report, 1935.

5. Government medical officers described Bechuanaland as "highly syphilized" and treated thousands of cases of syphilis each year in the 1930s, making syphilis by far the most prevalent problem that brought Batswana into their clinics and hospitals. There is much rich documentation from other parts of Africa of colonial doctors' confusion of yaws and syphilis. See Callahan, " 'Veni, VD, Vici?' "; Dawson, "The 1920's Anti-Yaws Campaigns and Colonial Medical Policy in Kenya." It is possible that this was also taking place in Bechuanaland, though the principle medical officer was clearly aware of the potential for confusion. He remarked, "Another explanation of the high Wasserman rate would be the occurrence of yaws in childhood, but yaws does not appear to be common in Bechuanaland. I was looking out for it particularly, having had much experience of yaws in West Africa, but I only saw one case which in a yaws country I should have diagnosed as that disease, and the same has been the experience in Bechuanaland of other officers who have had experience of yaws elsewhere." Report of the Commissioner Appointed by the Secretary of State for Dominion Affairs to Advise on Medical Administration in Bechuanaland Protectorate 1937, Secretariat Series 426/4/1, BNA. Though Callahan notes that disfigurement from yaws was the leading cause of labor rejection noted by colonial officials in Northern Rhodesia, it was not even noted as a primary cause in Bechuanaland. Much of the syphilis that was seen in Bechuanaland appears to have been tertiary syphilis.

6. Wylie, "The Changing Face of Hunger," 174.

7. Testimony by Mogwera in Appeal Case against the Senior Tribunal, October 6, 1938, 2 District Commissioner Molepolole Series 12/1, BNA; Report by Dispenser Booker to Principal Medical Officer Dyke, June 6, 1934, Secretariat Series 395/8–9, BNA.

8. This description is based on that of Resident Commissioner Sir Charles Rey in *Monarch of All I Survey*, 66.

9. Minutes of the 15th Session of the Bechuanaland Protectorate Native Advisory Council, July 10, 1933, BNA.

10. Dispenser Booker to Principal Medical Officer Dyke, June 6, 1934, Secretariat Series 395/5–8, BNA; Principal Medical Officer Dyke to Dr. Shepherd, May 4, 1931, Secretariat Series 176/4, BNA; Bechuanaland Annual Medical and Sanitary Report, 1933–1934.

11. Minutes of the 15th Session of the Native Advisory Council, July 10, 1933.

12. In several of the southeastern *merafe* during this period, political struggles and factionalism challenged what ideally should have been the unifying, mediating force of chiefship, leaving the populace trapped in the cycle of heat, dust, and drought, which facilitated the new types of responses to physical suffering: labor migration and distribution of rations. For examples of this political turmoil, see "Record of the Proceedings of an Interview Granted by His Excellency the High Commissioner to Certain Bechuana Chiefs at Government House, Capetown, on the 21 and 22 Nov, 1927," Secretariat Series 6/1, BNA; Chief Sebele II: Charged against His Councillors Kebohula and Moiteelaiso, 1927, Secretariat Series 23/5, BNA; "Transcript of Shorthand Notes Taken at Chief Molefi Pilane's Kgotla: Mochudi 12–17 November, 1934," Judicial File, Bangwato Administration 9/1, BNA.

13. Iliffe, *The African Poor,* Chapter 9, quotation on 143.

14. Landau, *The Realm of the Word,* esp. Chapter 3.

15. See, for example, Vaughan, *Curing Their Ills*; Hunt, "Le bebe en brousse"; Hunt, *A Colonial Lexicon*; Lyons, *The Colonial Disease*; Marks and Andersson, "Typhus and Social Control: South Africa, 1917–50"; Ranger, "Godly Medicine: The Ambiguities of Medical Mission in Southeastern Tanzania, 1900–1945"; White, "'They could make their victims dull'": Sadowsky, *Imperial Bedlam.*

16. At this point, each southeastern *morafe* was participating in the migrant labor economy to a different extent. The degree and nature of dependency on migrant income and the impetus for individuals to migrate differed from *morafe* to *morafe* as well as from family to family. Nonetheless, the 1930s saw the start of the trend across the southeast described here. For migrants' economic motives, see Report by Acting Additional Resident Magistrate Mochudi, July 1, 1935, Secretariat Series 436/12, BNA; Schapera field notebook 1/2, October 29, 1929, LSE.

17. Schapera, *Migrant Labour and Tribal Life,* Chapter 4.

18. Crush, Jeeves, and Yudelman, *South Africa's Labor Empire,* Table A:4.

19. Schapera, *Migrant Labour and Tribal Life,* 34.

20. Ibid., 39.

21. Ibid., 43. Schapera included the major central *morafe* of Gammangwato in this figure. The southeastern groups had even higher numbers; 96 percent of the Batlokwa and 86.8 percent of the Bangwaketse men had experience working abroad.

22. In 1910 the Protectorate was producing "large quantities of grain for sale"; Resident Commissioner to High Commissioner (no date) re: Economy and Labour in the Bechuanaland Protectorate, Resident Commissioner Series 2/48, BNA. For a description of the somewhat comparable case of Basutoland see Colin, *Families Divided,* 10–22.

23. Pim, *Financial and Economic Position,* 5.

24. Report by Resident Magistrate Gaberones District, July 1935, Secretariat Series 346/12, BNA; Schapera field notebook 1/2, October 16 and 17, 1929.

25. In July 1935, the resident commissioner for Gaberones District described in his report to the government secretary "an unparalleled exodus of natives from the Protectorate during 1933 and 1934." Secretariat Series 436/12, BNA.

26. Schapera, *Married Life in an African Tribe,* 152–153.

27. Author's interview with Konobule Kobue.

28. Pim, *Financial and Economic Position of the Bechuanaland Protectorate,* 26.

29. Schapera, ed., *The Political Annals of a Tswana Tribe*, August 15, 1912.

30. Author's interviews with Tshukudu Mokgele; Mololokane Makati; and Konobule Kobue.

31. Author's interview with Tshukudu Mokgele.

32. Schapera, *Married Life in an African Tribe*, 78.

33. Ibid., 62.

34. Author's interview with Mosito Makwapeng. See also author's interviews with Basejane Motlhalamme; Konobule Kobue; and Maiketso Momokgwe.

35. Cooper, *Marriage in Maradi, 1900–1989*, 103.

36. Schapera, *Migrant Labour and Tribal Life*, 51. Author's interviews with Tshukudu Mokgele; Goodson Selthare; and Wamona Arona Wangura.

37. They were actually 270 daily shift contracts, which usually worked out to longer than nine months, especially given the quota policies of mine work. For example, a man might not get credit for his day's work unless he had drilled a certain depth during that shift.

38. Schapera, *Migrant Labour and Tribal Life*, 53–58.

39. Recruitment of Labour: Native in Bechuanaland Protectorate, Adverse Effects of Excessive Recruiting and of Labour Migration, Statement by Councilor Kenaleman, Secretariat Series 387/5, BNA.

40. See Kuper, *Wives for Cattle*.

41. Minutes Bechuanaland Native Advisory Council, 1923, see especially statements by Isang Pilane, Secretariat Series 14/3, BNA.

42. Schapera, *Bogwera*, 14.

43. Minutes Bechuanaland Native Advisory Council, 1924, statement by Martinus Seboni, Secretariat Series 14/3, BNA.

44. Alverson, *Mind in the Heart of Darkness*; Jean Comaroff, *Body of Power*.

45. Author's interview with Pelonome Kebafetse.

46. Extracts from Minutes of the 17th Session of the Native Advisory Council Meeting, May 1936, statement by Sefako Pilane, Secretariat Series 387/5, BNA.

47. Ibid.

48. Native Advisory Council Minutes 1924, March 18, 1924, Secretariat Series 14/3, BNA.

49. See Summers, "Intimate Colonialism"; Bozzoli and Nkotsoe, *Women of Phokeng*; Murray, *Families Divided*.

50. Native Advisory Council Minutes, 1924, Secretariat Series 14/3, BNA.

51. Resident Commissioner to High Commissioner, February 16, 1923, Secretariat Series 14/3, BNA.

52. Report by Acting Assistant Resident Magistrate Molepolole to Government Secretary, July 2, 1935, Secretariat Series 436/12, BNA.

53. Report by the Resident Magistrate, Gaberones District, to the Government Secretary, July 1935, Secretariat Series 436/12, BNA. Though this quote is from a colonial official, he is repeating sentiments expressed to him by Batlokwa seniors. These feelings were voiced in other contexts; see Report by Bamalete Chief Seboko Mokgosi, June 28, 1935, and Report by Matlala Gaberones, June 5, 1935, both in same file.

54. Schapera, field notebook 1/2 (notebook A), October 18, 21, 22, and 25, 1929, LSE.

55. Schapera field notebook 1/2 (notebook A), October 21, 1929, and October 22, 1929, LSE.

56. Author's interviews with Mosito Makwapeng; Mololokane Makati; Tshukudu Mokgele; and Ephraim Motlhalame.

57. Author's interviews with Basejane Motlhalamme and Mololokane Makati.

58. As one elderly former miner explained, "Well, if the parents were at all refusing one

would just sneak out [to the recruiter]—go for these tests and then if at all you succeeded, on coming back you tell them, 'I managed to succeed so I will be going.' Now it's for the old man to say 'Okay, now I take you to this traditional doctor so that you can be strengthened, so that you can be safe going there.'" Author's interview with Ntshinogang Molefi.

59. When questioned specifically about the problems of tuberculosis and silicosis, these men agreed that the mines often contributed to such problems, but this apparently did not influence their overall characterization of the mine as a place where strength was acquired.

60. Author's interviews with Andrew Mmanthe (March 2, 1999); Basejane Motlhalamme; Mosito Makwapeng; Rra Molatlhwa; Peter Mokwena (March 12, 1999); Maiketso Momokgwe; Mololokane Makati; and Ntene Moilwa.

61. Author's interview with Konobule Kobue.

62. Jean Comaroff, *Body of Power*, 174–175.

63. Konobule Kobue was born in 1917; though he embraced a Tswana understanding of physiology, he never utilized the services of local *dingaka*. He only used "white doctors." Author's interview with Konobule Kobue.

64. Author's interviews with Andrew Mmanthe (March 5, 1999); Rra Molatlhwa; Ntshinogang Molefi; Peter Mokwena (March 12, 1999); Mosito Makwapeng; Basejane Motlhalamme; and Tshukudu Mokgele.

65. Guy and Thabane, "Technology, Ethnicity, and Ideology."

66. Author's interview with Konobule Kobue.

67. Author's interview with Mololokane Makati.

68. Author's interview with Tshukudu Mokgele.

69. Author's interview with Ephraim Motlhalamme.

70. Author's interview with Neo Moamogwe.

71. Ibid.; and author's interview with Peter Mokwena (March 12, 1999).

72. Author's interview with Peter Mokwena (March 12, 1999).

73. See Bamangwato to Rev. Dr. Tidman, no date, Mackenzie letters, 1858–1869, M. Mackenzie Folder #1, Africa Personal Box #2, LMSP, CWM; see also Iliffe, *The African Poor*, 6–7.

74. I suspect that this might be a regional (Balete) interpretation but one that is particular to a given historical context nonetheless. See author's interview with Andrew Mmanthe (March 6, 1999).

75. Author's interview with Gabotlhaleshwe Morwane.

76. Author's interview with Pulane Tshwene.

77. Some of the debilitated men appear to have been hired by white employers out of a sense of paternalism. See the case of Piet Mosimanigape from Modipane, who was hired by Petras Frederick Brink on his farm at Notwane. Brink reported that "the reason I gave him this work was because he suffered from epileptic fits and the work I gave him was easy work." Piet was also rumored to be a *ngaka*. Inquest entries for July 1945, District Commissioner Gaberones Series 1/13, Inquests, BNA; *King vs. Malefho Motsamaese*, October 16, 1945, District Commissioner Gaberones Series 24/3, BNA. Motsamaese was a Mongwato man about 50 years old.

78. Author's interviews with Pelonome Kebafetse and Gabotlhaleshwe Morwane.

79. Author's interview with Pulane Tshwene.

80. For examples from the 1930s, see Chief Kgari Sechele to Acting District Commissioner, Molepolole, September 5, 1938, District Commissioner Molepolole Series 1/22, BNA. This exemption from age was not automatic, however. See *Rex vs. Kgabo Tebele*, October 13, 1926, 2 District Commissioner Molepolole Series 13, BNA. Tebele was an 82-year-old man

who was fined £1.15 or 3 weeks' hard labor for failing to pay his hut tax. (He paid the fine rather than go to jail.) Once the hut tax and the property tax were separated, things changed some—wealthier men might give their assets to their sons while they were still alive to avoid paying property tax.

81. *Rex vs. Mathe Kelatlhilwe of Ramoutswa,* November 11, 1943, District Commissioner Gaberones Series 23/4, BNA.

82. *Rex vs. Kalete Mokoleti,* November 23, 1942, District Commissioner Gaberones Series 23/3, BNA. Kalete's case was unusual in that he returned to court to push his case for exemption, which was finally granted in 1943 when a new medical officer examined him.

83. *Rex vs. Ramatsimako Radipitsi,* August 1938, 2 District Commissioner Molepolole Series 21, BNA.

84. For examples during this period, see author's interviews with Konobule Kobue; Maiketso Momokgwe; Tshukudu Mokgele; and Ephraim Motlhalamme.

85. Packard, *White Plague, Black Labor,* Chapter 4.

86. The British divided the protectorate into districts that roughly corresponded to the various *merafe.* So "Gakwena" became "Kweneng District" in colonial parlance.

87. See Criminal Ledger, cases 1924–1936, 2 District Commissioner Molepolole Series 13, BNA.

88. Recruitment of Labour: Native in Bechuanaland Protectorate, Adverse Effects of Excessive Recruiting and of Labour Migration, 1936, Secretariat Series 387/5, BNA; Seboko Mokgosi Chief of the Bamalete to the Government Secretary, June 28, 1935; Matlala Gaberones to Government Secretary, June 5, 1935; Report from Resident Magistrate, Gaberones District, to Resident Commissioner, July 1935; and Report from Acting Resident Magistrate, Mafikeng, to Resident Commissioner, July 24, 1935, all in Secretariat Series 436/12, BNA.

89. Recruitment of Labour: Native in Bechuanaland Protectorate, Adverse Effects of Excessive Recruiting and of Labour Migration, 1936.

90. Extract from Minutes of the 17th Session of the Native Advisory Council Meeting, May 1936, Secretariat Series 387/5, BNA.

91. The end of rainmaking and initiation (and key changes in various other rituals such as the first fruits ceremonies) occurred at different times in different southeastern *merafe.*

92. As Paul Landau's work illustrates, Batswana played upon both the similarities and divergences between the two medical systems in their integration of missionary medicine into local systems of knowledge and political power. For an extended discussion of local integration of Christianity into *bongaka,* see Paul Landau, *The Realm of the Word,* Chapter 5.

93. Comaroff and Comaroff, *Of Revelation and Revolution,* vols. 1 and 2.

94. See various cases in the files of the District Commissioner Series 13 and 21 for Molepolole in the BNA; for example, *Rex vs. Kgopiso Galeboe Rasedie,* February 1939.

95. Minutes of a meeting to discuss request of Gabane people to have a medical mission dispensary held in Gabane, November 13, 1936, District Commissioner Series Molepolole 4/8, BNA.

96. In fact, these services were so identified with western medicine that chiefs referred specifically to specialties such as syphilis treatment and surgery when asking the colonial government to provide western medical services. See Sechele II, Paramount Chief of the Bakwena, to the Acting Resident Commissioner, Molepolole, September 8, 1911, "Acting Resident Commissioner's Visit to Molepolole and Kanye in September 1911: Applications by both Bakwena and Bangwaketsi for a Doctor," Secretariat Series 43/2, BNA.

97. See Foucault, *The Birth of the Clinic;* Fanon, *A Dying Colonialism;* Vaughan, *Curing Their Ills.* I am grateful to Jonathan Sadowsky for helping me to clarify this confluence.

98. A handful of recruiters began employing local doctors to perform group examinations of recruits shortly before 1935.

99. Report of Dr. P. M. Shepherd on the Poor Physique of Mine Recruits and Main Causes of Rejection, Secretariat Series 398/6, BNA.

100. Schapera, *Migrant Labour and Tribal Life,* 16–17.

101. Ibid.; author's interview with Dr. Alfred Merriweather.

102. Report of Dr. P. M. Shepherd on the Poor Physique of Mine Recruits and Main Causes of Rejection.

103. Circular to Medical Officers re: Standards Required for Recruits for Mines etc., x June 24, 1928 (retyped with revisions February 24, 1932), Labour, Native: Medical Examination of Recruits, Secretariat Series 426/4/1, BNA.

104. Author's interview with Dr. Alfred Merriweather.

105. Author's interview with Wamona Arona Anguru.

106. Author's interview with Dr. Alfred Merriweather.

107. Bechuanaland Director of Medical Services to Dr. Mackenzie, January 14, 1947, Medical Series 2/3/1, BNA; Molepolole Annual Report, Africa Reports 1941–50, LMSP, CWM.

108. Dr. E. E. Barnett to Cocker Brown re: Sources of Income, 1938 (no date), Africa Odds, Box 34, folder #2, LMSP, CWM; Cocker Brown to Senator J. D. Rheinallt Jones, January 11, 1939, Molepolole Annual Report, AF/45 folder Shepherd, P. M. 1939–48, Africa Reports 1941–50, LMSP, CWM.

109. Dr. E. E. Barnett to Cocker Brown re: Sources of Income.

110. Report of the Witwatersrand Mine Natives' Wages Commission of 1943, Analysis of Grants to Institutions in Bechuanaland (page 61 of the report), Secretariat Series 464/1, BNA.

111. Molepolole Annual Report 1939, Africa Reports, 1941–50, AF/45 folder Shepherd, P. M. 1939–48, LMSP, CWM.

112. For more on cursory medical examinations as barriers to opportunities, see Kraut, *Silent Travelers.*

113. See author's interviews with Peter Mokwena (March 12, 1999); Maiketso Momokgwe; Konobule Kobue; Mololokane Makati; Mosito Makwapeng; and Basejane Motlhalamme.

114. For more on the stethoscope and other technologies to probe "under the skin," see White, "'They could make their victims dull.'"

115. Author's interview with Mololokane Makati.

116. Author's interview with Konobule Kobue. The machines Rra Kobue refers to were X-ray machines. (This I gleaned through further conversation not quoted here.)

117. Feierman, "Explanation and Uncertainty in the Medical World of Ghaambo."

118. Vaughan, *Curing Their Ills,* esp. 1–28, 55–76.

119. District Commissioner Kanye to Principal Medical Officer, August 24, 1937, Secretariat Series 426/4/1, BNA.

4. Increasing Autonomy, Entangled Therapeutics, and Hidden Wombs

1. Peters, *Dividing the Commons,* Chapters 3 and 4.

2. Ka-Mbuya and Morton, "The South," 148. See also Annual Report, 1952 (Molepolole), Box AF/45, Africa Reports 1951–60, J–M, LMSP, CWM.

3. Jackson, *Botswana 1939–1945,* 151–155.

4. Comaroff and Roberts, "Marriage and Extra-Marital Sexuality"; Gulbrandsen, "To Marry—or Not to Marry."

5. Schapera, "Premarital Pregnancy and Native Opinion"; Gulbrandsen, "To Marry—or Not to Marry."

6. Comaroff and Roberts, "Marriage and Extra-Marital Sexuality." See also Griffiths, *In the Shadow of Marriage*; Thomas, *The Politics of the Womb*; Jeater, *Marriage, Perversion, and Power.*

7. Manaheng Lesotho to Kgosi Tshekedi Khama, April 2, 1944, Papers of Michael Crowder, Box 17A, Institute of Commonwealth Studies, University of London (hereafter ICS); see also Thebetsile Dihutso to T. Khama, September 20, 1944, Box 17F.

8. G. Tsladikae to Kgosi Khama, December 26, 1943, Box 17I; R. K. Fiego Lelokwane to Tshekedi Khama, February 29, 1944, Box 17H; Oletheng Ramoruwana to T Khama, n.d., Box 17H. All in Papers of Michael Crowder.

9. I am grateful to Lynn Thomas for sharing these letters with me.

10. Thomas, *The Politics of the Womb*, 132.

11. Jeater, *Marriage, Perversion, and Power*, 262.

12. Schapera, *Married Life in an African Tribe*, 202.

13. Crush, Jeeves, and Yudelman, *South Africa's Labor Empire*, Table A:4.

14. The meanings of *madi* (money) underwent similar changes with proletarianization and the emergence of a notion of individual rights/privileges. See Barber, "Money, Self-Realization and the Person in Yoruba Texts."

15. I do not have figures on school enrollment for the entire period in question. But the figures for the late colonial period provide some index of the growth of participation in western schooling. In the early 1930s, there was only one national primary school (and a handful of mission schools), but by 1965, the last year before Independence, 66,061 children were enrolled in primary school. This was out of a total population estimated at just under 500,000. Kwape, "Access to Education," 212.

16. Author's interview with Mma Lekile. See also author's interview with Mma Pule, Rra Molatlhwa, and friend.

17. Author's interview with Mma Pule, Rra Molatlhwa, and friend. In Thamaga, the family of Kenalemang Motlake reported that these activities stopped "at Independence in 1966." Author's interview with Kenalemang Motlake and family.

18. Author's interview with Andrew Mmanthe (March 6, 1999). In the neighboring village of Kumakwane, several men agreed that these practices ended in the mid-1960s and equate this collapse with Independence. Author's interview with Sebete Phatswana (and several of the guests at his beer drink).

19. Appeal against Bamalete Senior Tribunal, *L. S. Mokgosi vs. M. Maotonyana*, January 1961, District Commissioner Gaberones Series 28/4, BNA. See also Testimony of Baibai Mopogo aka John Motlokwa, January 1, 1952 and Chief to District Commissioner, December 13, 1955, both in District Commissioner Gaberones Series 9/5, Tribunals Batlokwa, BNA. I was able to access only the transcripts of cases that reached the District Court. Cases involving regimental labor were tried locally and reached the District Court only on appeal, as is the case with the appeal cited above. However, several pieces of correspondence between chiefs and district commissioners about other such cases combine with the oral sources cited above to support the suggestion that these instances of refusal were becoming more common.

20. *L. S. Mokgosi vs. M. Maotonyana*, January 1961.

21. For example, there was a major drought in 1952. Annual Report Molepolole, 1952, and M. T. Mogwe, African Ministers' Reports, 1952,, both in Africa Reports 1951–60, J–M, Box AF/45, LMSP, CWM.

22. Seeley, "The Reaction of the Batswana to the Practice of Western Medicine," 52.

23. Mkgapha Mathabanyane to Kgosi Tshekedi Khama, December 13, 1943 (Bundle A, Letter 166); Seanana Moloi to Kgosi Tshekedi Khama, December 29, 1943 (Bundle E, Letter 52); Oitsile Seakgoseng to Kgosi Tshekedi Khama, n.d. (Bundle E, Letter 81); Lomeletsang Ntshabe to Kgosi Tshekedi Khama, n.d. (Bundle H); Kgakanyane Mangole to Kgosi Tshekedi Khama, n.d. (Bundle H); Chechebele Machacha to Kgosi Tshekedi Khama, n.d. (Bundle J). All in Papers of Michael Crowder, Box 17 (1943–45), ICS.

24. Ganawabo Nsala to Kgosi Tshekedi Khama, n.d. (Bundle J), Papers of Michael Crowder, Box 17 (1943–45), ICS. As this letter illustrates, the fears could also be for their own safety should a wife or other relatives hire a *ngaka* in their absence. Nsala writes, "Recently I heard that a child died and while waiting to here [sic] from her, I learnt that they had sought the services of a traditional doctor. I was shocked and grieved by the news that doctor can come into my compound and attend to my child (*my own blood*) during my absence. So I sought for his name. They refused to give me the name and this action has hurt me even more. My feeling is that the doctor has intended to kill me, that is why they refused to give his name" (emphasis mine).

25. Author's interview with Neo Moamogwe.

26. Report of Sister-in-Charge, Deborah Retief Memorial Hospital, Mochudi, Bechuanaland Annual Medical and Sanitary Report, 1946.

27. Minutes of the 28th Session of the African Advisory Council, August 11–20, 1947, Secretariat Series 395/1/1, BNA, see especially remarks by Tshekedi Khama and Kgosi Bathoen. See Feierman, "Colonizers, Scholars, and the Creation of Invisible Histories."

28. Landau, *The Realm of the Word*, Chapter 4.

29. Lagerwerf, *"They Pray for You,"* Chapter 2.

30. Quotation from Ka-Mbuya and Morton, "The South," 151. See also Merriweather, *Desert Doctor Remembers*, 155.

31. On the LMS, see Merriweather, *Desert Doctor Remembers*, 144, 155. Lagerwerf also reports these universal sanctions among the established churches in the early 1970s and specifically cites this as a motivation for young women to join independent churches. Since it seems that there has been a loosening rather than a tightening of such rules over time, we can fairly safely assume that her observations in the 1970s were true for the earlier period as well. Lagerwerf, *"They Pray for You,"* 94–99.

32. Merriweather, *Desert Doctor Remembers*, 156.

33. Marion Ginger, Annual Report Serowe and Lobatse, 1959, Africa Reports: A–H 1951–60, LMSP, CWM. See also author's interview with Dr. Alfred Merriweather; District Missionary's Report 1956, Kanye District, Folder Henson, H. F. P. 1955–59, Africa Reports A–H 1951–60, LMSP, CWM. In the late 1990s, disabled and frail elderly people were among those who received such visits. I imagine that some disabled persons (who were not "sick" per se) also received such visits in the postwar period. For a description of the earlier meanings and contours of this practice in Serowe, see Landau, *The Realm of the Word*, 123–124.

34. Interested readers should consult, for example, Comaroff, *Body of Power, Spirit of Resistance*; Landau, *The Realm of the Word*; Klaits, "Care and Kinship in an Apostolic Church during Botswana's Time of AIDS"; Sundkler, *Bantu Prophets in South Africa*.

35. Sundkler, *Bantu Prophets*, 228.

36. Prayers were said for rain, of course, but women had no special subversive role in this process by virtue of their biological identity. Instead, the idiom of mother/sister/nurse was applied to visiting and caring for the sick and the needy. See the extensive and excellent

discussion of the historical role of women's spiritual and moral potency in determining and shaping women's participation in Christian activities in Hodgson, *The Church of Women.*

37. Livingston, "These Children of Today."

38. Thema, "The Changing Pattern of Tswana Social and Family Relations." Thema describes such changes as beginning in the late 1930s, when he first saw milk sold in glass bottles, and picking up pace since.

39. Author's interviews with Kenalemang Motlake and family; Nomsa Rapela; Malau Alita Seati; Naniso Seati granny of Kenalemang Seati; Neo Moamogwe; Alice Molele.

40. Author's interview with Neo Moamogwe; The King vs Mmapudi Thapelo a Molete Woman Age 20 Years and Also Clara Taukobong a Molete Woman Age 60 in Ramoutsa, September 3, 1945, District Commissioner Gaberones Series 24/3, BNA. In her testimony Moitoi Molebatsi reported that she fetched water for Clara, her "crippled" neighbor, while her daughter was sick.

41. Author's interview with Neo Moamogwe.

42. See, for example, the various cases (too many to list individually) in Unclaimed Compensation, Southern District Council Series 24/7; Exemption from Tax, Southern District Council Series 19/12; Exemption from Tax, Southern District Council Series 2/6; Exemptions from tax, District Commissioner Kanye Series 13/7; General Matters on Mine Recruits, Native Administration Series 1/4 (this includes attempts by the chief and his councilors to secure deferred pay for the mothers of absent miners). All in BNA.

43. Author's interview with Dr. Merriweather; see also Southern District Council: Subject: Destitutes, Reference: Medical Attention, which has numerous references to destitute patients whose care was paid for by Chief Bathoen and the Ngwaketse Tribal Treasury between 1955 and 1966. In Southern District Council Series 3/8, BNA.

44. Author's interviews with Mma Mosala; Kenalemang Motlake and family. Neighbors, of course, were often relatives of one type or another, given the way that residential wards were settled. Schapera, "The Social Structure of the Tswana Ward."

45. See for example, Inquest into the Death of Woman Gaushupele, November 10, 1942, District Commissioner Gaberones Series 1/13; The King vs Mmapudi Thapelo, a Molete Woman Age 20 Years, and Also Clara Taukobong, a Molete Woman Age 60 in Ramoutsa, September 3, 1945, District Commissioner Gaberones Series 23/3. Both in BNA.

46. Author's interview with Nomsa Rapela.

47. Labour Migration: Survey of Effects of on Economic Position of BP: Scottish Livingston Hospital Birth and Infant Mortality Rates January–August 1943, Secretariat Series 437/1/1, BNA; Circular Memorandum, No 10152 of the 15th April, 1957 (No. 82 of 1957), To All Heads of Departments, Divisional Commissioners, and District Commissioners, 13, Mss. Africa s. 1378, Papers of B. O. Wilkin, Rhodes House, Oxford. See also a better-documented and comparable rise in tuberculosis across the border in South Africa in Packard, *White Plague, Black Labor,* 251.

48. Author's interview with Malau Alita Seati.

49. Author's interview with Nomsa Rapela.

50. See, for example, author's interview with Senowe Mmilo; *King vs. Malefho Motsamaese,* October 16, 1945, District Commissioner Gaberones Series 24/3, BNA.

51. Rosenberg, "Framing Disease Illness, Society, and History."

52. Good, *Medicine, Rationality, and Experience: An Anthropological Perspective.*

53. Bechuanaland Annual Medical Report, 1950, 7.

54. Annual Medical Reports were not issued from 1959 to 1973, though the report from 1959 includes statistics up through 1963.

55. Some forms of debility, such as cerebral palsy (which was related to tuberculosis as an effect of tubercular meningitis), were for the most part uncounted and unnoticed. Most cases did not enter the public space of the clinic or hospital. Other debilitating afflictions were the source of continuing attention reaching over from the prewar period but began a distinct decline in incidence. For example, nonvenereal tertiary syphilis (whose incidence was concentrated in the Kalahari region in the west of Bechuanaland) continued to plague thousands in the late 1940s, but the numbers dwindled over time. The colonial medical service applied two forms of developmentalist zeal to the problem—magic bullets and education (in this case about hygiene)—and by 1955 close to 125,000 people "had been seen and treated, either curatively or as contacts." Bechuanaland Annual Medical and Sanitary Report, 1955 (quote on p. 13). On the concentration of nonvenereal tertiary syphilis in the Kalahari and the subsequent decline of the disease, see Merriweather, "Changing Disease Patterns in Botswana."

56. Annual Report Kanye, Bechuanaland Annual Medical and Sanitary Report, 1945.

57. Rev. Sandilands to Ronald Chamberlain, December 1, 1945 (folder S. Africa Correspondence, A. Sandilands, 1940–45); Nathan of Churt to Rev. Sandilands, cc: Doctor Harold A Moody, January 9, 1946, Rev. Sandilands to Dr. Harold Moody, n.d., Sir Nathan to Dr. Moody, February 16, 1946. All four in Africa Box AF/13, South Africa Correspondence, folder S. Africa Correspondence, A. Sandilands, 1946–50, LMSP, CWM.

58. Ibid.

59. Packard, *White Plague, Black Labor,* Chapter 4.

60. Circular Memorandum, No 10152 of the 15th April, 1957 (No. 82 of 1957), 13.

61. Bechuanaland Annual Medical and Sanitary Report, 1955, 11. Tuberculosis rates continued to climb in subsequent decades, and the Medical Department spent more money on TB than any other disease. Ministry of Health to All Tribal Authorities, Division Commissioners, District Commissioners, Medical Officers, and Medical Missionaries, cc: District Medical Service, March 3, 1961, Secretariat Series 590/1, BNA.

62. Bechuanaland Annual Medical and Sanitary Report, 1955. There was a gradual downward trend in the reporting of extrapulmonary cases as compared to pulmonary cases. For example, in 1943 the Annual Medical and Sanitary Report found 183 extrapulmonary cases out of a total of 420 reported cases of TB. This may in part represent increased diagnostic capacity for pulmonary TB and perhaps also a greater tendency for Batswana to send pulmonary cases to western medical sites.

63. For more on the relation of technology to the social construction of diagnosis, see Wailoo, *Drawing Blood.*

64. Tuberculosis in the Bechuanaland Protectorate: Annex I: Plan for Control Programmes: Suggestions for the Control of TB in Countries with Undeveloped and Underdeveloped Programmes, World Health Organization, n.d., Secretariat Series 438/2/2, BNA.

65. For example, Dr. Alfred Merriweather takes a very expansive view of tuberculosis in his 1969 memoir about his experiences at the United Free Church mission hospital in Molepolole. He opens his chapter on TB, entitled "Captain of the Men of Death," with the following description: "Tuberculosis is still the greatest medical problem facing Botswana. No other disease causes so much morbidity or mortality. It is the greatest deceiver, presenting itself in many forms; affecting lungs, glands, kidneys, intestines, bones, joints, covering membranes of heart and lungs, and the central nervous system. Whenever a patient complains of a cough or weakness or fever or swelling, we say, 'This is tuberculosis until proved otherwise.'" Merriweather, *Desert Doctor,* 50.

66. Bechuanaland Annual Medical and Sanitary Report, 1950, quote on p. 7.

67. Author's interview with Dr. Alfred Merriweather; see also Bechuanaland Annual Medical and Sanitary Reports for this period. I should note that this continued to be the case well into the 1990s, though the dialogue was now shaped by a national medical service and the language of international health, even though I saw many people debilitated by extra-pulmonary tuberculosis in the course of visits from health care workers who provided community-based rehabilitation.

68. Author's interview with Dr. Alfred Merriweather.

69. Author's interview with Dr. Karl Seligmann.

70. Author's interviews with Dr. Karl Seligmann and Dr. Alfred Merriweather; Bechua-naland Annual Medical and Sanitary Report, 1951.

71. Author's interview with Dr. Alfred Merriweather.

72. In the late 1970s, when the Red Cross began providing technical aids (calipers, arti-ficial limbs, etc.) to disabled Batswana, polio survivors were a significant portion of the pa-tients seen. List of Patients to be Seen at Next Clinic, September 1978, Botswana Red Cross Series 7/3a, BNA.

73. Bechuanaland Annual Medical and Sanitary Report, 1948; Chief Bathoen to District Commissioner re: Circular 15, May 7, 1948, Southern District Council Series 9/2, BNA.

74. Bechuanaland Protectorate Annual Medical and Sanitary Report 1948.; in the 1944–1945 outbreak in the Transvaal, Europeans had an incidence rate of 40.98 per 100,000, while Africans had an incidence rate of only 3.65 per 100,000. The total number of European cases was 808; there were 572 non-European cases. *Poliomyelitis: Papers and Discussions Presented at the First International Poliomyelitis Conference* (Philadelphia: J. B. Lippincott Company, 1949), 348. In 1948, in urban South Africa, the disproportion remained: the polio rate per 100,000 for whites was 57.57 and for Africans it was 5.40. Gear et al., "Poliomyelitis in an Urban Native Township during a Non-Epidemic Year," 297. Several missionary doctors and colonial officials and their family members suffered disabling or even fatal polio infections in these years. Author's interviews with Dr. Karl Seligmann and Barry Eustace.

75. High Commissioner's Notice no. 100 (April 18, 1948) Amending the Public Health Regulations (High Commissioner's Notice No. 16 of 1938) in Respect of Acute Anterior Poliomyelitis, Bechuanaland Protectorate Annual Medical and Sanitary Report, 1948.

76. Rogers, *Dirt and Disease: Polio Before FDR*, 125–126.

77. Bechuanaland Annual Medical and Sanitary Report 1956; Bechuanaland Annual Medical and Sanitary Report 1958 (contains statistics through 1963).

78. Both polio and tuberculosis could cause meningitis and a number of other bacterial and/or viral infections. Dr. Merriweather remembers parents bringing many, many chil-dren in with meningitis infections in the 1950s and 1960s. Author's interview with Dr. Alfred Merriweather.

79. Dr. Alexander Jokl, Blind Africans in the High Commission Territories: Report on a Tour through the Bechuanaland Protectorate, 1944 and Dr. Alexander Jokl, Report on a Tour through the Northern Bechuanaland Protectorate, 1945, both in Secretariat Series 276/2/1, BNA; Bechuanaland Protectorate Census 1946, Native Administration Series 2/10, BNA; Bechuanaland Protectorate Annual Medical and Sanitary Report, 1955; British Empire So-ciety for the Blind, Report of a Director's Visit to Bechuanaland Protectorate, November 1955, Secretariat Series 548/5, BNA.

80. Director of Medical Services to the Government Secretary, Blind Africans in the High Commission Territories, February 22, 1947; Dr. Mackenzie to Dr. Jokl, February 21, 1947. Both documents in Secretariat Series 276/2/2, BNA.

81. British Empire Society for the Blind, Report of a Director's Visit to the Bechuanaland Protectorate, November 1955.

82. Ibid.

83. The same in all probability might be said for the Transvaal and the Central African regions, where comparable figures were found. Ibid.

84. Cataract surgery appears to have also been intermittently practiced at mission hospitals. See, for example, Main, "The Opening of the Sefhare Hospital."

85. Blind Africans in the High Commission Territories: Report on a Tour through the Bechuanaland Protectorate by Dr. Alexander Jokl, 1944, Secretariat Series 276/2/1, BNA. See also similar statements by the Acting Director of Medical Services, which on the one hand shift blame onto Tswana parents for neglecting their children and on the other argue against the provision of "weak" eyeglasses; Acting Director of Medical Services to the Government Secretary re: Blind Africans, June 5, 1946, Secretariat Series 276/2/2, BNA.

86. On developmentalism, see Cooper, "Modernizing Bureaucrats"; Packard, "Visions of Postwar Health and Development."

87. See Livingstone, *Missionary Travels and Researches in South Africa*, 145.

88. In other African colonies at the time there was a well-developed interest in women's reproductive health; see Hunt, *A Colonial Lexicon*. But in the southeastern protectorate at the time, there was only limited talk about midwifery. In Serowe to the north however, nurse Evelyn Haile of the London Missionary Society worked for decades as a nurse/midwife in an effort to "educate" local women and improve local midwifery practices. E. Haile, 9th Annual Report of Maternity Work, Serowe Bechuanaland Protectorate, 1941; "Report of Work among Mothers and Girls in Serowe, Bechuanaland Protectorate, 1940"; 11th Annual Report Maternity Work, 1943. All three in Africa Reports 1941–1950, folder Haile, E. A., LMS, CWM.

89. See annual medical reports for this period.

90. Worboys, "The Discovery of Colonial Malnutrition between the Wars." See Director Medical Service to All Medical Officers and Medical Missionaries re: Nutritional State of People in the BP, October 22, 1952, District Commissioner Lobatse Series 18/11, BNA.

91. Cooper, "Modernizing Bureaucrats," 64–92; Packard, "Visions of Postwar Health and Development," 93–115.

92. Extract District Commissioners' Conference, Agenda: Lunatics, August 11, 1947 and Minutes of Meeting Held at Mafikeng, April 24–27, 1944, both in Secretariat Series 399/6/1, BNA.

93. Bechuanaland Annual Medical and Sanitary Report, 1926; DDMS (Dr. Mackenzie) to Government Secretary, June 26, 1944 and Extract from Resident Commissioner's Report on Visit to Southern Protectorate, November 1935, both in Secretariat Series 399/6/1, BNA.

94. Extract Annual Report, 1943, Ngwato District, Secretariat Series 399/6/1, BNA.

95. DDMS (Dr. Mackenzie) to Government Secretary, June 26, 1944; Minutes of Meeting Held at Mafikeng, April 24–27, 1944; Extract District Commissioners' Conference, August 11, 1947.

96. Director Medical Services to Government Secretary, June 26, 1944; Annual Report: Molepolole, Medical Department Annual Report, 1940, Medical Series 1/2; Annual Report: Serowe, Medical Department Annual Report, 1945, Medical Series 1/6; Annual Report: Lobatse District, Medical Department Annual Report, 1946, Medical Series 1/7. All in BNA.

97. Director of Medical Services to Government Secretary re: Construction of a Mental Home, August 30, 1945, Secretariat Series 399/6/1, BNA.

98. There are numerous instances of this. See Chief Bathoen to District Commissioner Kanye, December 11, 1956; Dr Manson to District Commissioner Kanye, December 12, 1956. Both in District Commissioner Kanye Series 16/12, BNA.

99. See Tribal Secretary Bome to DC Kanye, May 5, 1966, re: Mosetsanakhumo Katshoma; District Commissioner to Tribal Secretary, May 12, 1966, re: Mosetsanakhumo Katshoma. Both in Southern District Council Series 2/11, BNA.

100. There is some internal variation of ideas and practices and debate within *bongaka*, but this discussion will focus mainly on broad areas of agreement and commonality within the therapeutic system. Uneasy comparisons and entanglements of biomedical and other diagnostic nosologies occur within both popular and professional discourses that to some extent transcend these internal distinctions. See Cohen, *No Aging in India*.

101. This phenomenon persists. Suzette Heald's work illustrates how this flexibility has facilitated interpretations of the biomedical disease HIV/AIDS as a form of *boswagadi*. Heald, "It's Never as Easy as ABC."

102. Kuriyama, *The Expressiveness of the Body*, especially Part One.

103. Giles-Vernick, "Leaving a Person Behind."

104. I am grateful to Paul Landau for helping me think through these issues. See Landau, "Nineteenth Century Transformations in Consciousness."

105. Karp and Jackson, "Introduction"; Kleinmann, *The Illness Narratives*; Comaroff, "Healing and the Cultural Order."

106. This "*pelo*" has historically referred to a broader domain than the single organ biomedicine calls "heart." It is unclear the extent to which exposure to biomedical models has narrowed "*pelo*"—but in the late-nineteenth- and early-twentieth-century missionary W. C. Willoughby referred to "the contents of the chest cavity, these last being loosely and generally referred to as the 'heart,' though every Native can give a distinct name to each chest organ if he stays to think about it." Willoughby, *The Soul of the Bantu*, 5.

107. Alverson, *Mind in the Heart of Darkness*, 112. See also Schapera field notebook 2/3, "Identity," John Sejwe 1930, LSE; author's interview with Rra Seleka.

108. Schapera field notebook 2/3, "Identity," John Sejwe 1930, Sofonia 1930, LSE; author's interview with Rra Seleka.

109. Alverson, *Mind in the Heart of Darkness*, 112–114.

110. Ibid., 113–114.

111. For more on the shift from the heart to the brain as the central organ of personhood in the west, see Lock, *Twice Dead*. Nor are all African cultures similarly heart-centric in this sense. Yoruba people place the locus of self in the belly. Hallen, *The Good, the Bad, and the Beautiful*, 47.

112. This is not to suggest that there is no sense of emotion, intellect, mind, and body—but rather that they bleed into one another, across corporeal boundaries, and are configured in relation to one another in radically different ways. "Mind" is often located in one's heart, not one's brain. See Lambek, "Body and Mind in Mind, Body and Mind in Body"; Klaits, "Care and Kinship in an Apostolic Church During Botswana's Time of AIDS"; Lambek and Solway, "Just Anger."

113. It is no accident that relatives are called *losika* (people of the vein). In marriage payments, thus, cattle are exchanged for the blood of the wife's lineage. Kuper, *Wives for Cattle*, 17.

114. See Schapera field notebook 2/3, "Protection (Birth)," Rapedi, September 22, 1932; Sofonia, October 11, 1932.

115. *Boswagadi*, a disease of widow(er)s, gained in prevalence during the prewar period, amid the dislocations and dangers of migrant mining. With *boswagadi* the blood of one spouse missed the (now deceased) other, so the widow(er) underwent a yearlong period of mourning, abstinence, and ritual purification to cool his or her blood. But this disease,

though stemming out of the sexual mixing of blood and procreation of spouses, focused more on the intestines (*mala*) than the uterus (*popelo*). Schapera, "Kgatla Notions of Ritual Impurity."

116. Schapera field notebook 2/3, "Death (Causes)," Sofonia, September 21, 1932, LSE.

117. Feierman, "Explanation and Uncertainty in the Medical World of Ghaambo," 329. See also Jean Comaroff, "Healing and the Cultural Order."

118. Werbner, *Ritual Passage, Sacred Journey,* Chapter 1.

119. For more specifically on *dibeela,* see Schapera field notebook 2/3, Rapedi, June 4, 1931, Rapedi, May 9, 1931, Sofonia, October 5, 1932, Sofonia, January 19, 1934, LSE.

120. Schapera, *Married Life in an African Tribe,* 68, 223.

121. *Regina vs. Makgaribe Polaki,* November 16, 1964, 2 District Commissioner Series Molepolole 2/23, BNA; see also *The Queen versus Nthomme Teko,* September 23, 1964, *The Queen versus Phologotswana Ramme,* August 28, 1964, and *The Queen versus Dineonyane Barupi,* October 7, 1964, all in 2 District Commissioner Series Molepolole 2/23; *Tshiri Pilane versus Moji Mageta,* March 12, 1948, District Commissioner Gaberones Series 27/2, BNA.

122. *Rex vs. Obamang Reakae,* February 12, 1964, 2 District Commissioner Series Molepolole 22; BP Police Serowe to BP Police Commissioner, Mafikeng, February 10, 1959; *Rex vs. Arekile Baganetseng,* September 29, 1958; *Rex vs. Chombo Monyana, Tikanyetso Letsatsi, and Sundano Nsiko,* September 3, 1958; *Rex vs. Ampeng Kelesemetswe, Tshukudu Tawana, Tubang, Tsubang Bile, Leteleng Leshibogo, Rebeetsweng Keagomang, Moeng Nkoi, Mosimane Wakiri,* July 1, 1954; *Rex vs. Amegeng Kelesemetswe and Mathare Kelefekae,* May 14, 1958. All in Secretariat Series 575/2, BNA.

123. Lambek and Solway, "Just Anger," 56–57.

124. See *Gotlanna Baitlotli vs. Senior Tribunal,* Molepolole, July 29, 1961, 2 District Commissioner Series Molepolole 2/22, BNA.

125. Author's interview with Andrew Mmanthe (March 2, 1999).

126. Author's interview with Sebete Phatswana.

127. Anderson and Staugard, *Traditional Midwives,* 125.

128. Schapera field notebook 2/3, "Compiled Notes on Boloi," Marobela, January 30, 1935; Edirilwe, July 22, 1935, LSE.

129. Schapera, *Married Life in an African Tribe,* 202.

130. See author's interviews with Sebete Phatswana; Peter Mokwena (March 12, 1999); and Esther Kenalemang.

131. Author's interview with Esther Kenalemang.

132. While not exactly mirroring *mopakwane,* the symptoms overlap and potentially refer to one another, just as severe diarrhea might also be associated with big tummies and muscle-wasting and so forth. Romero-Daza and Himmelgreen, "More Than Money for Your Labor," 194.

133. Merriweather, *English-Setswana Medical Phrasebook and Dictionary.*

134. For a description of some previous restrictions on male sexuality see Schapera, *Married Life in an African Tribe,* 194–201. Schapera refers to changes in some of these restrictions as they are practiced, though he is not describing the rise of a new model of male sexuality such as that described by some of my informants. See author's interviews with Modise Thebe; Ntene Moilwa; and Mma Mantshadi.

135. Author's interviews with Mma Pule, Rra Molatlhwa, and friend; Sebete Phatswana; and Mma Mantshadi.

136. In the late 1990s, people appeared to use these terms interchangeably. I asked several people to outline the differences between the three, but no pattern emerged in their re-

sponses. I only found a few letters written in Setswana to the Ngwaketse chief from persons requesting confinement for their ill relatives in the 1950s and 1960s. They seem to use a variant of *botsenwa/ditsenwa* or to simply use the generic term *bolwetsi* (illness). See Daniel Oaitse to Bathoen, October 14, 1963; K. R. Bome to Daniel Oaitse, October 17, 1963. Both in Southern District Council Series 2/11, BNA.

137. Author's interview with Mma Lekile.

138. Statement by Chief Tshekedi Khama, in Extract of Minutes of African Advisory Council 25th session, April 1944, Secretariat Series 399/6/6, BNA.

139. Author's interviews with Mpho Lekile; Mmabojale Tshukunono; Modise Thebe; and Mma Pule, Rra Molatlhwa, and friend.

140. Author's interviews with Andrew Mmanthe (March 5, 1999) and Peter Mokwena (March 12, 1999).

141. I did know one man in Botswana in the late 1990s who explicitly used the word *boboko* (brain) when we talked about mental illness, but he was an unusual man in terms of his educational accomplishments for someone of his age. He worked for the Native Recruitment Corporation as a clerk and embraced western medical epistemology and terminology in several instances. But his terminology reminds us that the process of entanglement unfolds somewhat unevenly across popular knowledge. See author's interview with Chum Sejabadila.

142. Author's interviews with Andrew Mmanthe (March 5, 1999); Mma Pule, Rra Molatlhwa, and friend; Ntshinogang Molefi; Peter Mokwena (March 12, 1999); Mosito Makwapeng; Basejane Motlhalamme; Tshukudu Mokgele; and Konobule Kobue.

143. Author's interviews with Chum Sejabadila; Mma Mosala; and Mmabojale Tshukunono.

144. Author's interview with Modise Thebe.

145. Intergenerational tensions leading to suspicions of *boloi* committed by elders against their juniors were not new in the postwar period. See Schapera field notebook 2/3, "Watching Graves," Kgampu May 1938, Ngwaketse; Schapera, ed., *The Political Annals of a Tswana Tribe*, August 15, 1912. But there is the strong possibility that new types of boloi emerged or became more popular.

146. Schapera field notebook 2/3, "Compiled Notes on Boloi," Simon Kobe 1931; Rrakgomo, November 13, 1929, Rapedi, April 18, 1931, LSE.

147. Author's interview with Mma Pule, Rra Molatlhwa, and friend.

148. Schapera field notebook 2/3, "Compiled Notes on Boloi," Sofonia, October 20, 1932, Maswe, August 14, 1934.

149. Author's interviews with Andrew Mmanthe (March 5, 1999) and Rra Seleka.

150. Many people in Diphaleng knew this story and told it to me. Others told me of similar stories, and I met several people who were injured in this way by their parents, though not necessarily in the time period in question. See author's interview with Peter Kgosietsile.

151. Author's interviews with Mpho Lekile; Modise Thebe; and Peter Mokwena (March 12, 1999).

152. District Commissioner Kanye Series 16/12; District Commissioner Series 9/7; Southern District Council Series 2/11, all in BNA. There are too many cases to list them each individually here; instead the reader should note the general trends indicated.

153. Author's interviews with Peter Mokwena (March 12, 1999) and Mpho Lekile.

154. Ibid.; author's interview with Norah Kgosietsile.

155. Landau, "Strategy and Selfhood among the Samuelites of Thaba Nchu."

156. Draft of Talks on TB and Smallpox by H. F. Hilson, Government Inspector of Health,

Lobatse, 1947, District Commissioner Lobatse Series 18/11, BNA. Merriweather, *English-Setswana Medical Phrasebook and Dictionary,* 64.

157. Anderson and Staugard, *Traditional Midwives,* 125.

158. In the late 1990s I never heard the term *thibamo* used by patients to describe a tubercular spine or cerebral tuberculosis, though given the fluidity of diagnosis, it is possible for the association to yet arise. Anderson and Staugard mention the bloody cough of tuberculosis only as a sign of *thibamo,* not symptoms of other possible types of tubercular infection. Anderson and Staugard, *Traditional Midwives,* 123–126.

159. Draft of Talks on TB and Smallpox by H. F. Hilson.

160. "Expansion and Improvement of Medical Services," in *Minutes of the Bechuanaland Protectorate African Advisory Council, 1960* (Mafikeng, South Africa: Government Printer, 1960).

161. Author's interview with Dr. Alfred Merriweather.

162. Draft of Talks on TB and Smallpox by H. F. Hilson.

163. Author's interview with Ntene Moilwa.

164. Brown, *Among the Bantu Nomads,* 158.

165. For an anecdotal example, see Merriweather, *Desert Doctor,* 51–55.

166. Author's interviews with Mma Rabasimane; Thuso Sethata; and Kekgabile Molefi.

167. Some elderly women today who care for their disabled grandchildren still use the opportunity of meeting one another in the hospital and clinic waiting rooms to ridicule their daughters in their absence for "breaking the rules." Author's interview with Mma Phofuetsile.

168. Author's interviews with Dr. Karl Seligmann and Dr. Alfred Merriweather.

169. District Commissioner to Medical Officer, Lobatse, re: Noah Kubyade, September 15, 1960, District Commissioner Mochudi Series 9/7; Post Commander Bechuanaland Protectorate Police to District Commissioner Kanye, December 16, 1957, District Commissioner Kanye Series 16/12. Both in BNA.

170. Chief Bathoen to District Commissioner, Kanye, December 11, 1956, District Commissioner Kanye Series 16/12, BNA.

171. Dr Manson to District Commissioner Kanye, December 12, 1956, District Commissioner Kanye Series 16/12, BNA.

172. This is very similar to what Nancy Hunt describes in the Belgian Congo during this period. Hunt, *A Colonial Lexicon,* 23–24.

173. Vaughan, *Curing Their Ills,* 1–26.

174. See Thomas, *The Politics of the Womb.*

175. Klaits, "Care and Kinship in an Apostolic Church During Botswana's Time of AIDS," 273.

176. Mkgapha Mathabanyane to Kgosi Tshekedi, Khama, December 13, 1943 (Bundle A); Seanana Moloi to Kgosi Tshekedi, Khama, December 29, 1943 (Bundle E). Both in Papers of Michael Crowder, Box 17, ICS.

177. See author's interviews with Malau Alita Seati and Mmamosweu Koloi.

178. The latter group were no doubt encouraged by postcolonial public health campaigns designed to increase awareness of disability. See author's interviews with Cerebral Palsy Mother's Group, Diphaleng, October 6, 1997 and Mma Mosala.

179. Quotations from interviews with Chum Sejabadila and Mma Segokgo.

180. Ingstad, "The Myth of the Hidden Disabled."

181. Author's interviews with Thuso Sethata; Mma Rabasimane; and Kekgabile Molefi.

182. Dr. Merriweather to Director Medical Services April 18, 1950, re: T. B. Shelter, Medical Series 2/3/1, BNA.

183. Merriweather, *Desert Doctor*, 51–55.

184. Author's interview with Mpho Lekile.

185. Author's interview with Esther Gopane.

186. Author's interview with family of Kenalemang Motlake.

187. Author's interviews with Thuso Odirilwe and Esther Gopane.

188. This was clearly the case in the post-Independence period. See author's interview with Mma Rabasimane.

189. Author's interview with Mma Phofuetsile.

190. Author's interview with Mary Leburane.

191. Author's interview with Tshepo Dinare.

192. Author's interview with Thuso Sethata and daughters.

193. Author's interview with Mpho Lekile.

194. Ibid. For more on sitting, see Mary Leburane.

195. Author's interview with Norah Kgosietsile. For more on saliva, see author's interview with Oagile Tabola.

196. Merriweather, *Desert Doctor*, 34.

197. Merriweather, *Desert Doctor Remembers*, 176.

198. Weiss, *Conditional Love*.

199. Durham and Klaits, "Funerals and the Public Space of Sentiment in Botswana," quote on p. 778.

200. Meswele, "Death, Burial, and Ritual," 30–31. Children are often still buried in their mother's compounds. So it is not that mother's love did not continue to infuse this space but that the place of the *segotlo* in the moral imagination grew more ambiguous.

201. Author's interviews with Boitumelo Dinare and Thuso Sethata.

202. Author's interview with Alice Molele.

203. Author's interview with Thuso Sethata.

204. Author's interview with Peter Mokwena (March 12, 1999).

205. J. A. Hay, MD, to District Commissioner Kanye, September 16, 1956, re: Mepeki Keolese, District Commissioner Kanye Series 16/12, BNA.

206. District Commissioner to Medical Officer, Lobatse, June 23, 1948; District Commissioner to Government Secretary, March 17, 1949, re: Ramohibidu Piti; Radio message District Commissioner Kanye to Impilo, March 22, 1957. All in District Commissioner Kanye Series 16/12, BNA.

207. Extract District Commissioners' Conference, Agenda: Lunatics, August 11, 1947, Secretariat Series 399/6/1, BNA.

208. District Commissioner Serowe to Director Medical Services, August 14, 1944, Secretariat Series 399/6/1, BNA.

209. Deputy Director Medical Service to Government Secretary, August 30, 1945, Secretariat Series 399/6/1, BNA.

210. Author's interviews with Peter Mokwena (March 12, 1999) and Mary Leburane; Dr. Manson to District Commissioner Kanye re: Raiseelele Lenkutu, January 12, 1956, District Commissioner Kanye Series 16/12, BNA.

211. District Commissioner to Medical Officer, Lobatse, October 1, 1952, District Commissioner Kanye Series 16/12, BNA; author's interview with Dr. Alfred Merriweather.

212. One case I saw in the late 1990s involved a woman whose grandmother, her sole caretaker, kept her tied to the center pole of their one-room house. She felt forced to do this because she feared for her granddaughter's safety if she were allowed to wander. Whenever the young woman got the chance, she ran away and roamed the village, often going to the

local bars, where men would buy her drinks and, the FWEs suspected, have sex with her. When I saw her in 1997 she appeared to be pregnant. See also Ingstad, "The Myth of the Hidden Disabled," 229–230.

213. Bathoen to District Commissioner Kanye, January 8, 1956, re: Raiseelele Lenkutu; Bathoen to DC Kanye, re: EC 910 Ramohibidu Piti, March 14, 1949; D. Gasaitsiwe to District Commissioner Kanye re: Mental Patient—Botsetsa Moitloubu, September 15, 1949. All in District Commissioner Kanye Series 16/12, BNA.

214. Extract District Commissioners' Conference, Agenda: Lunatics, August 11, 1947, Secretariat Series 399/6/1, BNA.

215. Mr. Mackenzie's comment, Minutes of Meeting Held at Mafikeng, April 24–27, 1944; Chief Tshekedi Khama's comment, Extract of Minutes of African Advisory Council 25th session, April 1944; author's interview with Mpho Lekile.

216. Bathoen to District Commissioner, Kanye, re: Setanke Ketlaaren: Attempted Suicide, September 29, 1948, District Commissioner Kanye Series 16/12, BNA.

5. Postcolonial Development and Constrained Care

1. The real GDP per capita in Botswana more than doubled in the 1980s, rising from US$2,510 in 1985 to US$5,220 in 1993. Siwawa-Ndai, "Some Facts and Figures about Quality of Life in Botswana," 28.

2. Urbanization levels rose sharply in the postcolonial period. The Botswana Central Statistics Office reported a rise in the percentage of urban Batswana from 4 percent in 1964 to 49 percent in 1996. Mazonde, "Poverty in Botswana," 63.

3. Some of the historically large villages were also centers of moderate employment, so the urban-rural picture I am painting is more complicated. But even in these large villages, such as Molepolole or Mochudi, many people had to leave for work (sometimes to another large village).

4. Durham and Klaits, "Funerals and the Public Space of Sentiment in Botswana"; Durham, "Love and Jealousy in the Space of Death"; Klaits, "Care and Kinship in an Apostolic Church during Botswana's Time of AIDS."

5. For a detailed analysis of these processes, see Samatar, An African Miracle.

6. Staugard, "Traditional Health Care in Botswana."

7. Tlou, "Indicators of Health," 306.

8. Festus G. Mogae, "Opening Speech," in Nteta, Jermans, and Jeskova, eds., Poverty and Plenty, 12. Sadly, the AIDS epidemic has lowered life expectancy. The figure has become highly contested; the United Nations Development Programme reports 40.3 years and the Government of Botswana 52.1 years; Mmegi, August 16–22, 2002. A quick Internet search brings up numerous other possible figures.

9. Botswana Government, Selected Demographic Statistics, 2000, Central Statistics Office, available online at http://www.cso.gov.bw/cso (accessed August 2002). The total population of the country doubled between 1971 and 1991, so I am not suggesting that the proportion of older people grew, only their raw numbers. Nonetheless, popular experiences of an aging population through a rise in the total numbers of elderly in any given family or community contribute to perceptions that there are many more elderly people now than there were long ago.

10. Tlou, "Indicators of Health," 308.

11. Ibid. For more on the steady rise in the incidence of accidents between 1960 and 1980, see Pule, "The Socio-Economic Implications of Accidents in Botswana."

12. Maganu, "Access to Health Facilities in Botswana," 297.

13. Community-Based Rehabilitation Closed Case Notes, Cheshire Foundation of Botswana, 1993–1999.

14. "Massive TB Campaign Planned," *Botswana Daily News*, December 17, 1974; "Smallpox Cases Drastically Reduced in 1973," *Botswana Daily News*, January 4, 1974.

15. As in the colonial period, the focus remained on pulmonary disease, but gains were significant. Many people with nonpulmonary tuberculosis also received intensive in-patient treatment, and regular follow-up. However, pathways through the health system to effective therapy were not as clear-cut for disseminated, spinal, bone, and other forms of tuberculosis as they were for lung cases.

16. "Table 1: 1975–1985—Botswana: Annual Notification of Tuberculosis Cases, Deaths," *Botswana Epidemiological Bulletin* 6, no 4 (1985): 226.

17. Livingston, "Reconfiguring Old Age"; Livingston, "Pregnant Children and Half-Dead Adults."

18. Author's interview with Mma Pule, Rra Molatlhwa, and friend.

19. See author's interviews with Malau Alita Seati; Mma Phofuetsile; and Pelonome Kebafetse.

20. Author's interview with Lorato Molapo.

21. The term "disability" appears to have been used quite broadly in these programs and in many ways resonates more with my term "debility" than with the Tswana term *bogole*. See Matthew Kohrman on the difficulties of defining disability: Kohrman, "Why Am I Not Disabled?"

22. Untitled report (reviewing origins of the rehabilitation center), n.d., Rehabilitation Centre Correspondence, Botswana Red Cross Series 8/3, BNA.

23. "Notes—August 1977: Old and Poor People in Old Naledi," Destitutes, Botswana Red Cross Series 12/10, BNA. See also the rest of the correspondence in this file which discusses many other cases of destitution.

24. E. D. Mosielele, Thamaga Group Botswana Red Cross Society (BRCS), to Director General, BRCS, July 18, 1972 and Mrs Mogobojwa, Secretary Thamaga BRCS, to Sec BRCS, December 5, 1973, both in Botswana Red Cross Series 12/5, Thamaga Division, BNA.

25. Untitled report (reviewing origins of the rehabilitation center), n.d.; Physically disabled clinic correspondence, Botswana Red Cross Series 7/3. Both in BNA.

26. See "R500 Given to Red Cross by the Grain Company," *Botswana Daily News*, April 5, 1974; "General Motors Donate R1000 to Red Cross," *Botswana Daily News*, September 11, 1973; "Lady Khama Receives Cheques," *Botswana Daily News*, December 18, 1973; "Maru-a-Pula, Red Cross Get R2500 Each from Oil Company," *Botswana Daily News*, April 16, 1975; "500 More Blankets for the Needy," *Botswana Daily News*, July 11, 1974; "Red Cross Measures Disabled," *Botswana Daily News*, September 26, 1973; "Botswana Red Cross to Build Rehabilitation Centre," *Botswana Daily News*, June 15, 1973; "UBLS Students Present Cheque to School for the Blind," *Botswana Daily News*, December 14, 1973.

27. In this way, programs to provide rehabilitation and prosthetics in postcolonial Botswana were part of larger political, ideological, economic, and cultural changes in ways that often happen after war. See Herschbach, "Prosthetic Reconstructions"; Koven, "Remembering and Dismemberment."

28. See the description in Nordholm and Lundgren-Lindquist, "Community-Based Rehabilitation in Moshupa Village, Botswana."

29. See the much longer discussion of these issues in Livingston, "Maintaining Local Dependencies."

30. Ingstad, "Mpho ya Modimo—A Gift from God."

31. For a thoughtful discussion of these matters, see Ingstad, "The Myth of the Hidden Disabled," 15–25; Ingstad, "Public Discourses on Rehabilitation."

32. Author's interview with Mma Mosala.

33. Author's interview with Matshediso Fitlhile.

34. Durham, "Soliciting Gifts and Negotiating Agency."

35. As far as I could see, this dynamic did not extend to the professional nurses who headed local clinics.

36. It would be a mistake to assume that this meant she had no suitors. When we visited her one time she had been forced to sleep with a bureau pushed against her door to fend off an overly aggressive would-be boyfriend.

37. Mazonde, "Poverty in Botswana," 71.

38. A cost-of-living increase is built into the pension program, so the monthly payment is now higher.

39. Author's interview with Nomsa Rapela.

40. Livingston, "Reconfiguring Old Age."

41. Klaits, "Care and Kinship in an Apostolic Church During Botswana's Time of AIDS."

42. Emphasis mine. Mazonde, *A Study of Attitudes towards the Disabled in Botswana*, 17.

43. Author's interview with Isaac Mokwena.

44. Author's interview with Connie Diphuti.

45. Mazonde, *A Study of Attitudes towards the Disabled in Botswana*.

46. Ingstad, "Myth of the Hidden Disabled."

47. For an excellent discussion of the relationship between polluted wombs/female sexuality and HIV/AIDS in Botswana, see Heald, "It's Never as Easy as ABC."

48. Gulbrandsen, "To Marry—or Not to Marry." Relationships with men are of course also incredibly important to women, even those who are household heads, in both economic and legal terms. But since it is women who provide most palliative care through their identities as mothers and daughters, the mother-daughter relationship is particularly important in terms of caregiving dynamics. For women's legal relationships, see Griffiths, *In the Shadow of Marriage*. For men and the household economy, see Townsend, "Men, Migration, and Households in Botswana." Some women, of course, are not able to become mothers, and infertility is a very fraught experience for women in Botswana. This subject is, unfortunately, beyond the scope of this book, though it is clearly related to questions of disability and able-bodiedness. Interested readers should consult Rebecca Upton's dissertation on the subject, "'Our Blood Does Not Agree'"; and Upton, "'Infertility Makes You Invisible.'"

49. Mazonde, "Poverty in Botswana," 64.

50. Ibid, 65.

51. For a discussion of older women's manipulation of negative discourse and complaint, see Guillette, "Finding the Good Life," 192–197; see also Mutongi, "'Worries of the Heart.'"

52. Durham, "Did You Bathe This Morning? Baths and Morality in Botswana,"; Durham, "Disappearing Youth."

53. Ibid.

54. Author's interview with Mma Lekile.

55. Author's interview with Lucy Molefi.

56. Author's interview with Connie Diphuti. For a related discussion on local explanatory models of disability, see Ingstad, "Mpho ya Modimo—A Gift from God."

57. Some of these women have maids working for them. Maids are fairly common in

Tswana households that can afford to employ them; their pay is very low. In some cases, daughters with disabled children hire maids to help their mothers with the domestic work, but in most such cases I observed, while the maid helped with cooking cleaning and some child care, the grandmother retained primary responsibility for the disabled child. This is in part a reflection of grandmotherly desire and in part a reflection of how difficult it is to find a maid willing to care for such a child over the long term.

58. Klaits, "Care and Kinship in an Apostolic Church During Botswana's Time of AIDS," 259.

59. Author's interview with Mma Phofuetsile.

60. Author's interview with Dinki Moloi.

61. Author's interview with Lucy Molefi.

62. Delius, *A Lion amongst the Cattle,* 187–204.

63. Author's interview with Mma Mosala.

64. See interviews with Lucy Molefi (interviewed by the author); Mary Dinare (interviewed by the author); Kamofera Phuti (interviewed by Tshepiso Moremi); Cindy Molome (interviewed by Tshepiso Moremi); and Sedipe Phiri (interviewed by Tshepiso Moremi).

65. Staffing problems, especially for nurses, have been acknowledged, but such difficulties did not detract from overall images of success.

66. Maganu, "Access to Health Facilities in Botswana."

67. Livingston, "AIDS as Chronic Illness."

68. Author's interview with Mma Mosala; casual conversation with mother of Lucy Molefi (a former family welfare educator), January 1999.

69. "Lack of Medical Services—Great Concern—Minister Nwako," *Botswana Daily News,* September 26, 1973; "Hospital Denies Charges of Non-Treatment," *Botswana Daily News,* January 2, 1974.

70. "No Holidays for Hospitals or We'll Die!" letter to the editor, *Botswana Daily News,* December 16, 1974; "Lazy Doctors Rapped," *Botswana Daily News,* October 8, 1974; "Doctors, Nurses Are Not Fair to Patients," letter to the editor, *Botswana Daily News,* October 17, 1973; "Why No Doctors at Night?" letter to the editor, *Botswana Daily News,* October 31, 1973; "Outpatient Query," *Botswana Daily News,* April 1, 1975; "Hospital Denies Charges of Non-Treatment," *Botswana Daily News,* January 2, 1974.

71. "DC Urges Nurses to Practice Patience," *Botswana Daily News,* June 27, 1974.

72. Over time, the length of training was increased.

73. Author's interview with Mma Mosala.

74. Tlou and Sandberg, "The Elderly and Their Use of the Health Care System," 97.

75. Author's interview with Cerebral Palsy Mother's Group, Diphaleng, October 6, 1997.

76. Tshepiso Moremi's interview with Sedipe Phiri.

77. Author's interview with Peter Mokwena. Peter Mokwena was not the only person to rhetorically linked post-Independence politics with post-Independence health care development in sometimes subtle ways. See author's interviews with Thuso Sethata; Mma Pule, Rra Molatlhwa, and friend; and Mpho Lekile (March 17, 1999).

78. Author's interviews with Andrew Mmanthe, March 2, 5, and 6, 1999. This is a longstanding practice; see Schapera, *Rainmaking Rites.* For how this has changed over time with the rise of Christianity, see Jean Comaroff, "Healing and Cultural Transformation."

79. Author's interviews with Nomsa Rapela and Esther Gopane. Narratives about missionary medical care might center on the moment when the doctor and patient would kneel down together and pray to Modimo and might minimize or marginalize descriptions of biomedical therapies. Furthermore, many people in the 1990s who refused to seek treatment

at the central hospital in Gaborone would still travel to see the closest missionary doctor, Dr. Merriweather, who had worked in the large village of Molepolole since the 1940s. Since Independence, it has been more difficult for mission hospitals to provide doctors who are also missionaries, and many mission hospitals are now staffed at least partially by secular medical personnel. As a result, prayer is now increasingly separate from medical care at these institutions. See author's interview with Kekgabile Molefi.

80. See the press reports on the handing over of the Scottish Livingstone hospital in Molepolole in 1975. Dr. Merriweather, who was immensely popular with patients and family members, stayed on. In the late 1990s, many people in the region would still travel to Molepolole, bypassing closer clinics and hospitals, to see Dr. Merriweather, who was by then semi-retired. "Problems of Running Hospital Grow Complex," *Botswana Daily News,* December 12, 1973; "Scottish Livingstone Hand-Over Talks to Peak during September," *Botswana Daily News,* September 6, 1974; "No Change of Hospital Head on Take-Over by Gov't in 3 Months," *Botswana Daily News,* January 2, 1975; "MP Alleges Intimidation of Molepolole Hospital Staff," *Botswana Daily News,* March 19, 1975; "Scottish Livingstone Hospital Officially Handed Over to Government," *Botswana Daily News,* April 2, 1975.

81. See author's interview with Pelonome Kebafetse, which described debates among people about health care: "Before [Independence] we would get to *dingaka* and get cured, now we no longer have those *dingaka.* . . . [S]ometimes now even if the *ngaka* is there and someone is sick and you want to go and see them you will be told 'Never go to see them.' You will be spending a lot of money on them and they won't do anything good for you and you end up going to the hospital, where you'll be given some medication only to calm not to actually cure the disease."

82. See author's interviews with Peter Mokwena and Norah Kgosietsile.

83. Author's interview with Mpho Lekile (March 17, 1999).

84. Community-Based Rehabilitation Closed Case Notes, Cheshire Foundation of Botswana, 1993–1999. This difficulty in maintaining supplies and accessing appropriate technical aids was something I witnessed.

85. Author's interview with Mma Lekile.

86. Author's interview with Mmamosweu Koloi.

87. Author's interview with Goodson Setlhare.

88. Author's interviews with Alice Molele; Goodson Setlhare; and Andrew Mmanthe, March 2, 1999.

89. See author's interviews with mother of Bantle Segokgo; Goodson Setlhare; Mma Pule, Rra Molatlhwa, and friend; and Dinki Moloi. Doctors have always been ambiguous or suspect individuals because of their ability to make sorcery substances as well as healing medicines and because of the historical role of some as political subversives. But the profit motives raise new questions, not only because money may constitute another impetus for malevolence but also because desire for profit might diminish the basic efficacy and training of many doctors.

90. Author's interviews with Pulane Tshwene and Kenalemang Seati and Naniso Seati.

91. Cf. Last, "The Importance of Knowing about Not Knowing."

92. Author's interview with Thuso Sethata.

Conclusion

1. The pioneer in this field is anthropologist John Janzen, whose research on the history of African therapeutics is broad and deep. His work stands as an important exception to

dominant trends in African medical historiography. See Janzen, *Lemba, 1650–1930*. Janzen and Steven Feierman both pointed to the significance of familial care over two decades ago. Janzen, *The Quest for Therapy in Lower Zaire*; Feierman, "Popular Control over the Institutions of Health."

2. http://www.unbotswana.org.bw/unaids.html (accessed August 9, 2004).

3. I take this term and model of transmuted illness from Feudtner, *Bittersweet*.

4. "PS Fumbles over 'Rotting Patient,'" *Mmegi*, November 7, 2003; "Mother Blames Marina for Son's Death," *Mmegi*, November 10, 2003; "Medical Authorities Should Wake Up," letter to the editor by Nkagelang Mothanka, *Mmegi*, November 17, 2003. See also "No Person 'Rotting' at Marina Hospital? Ministry," *Botswana Daily News*, November 12, 2003.

5. "Marina Must Overhaul Its Act," editorial, *Mmegi*, November 10, 2003. Three days later, the editors also took incompetent and unethical *dingaka* to task, "Traditional Doctors Must Overhaul Their Act," editorial, *Mmegi*, November 13, 2003. See also "Traditional Doctor 'Costs a Leg,'" which leads with "A diabetic father of four, who has lost faith in Western medicine, has lost his leg after being treated by a traditional doctor," *Mmegi*, November 13, 2003.

6. "Declining Commitment of Nurses towards Patients Worrisome," *Botswana Daily News*, July 5, 2004.

Sources

Primary Material: Archival

Botswana National Archives and Records Services, Gabarone (BNA)
    Botswana Red Cross Series
    District Commissioner Series
        Gaberones
        High Commissioner Series
        Kanye
        Lobatse
        Mochude
        Molepolole
        Medical Series
        Native Administration
        Native Advisory Council Minutes
    Protectorate Annual Medical and Sanitary Reports
    Resident Magistrate Series
    Secretariat Series
    Social Welfare Series
    Southern District Council Series
Cheshire Foundation of Botswana, Mogoditshane
    Client Case Files
Institute of Commonwealth Studies, University of London
    Papers of Michael Crowder
        Box 17 (courtesy of Lynn Thomas)
London School of Economics (LSE)
    Papers of Isaac Schapera (field notes)
Rhodes House, Oxford
    Papers of B. O. Wilkin
School of Oriental and African Studies, University of London
    London Missionary Society Papers, Council for World Mission (CWM)
        Africa Correspondence
        Africa Odds
        Africa Personal
        Africa Reports
        Africa Subjects
        The Chronicle of the London Missionary Society (periodical)

Newspapers

Botswana Daily News
Botswana Gazette
Mmegi: The Reporter

Primary Material: Oral Interviews

I have included the names of all those "officially" interviewed whether cited in the text or not, since the recollections and ideas they offered were integral to my research and conclusions. Some of the names listed have been changed to protect the subject's anonymity, others are listed as they identified themselves. Place names are correct, except in the case of the psuedonymous village of Diphaleng. All interviews unless otherwise indicated (Eng. = English) were conducted in Setswana and translated with the assistance of either Dikeledi Moloi, Tshepiso Moremi, or Condril Mosala. Several interviews were conducted by Tshepiso Moremi alone; they are designated as such (TM). Less formal conversations are not noted here.

Anguru, Wamona Arona, Diphaleng, November 24, 1997
Babedi, Seswaba, Diphaleng, April 15, 1999 (TM)
Bathodi, Banyana, Kubung, July 13, 1999
Batshegi, Mothibedi, Thamaga, October 30, 1997
Cerebral Palsy Mother's Group, Diphaleng, October 6, 1997
Dinare, Lesego, Boitumelo Dinare, and Tshepo Dinare, Diphaleng, December 10, 1998
Dinare, Mary, Diphaleng, June 24, 1999
Diphoko, Sethato, Diphaleng, November 19, 1997
Diphuti, Connie, Diphaleng, February 5, 1999
Eustace, Barry, Gaborone, September 30, 1997 (Eng.)
Fitlhile, Matshediso, Diphaleng, October 27, 1997
Gabarongwe, Wampona Jackson, Thamaga, April 14, 1999
Gopane, Esther, Metsimotlhabe, June 25, 1999 (Eng.)
Kebafetse, Pelonome, Diphaleng, November 8, 1998
Kedisang, Matsimo, Thamaga, April 9, 1999
Kenalemang, Esther, Thamaga, June 24, 1999
Kgosietsile, Norah, Thamaga, April 11, 1999
Kgosietsile, Peter, Diphaleng, May 14, 1999
Kobue, Konobule, Diphaleng, March 27, 1999
Koloi, Mmamosweu, Diphaleng, January 20, 1999
Leburane, Mary, Diphaleng, February 5, 1999
Lekile, Mma, Diphaleng, January 5, 1999
Lekile, Mpho, Lentsweletau, March 17 and 18, 1999
Lentswe, Sitiwa, Kubung, August 4, 1999
Makati, Mololokane, Diphaleng, March 31, 1999
Makwapeng, Mosito, Diphaleng, March 27, 1999
Mantshadi, Mma, Kumakwane, July 2, 1999
Merriweather, Dr. Alfred, Molepolole, October 8, 1997 (Eng.)
Mmanthe, Andrew Ramokwakwa, Mmopane, March 2, 5, and 6, 1999
Mmilo, Senowe, Diphaleng, July 21, 1999
Mmontsho, Mogae, Thamaga, November 19, 1997
Moamogwe, Neo, Thamaga, December 9, 1998
Moilwa, Ntene, Kumakwane, August 3, 1999
Mokgele, Tshukudu, and Mma Mokgele, Diphaleng, April 15, 1999
Mokwena, Isaac, Gaborone, July 1, 1999 (Eng.)

Mokwena, Peter, Kopong, March 12 and 13, 1999
Molapo, Lorato, Diphaleng, November 12, 1997
Molalthwa, Rra, Diphaleng, March 1999 (n.d., Eng.)
Molefi, Kekgabile, Thamaga, June 24, 1999
Molefi, Lekololwane, Diphaleng, April 15, 1999 (TM)
Molefi, Lucy, and her mother, Diphaleng, January 15, 1999
Molefi, Ntshinogang, Thamaga, December 9, 1998
Molele, Alice, Diphaleng, January 22, 1999
Moloi, Dinki, Diphaleng, February 24, 1999
Molome, Cindy, Diphaleng, April 19, 1999 (TM)
Momokgwe, Maiketso, Diphaleng, March 24, 1999
Mooki, Ditirwa, Diphaleng, May 14, 1999
Moremi, Lesego, Kumakwane, April 13, 1999
Morwa, Moreki, Diphaleng, February 10, 1999
Morwane, Gabotlhaleshwe, Kubung, July 27, 1999
Morwane, Gasetsewa, Kubung, July 27, 1999
Mosala, Mma, Mogoditshane, December 1, 1998
Molatlhwa, Rra. See Mma Pule.
Motlake, Kenalemang and family, Thamaga, June 24, 1999
Motlhalamme, Basejane, Diphaleng, March 31, 1999
Motlhalamme, Ephraim, Diphaleng, April 15, 1999
Motshididi, Ntontwane, Thamaga, August 9, 1999
Motshididi, Tebogo, Thamaga, April 7, 1999
Odirilwe, Thuso, Diphaleng, November 24, 1998
Opini, Mma, Kubung, July 27, 1999
Phatswana, Sebete, Kumakwane, July 2, 1999
Phiri, Sedipe, Diphaleng, April 18, 1999 (TM)
Phofuetsile, Mma, Diphaleng, October 15, 1997
Phuti, Kamofera, Diphaleng, April 18, 1999 (TM)
Pogiso, Nonyane, Diphaleng, August 3, 1999
Pule, Mma, Rra Molatlhwa, and friend, Diphaleng, February 17, 1999 (Eng.)
Rabasimane, Mma, Diphaleng, January 22, 1999
Ramotsisi, Mmantsie, Diphaleng, April 16, 1999 (TM)
Ranatse, Sebokolodi, Kubung, July 27, 1999
Rantsemele, Maria, Diphaleng, February 3, 1999
Rapela, Nomsa, Diphaleng, January 29, 1999
Seati, Kenalemang, and Naniso Seati, Kumakwane, December 3, 1998
Seati, Malau Alita, Diphaleng, October 13, 1997
Segokgo, Mma Bantle, Thamaga, November 5, 1997
Segwatse, Mmamonthso, Diphaleng, April 18, 1999 (TM)
Seisabogadi, George, Diphaleng, February 10, 1999
Sejabadila, Chum, Thamaga, December 10, 1998
Seleka, Rra, Kumakwane, April 11, 1999
Selema, Dikeledi, and Honey Ntomile, Diphaleng, January 20, 1999
Seligmann, Dr. Karl, Gaborone, August 3, 1999 (Eng.)
Sengape, Otladisa, Kubung, July 7, 1999
Sethata, Onkaetse, Gaborone, August, 9, 1999
Sethata, Thuso, and daughters, Diphaleng, January 22, 1999

Setlhare, Goodson, and Mma Setlhare, Diphaleng, January 15, 1999
Tabola, Oagile, Thamaga, April 8, 1999
Thebe, Modise, Kumakwane, July 16, 1999
Tlalang, Diralanang, Thamaga, April 7, 1999
Tshukudu, Mmasetadile Seneo, Diphaleng, April 18, 1999 (TM)
Tshukunono, Mmabojale, Kumakwane, April 13, 1999
Tshwene, Pulane, Diphaleng, January 29, 1999
Tswane, Kweetse, Diphaleng, January 29, 1999
Wanguru, Wamana Arona, Diphaleng, November 24, 1997

Books and Articles

Alverson, Hoyt. *Mind in the Heart of Darkness: Value and Self-Identity among the Tswana of Southern Africa*. New Haven, Conn.: Yale University Press, 1978.

Anderson, Sandra, and Frants Staugard. *Traditional Midwives: Traditional Medicine in Botswana*. Gaborone: Ipelegeng Publishers, 1986.

Arkles, Rachel. "The Social Consequences of Industrial Accidents: Disabled Mine Workers in Lesotho." Master's thesis, University of Witwatersrand, 1993.

Barber, Karin. "Money, Self-Realization and the Person in Yoruba Texts." In Jane Guyer ed., *Money Matters: Instability, Values, and Social Payments in the Modern History of West African Communities*, 205–224. Portsmouth, N.H.: Heinemann, 1994.

Bay, Edna. *Wives of the Leopard: Gender, Politics, and Culture in the Kingdom of Dahomey*. Charlottesville: University of Virginia Press, 1998.

Baynton, Douglas. "Disability and the Justification of Inequality in American History." In Paul Longmore and Laurie Umansky, eds., *The New Disability History*, 33–57. New York: New York University Press, 2001.

Beidelman, T. O. "Swazi Royal Ritual." *Africa* 36 (1966): 373–405.

———. *Moral Imagination in Kaguru Modes of Thought*. Bloomington: Indiana University Press, 1986.

Bell, Heather. *Frontiers of Medicine in the Anglo-Egyptian Sudan, 1899–1940*. Oxford: Clarendon Press, 1999.

Berry, Sara. *Fathers Work for Their Sons: Accumulation, Mobility and Class Formation in an Extended Yoruba Community*. Berkeley: University of California Press, 1985.

Bledsoe, Caroline. *Contingent Lives: Fertility, Time, and Aging in West Africa*. Chicago: University of Chicago Press, 2002.

Boddy, Janice. *Wombs and Alien Spirits: Men, Women, and the Zar Cult in Northern Sudan*. Madison: University of Wisconsin Press, 1989.

Bozzoli, Belinda, and Mmantho Nkotsoe. *Women of Phokeng: Consciousness, Life Strategy, and Migrancy in South Africa, 1900–1983*. Portsmouth, N.H.: Heinemann, 1991.

Briggs, Charles, and Clara Mantini-Briggs. *Stories in the Time of Cholera: Racial Profiling During a Medical Nightmare*. Berkeley: University of California Press, 2002.

Brown, Rev. J. Tom. "Circumcision Rites of the Becwana Tribes." *Journal of the Royal Anthropological Institute of Great Britain and Ireland* 51 (1922): 419–427.

———. *Among the Bantu Nomads: A Record of Forty Years Spent among the Bechuana, a Numerous and Famous Branch of the Central South African Bantu, with the First Full Description of Their Ancient Customs, Manners and Beliefs.* London: Seeley, 1926.

Burke, Charlanne. "Life at the Margins in Botswana: From Sitting in Class to Sitting and Doing Nothing." Paper presented at the workshop Recovering the Legacy of Schapera, University of Botswana, Gaborone, May 25-26, 2000.

Burns, Catherine. "'A Man Is a Clumsy Thing Who Does Not Know How to Handle a Sick Person': Aspects of the History of Masculinity and Race in Shaping of Male Nursing in South Africa, 1900–1950." *Journal of Southern African Studies* 24 (1998): 695–718.

Callahan, Bryan. "'Veni, VD, Vici'? Reassessing the Ila Syphilis Epidemic, 1900–1963." *Journal of Southern African Studies* 23 (1997): 421–440.

Carton, Benedict. *Blood from Your Children: The Colonial Origins of Generational Conflict in South Africa.* Durban: Natal Press, 2000.

Cassell, Eric. "The Nature of Suffering and the Goals of Medicine." *New England Journal of Medicine* 306 (1982): 639–645.

Cohen, Lawrence. *No Aging in India: Alzheimer's, the Bad Family, and Other Modern Things.* Berkeley: University of California Press, 1998.

Cohen, Stephanie. "Community Based Rehabilitation in Botswana: Theory and Practice in a Dynamic Context." Unpublished paper, 1999.

Cole, Jennifer. *Forget Colonialism? Sacrifice and the Art of Memory in Madagascar.* Berkeley: University of California Press, 2001.

Comaroff, Jean. "Healing and the Cultural Order: The Case of the Barolong-boo-Ratshidi of Southern Africa." *American Ethnologist* 7 (1980): 637–657.

———. "Healing and Cultural Transformation: The Tswana of Southern Africa." *Social Science and Medicine* 15b (1981): 367–378.

———. *Body of Power, Spirit of Resistance: The Culture and History of a South African People.* Chicago: University of Chicago Press, 1985.

———. "The Diseased Heart of Africa: Medicine, Colonialism, and the Black Body." In S. Lindenbaum and M. Lock, eds., *Knowledge, Power, and Practice: The Anthropology of Medicine and Everyday Life.* Berkeley: University of California, 1993.

Comaroff, Jean, and John L. Comaroff. *Of Revelation and Revolution.* Vol. 1, *Christianity, Colonialism, and Consciousness in South Africa.* Chicago: University of Chicago Press, 1991.

———. *Of Revelation and Revolution.* Vol. 2, *The Dialectics of Modernity on a South African Frontier.* Chicago: University of Chicago Press, 1997.

Comaroff, John. "Competition for Office and Political Processes among the Barolong Boo Ratshidi." Ph.D. diss., University of London, 1973.

———. "Rules and Rulers: Political Processes in a Tswana Chiefdom." *Man* 13 (1978): 1–20.

Comaroff, John L., and Jean Comaroff. "On Personhood: An Anthropological Perspective from Africa." *Social Identities* 7, no. 2 (2001): 267–283.

Comaroff, John L., and Simon Roberts. "Marriage and Extra-Marital Sexuality: The Dialectics of Legal Change among the Kgatla." *African Journal of Law* 20 (1977): 97–123.

———. *Rules and Processes: The Cultural Logic of Dispute in an African Context.* Chicago: University of Chicago Press, 1981.

Cooper, Barbara. *Marriage in Maradi, 1900–1989: Contestations and Contradictions.* Portsmouth, N.H.: Heinemann, 1996.

Cooper, Frederick. "Modernizing Bureaucrats, Backwards Africans, and the Development Concept." In Frederick Cooper and Randall Packard, eds., *International Development and the Social Sciences: Essays on the History and Politics of Knowledge*, 64–92. Berkeley: University of California Press, 1997.

Cousins, Rev. George, ed. *The Chronicle of the London Missionary Society*, vol. V. (1896).

Crais, Clifton. *The Politics of Evil: Magic, State Power, and the Political Imagination in South Africa*. Cambridge: Cambridge University Press, 2002.

Crush, J. S., Alan Jeeves, and David Yudelman. *South Africa's Labor Empire: A History of Black Migrancy to the Gold Mines*. Boulder, Colo.: Westview Press, 1991.

Das, Veena, and Renu Addlakha. "Disability and Domestic Citizenship: Voice, Gender, and the Making of the Subject." *Public Culture* 13 (2001): 511–531.

Davis, Lennard. *The Disability Studies Reader*. London: Routledge, 1997.

———. *Enforcing Normalcy: Disability, Deafness, and the Body*. New York: Verso, 1995.

Dawson, Marc. "The 1920's Anti-Yaws Campaigns and Colonial Medical Policy in Kenya." *International Journal of African Historical Studies* 20 (1987): 220–240.

Delius, Peter. *A Lion amongst the Cattle: Reconstruction and Resistance in the Northern Transvaal*. Portsmouth, N.H.: Heinemann, 1996.

Dennis, Caroline. "The Role of Dingaka tsa Setswana from the 19th Century to the Present." *Botswana Notes and Records* 10 (1978): 53–66.

Dreger, Alice. *One of Us: Conjoined Twins and the Future of Normal*. Cambridge, Mass.: Harvard University Press, 2004.

Duden, Barbara. *The Woman beneath the Skin: A Doctor's Patients in Eighteenth-Century Germany*. Cambridge, Mass.: Harvard University Press, 1997.

Durham, Deborah. "Soliciting Gifts and Negotiating Agency: The Spirit of Asking in Botswana." *Journal of the Royal Anthropological Institute* n.s. 1 (1995): 111–128.

———. "Civil Lives: Leadership and Accomplishment in Botswana." In John Comaroff and Jean Comaroff, eds., *Civil Society and the Political Imagination in Africa*, 192–218. Chicago: University of Chicago Press, 1999.

———. "The Predicament of Dress: Polyvalency and the Ironies of a Cultural Identity." *American Ethnologist* 26, no. 2 (1999): 389–411.

———. "Love and Jealousy in the Space of Death." *Ethnos* 67 (2002): 155–180.

———. "Disappearing Youth: Youth as a Social Shifter in Botswana." *American Ethnologist* 31, no. 4 (Nov. 2004): 589–605.

———. "Did You Bathe This Morning? Baths and Morality in Botswana." In Adeline Masquelier, ed., *Dirt, Undress, and Difference*. Forthcoming.

———. "Empowering Youth: Making Youth Citizens in Botswana." In Deborah Durham and Jennifer Cole, eds., *Generations and Globalization: Family, Youth, and Age in the New World Economy*. Bloomington: Indiana University Press, in press.

Durham, Deborah, and Frederick Klaits. "Funerals and the Public Space of Sentiment in Botswana." *Journal of Southern African Studies* 28 (2002): 777–796.

Echenberg, Myron. *Black Death, White Medicine: Bubonic Plague and the Politics of Public Health in Colonial Senegal, 1914–1945*. Portsmouth, N.H.: Heinemann, 2002.

Evans-Pritchard, E. E. *Witchcraft, Oracles, and Magic among the Azande*. Oxford: Clarendon Press, 1937.

Fabian, Johannes. *Remembering the Present: Painting and Popular History in Zaire*. Berkeley: University of California Press, 1996.

Fanon, Frantz. *A Dying Colonialism*. New York: Grove Press, 1965.

Feierman, Steven. *The Shambaa Kingdom*. Madison: University of Wisconsin Press, 1974.

———. "Struggles for Control: The Social Roots of Health and Healing in Modern Africa." *African Studies Review* 28 (1985): 73–145.

———. "Popular Control over the Institutions of Health: A Historical Study." In Murray Last and G. L. Chavunduka, eds., *The Professionalization of African Medicine*, 205–220. Manchester: Manchester University Press, 1986.

———. *Peasant Intellectuals: Anthropology and History in Tanzania*. Madison: University of Wisconsin Press, 1990.

———. "Colonizers, Scholars, and the Creation of Invisible Histories." In Victoria Bonnell and Lynn Hunt, eds., *Beyond the Cultural Turn: New Directions in the Study of Society and Culture*, 182–216. Berkeley: University of California Press, 1999.

———. "Explanation and Uncertainty in the Medical World of Ghaambo." *Bulletin of the History of Medicine* 74 (2000): 317–344.

Ferguson, James. *Expectations of Modernity: Myths and Meanings of Urban Life on the Zambian Copperbelt*. Berkeley: University of California Press, 1999.

Feudtner, Chris. *Bittersweet: Diabetes, Insulin, and the Transformation of Illness*. Chapel Hill: University of North Carolina Press, 2003.

Foucault, Michel. *The Birth of the Clinic*. New York: Vintage, 1975.

Frank, Gelya. *Venus on Wheels: Two Decades of Dialogue on Disability, Biography, and Being Female in America*. Berkeley: University of California Press, 2000.

Gaye, Pippa. *Better than Light*. London: Mowbray, 1983.

Gear, J., et al. "Poliomyelitis in an Urban Native Township during a Non-Epidemic Year." *South African Medical Journal* 25, no. 18 (1951).

Geurts, Kathryn Linn. *Culture and the Senses: Bodily Ways of Knowing in an African Community*. Berkeley: University of California Press, 2002.

Giles-Vernick, Tamara. "Leaving a Person Behind: History, Personhood, and Struggles over Forest Resources in the Sangha Basin of Equatorial Africa." *International Journal of African Historical Studies* 32 (1999): 311–338.

Goffman, Erving. *Stigma: Notes on the Management of a Spoiled Identity*. Englewood Cliffs, N.J.: Prentice Hall, 1963.

Good, Byron. *Medicine, Rationality, and Experience: An Anthropological Perspective*. Cambridge: Cambridge University Press, 1994.

Grant, Sandy, and Elinah Grant. *Decorated Homes in Botswana*. Mochudi: Phutadikobo Museum, 1995.

Griffiths, Anne. *In the Shadow of Marriage: Gender and Justice in an African Community*. Chicago: University of Chicago Press, 1997.

Guillette, Elizabeth. "Finding the Good Life in the Family and Society: The Tswana Aged of Botswana." Ph.D. diss., University of Florida, 1992.

Gulbrandsen, Ornulf. "To Marry—or Not to Marry: Marital Strategies and Sexual Relations in a Tswana Society." *Ethnos* 51 (1986): 7–28.

Guy, Jeff, and Motlatse Thabane. "Technology, Ethnicity, and Ideology: Basotho Miners and Shaft Sinking on the South African Gold Mines." *Journal of Southern African Studies* 14 (1988): 254–270.

Hallen, Barry. *The Good, the Bad, and the Beautiful: Discourse about Values in Yoruba Culture*. Bloomington: Indiana University Press, 2000.

Hamlin, Chris. *Public Health and Social Justice in the Age of Chadwick*. Cambridge University Press, 1997.

Heald, Suzette. *Manhood and Morality: Sex, Violence, and Ritual in Gisu Society.* London: Routledge, 1999.

———. "It's Never as Easy as ABC: Understandings of AIDS in Botswana." *African Journal of AIDS Research* 1 (2002): 1–11.

Hepburn, Rev. J. D. *Twenty Years in Khama's Country and Pioneering among the Batuana of Lake Ngami.* London: Hodder and Stoughton, 1895.

Herschbach, Lisa. "Prosthetic Reconstructions: Making the Industry, Re-Making the Body, Modeling the Nation." *History Workshop Journal* 44 (1997): 23–57.

Hodgson, Dorothy L. *The Church of Women: Gendered Encounters between Maasai and Missionaries.* Bloomington: Indiana University Press, 2005.

Holzer, Brigitte, Arthur Vreede, and Gabriele Weigt, eds. *Disability in Different Cultures: Reflections on Local Concepts.* New Brunswick, N.J.: Transaction Publishers, 1999.

Hunt, Nancy. "Le bebe en brousse: European Women, African Birthspacing, and Colonial Intervention in Breast Feeding in the Belgian Congo." *International Journal of African Historical Studies* 21 (1988): 401–432.

———. *A Colonial Lexicon: Of Birth Ritual, Medicalization, and Mobility in the Congo.* Durham, N.C.: Duke University Press, 1999.

Iliffe, John. *The African Poor: A History.* Cambridge: Cambridge University Press, 1987.

Ingstad, Benedicte. "Mpho ya Modimo—A Gift from God: Perspectives on 'Attitudes toward Disabled Persons.'" In Benedicte Ingstad and Susan Reynolds Whyte, eds., *Disability and Culture,* 246–263. Berkeley: University of California Press, 1995.

———. "Public Discourses on Rehabilitation: From Norway to Botswana." In Benedicte Ingstad and Susan Reynolds Whyte, eds., *Disability and Culture,* 174–195. Berkeley: University of California Press, 1995.

———. "'The Myth of the Hidden Disabled': A Study of Community-Based Rehabilitation in Botswana." Working Paper no. 1. University of Oslo, Institute of Community Medicine, Section for Medical Anthropology, 1992.

Ingstad, Benedicte, and Frank Bruun. "Elderly People as Care Providers and Care Receivers." In Frank Bruun, Mbulawa Mugabe, and Yolanda Coombs, eds., *The Situation of the Elderly in Botswana: Proceedings from an International Workshop.* Gaborone and Oslo: University of Botswana National Institute of Research and University of Oslo, 1991.

Ingstad, Benedicte, Frank Bruun, Edwin Sandberg, and Sheila Tlou. "Care for the Elderly, Care by the Elderly: The Role of Elderly Women in a Changing Tswana Society." *Journal of Cross-Cultural Gerontology* 7 (1992): 379–398.

Ingstad, Benedicte, and Susan Reynolds Whyte, eds. *Disability and Culture.* Berkeley: University of California Press, 1995.

Jackson, Ashley. *Botswana 1939–1945: An African Country at War.* Oxford: Oxford University Press, 1999.

Jackson, Michael, and Ivan Karp, eds. *Personhood and Agency: The Experience of Self and Other in African Cultures.* Washington, D.C.: Smithsonian Institution Press, 1990.

Janzen, John. *The Quest for Therapy in Lower Zaire.* Berkeley: University of California Press, 1978.

———. *Lemba, 1650–1930: A Drum of Affliction in Africa and the New World.* New York: Garland Publishing, 1982.

——. *Ngoma: Discourses of Healing in Central and Southern Africa.* Berkeley: University of California, 1992.

Jeater, Diana. *Marriage, Perversion, and Power: The Construction of Moral Discourse in Southern Rhodesia, 1894–1930.* Oxford: Oxford University Press, 1993.

Jennings, A. E. "Maphakela: The Witch-Doctor's Son." *Chronicle of the London Missionary Society* XL (April 1932).

Ka-Mbuya, Titus, and Fred Morton. "The South." In Fred Morton and Jeff Ramsay, eds., *The Birth of Botswana: A History of the Bechuanaland Protectorate from 1910 to 1966.* Gaborone: Longman Botswana, 1987.

Karp, Ivan. "Persons, Notions of." In J. Middleton, ed., *Encyclopedia of Africa,* 392–393. New York: Charles Scribner and Sons, 1997.

Karp, Ivan, and Michael Jackson. "Introduction." In Michael Jackson and Ivan Karp, eds., *Personhood and Agency: The Experience of Self and Other in African Cultures,* 15–30. Washington, D.C.: Smithsonian Institution Press, 1990.

Kinsman, Margaret. "Beasts of Burden: The Subordination of Tswana Women, ca. 1800–1840." *Journal of Southern African Studies* 10 (1983): 39–54.

Klaits, Frederick. "Care and Kinship in an Apostolic Church during Botswana's Time of AIDS." Ph.D. diss., Department of Anthropology, Johns Hopkins University, 2002.

Kleinmann, Arthur. *The Illness Narratives: Suffering, Healing, and the Human Condition.* New York: Basic Books, 1988.

Kohrman, Matthew. "Motorcycles for the Disabled: Mobility, Modernity and the Transformation of Experience in Urban China." *Culture, Medicine and Psychiatry* 23 (1999): 133–155.

——. "Why Am I Not Disabled? Making State Subjects, Making Statistics in Post-Mao China." *Medical Anthropology Quarterly* 17 (2003): 5–24.

Koven, Seth. "Remembering and Dismemberment: Crippled Children, Wounded Soldiers and the Great War in Great Britain." *American Historical Review* (1994): 1167–1199.

Kratz, Corinne, " 'We've Always Done It Like This . . . Except for a Few Details': 'Tradition' and 'Innovation' in Okiek Ceremonies." *Comparative Studies in Society and History* 35 (1993): 30–65.

Kraut, Alan. *Silent Travelers: Germs, Genes, and the "Immigrant Menace."* Baltimore: Johns Hopkins University Press, 1994.

Kudlick, Catherine. "Disability History: Why We Need Another 'Other.' " *American Historical Review* 108 (2003): 763–793.

Kuper, Adam. *Kalahari Village Politics: An African Democracy.* Cambridge: Cambridge University Press, 1970.

——. *Wives for Cattle: Bridewealth and Marriage in Southern Africa.* London: Routledge, 1982.

Kuriyama, Shigehisa. *The Expressiveness of the Body and the Divergence of Greek and Chinese Medicine.* New York: Zone Books, 1999.

Kwape, Irene. "Access to Education." In Doreen Nteta and Janet Hermans with Pavla Jeskova, eds., *Poverty and Plenty: The Botswana Experience.* Gaborone: The Botswana Society, 1997.

La Berge, Ann. "The Early Nineteenth-Century Public Health Movement: The Disciplinary Development and Institutionalization of Hygiene Publique." *Bulletin of the History of Medicine* 58 (1984): 363–379.

Lagerwerf, Leny. *"They Pray for You . . . ": Independent Churches and Women in Botswana.*

IIMO Research Pamphlet no. 6. Leiden: Interuniversitair Instituut Voor Missiologie En Oecumenica, 1984.

Lamb, Sarah. *White Saris and Sweet Mangoes: Aging, Gender, and the Body in North India.* Berkeley: University of California Press, 2000.

Lambek, Michael. "Body and Mind in Mind, Body and Mind in Body: Some Anthropological Interventions in a Long Conversation." In Michael Lambek and Andrew Strathern, eds., *Bodies and Persons: Comparative Perspectives from Melanesia,* 103–123. Cambridge: Cambridge University Press, 1998.

Lambek, Michael, and Jacqueline Solway. "Just Anger: Scenarios of Indignation in Botswana and Madagascar." *Ethnos* 66 (2002): 49–72.

Landau, Paul. *The Realm of the Word: Language, Gender and Christianity in a Southern African Kingdom.* Portsmouth, N.H.: Heinemann, 1995.

———. "Strategy and Selfhood among the Samuelites of Thaba Nchu, South Africa, 1928–1940." Paper presented at the Northeastern Workshop on Southern Africa, Burlington, Vermont, 2000.

———. "Nineteenth Century Transformations in Consciousness." In Robert Ross, Carolyn Hamilton, and Bill Nasson, eds., *Cambridge History of South Africa,* vol. 1. Forthcoming.

Last, Murray. "The Importance of Knowing about Not Knowing: Observations from Hausaland." In Steven Feierman and John Janzen, eds., *The Social Basis of Health and Healing in Africa,* 393–406. Berkeley: University of California Press, 1992.

Leavitt, Judith. *The Healthiest City: Milwaukee and the Politics of Health Reform.* Princeton, N.J.: Princeton University Press, 1982.

Lienhardt, Godfrey. *Divinity and Experience: The Religion of the Dinka.* Oxford: Oxford University Press, 1961.

Linton, Simi. *Claiming Disability: Knowledge and Identity.* New York: New York University Press, 1998.

Livingston, Julie. "These Children of Today: Older Women's Narratives of Domestic Caring and Conflict in Twentieth Century Botswana." Paper presented at the Berkshire Conference on Women's History, University of Rochester, May 1999.

———. "Pregnant Children and Half-Dead Adults: Modern Living and the Quickening Life-Cycle in Botswana." *Bulletin of the History of Medicine* 77 (2003): 133–162.

———. "Reconfiguring Old Age: Elderly Women and Concerns over Care in Southeastern Botswana." *Medical Anthropology* 22, no. 2 (2003): 205–231.

———. "AIDS as Chronic Illness: Epidemiological Transition and Health Care in Southeastern Botswana." *African Journal of AIDS Research.* In press.

———. "Maintaining Local Dependencies: Elderly Women and Global Rehabilitation Agendas in Botswana." In Jennifer Cole and Deborah Durham, eds., *Generations and Globalization: Family, Youth, and Age in the New World Economy.* Indiana University Press, in press.

Livingstone, David. *Missionary Travels and Researches in South Africa.* New York: Harper and Brothers, 1872.

Lock, Margaret. *Encounters with Aging: Mythologies of Menopause in Japan and North America.* Berkeley: University of California Press, 1993.

———. *Twice Dead: Organ Transplants and the Reinvention of Death.* Berkeley: University of California Press, 2002.

Longmore, Paul, and Lauri Umansky, eds. *The New Disability History: American Perspectives.* New York: New York University Press, 2000.

Lutz, Catherine. *Unnatural Emotions: Everyday Sentiments on a Micronesian Atoll and Their Challenge to Western Theory.* Chicago: University of Chicago Press, 1988.

Lyons, Maryinez. *The Colonial Disease: A Social History of Sleeping Sickness in Northern Zaire, 1900–1940.* Cambridge: Cambridge University Press, 1992.

Mackenzie, Rev. John. *Ten Years North of the Orange River: A Story of Everyday Life and Work among the South African Tribes, from 1859 to 1869.* Edinburgh: Edmonston and Douglas, 1871.

MacRae, D. "The Bechuanaland Protectorate: Its People and Prevalent Diseases—With a Special Consideration of the Effects of Tropical Residence and Food in Relation to Health and Disease." M.D. thesis, University of Edinburgh, 1920.

Maganu, Edward. "Access to Health Facilities in Botswana and Its Impact on Quality of Life." In Doreen Nteta and Janet Hermans with Pavla Jeskova, eds., *Poverty and Plenty: The Botswana Experience,* 296–298. Gaborone: The Botswana Society, 1997.

Mairs, Nancy. *Waist-High in the World: A Life among the Nondisabled.* Boston: Beacon Press, 1996.

Malkki, Liisa. *Purity and Exile: Violence, Memory, and National Cosmology among Hutu Refugees in Tanzania.* Chicago: University of Chicago Press, 1995.

Marks, Shula. *Divided Sisterhood: Class, Race and Gender in the Nursing Profession in South Africa.* Basingstoke: Macmillan, 1994.

Marks, Shula, and Niel Andersson. "Typhus and Social Control: South Africa, 1917–50." In Roy Macleod and Milton Lewis, eds., *Disease, Medicine, and Empire: Perspectives on Western Medicine and the Experience of European Expansion.* London: Routledge, 1988.

Mazonde, Isaac. *A Study of Attitudes towards the Disabled in Botswana.* Working Paper no. 53. Gaborone: University of Botswana, National Institute of Research and Documentation, 1988.

———. "Poverty in Botswana and Its Impact on the Quality of Life." In Doreen Nteta and Janet Hermans with Pavla Jeskova, eds., *Poverty and Plenty: The Botswana Experience,* 61–76. Gaborone: The Botswana Society, 1997.

Merriweather, Alfred. *English-Setswana Medical Phrasebook and Dictionary/Puisanyo ya Bongaka ka Sekgoa le Setswana.* Gaborone: Botswana Book Centre, 1965.

———. *Desert Doctor: Medicine and Evangelism in the Kalahari Desert.* London: Lutterworth Press, 1969.

———. "Changing Disease Pattern in Botswana." *Journal of the Medical and Dental Association of Botswana* 9, no. 3 (1979): 85–93.

———. *Desert Doctor Remembers: The Autobiography of Alfred Merriweather.* Gaborone: Pula Press, 1999.

Meswele, Gladness Diana. "Death, Burial, and Ritual: An Ethnohistorical Study of the Changing Practices among Bakgatla Ba-Ga Kgafela from c. 1870 to the Present." B.A. honors thesis, Department of History, University of Botswana, 2002.

Moffat, Robert. *Missionary Labors and Scenes in Southern Africa.* Pittsburgh: Robert Carter, 1843.

Molefi, Rodgers, Fred Morton, and Leonard Ngcongco. "The Modernists: Seepapitso, Ntebogang and Isang." In Fred Morton and Jeff Ramsay, eds., *The Birth of Botswana: A History of the Bechuanaland Protectorate from 1910 to 1966,* 11–29. Gaborone: Longman Botswana, 1987.

Morton, Fred, and Jeff Ramsay, eds. *The Birth of Botswana: A History of the Bechua-naland Protectorate from 1910 to 1966.* Gaborone: Longman Botswana, 1987.

Morton, R. Fred. "Chiefs and Ethnic Unity in Two Colonial Worlds: The Bakgatla baga Kgafela of the Bechuanaland Protectorate and the Transvaal, 1872–1966." In A. I. Asiwaju, ed., *Partitioned Africans: Ethnic Relations across Africa's Interna-tional Boundaries, 1881–1984,* 127–154. London: C. Hurst, 1985.

Motzafi-Haller, Pnina. *Fragmented Worlds, Coherent Lives: The Politics of Difference in Botswana.* Westport, Conn.: Greenwood, 2002.

Mugabe, Mbulawa. "Social Welfare Issues and the Quality of Life in Botswana." In Doreen Nteta and Janet Hermans with Pavla Jeskova, eds., *Poverty and Plenty: The Botswana Experience,* 175–192. Gaborone: The Botswana Society, 1997.

Murray, Colin. *Families Divided: The Impact of Migrant Labour in Lesotho.* Cambridge: Cambridge University Press, 1981.

Mutongi, Kenda. "'Worries of the Heart': Widowed Mothers, Daughters and Mascu-linities in Maragoli, Western Kenya, 1940–1960." *Journal of African History* 40 (1999): 67–86.

Ngubane, Harriet. *Body and Mind in Zulu Medicine: An Ethnography of Health and Dis-ease in Nyuwasa-Zulu Thought and Practice.* London: Academic Press, 1977.

Nordholm, Lena, and Birgitta Lundgren-Lindquist. "Community-Based Rehabilitation in Moshupa Village, Botswana." *Disability and Rehabilitation* 21 (1999): 515–521.

Packard, Randall. "The Arudy of Historical Processes in African Traditions of Genesis: The Bashu Myth of Muhiyi." In Joseph Miller, ed., *The African Past Speaks.* London: Dawson Publishing, 1980.

———. *Chiefship and Cosmology: An Historical Study of Political Competition.* Bloom-ington: Indiana University Press, 1981.

———. "Social Change and the History of Misfortune among the Bashu of Eastern Zaire." In Ivan Karp and Charles Bird, eds., *Explorations in African Systems of Thought,* 237–268. Washington, D.C.: Smithsonian Institution Press, 1981.

———. 'The 'Healthy Reserve' and the 'Dressed Native': Discourses on Black Health and the Language of Legitimation in South Africa." *American Ethnologist* 16 (1989): 77–93.

———. *White Plague, Black Labor: Tuberculosis and the Political Economy of Health and Disease in South Africa.* Berkeley: University of California Press, 1989.

———. "Visions of Postwar Health and Development and Their Impact on Public Health Interventions in the Developing World." In Frederick Cooper and Randall Packard, eds., *International Development and the Social Sciences: Essays on the History and Politics of Knowledge,* 93–115. Berkeley: University of California Press, 1997.

Parsons, Q. N. "Khama III, the Bamangwato, and the British, with Special Reference to 1895–1923." Ph.D. thesis, University of Edinburgh, 1973.

Peters, Pauline. *Dividing the Commons: Politics, Policy, and Culture in Botswana.* Char-lottesville: University of Virginia Press, 1994.

Pigg, Stacy. "Inventing Social Categories through Place: Social Representations and Development in Nepal." *Comparative Studies in Society and History* 34, no. 3 (1992): 491–513.

———. "The Credible and the Credulous: The Question of 'Villagers' Beliefs' in Nepal." *Cultural Anthropology* 11, no. 2 (1996): 160–201.

———. "'Found in Most Traditional Societies': Traditional Medical Practitioners between Culture and Development." In Frederick Cooper and Randall Packard, eds., *International Development and the Social Sciences,* 259–290. Berkeley: University of California Press, 1997.

Pim, Sir Alan. *Financial and Economic Position of the Bechuanaland Protectorate: Report of the Commission Appointed by the Secretary of State for Dominion Affairs.* Cmd. 4368. London: HMSO, 1933.

Plaatje, Solomon. *Sechuana Proverbs with Literal Translations and Their European Equivalents.* London: Kegan Paul, Trench, Trubner, and Company, 1916.

Porter, Dorothy. *Health, Civilization and the State: A History of Public Health from Ancient to Modern Times.* London: Routledge, 1999.

Pule, Theresia. "The Socio-Economic Implications of Accidents in Botswana." B.A. Sociology Research Paper, University of Botswana, 1986.

Ramsay, Jeff. "The Neo-Traditionalist: Sebele II of the Bakwena." In F. Morton and J. Ramsay, eds., *The Birth of Botswana: A History of the Bechuanaland Protectorate from 1910 to 1966,* 30–44. Gaborone: Longman Botswana, 1987.

———. "The Rise and Fall of the Bakwena Dynasty of South-Central Botswana, 1820–1940." Ph.D. diss., Boston University, 1991.

Ramsay, Jeff, Fred Morton, and Barry Morton. *Historical Dictionary of Botswana.* 3rd ed. London: Scarecrow Press, 1996.

Ranger, Terence. "Godly Medicine: The Ambiguities of Medical Mission in Southeastern Tanzania, 1900–1945." In John Janzen and Steven Feierman, eds., *The Social Basis of Health and Healing in Africa,* 256–283. Berkeley: University of California Press, 1992.

Rapp, Rayna. "Extra Chromosomes and Blue Tulips: Medico-Familial Conversations." In Alberto Cambrosio, Margaret Lock, and Allan Young, eds., *Living and Working with the New Medical Technologies,* 184–208. Cambridge: Cambridge University Press, 2000.

Rapp, Rayna, and Faye Ginsburg. "Enabling Disability: Rewriting Kinship, Reimagining Citizenship." *Public Culture* 13 (2001): 533–556.

Republic of Botswana, Central Statistics Office. *Living Conditions in Botswana, 1986–1994: Socio-Economic Indicators Based on the 1985/6 HIES, 1991 Census and 1993/4 HIES.* Gaborone: Government Printer, 1996.

Rey, Sir Charles. *Monarch of All I Survey: Bechuanaland Diaries 1929–37.* Ed. Neil Parsons and Michael Crowder. Gaborone: Botswana Society, 1988.

Riseman, Paul. "The Person and the Life-Cycle in African Social Life and Thought." *African Studies Review* 29 (1986): 72–198.

Risse, Guenter. *Mending Bodies, Saving Souls: A History of Hospitals.* Oxford: Oxford University Press, 1999.

Rogers, Naomi. *Dirt and Disease: Polio Before FDR.* New Brunswick, N.J.: Rutgers University Press, 1992.

Romero-Daza, Nancy, and David Himmelgreen. "More than Money for Your Labor: Migration and the Political Economy of AIDS in Lesotho." In Merrill Singer, ed., *The Political Economy of AIDS.* New York: Baywood Publishing, 1998.

Rosenberg, Charles. *The Cholera Years: The United States in 1832, 1849, and 1866.* Chicago: University of Chicago Press, 1962.

———. "Framing Disease: Illness, Society, and History." In Charles E. Rosenberg and Janet Lynne Golden, eds., *Framing Disease: Studies in Cultural History,* xiii–xxvi. New Brunswick, N.J.: Rutgers University Press, 1992.

Sadowsky, Jonathan. *Imperial Bedlam: Institutions of Madness in Colonial Southwestern Nigeria.* Berkeley: University of California Press, 1999.

Samatar, Abdi Ismail. *An African Miracle: State and Class Leadership and Colonial Legacy in Botswana Development.* Portsmouth, N.H.: Heinemann, 1999.

Schapera, Isaac. "Premarital Pregnancy and Native Opinion: A Note on Social Change." *Africa* 6 (1933): 59–89.

———. "The Social Structure of the Tswana Ward." *Bantu Studies* 9 (1935): 203–224.

———. *Handbook of Tswana Law and Custom.* London: Frank Cass, 1938.

———. *Married Life in an African Tribe.* London: Faber and Faber, 1940.

———. *Migrant Labour and Tribal Life.* New York: Oxford University Press, 1947.

———. "Sorcery and Witchcraft in Bechuanaland." *African Affairs* 51 (1952): 41–50.

———. *Tribal Innovators: Tswana Chiefs and Social Change 1795–1940.* London: Athlone Press, 1970.

———. *Rainmaking Rites of Tswana Tribes.* Leiden: Afrika-Studiecentrum, 1971.

———. *Bogwera: Kgatla Initiation.* Pamphlet. Mochudi: Phutadikobo Museum, 1978.

———. "Kgatla Notions of Ritual Impurity." *African Studies* 38, no. 1 (1979): 3–15.

Schapera, Isaac, ed. *The Political Annals of a Tswana Tribe: Minutes of Ngwaketse Public Assemblies, 1910–1917.* Communications from the School of African Studies, University of Cape Town, new ser., 18 [Cape Town: School of African Studies, University of Cape Town], 1947.

———. *Livingstone's Private Journals, 1851–1853.* London: Chatto and Windus, 1960.

Schapera, Isaac, and John L. Comaroff. *The Tswana.* Revised ed. London: International Africa Institute, 1991.

Scheper-Hughes, Nancy. *Death without Weeping: The Violence of Everyday Life in Brazil.* Berkeley: University of California Press, 1993.

Scheper-Hughes, Nancy, and Margaret Lock. "The Mindful Body: A Prolegomenon to Future Work." *Medical Anthropology* 1 (1987): 6–41.

Seeley, Caroline Frasier. "The Reaction of the Batswana to the Practice of Traditional Medicine." M.Phil. thesis, University of London, 1973.

Silla, Eric. *People Are Not the Same: Leprosy and Identity in Twentieth-Century Mali.* Portsmouth, N.H.: Heinemann, 1998.

Siwawa-Ndai, Pelani. "Employment Opportunities and Their Impact on the Quality of Life in Botswana." In Doreen Nteta and Janet Hermans with Pavla Jeskova, eds., *Poverty and Plenty: The Botswana Experience, Proceedings of a Symposium Organised by the Botswana Society, October 15–18, 1996.* Gaborone: The Botswana Society, 1997.

———. "Some Facts and Figures about the Quality of Life in Botswana." In Doreen Nteta and Janet Hermans with Pavla Jeskova, eds., *Poverty and Plenty: The Botswana Experience, , Proceedings of a Symposium Organised by the Botswana Society, October 15–18, 199,.* 25–32. Gaborone: The Botswana Society, 1997.

Staugard, Frants. "Traditional Health Care in Botswana." In Murray Last and G. L. Chavunduka, eds., *The Professionalization of African Medicine,* 51–86. Manchester: Manchester University Press, 1986.

Summers, Carol. "Intimate Colonialism: The Imperial Production of Reproduction in Uganda." *Signs* 16 (1991): 787–807.

Sundkler, Bengt. *Bantu Prophets in South Africa.* London: Oxford University Press, 1960.

"Table 1: 1975–1985—Botswana: Annual Notification of Tuberculosis Cases, Deaths." *Botswana Epidemiological Bulletin* 6 (1985): 226.

Taylor, Christopher. *Milk, Honey, and Money: Changing Concepts of Rwandan Healing.* Washington, D.C.: Smithsonian Institution Press, 1992.

Thema, B.C. "The Changing Pattern of Tswana Social and Family Relations." *Botswana Notes and Records* 4 (1972): 39–43.

Thomas, Lynn. *The Politics of the Womb: Women, Reproduction, and the State in Kenya.* Berkley: University of California Press, 2003.

Thomson, Rosemarie Garland. *Extraordinary Bodies: Figuring Physical Disability in American Culture and Literature.* New York: Columbia University Press, 1997.

Tlou, Sheila Dinotshe. "Indicators of Health." In Doreen Nteta and Janet Hermans with Pavla Jeskova, eds., *Poverty and Plenty: The Botswana Experience,* 303–317. Gaborone: The Botswana Society, 1997.

Tlou, Sheila, and Edwin Sandberg. "The Elderly and Their Use of the Health Care System." In Frank Bruun, Mbulawa Mugabe, and Yolanda Coombes, eds., *The Situation of the Elderly in Botswana: Proceedings from an International Workshop.* Gaborone: National Institute of Research, 1994.

Tomes, Nancy. "The Private Side of Public Health: Sanitary Science, Domestic Hygiene, and the Germ Theory, 1870–1900." In Judith Walzer Leavitt and Ronald L. Numbers, eds., *Sickness and Health in America,* 3rd ed., 506–528. Madison: University of Wisconsin Press, 1997.

Townsend, Nicholas. "Men, Migration, and Households in Botswana: An Exploration of Connections over Time and Space." *Journal of Southern African Studies* 23 (1997): 405–420.

Upton, Rebecca. "'Our Blood Does Not Agree': Negotiating Infertility in Northern Botswana." Ph.D. diss., Anthropology Department, Brown University, 1999.

———. "'Infertility Makes You Invisible': Gender, Health and the Negotiation of Childbearing in Northern Botswana." *Journal of Southern African Studies* 27, no. 2 (2001): 349–362.

Vail, Leroy, and Landeg White. *Power and the Praise Poem: Southern African Voices in History.* London: James Currey, 1991.

van Onselen, Charles. *The Seed Is Mine: The Life of Kas Maine, a South African Sharecropper, 1894–1985.* New York: Hill and Wang, 1986.

Vaughan, Megan. *The Story of an African Famine: Gender and Famine in Twentieth Century Malawi.* Cambridge: Cambridge University Press, 1987.

———. *Curing Their Ills: Colonial Power and African Illness.* Stanford, Calif.: Stanford University Press, 1991.

Wailoo, Keith. *Drawing Blood: Technology and Disease Identity in Twentieth Century America.* Baltimore: Johns Hopkins University Press, 1997.

Weiss, Meira. *Conditional Love: Parents' Attitudes toward Handicapped Children.* Westport, Conn.: Bergin and Garvey, 1994.

Werbner, Richard. *Ritual Passage, Sacred Journey.* Washington, D.C.: Smithsonian Institution Press, 1989.

Werbner, Richard, and Deborah Gaitskell, eds. *Minorities and Citizenship in Botswana.* Special issue of *Journal of Southern African Studies* 28, no. 4 (2002).

White, Luise. "'They could make their victims dull': Genders and Genres, Fantasies and Cures in Colonial Southern Uganda." *American Historical Review* 100 (1995): 1379–1402.

———. *Speaking with Vampires: Rumor and History in Colonial Africa.* Berkeley: University of California Press, 2000.

Whyte, Susan Reynolds, and Benedicte Ingstad. "Disability and Culture: An Overview." In Benedicte Ingstad and Susan Reynolds Whyte, eds., *Disability and Culture,* 3–32. Berkeley: University of California Press, 1995.

Willoughby, Rev. W. C. "Notes on the Initiation Ceremonies of the Becwana." *Journal of the Royal Anthropological Institute of Great Britain and Ireland* 39 (1909): 228–245.

———. *The Soul of the Bantu.* 1928; reprint, Westport, Conn.: Negro Universities Press, 1970.

Worboys, Michael. "The Discovery of Colonial Malnutrition between the Wars." In David Arnold, ed., *Imperial Medicine and Indigenous Societies,* 208–226. Manchester: Manchester University Press, 1988.

Wylie, Diana. "The Changing Face of Hunger in Southern African History, 1880–1980." *Past and Present* 22 (1988): 159–199.

Index

Numbers in *italics* refer to illustrations.

223, 228–229; universalistic human body of, 165. *See also* doctors, European

blindness, 101–102, 119, 128–129, 152, 251n19; age and, 36–37; prevalence of, 158

boaga (building), 15, 30, 46, 56

bodies: African bodies and European assumptions, 140, 154; African cultures and, 4; age and, 91–98; heat of female body, 98; history experienced in, 1, 234; male bodies and labor migration, 110; mind-body dichotomy, 4; normative views of, 10; persons and, 2–5; postcolonial changes and, 198–201; ritual power of, 88; self-making and, 209–212; universalistic body of western medicine, 165. *See also* able-bodiedness

bogole (disability), definition of, 7–10, 102

bogwera (boys' initiation) ritual, 81, 92, 93, 94–96, 128; demise of, 190, 259n122; fading of, 110; illicit continuation of, 143; labor migration as replacement for, 120–122; rules of sexual conduct, 118; secrecy of, 94

bojale (girls' initiation) ritual, 94, 95–96, 167, 190

boloi (sorcery, witchcraft), 21, 24, 40, 76, 147, 150; bush medicines and, 67; collapsing public health and, 195; colonial laws against, 89, 148; in competitive relationships, 171; diagnosis and, 163, 168; *dingaka/ngaka* and, 82, 85; gender and, 87; mental illness and, 52, 177; misfortune attributed to, 86–90; negative emotions and, 78; women suspected of, 85, 148, 220–222

bongaka (Tswana medicine), 16, 17, 24, 45, 85–86, 198; biomedicine entangled with, 179–184, 230–232, 234, 239; changing landscape of, 133–134; colonial policies and, 236; criminalization of, 89, 112; decline of, 141; new meanings of, 109; personhood and, 166; postcolonial care and, 222–223, 228, 231–232; women's access to, 148. *See also* *dingaka/ngaka* (Tswana doctors)

bonyatsi/nyatsi relationships, 143, 171

bopelotelele (long-heartedness, patience), 217, 222

boso (retarded, "feeble-minded"), 173

boswagadi (disease of unpurified widows), 172, 273–274n115

botsenwa (mental illness), 169, 176–179; confinement and, 187, 193–194; diagnoses of western medicine and, 182–183; nursing care and, 184

botsetse (confinement), 100

botsofe/mostofe (old age), 60, 61, 102, 200

Botswana: diamond boom in, 196, 198; disability in, 7–11; ecology of, 22; economic situation of, 30–31; elderly population of, 3; geography of, 64; health care systems, 16–19, 33, 34, 223; historical transformations in, 1–2; Independence (1966), 17, 142, 146, 186, 218, 235; military forces

of, 131, 211, 240; Ministry of Health, 34, 36–37, 187, *188*, 198, 203, 225; "modernization" in, 5, 13; postcolonial changes, 198–201; precolonial society in, 10–11; Society for People with Disabilities, 38–39. *See also* Bechuanaland Protectorate

boys, 70, 78, 92–95, *93*, 120. *See also* *bogwera* (boys' initiation) ritual; *magwane/legwane* (boy initiates); men

breast-feeding, 92, 173, 174

bridewealth, 68, 116, 131, 167

British Empire Society for the Blind, 158

British imperialism, 113

Brown, J. Tom, 94

Bruun, Frank, 43

building. *See boaga* (building)

bureaucracy, 196

bush (*naga*), 66–67, 71, 83, 98, 123, 181

cancer, 199, 200, 229

canes, walking with, 35, 102

capitalism, global/western, 1, 141, 231, 232, 248n36; "modernization" and, 4, 5; social dislocations of, 13

caregiving, 18, 145; AIDS patients, 32; developmental ethos and, 202; disputes relating to, 47; national politics of care, 212; postcolonial changes and, 197; relationships and, 28

Carton, Benedict, 68

case studies, 27–28, 56–58, 62–63; Kago, 40–46, 90, 150, 232, 241; Lesego Dinare, 58–62; Moreki Morwa, 46–47; Nanki, 47–51; Obabeng Mmilo, 51–56

cataracts, 37, 158

Catholicism, 104

cattle, 21, 73, 138, 145; bought with wages, 116; as bridewealth, 144, 167; community importance of, 67–68, 255n44; diseases of, 68, 110–111; donkeys as replacement for, 26; in dry season, 64; kraals, 66, 79, 85, 147, 177; *mafisa* labor system and, 77, 142; raiding of, 65

cattle posts (*meraka*): as male domain, 64–65, 67, 69, 113; as shelters for patients, 180–181, 184, 195

CBR (community-based rehabilitation services) programs, 29, 30, 32, 34, 53

cemeteries, 98, 192

cerebral palsy, 39, 40, 43, 47–48, 181, 270n55

Chamber of Mines, 135

Cheshire Foundation, 29, 30, 251n12

chiefs/chiefship, 64, 65; British colonial policy and, 64, 75, 112; community and, 73–82; declining power of, 133, 196; *dingaka/ngaka* and, 82–

colonial care and, 230–232; postwar epidemiology and, 153; sorcery and, 87–88, 90; spiritual weakening of, 112; training of, 85–86; treatment of arthritic disease, 104–105; western doctors and, 84–85; women and, 146–147. *See also* *bongaka* (Tswana medicine)

Diphaleng (pseudonymous village), 26–30, 29, 52, 146, 178; CBR program in, 53; *digole* in, 39; professional health care in, 32–36, *33*

Diphuti, Connie, 212

Diphuti family, 38, 39

disability, 6–11, 18, 36–40

disabled activists, 29

diseases, 3, 98, 104, 127; of animals (epizootic), 68, 110–111, 147; decline of infectious diseases, 222; incidence of, 199; Tswana diagnosis of, 168. *See also specific diseases*

disfigurement, 2, 247n4

Ditaba, Frances, 37–39, 240–241

ditaola (divining bones), 138, 168–169

ditsenwa/setsenwa (persons with mental illness), 176, 177–178, 183, 184, 193–195

divination, 87, 89, 112, 133, 138, 168–169

doctors, European, 104, 112, 202; changing medical landscape and, 133; colonial taxes and, 130–131; missionary, 29, 133–134, 137, 179, 228; physical fitness exams conducted by, 135–140; in South African mines, 122. *See also* biomedicine (western medicine)

Down's syndrome, 39, 43, 189

droughts, 74, 75, 112, 151; in Depression era, 107, 110; impoverishment of Bechuanaland and, 198; as "miscarriage" of clouds, 77; relief for, 31; ritual murder and, 88; social disruption and, 78

dry season, 64, 71–72

Durham, Deborah, 5, 192

ecology, 16, 18, 21; balance of, 73–74; chiefs and, 78; disruptions of, 65; dry and rainy seasons, 71–73; labor migration and, 109, 111

economic contexts, 30–32

education, 39, 198, 209, 216, 267n15

egalitarian ethos, 5

elderly people, 6, 29, 99; bush knowledge and, 67; children as company for, 214; Depression-era hardship and, 111; gifts from kin, 208; kinship networks and, 57; moral imagination and, 19, 21; nursing care of, 185–186; pensions and, 31, 57–58; population of, 199, 278n9; senescence and, 96–97; sociopolitical power of, 119; spiritual power of, 110; veneration of, 86; welfare and, 201

entrepreneurship, 150

epidemiology, 24, 127, 145, 195; biomedical, 154–163; diagnosis as history, 152–154; postcolonial care and, 222–232; Tswana, 163–179, 183

epilepsy, 12, 130–131, 152, 238

ethnicities, 123–124

eugenics, 10

Evans-Pritchard, E. E., 35

eyeglasses, 37, 101, 159, *160*

facial deformities, 191

families, 15, 106; age position in, 20; burden of caregiving and, 56–57; greeting relatives, 44; health care and, 28–29, 231; polygynous, 70; public life and, 69; wage work and, 116; welfare programs and, 208–209; women's agricultural work and, 184. *See also* generational struggle; kinship/lineage; mother-daughter relationships

family welfare educators (FWEs), 29–30, 33, 34, 47; case studies and, 56, 61, 62; developmental ethos of progress and, 205, 206

famine, 109

Feast of the First Fruits, 77, 81

Feierman, Steven, 74, 168

fertility, 118

floods, 241

funerals, 18, 49, 101, 192, 197

Gabane village, 134

Gaberones (village), 102–103, *108*, 119

Gaborone (capital city), 26, 37, 44, 60, 207, 237; beggars in, 201; established after Independence, 196; hospital in, 230; Lion's Club, 39, 202; Princess Marina Hospital, 34, 42, 219, 238–239

Gagoangwe (queen/regent), 76, 254n35

Gaseitsiwe, Chief, 87

gender, 5, 20, 22, 39, 234; caregiving and, 99–100; cosmological well-being and, 81; ecological balance and, 73, 74; historical memory and, 23–24; personhood and, 165; sexual morality and, 175; space and, 12; trees and, 77

generational struggle, 22, 105, 197, 212, 220. *See also* families

gerontocracy, 145, 153, 177, 197; building (*boaga*) and, 15; wage work and, 107; weakening of, 144, 172, 200

Geurts, Kathryn, 12

gifts, 19, 20, 30, 97, 129; food, 62, 151, 208; material objects, 57; money, 18; from returning migrant laborers, 208; as social capital, 117

Ginsburg, Faye, 9

girls, 26, 70, 78; agricultural labor of, 69; initia-

ings and, 44, 69; heart as central organ of, 97; medicine and, 17; in Tswana culture, 165–168; visiting as reaffirmation of, 225

physical fitness, 134–140, 146, 209, 211, 212. *See also* able-bodiedness

Pilane, Sefako, 119

Pim, Sir Alan, 113

poisonous substances (*sejeso*), 86–87, 89, 104, 152, 170. *See also dibeela* (toxins)

polio, 155, 157–158, 187, 188, 189

pollution, 101, 104, 111, 184; *mopakwane* and, 173, 174; polluted blood, 122; returning migrants and, 147

polygyny, 70, 143, 173

poverty, 31, 111, 186, 193

pregnancy, 77, 78, 92, 98; Christian deacons and, 149; premarital, 144; *thibamo* disease and, 172

primitivism, 203

Princess Marina Hospital, 34, 42, 219, 238–239

privacy, 70, 71

prosthetics, 35, 230

proverbs, 20, 22; on absence of young men, 107; on boy initiates, 92–93; on cripples, 1, 101, 107, 128; on healing power of visits, 64, 99; on heart as medicine, 142; on houses and secrets, 142; on love, 234; on misfortune, 234; on mothers and children, 196; on paying for health care, 196; on ritual murder, 88–89; on wealth and poverty, 26

public space, 11, 12

Radipitsi, Ramatsimako, 131

rain/rainmaking, 21, 74, 75, 76–77, 112; cosmological significance of, 71–73; demise of rainmaking rituals, 133, 149; diagnosis and, 168; dry season and, 64; floods, 241; meaning and, 22, 23

Ramotswa village, 39, 60, *108*, 146, 218

Rapela, Nomsa, 102, 150, 152, 187

Rapp, Rayna, 9

Red Cross, 201, 205–206, 224

rehabilitation, 10, 43, 201–209, *204*

residential wards, 57

Rhodesia, 74, 110

road accidents, 32, 46, 103, 199

Sanitation Day, 226

Schapera, Isaac, 65–66, 75, 78, 80, 164; on initiation of boys, 92–93, 94, 95; on labor migration, 113; on *mopakwane*, 174; on sexual taboo, 144; on tribal dispute resolution, 86; Tswana diagnosis and, 168; on witchcraft, 87

schizophrenia, 162

science, 16, 112, 133, 228

seasons, 66–73

Seati, Alita, 1, 151–152, 187

Sebele II, Chief, 90, 120

Sebobi, Pitoro, 182

Seboni, Martinus, 118–119

Sechele, Chief, 102, 105

secrecy, 78, 142, 184, 195; gossip and, 70; privacy and, 71; women's sexual autonomy and, 172

Seepapitso, Chief, 70, 76, 87, 115, 254n35, 255n44

segole. See digole/segole (disabled persons)

segotlo (backyard of compound), 71, *72*, 92, 192–193

Sejabdila, Chum, 104

senescence, 6, 11, 16, 91, 96–97

Setswana language, 7, 23, 29, 122, 247n3, 250n4; jokes in, 66; medical terms, 125, 169–170; seasonal change reflected in, 72; translation difficulties, 36, 139–140, 179, 234

sexuality, 2, 23, 67; changes in sexual morality, 109, 110; clear rules regulating, 90; community constraints on, 78, 172, 173; cultural changes in behavior, 169; European views of African sexuality, 154; extramarital/premarital, 163; female, 17, 144–145, 163, 167; hot blood and, 104, 172, 180; initiation rituals and, 94, 95–96; jealousy/envy (*lefufa*) and, 171; post-Independence social changes and, 218; postpartum abstinence, 173; rules of conduct, 94, 118; taboos, 39, 48

Shambaa people (Tanzania), 168

Shepherd, Dr., 135, 136, 137–138, 180

silicosis, 132, 264n59

smallpox, 199

soldiers, 143–144, 155, 176–177, 211

Solway, Jacqueline, 171

sorcery. *See boloi* (sorcery, witchcraft)

South Africa, 14, 202, 252n1; Batswana women employed in, 58; blindness rates in, 158; economic growth in, 74; foot-and-mouth disease from, 111; miners establishing new families in, 117–118; polio in, 157; as regional power, 113; repressive racist government of, 142; witchcraft accusations in, 220–221; women in domestic service in, 145

South African mines, 48, 82, 85, 103, 256n59; Depression era and, 111, 112–113; gold mines, 41; localization of workforce in, 196; map, *108*; medical exams in, 134; Tswana labor harvested by, 109–110

space: affect and, 11–13; season and, 66–73

starvation, 114

Staugart, Frants, 172, 180

stroke, 60, 61, 105, 199

suffering, 1, 5, 159, 235; Christianity and, 150;

community of, 39; ecological crises and, 111, 112; human nature and, 166; labor migration and, 127, 141

suicide, 72, 182, 194, 210

Sundkler, Bengt, 149

syphilis, 109, 133, 134, 191, 261n5

Tamocha, Joyce, 239

Tanzania, 168

taxes, 82, 112, 114; collection of, 130; court cases involving, 130–131, 132; disabled persons and, 129–131, 133; failure to pay, 117–118; impoverishment of Bechuanaland and, 198; inability to pay, 119

technologies, 3, 142, 161; "appropriate," 198; biomedical, 163; medical, 156; modernization of health services and, 230; postcolonial care and, 236; sewing machines, 206; therapeutic, 153

television, 27

Thabane, Motlatse, 123–124

Thebe, Modise, 177

Thema, B. C., 150

thibamo (disease associated with childbirth), 169, 171–173, 174, 175; confinement and, 187–188; missionary doctors and, 179; nursing care and, 184; tuberculosis and, 179–181

Thomas, Lynn, 5, 144

trachoma, 155, 158–159

Trans-Kalahari Highway, 26

trees, 77

Tshekedi, Chief, 90

Tswana people, 4–5, 66, 107; aristocracy, 131, 142; developmental ethos of modernity and, 203; emotional lives, 12–13; historical change and, 2; homes of, 26–27; laws of, 94, 102; life cycle of, 91, 96–97; as minority in South Africa, 124; moral imagination and, 20; neighboring peoples and, 84–85; nursing practices, 43; personhood understood by, 154–168; social values, 78, 115; "traditional" values of, 57

Tswapong people, 169

tuberculosis, 104, 109, 127, 151, 159; AIDS epidemic and, 237; colonial medical service and, 261n4; European doctors and, 133; physical fitness exams and, 135; prevalence of, 155–156; tax defaulters with, 132; TB Awareness Day, 226; *thibamo* diagnosis and, 179–181; WHO campaign against, 199–200. *See also* cerebral palsy; meningitis

unemployment, 30–31, 48, 215

UNICEF, 225

United Free Church, 135

United Free Church Moffat Hospital, 182, 270n65

United States, 9, 10, 157, 158

uterus, cosmological invocation of, 69, 71, 98, 167–168; *mopakwane* and, 173, 174, 175; motherly care in changing moral landscape, 184–195; polluted wombs, 213. *See also* wombs (*dipopelo/popelo*)

vaccination campaigns, 156

Vaughan, Megan, 109, 140

Vernick, Tamara Giles, 164

Village Development Committee, 36

villages, 64–65, 66, 197

wage work, 30, 68; kin-based production contrasted with, 118–119, 122; physical fitness and, 128; village labor obligations versus, 146; wage reallocations, 116–117

Wanguru, Wamona, 105

wards, 65, 75

wars, 65, 74; amputations in, 102; headmen and, 76; mental breakdowns and, 177, 182; South African (Boer) war, 113

water supplies, 27, 31, 36, 196, 198, 208

weddings, 49, 116, 197

Weiss, Meira, 192

welfare programs, 31, 201–209

Werber, Richard, 169

wheelchairs, 35, 40, 207

Whyte, Susan Reynolds, 18

widows, 77, 78, 98; *bojale* ritual led by, 95; *boswagadi* disease and, 172, 273–274n115; purification of, 86; sexual relations with, 172

Willoughby, W. C., 77, 81, 88, 94, 273n106

witchcraft. *See boloi* (sorcery, witchcraft)

Witchcraft Proclamation Act (1927), 89, 90

wombs (*dipopelo/popelo*), 167, 203, 234, 239. *See also* uterus, cosmological invocation of

women, 26, 82, 156; AIDS epidemic and, 237–238; caregiving of, 98–100; Christian churches and, 77, 195, 215, 225, 235; excluded from mine employment, 14, 110; farming and, 32; female sexuality, 17, 144–145, 163, 167; heat of, 98, 111; home compounds of, 70–71; increase in female autonomy, 143, 147–150; maids hired by, 55, 280–281n57; moral debate on debility and, 28–29, 62; nurturing qualities, 74, 79; political power and, 76, 254n37; in postpartum confinement, 185–186; rainmaking and, 79–81, 80; suspected of sorcery, 85, 148, 216; travel passes for, 120; Tswana nursing practices and,

43; unemployment and, 31. *See also* girls; labor migration, female; mother-daughter relationships; pregnancy

Worboys, Michael, 161

World Health Organization (WHO), 32, 156, 199, 203, 205

World War I, 134

World War II, 107, 161, 176–177

Zimbabwe, 33

Zionist churches, 35, 36, 148, 149

Zululand, 68

JULIE LIVINGSTON is a historian at Rutgers University with a background in public health and anthropology. She has worked in Botswana since the mid-1990s. Julie grew up in the Boston area but now lives in New York City with her husband, daughter, and dog.